Transatlantic economic relations are dominated by three factors which are of major historical significance. The first and most important is the multilateral process for trade liberalization, deregulation of financial markets, and macro-economic policy coordination. The second factor is a transatlantic environment of national and regional idiosyncrasies exemplified by protectionist initiatives, a significant weakening of the EMS, and changes in central bank statutes. The second factor is in part a political backlash against the first. The third factor affecting transatlantic economic relations is of course the emergence of regional economic relationships within the transatlantic economy, and a treaty calling for a common currency in Europe. In this volume, specialists in international trade, international finance, and political economy analyse the cause of these three factors, and their implications.

T0300491

The new transatlantic economy

The Center for German and European Studies

The Center for German and European Studies of Georgetown University, Washington, DC, was founded in 1990 with the generous support of the German government. Its purpose is the promotion of scholarship and teaching on domestic and international topics relating to Germany and Europe in general. It offers a two-year degree programme leading to the Master of Arts in German and European Studies; students may also be enrolled simultaneously in PhD programmes in the departments of Government, History, Economics and German. Financial aid is available on a competitive basis. The Center hosts at least two postdoctoral scholars each year, as well as short-term visitors, speakers, and conferences and symposia.

Director
Professor Samuel H. Barnes

Director of Programs
Professor Gregory Flynn

Centre for Economic Policy Research

The Centre for Economic Policy Research is a network of over 300 Research Fellows, based primarily in European universities. The Centre coordinates its Fellows' research activities and communicates their results to the public and private sectors. CEPR is an entrepreneur, developing research initiatives with the producers, consumers and sponsors of research. Established in 1983, CEPR is a European economics research organization with uniquely wide-ranging scope and activities.

CEPR is a registered educational charity. Institutional (core) finance for the Centre is provided by major grants from the Economic and Social Research Council, under which an ESRC Resource Centre operates within CEPR; the Esmée Fairbairn Charitable Trust; the Bank of England; 20 other central banks; and 40 companies. None of these organizations gives prior review to the Centre's publications, nor do they necessarily endorse the views expressed therein.

The Centre is pluralist and non-partisan, bringing economic research to bear on the analysis of medium- and long-run policy questions. CEPR research may include views on policy, but the Executive Committee of the Centre does not give prior review to its publications, and the Centre takes no institutional policy positions. The opinions expressed in this volume are those of the authors and not those of the Centre for Economic Policy Research.

The new transatlantic economy

Edited by

MATTHEW B. CANZONERI,
WILFRED J. ETHIER,

and

VITTORIO GRILLI

CAMBRIDGE
UNIVERSITY PRESS

CAMBRIDGE UNIVERSITY PRESS
Cambridge, New York, Melbourne, Madrid, Cape Town, Singapore,
São Paulo, Delhi, Dubai, Tokyo

Cambridge University Press
The Edinburgh Building, Cambridge CB2 8RU, UK

Published in the United States of America by Cambridge University Press, New York

www.cambridge.org
Information on this title: www.cambridge.org/9780521142625

First published 1996
This digitally printed version 2010

A catalogue record for this publication is available from the British Library

ISBN 978-0-521-56205-8 Hardback
ISBN 978-0-521-14262-5 Paperback

Contents

xii **Contents**

Figures

Tables

Preface

This book is the outcome of the conference on 'The New Transatlantic Economy' held at Georgetown University on 5–6 May 1994. It was sponsored by the Centre for Economic Policy Research, the Center for German and European Studies at Georgetown University, and the Program for International Economic Studies, also at Georgetown University. The conference was made possible by the following grants: to CEPR from the Commission of the European Communities' Human Capital and Mobility Programme (no. ERBCHRXCT930234) under the Centre's research project on 'Macroeconomics, Politics and Growth in Europe', and from the Ford Foundation (no. 920–1265) as part of the Centre's project on 'Market Integration, Regionalism and the Global Economy'; and to the Center for German and European Studies from the government of the Federal Republic of Germany.

The conference also included a panel discussion on the direction of transatlantic economic relations and after-dinner remarks presented by Michael Mussa, Director of the Research Department at the International Monetary Fund.

We would like to thank Brad Billings and Kelli McTaggart of Georgetown University for organizing the conference, CEPR's Programme Officer, Peter Johns, for his contributions during the preparations for the conference, Kate Millward at CEPR for patiently guiding the present volume to press, and Liz Paton for her work as Production Editor.

Matthew B. Canzoneri
Wilfred J. Ethier
Vittorio Grilli

October 1995

Conference participants

Giorgio Basevi *Università degli Studi di Bologna*
Bradley Billings *Georgetown University*
Stanley Black *University of North Carolina*
Eric Bond *Pennsylvania State University*
Matthew Canzoneri *Georgetown University and CEPR*
Susan Collins *Georgetown University and CEPR*
Max Corden *Johns Hopkins University*
Robert Cumby *Georgetown University*
Alan Deardorff *University of Michigan*
Barry Eichengreen *University of California and CEPR*
Gwen Eudey *Georgetown University*
Robert Flood *International Monetary Fund*
Gregory Flynn *Georgetown University and Center for German and European Studies*
Joseph Gagnon *US Department of Treasury*
Konstantine Gatsios *Athens University of Economics and Business and CEPR*
Alberto Giovannini *Consiglio degli Esperti, Ministero del Tesoro, Rome, and CEPR*
Vittorio Grilli *Consiglio degli Esperti, Ministero del Tesoro, Rome, and CEPR*
Dale Henderson *Board of Governors – Federal Reserve System*
Arye Hillman *Bar-Ilan University*
Andrew Hughes Hallett *Strathclyde University and CEPR*
Karen Johnson *Board of Governors – Federal Reserve System*
Mitch Kaneda *Georgetown University*
Ben Lockwood *University of Exeter and CEPR*
James Markusen *University of Colorado*
Paul Masson *International Monetary Fund*
Jacques Mélitz *INSEE and CEPR*

Marcus Miller *University of Warwick and CEPR*
Peter Moser *SIASR*
Michael Mussa *International Monetary Fund*
Richard Portes *CEPR and Birkbeck College, London*
Martin Richardson *Georgetown University*
Andrew Rose *University of California, Berkeley, and CEPR*
Nouriel Roubini *Yale University and CEPR*
Alasdair Smith *University of Sussex and CEPR*
Robert Staiger *University of Wisconsin*
Constantinos Syropoulos *Pennsylvania State University*
Richard Sweeney *Georgetown University*
Vito Tanzi *International Monetary Fund*
Axel Weber *Universität-GH Siegen and CEPR*
L. Alan Winters *The World Bank and CEPR*
Paul Wonnacott *Institute for International Economics*
Paul Wood *Board of Governors – Federal Reserve System*
Lei Zhang *University of Warwick*

1 Introduction

MATTHEW B. CANZONERI, WILFRED J.
ETHIER, and VITTORIO GRILLI

Present transatlantic economic relations are dominated by three factors that are of major historical significance. The first, and no doubt most important, is the multilateral process for trade liberalization and macroeconomic policy coordination, which is embodied in the General Agreement on Tariffs and Trade (GATT) and in ongoing Group of Seven (G7) ministerial meetings. The GATT system has produced decades of extremely liberal transatlantic trade, accompanied by a steady convergence of the individual transatlantic economies. Financial deregulation on both sides of the Atlantic has produced a truly international capital market but, in sharp contrast with the history of GATT, episodes of macroeconomic policy coordination have been sporadic and short lived.

The GATT system has of course been around for many years, but it seems to be at something of a crossroads. The gradual liberalization of trade in manufactured goods is largely complete, and the prospects of successfully extending the multilateral system to other spheres remain uncertain; negotiations have become increasingly difficult, with the recently completed Uruguay Round the longest and most contentious yet, and there seems to be little enthusiasm for embarking on yet another round. Similarly, the international monetary system seems to be at a crossroads. Huge movements of capital are making nominal exchange rates fluctuate rapidly, putting new pressures on central banks and international agencies such as the International Monetary Fund (IMF). The remaining two factors that are dominating transatlantic relations can be seen, at least in part, as responses to a growing dissatisfaction with GATT prospects and the new pressures brought by capital mobility.

The second factor is a transatlantic environment of national and regional idiosyncrasies exemplified by protectionist initiatives, a significant weakening of the European Monetary System (EMS), and independence for some of the central banks in Europe and an enhanced role in

1

policy-making for others. The protectionist initiatives are in part a
political backlash against the liberal trade order. This has been present
almost from the beginning of the GATT system, but it has grown in
significance as rapidly industrializing countries, which had not originally
shared with the transatlantic economy the benefits of multilateral liberalization, increasingly began to exploit its basically non-discriminatory
character. The changing monetary arrangements in Europe are a natural
outcome of the recent acceleration of financial integration and the free
flow of capital that it engendered; these new arrangements also reflect the
uncertain advance toward a common currency, which is of course a
politically charged issue. This second factor implies a growing importance for the link between political economy and transatlantic relations.

The third factor affecting transatlantic economic relations is the
emergence of regional economic relationships within the transatlantic
economy. Such relationships are not themselves new – there were many
regional initiatives during the 1950s and 1960s. But the formation of the
European Economic Community (EEC) and the European Free Trade
Area (EFTA), despite initial trepidation, apparently spawned the
Kennedy Round and so came to be seen as complementary to multilateral liberalization, and most of the other earlier trade initiatives never
in fact came to much. Similarly, the earlier attempts at monetary union
petered out; they did rather little to change the G7 approach to
macroeconomic coordination or to integrate European capital markets.

The more recent 'new regionalism', however, appears to be altering the
nature of the transatlantic economy, with consequences that are unclear.
The trade initiatives involve, in North America, the Canadian–US Free
Trade Agreement and its subsequent extension to the North American
Free Trade Agreement (NAFTA). Further enlargement within the
western hemisphere appears a distinct possibility. In Europe, we have the
completion of the internal market within the European Union (EU)
followed by the extension of the central provisions of that completion to
the EFTA nations by means of the European Economic Area (EEA). In
addition, we have the extension of the EU itself, most immediately by
the accession of Austria, Finland, and Sweden, but ultimately by the
prospective incorporation of states in Central and Eastern Europe. The
latter have become loosely linked to the EU by the recent Europe
Agreements. On the financial side, the dramatic changes are in the EU,
where capital controls have been virtually eliminated and where the
Maastricht Treaty now provides a legal and institutional framework for
monetary union anytime the member states wish to proceed. On the
American side of the Atlantic, capital moves freely but little thought is
given to deeper monetary integration; there is, however, a growing

concern in Washington about the implications of a single currency in Europe. The ramifications of the new regionalism have become a great concern to economists and policy makers alike.

The papers in this volume attempt to address all three basic factors. The paper by Markusen and Venables (chapter 6) concerns – as does the first of the three factors – the increasing similarity of the transatlantic economies as their mutual trade steadily expands. Markusen and Venables address, specifically, the fact that direct investment between these economies has grown even more rapidly than their trade, in sharp contrast to much theory, which apparently predicts that direct invest-ment is induced by *dissimilarities* between economies and *substitutes* for international trade. They develop an oligopoly model in which locational considerations (specifically, tariffs and transport costs) help induce direct investment in conventional fashion, and then effectively employ numer-ical simulation to picture the effects of growth and convergence of various sorts. By giving us a model in which direct investment can grow relative to trade even as national economic characteristics converge, Markusen and Venables draw a picture of transatlantic development of more general interest.

The paper by Weber (chapter 3) also addresses the first factor by examining coordinated exchange rate intervention following the Plaza and Louvre agreements in 1985, and by comparing it with the EMS experience prior to the exchange rate crises of 1992. Weber makes the interesting observation that the wider exchange rate mechanism (ERM) bands instituted after these crises are comparable to the bands thought by some to characterize the post-Louvre regime. Thus, the post-Louvre experience may yield some important lessons for the 'new' EMS, and the old EMS experience may have some lessons for those who would reform the current rules of Group of Three (G3) intervention. Weber uses intervention data that have only recently been released by central banks and lays out the facts about both G3 and EMS intervention in a much more comprehensive way than is available elsewhere in the literature. He also uses new techniques to test widely held views about exchange rate intervention. He finds that the chief difference between the old EMS and G3 intervention was that the former was more likely to commit interest rates to the cause. It remains an open issue whether that or the existence of capital controls was responsible for the success of the EMS in the late 1980s. In any case, Weber finds little evidence for the effectiveness of sterilized intervention, and this has obvious implications both for G3 coordination and for the new EMS.

Four papers address the second factor dominating transatlantic economic relations. Two of them – the paper by Hillman and Moser

4   **Matthew B. Canzoneri, Wilfred J. Ethier, and Vittorio Grilli**

(chapter 10) and the paper by Fung and Staiger (chapter 9) – address the link between trade liberalization and political economy. These papers take complementary views, with Hillman and Moser looking at the big picture, and Fung and Staiger focusing narrowly on a specific, illustrative issue. Two others – the paper by Lockwood, Miller, and Zhang (chapter 8) and the paper by Eichengreen, Rose, and Wyplosz (chapter 7) – address the new monetary arrangements in Europe and the exchange rate crises that followed the liberalization of capital markets. These papers also take complementary views, with Eichengreen et al. looking at a problem that confronts all central banks on both sides of the Atlantic, and Lockwood et al. focusing on independence for the national central banks of Europe.

Hillman and Moser offer an explanation of how political-economic dominance by special interests in policy-making can nevertheless be consistent with trade liberalization, as experienced over time by the transatlantic economy. Many years ago Harry Johnson analysed 'retaliatory' tariff-setting by national governments concerned with maximization of national welfare, and a significant literature concerned with this problem has developed over the years. Hillman and Moser demonstrate that the conclusions of this literature by and large apply to a more realistic setting in which special-interest groups influence commercial policy.

Fung and Staiger examine a specific policy tool – trade adjustment assistance. Although some special interests always find free trade disadvantageous, the theory of comparative advantage implies that the gainers from such a policy (relative to no trade) always gain enough to compensate the losers. The problem is to find a practical method to effect such compensation. Trade adjustment assistance has been regarded as a way to make free trade more palatable by offering losers some compensation and by easing the pains of reallocating resources out of comparatively disadvantaged sectors. But economists have often been sceptical about such a policy because it offers import-competing sectors a subsidy, in the form of insurance, denied to other sectors, and because in practice it often seems to enable recipients to 'sit tight', thereby retarding adjustment rather than assisting it. Fung and Staiger expose a new link between trade adjustment assistance and the process of trade liberalization, showing how the availability of such assistance might enhance tariff cooperation between governments.

Eichengreen et al. are the first systematically to characterize the stylized facts leading up to currency crises and then test competing views about their causes. Although Weber found that policy coordination was deeper within the EMS than among the G3, this was not sufficient to preserve exchange rate stability once capital became fully mobile in the 1990s. The Bretton Woods period was still a time of limited capital mobility, and currency crises were generally preceded by a period of clearly diverging macroeconomic behaviour in the country in question; this divergence triggered a 'classic' speculative attack. The authors argue that the attacks of the 1990s were not of the 'classic' type, but were instead of a self-fulfilling nature. There was no significant difference in macroeconomic behaviour leading up to these crises. The attacks were not provoked by divergent macroeconomic indicators but, in some cases, they were the cause of subsequent divergence in macroeconomic policies. This view of currency crises has strikingly different implications for policy than the 'classic' view. Contrary to the official view taken after the exchange rate crises of 1992, it may not be sufficient for exchange rate stability – either within Europe or across the Atlantic – simply to monitor macroeconomic behaviour and take corrective measures after divergences are clearly visible.

Lockwood *et al.* revisit an old question: how can newly independent central banks establish credibility for low-inflation policies while at the same time maintaining the flexibility necessary for stabilization? The authors combine two strands of the existing literature – one on trigger mechanisms, the other on delegation – and they add an interesting new element – the degree of nominal wage rigidity. Their discussion comes at a time when many of the central banks in Europe are sailing through uncharted waters. For these central banks, exchange rate stabilization no longer serves as the operating procedure, or as the linchpin for inflation credibility. In addition, institutional change is in the wind: the central banks of France and Spain are being granted independence, and the banks of Italy, the UK, Belgium, and the Netherlands are being given a more important role in policy formulation; moreover, the Maastricht process requires that national central banks be given independence from their governments before they can participate in economic and monetary union (EMU). The literature on central bank independence serves as a guide for these new institutions, and the Federal Reserve System in the United States is often held up as an example to be emulated. However, Lockwood *et al.* show, among other things, that the Federal Reserve experience may not be relevant in a European context, because the degree of nominal wage rigidity is quite different on the two sides of the Atlantic.

The three remaining papers address the third factor dominating transatlantic economic relations: the 'new regionalism'. Two – the paper by Bond and Syropoulos (chapter 4) and the paper by Deardorff (chapter 5) – address the relation between multilateral trade liberalization and the formation of regional trading arrangements. The third – the paper by Hughes Hallett and Ma (chapter 2) – looks at macroeconomic interaction between the blocs. Again the three papers are complementary, and together they provide us with a comprehensive picture of the multilateral–regional relationship characteristic of the new transatlantic economy.

Bond and Syropoulos examine the implications of trading blocs for trade liberalization between blocs, that is, for multilateralism. They hypothesize an exogenous increase in, alternatively, the number of regional blocs and the relative size of a given bloc, and analyse the effects of multilateral liberalization, where the latter is the outcome of an infinitely repeated game between the blocs. Thus Bond and Syropoulos directly analyse a problem of prominent contemporary concern.

Deardorff, by contrast, looks at the effects of multilateral liberalization on individual countries that belong to regional blocs (or, alternatively, on distinct regions within a single country). This problem is a natural complement to that examined by Bond and Syropoulos but it has attracted very little attention, so Deardorff breaks new ground. He employs standard comparative advantage analysis to great effect, clarifying a complex model and showing how regional effects of liberalization depend upon initial patterns of production.

Hughes Hallett and Ma use large macro-econometric models to address the question of macroeconomic coordination between blocs. Whereas many studies have found little or no gain from the coordination of macroeconomic policies, these authors find just the opposite. In particular, they argue that coordination can be important even when transatlantic spillovers are small; they also argue that forming blocs is a poor substitute for full cooperation. But perhaps the most novel part of this paper is the authors' analysis of 'regime' coordination, or reform of the economic environment. The most interesting example of this is deregulation of labour markets in Europe; the authors find that deregulation has big spillover effects, both within Europe and across the Atlantic. Given the recent political sensitivity to the persistently high rates of unemployment in Europe, and the concern with labour market reform that this new awareness has engendered, the result is quite important. This paper, together with the paper by Lockwood *et al.*, suggests that a rush to reform labour markets may have unintended, and essentially unknown, effects on transatlantic policy coordination.

Taken together, the ten papers in this volume only begin to address the three basic factors that are shaping transatlantic economic relations. However, a beginning has been made, and that was the intention of the editors.

2 Transatlantic policy coordination with sticky labour markets: the reality of the real side

A. J. HUGHES HALLETT and YUE MA

1   Introduction

The early years of the 1990s have seen big changes in the interactions between the industrialized economies. Changes have taken place on both sides of the Atlantic. For Europe, there has been the single market, the Maastricht Treaty, and the collapse and suspension of the exchange rate mechanism (ERM). For the USA there has been the signing of the North American Free Trade Agreement (NAFTA) treaty and a change of fiscal course within the Clinton administration.

One might expect that these changes would alter the nature of the interactions between the European, American and Japanese economies, and therefore alter the incentives and scope for coordination between them – not to mention the distribution of the gains. The purpose of this paper is to investigate these issues. With the example of German unification before us, and the collapse of the exchange rate mechanism in a period of falling inflation and monetary convergence, we take the view that much of the coordination and economic control has to do with the real side. Indeed we argue that uncoordinated and potentially unsustainable fiscal policies produce a lack of credibility in the same way that monetary policies do, but with potentially larger consequences.

We also show that extending the domain of policies through monetary integration or coordinated decision-making can be very helpful if sufficient commitment to the regime is made, whereas simply trying to unify preferences and actions by imposing a tight ERM regime is not. 'Tying the policy makers' hands' in this way may have moved Europe in the wrong direction therefore. This is important for the design of policies on a monetary union because that automatically involves extensions of the policy domain. However, we find that these things have little impact outside Europe. By contrast, it is the policy regimes that these

7

developments may impose on their markets that matter. Here transatlantic policy coordination continues to be important.

2   The decision-making framework

2.1   Procedures vs. regimes

In this paper we distinguish between the *way* in which policy makers reach their decisions and the *regime* within which those decisions are intended to operate. Our purpose is to examine the consequences of adopting different decision procedures, conditional on certain policy regimes. We then investigate the spillovers under each regime, and the importance of, and scope for, transatlantic (or G7) coordination. There are various possibilities.

(a) **Policy makers could agree to full and explicit cooperation**. However, bargains across all the targets and instruments of policy are politically very difficult to achieve, and may be too sensitive to errors and disagreements about how the world works to be a practical proposition. In that case, the following might serve as substitutes:

(b) **A hard target zone regime**. The leading central bank exploits its reputation for credible monetary policies, and the remaining countries act as followers, with reaction functions determined by their commitment to stay within a set exchange rate. Arguably this was the position of the Bundesbank in Europe until the suspension of the European Monetary System (EMS) regime in 1993. The extension to a G7-wide target zone regime is not under active consideration, so we restrict this regime to Europe only.

(c) **The preference transfer solution**. As an alternative, we consider what happens when the exchange rate bands become very narrow and realignments are ruled out. Nominal interest rates then converge, and European monetary policy is set by the Bundesbank. To achieve this outcome the non-German economies have to acquire not only the policies but also the preferences of Germany – for monetary policy at least. This is an extreme version, where inflation-prone economies 'buy' the policy credibility of low-inflation economies through a commitment to fixed exchange rates. But to achieve the same results in a looser world, where exchange rates are not completely fixed, where fiscal policies may differ, and where structures and shocks vary over countries (so that what suits Germany may not be suitable elsewhere), policy makers would have to use the preferences and priorities of Germany in their own policy decisions. This is a weaker form of 'tying one's hands': the narrow bands would be 'soft' but realignments or deviations heavily penalized.

(d) **The domain solution.** If the goal is to improve European economic performance on average, then it might be better to have the Germans target *average* European variables directly (rather than their own national variables) and to have other countries target deviations from the average using the instruments remaining at their disposal; all of this happening under an agreed set of preferences. Those preferences might be the original German preferences, or non-German preferences, or some compromise between the two. In this scenario the Germans extend the domain of their policies to all of Europe, instead of simply following their own national goals and forcing the other countries to follow suit (see Masson and Meredith, 1990, or Kenen, 1992).

(e) **Variants of the domain solution.** We examine two variants of the domain solution in order to show the gains and losses for each participant over standard non-cooperative policies. In the first variant, each country makes its decisions, subject to the constraints of the domain solution, according to its own national preferences, while the lead country (Germany) has to design policy for the system at the system's average preferences. The results can be evaluated using national preferences to show the incentives for individual countries to follow this decision strategy, compared with non-cooperative policy-making. But they can also be evaluated at the average of the national preferences to show the incentives for adopting this strategy when policy makers wish to improve the social welfare of the system as a whole, as opposed to just their own national objectives. The second variant, however, is the one foreseen in the Maastricht Treaty. Here a domain solution is created by using the lead country's (in this case German) preferences for policy selection in every country but national preferences to evaluate the results.

It is clear from this discussion that possibility (b) is a policy *regime* imposed on the currency markets, whereas possibilities (a), (c), and (d), or (e), are decision *procedures* that policy makers might wish to use. This contrast is deliberate, although the operating distinctions between (b) and (c) – if not between (a) and (d) as well – may be very small. The distinction is important because it makes the point that it is the regimes that regulate economic performance, and not the procedures by which policies are chosen, that matter and need coordination. In fact we show that regime (b) has profound spillover effects both within Europe and across the G7, while its apparently close substitute – decision procedure (c) – has few transatlantic spillovers, and relatively few even within Europe. We underline this result by showing that the same thing happens with regimes involving labour market regulation, or trading restrictions, or fiscal consolidation. The case for coordinating regimes rather than the policy decisions themselves is therefore made.

2.2   Optimal non-cooperative policies

Consider the case of two countries. Define y_t^A as the vector of deviations of country A's targets from their ideal values at time t; y_t^{Ad}. Then $y^{A'} = (y_1^{A'} \ldots y_T^{A'})$ is the vector of target 'failures' over the decision periods $1 \ldots T$. Similarly let $x^{A'} = (x_1^{A'} \ldots x_T^{A'})$ be the vector of deviations of country A's instruments from their ideal values.

Now define a conventional quadratic loss function for country A:

$$w^A = y^{A'} C^A y^A + x^{A'} E^A x^A, \tag{1}$$

where C^A and E^A are positive definitive symmetric matrices. This loss function will be minimized subject to a set of linear constraints:

$$y^A = R_{AA} x^A + R_{AB} x^B + s^A, \tag{2}$$

where R_{AA} and R_{AB} are matrices of dynamic multipliers,[1] and s^A represents the non-controllable (and random) influences on y^A. If the instrument values of the other player, B, are treated as given, the first-order conditions yield a set of linear reaction functions:

$$x^A = -(R_{AA}' C^A R_{AA} + E^A)^{-1} R_{AA}' C^A (R_{AB} x^B + s^A). \tag{3}$$

Meanwhile country B will have a loss function $w^B = (y^{B'} C^B y^B + x^{B'} E^B x^B)$ and face the constraints $y^B = R_{BA} x^A + R_{BB} x^B + s^B$. Hence a reaction function for B, analogous to (3), can be solved simultaneously with (3) to yield the Nash equilibrium values x^A and x^B:[2]

$$\begin{bmatrix} R_{AA}' C^A R_{AA} + E^A & | & R_{AA}' C^A R_{AB} \\ - & - & - \\ R_{BB}' C^B R_{BA} & | & R_{BB}' C^B R_{BB} + E^B \end{bmatrix} \begin{bmatrix} x^A \\ x^B \end{bmatrix} = - \begin{bmatrix} R_{AA}' C^A s^A \\ R_{BB}' C^B s^B \end{bmatrix} \tag{4}$$

2.3   Cooperative decision-making

Pareto optimal outcomes may be calculated by minimizing the collective loss function, subject to the constraints represented by (2) and its counterpart for $\mathbf{y}^B$:

$$w = \alpha w^A + (1 - \alpha)w^B \quad 0 < \alpha < 1. \tag{5}$$

That yields the following expression for the optimal cooperative policies:

$$\begin{bmatrix} \alpha(R'_{AA}C^A R_{AA} + E^A) + (1-\alpha)R'_{BA}C^B R_{BA} \mid \alpha R'_{AA}C^A R_{AB} + (1-\alpha)R'_{BA}C^B R_{BB} \\ - \quad - \quad - \\ \alpha R'_{AB}C^A R_{AA} + (1-\alpha)R'_{BB}C^B R_{BA} \mid \alpha R'_{AB}C^A R_{AB} + (1-\alpha)(R'_{BB}C^B R_{BB} + E^B) \end{bmatrix}$$

$$\begin{bmatrix} x_A \\ x_B \end{bmatrix} = - \begin{bmatrix} \alpha R'_{AA}C^A s^A + (1 - \alpha)R'_{BA}C^B s^B \\ \alpha R'_{AB}C^A s^A + (1 - \alpha)R'_{BB}C^B s^B \end{bmatrix} \tag{6}$$

2.4   The preference transfer solution

If Germany is country A, and the rest of Europe country B, the only change from the Nash equilibrium in (4) would be that C^A and E^A replace C^B and E^B in the lower matrix equation. But would the rest of Europe – and Germany too for that matter – be better or worse off?

To a first approximation, the rest of Europe will be unambiguously worse off (unless both economies are subject to identical shocks and preferences, in which case nothing will happen). This is because, if Germany and the Bundesbank carry out their policies exactly as previously announced, then the only change for the rest of Europe will come from their own policy changes driven by their new (German) preferences. Yet Germany may be better off because other countries are not following policies more in line with Germany's needs, and that in turn may improve the average outcomes for Europe. This presumably is what policy makers had hoped for when they appeared to adopt this solution in the early 1990s. Yet it imposes a tremendous load on German 'locomotive' power, and it assumes (unjustifiably) that every economy is structured and responds just like the German one.

2.5   The domain solution

The domain solution requires German policies to minimize

$$w^D = \mathbf{y}'C\mathbf{y}, \tag{7}$$

where $\mathbf{y} = \frac{1}{2}(\mathbf{y}^A + \mathbf{y}^B)$ and C is the agreed set of preferences across the union of national targets. Hence

$$w^D = \frac{1}{4}(\mathbf{y}^{A'}C\mathbf{y}^A + \mathbf{y}^{B'}C\mathbf{y}^B + 2\mathbf{y}^{A'}C\mathbf{y}^B) = \frac{1}{2}(w + \mathbf{y}^{A'}C\mathbf{y}^B), \tag{8}$$

where w comes from (5) evaluated at $\alpha = \frac{1}{2}$. Now, if there exists an incentive-compatible bargain at $\alpha = \frac{1}{2}$ relative to the Nash (non-cooperative) equilibrium – which is likely for two equal-sized economies, although they are not assumed to have identical structures – then it will always be possible to choose $\mathbf{y}^A$ and $\mathbf{y}^B$ from the incentive-compatible range. As a result, $w = \frac{1}{2}w^A_{CP} + \frac{1}{2}w^B_{CP}$ where $w^A_{CP} < w^A_{NC}$ and $w^B_{CP} < w^B_{NC}$, the subscript CP denoting 'evaluated in the incentive-compatible range' and subscript NC denoting 'evaluated at the optimal non-cooperative policies'. Hence

$$w^D < \frac{1}{2}\left(\frac{w^A_{NC} + w^B_{NC}}{2}\right) + \frac{1}{2}\mathbf{y}^{A'}C\mathbf{y}^B \tag{9}$$

and the domain solution *always* produces a better outcome for Europe as a whole, i.e. w^D is less than the *average* non-cooperative outcome, so long as $\mathbf{y}^{A'}C\mathbf{y}^B$ is less than the average of the non-cooperative outcomes.[3] Thus the domain solution always improves on non-cooperative policies with the same set of preferences: (a) for two identically symmetric economies; (b) for Europe on average; (c) for the worse-performing of the two economies; (d) for both economies individually if the dispersion of $w^A_{NC} + w^B_{NC}$ is less than half the average of the non-cooperative outcomes; (e) but necessarily for the better-performing economy otherwise.

All these conclusions are conditional on finding $\mathbf{y}^A$ and $\mathbf{y}^B$ in the incentive-compatible range such that $\mathbf{y}^{A'}C\mathbf{y}^B \le \frac{1}{2}(w^A_{NC} + w^B_{NC})$. That means the domain solution works when policies can be chosen to make price reductions in one country match price rises in another (so that $\mathbf{y}^{A'}\mathbf{y}^B \le 0$), or to match output gains in one country with losses in another, or by making the larger rises in one variable match smaller rises in the same variable elsewhere. Nevertheless, we have been unable to show that the Germans would be better off under their own or the average preferences. So the political feasibility of the scheme has still to be verified.

3   The simulation exercises

3.1   The model

To explore the interdependence and interactions between the trans-atlantic economies, we have modified one of the standard empirical multicountry models – the IMF's MULTIMOD – which contains linked models for each of the G7 economies (the USA, Japan, Canada, Germany, France, Italy, and the UK). It also contains fully specified models for the smaller European Union (EU) economies as a bloc (the 'rest of the EMS') and for the rest of the OECD as a bloc. Then there are also models for the OPEC country bloc, and for the developing countries in Africa, Asia, and Latin America. Each of these national or regional models is linked to the others through bilateral trade flows, capital movements, and exchange rates, which in turn influence domestic financial markets. Our modifications involve, first, a proper modelling of the unification process in Germany: that is, a separate eastern region in Germany so that we can track the recent changes in output, capital, (un)employment, and fiscal expenditures in the east; also separate wages and migration, so that we can assess the impact of labour market developments properly. Second, we allow for changes in the European exchange rate mechanism in 1992/3, and consider alternative replace-ments. All of these modifications are needed for any assessment of the impact of events in Europe on transatlantic coordination. They are detailed in the appendix to this paper.

MULTIMOD is an annual multicountry econometric model. The model's specification explains the main expenditure categories and production flows in each country, from which employment, investment, prices, interest rates and exchange rates are determined. Financial markets, trade flows, and capital movements (including loans and interest payments) are included. Trade is divided into three markets: oil, primary commodities, and manufactured goods. Perfectly flexible prices clear the commodity markets, where demands are driven by activity levels and supplies by prices and a predetermined capacity. Manufactured goods are produced and traded everywhere. Aggregate demand is then built up from consumption (based on current *and* expected future earnings, asset values), investment (based on market evaluations of firms' current *and* expected future earnings), trade, and the net fiscal position. This determines output in the short run. Long-run or potential output is determined by a production function, so capacity utilization (the ratio of actual to potential output) can vary. Domestic output prices are subject to a Phillips curve, such that the higher the capacity utilization the

Table 2.1. Policy preferences, 1990–6 inclusive

Country	Ideal values[1]				Relative priorities			
	$G\dot{D}P\%$	$\dot{P}\%$	$G/Y\%$	$RS\%$	$G\dot{D}P$	$\dot{P}$	G/Y	RS
USA	3.0	2.7	19.0→17.6	4.5	1	1	1	1
Japan	3.0	1.5	14.8→15.1	4.0	1	1	1	1
Canada	3.0	2.0	22.6→21.7	5.0	1	1	1	1
Germany	3.0	2.0	20.6→21.2[2]	6.0	1	5	1	1
UK	3.0	4.0	22.8→24.0	5.0	1	1	1	1
France	3.0	2.0	21.3→21.0	5.0	1	1	1	1
Italy	3.0	4.0	20.1→19.6	6.0	1	1	1	1

[1] Units: $G\dot{D}P$ and $\dot{P}$ in % growth p.a.; G/Y = government expenditures as % of national income; RS in % points.
[2] Via 22.6 in 1991/2; the actual and baseline figures are rather higher.

greater the inflation pressure. So there is no absolute output constraint, and prices change by an amount depending on the remaining spare capacity and the state of the labour markets. Prices are therefore partly sticky and partly forward looking, depending on wage contracts, international competitiveness, and capacity utilization.

In the government sector, non-ERM exchange rates are determined by open interest parities and the *expected* depreciations consistent with a complete model solution. The non-German ERM rates, however, are obliged to stay within a 2.5 per cent band around pre-assigned parity values. Monetary policy, for ERM members, therefore consists of forcing interest rates to follow a reaction function that targets the given DM parity and maintains the currency within its band. For other countries, and for Germany, a pre-assigned monetary growth rate is targeted, with interest rates set gradually to reduce the gap between actual and targeted money growth. Likewise tax rates adjust to eliminate the gap between actual and targeted debt levels, subject to an inter-temporal budget constraint. Fiscal expenditures are therefore also partly exogenous and partly endogenized. A full description of MULTIMOD's properties and simulation characteristics is given in Masson et al. (1990), and comparisons with other models in Bryant et al. (1993). Hughes Hallet and Ma (1994) review a number of sensitivity tests of the model's simulation properties.

3.1.1 The policy preferences
Table 2.1 summarizes the reference solution preferences over the declared targets and instruments of policy: output growth ($G\dot{D}P$), inflation ($\dot{P}$),

aggregate fiscal expenditures as a proportion of GNP (G/Y), and short-term interest rates (R/S).[4] The ideal values are simply set at levels rather better than recent experience. Since they are infeasible, but represent the sort of values that the policy makers themselves say they wish to aim for, they should not prove very controversial.

Our *relative* priorities are set so that each percentage point failure (in each variable in each period) is penalized equally, except for German inflation, which is penalized at five times that rate. That is a plausible starting point for looking at the relative performance of different policy rules or regimes, given that all policy variables are measured in equivalent units.

Nevertheless there is something unavoidably arbitrary in *any* preference specification, in that these preferences might not be the ones the policy makers would wish to choose. If not, the baseline will look poor, and unfairly so, in comparison with optimized non-cooperative policies under the specified preferences. However, that criticism is not important because it is the comparison between the reference (non-cooperative) solution and the various cooperative, domain, and preference transfer solutions derived from the *same* preferences that is at issue here; not the comparison with a particular choice of baseline, which is for orientation only. Indeed, given the usual relative insensitivity of policies to changes in the penalties (Hughes Hallett, 1987b), it would take implausibly large changes in the relative priorities to upset the ranking of the policy rules and regimes. A five-fold increase in inflation penalties, for example, produces only relatively small changes in the target outcomes for the EU countries between simulation A and simulation C in table 2.4 below.

The difficulty is that the alternative, which is to calculate the preferences implicit in the baseline/historical policies (e.g. Oudiz and Sachs, 1984), is equally arbitrary and perhaps less plausible. Not only are half the figures projections rather than actual policy choices, but it is assuming a lot to

Table 2.2. ERM parities/weights

	1990	1991	1992	1993	1994	1995	1996
DM/£	2.95	2.95	2.95	2.43	2.43	2.43	2.43
(Weight)	(1500)	(1000)	(1000)	(1)	(1)	(1)	(1)
Fr/DM	3.35	3.35	3.35	3.35	3.35	3.35	3.35
(Weight)	(100000)	(100000)	(200000)	(100000)	(1)	(1)	(1)
Lira/DM	0.748	0.748	0.748	1.007	1.007	1.007	1.007
(Weight)	(5000)	(5000)	(5000)	(1)	(1)	(2000)	(2000)

Note: The bands of $\pm$ 2.5% are maintained throughout

say that the authorities actually did optimize their choices, that they used exactly this model and knew both its information set and each others' reaction functions without error. If these assumptions are not correct then these calculated preferences would become contaminated with model, and information, optimization errors.

3.1.2   The baseline and information set

All the simulations that follow work from a baseline composed of the historical values of the model's variables plus projections forward to some terminal period (in this case forty years from our start date of 1990). The model is then solved sufficiently far ahead so as to remove any influence of the terminal conditions on our simulation results. We report the results for 1990 to 1996 inclusive, to cover the period of German unification, the Maastricht Treaty, the breakdown of the European Monetary System in 1992/3, the signing of NAFTA and the Uruguay Round, and the introduction of a new fiscal programme in the USA (see table 2.A1 in the appendix). The baseline itself is identical to that used by the IMF in its own work with MULTIMOD; the endogenous and exogenous variables are made to follow the 1993 projections in the IMF's *World Economic Outlook*. Forward-looking expectations are then solved to be equal to the outcome projected for the relevant future period. This baseline therefore defines our information set except in so far as we have had to model the unification of Germany explicitly.[5]

Except for the one exercise where no realignments are allowed, each ERM country is obliged to accept its official 1990 parity against the DM and to maintain its 2.5 per cent band around that for the duration of the simulation (1990–6). However, Italy and the UK *are* allowed to realign their currencies down during 1992, from DM 1.33 ± 2.5 per cent to 0.993 ± 2.5 per cent per 1000 lire, and from DM 2.95 ± 2.5 per cent to 2.43 ± 2.5 per cent per pound, roughly as happened. But, for the purposes of this paper, both currencies are required to stay within the ERM system after 1992. France, of course, is allowed no realignments; we retain 3.35 ± 2.5 per cent francs per DM throughout and do not attempt to include the 1993 widening of the bands to 15 per cent (that is left to a later exercise). These figures are summarized in table 2.2, together with the penalty function weights that are necessary to keep the currencies within their 2.5 per cent bands. Notice, in that table, the extreme pressure on the French franc in 1990–1993, as reflected in the huge penalties necessary to maintain the franc's bands (20 to 200 times greater than those necessary to hold the pound and lira in place). Moreover, the pressure on the realigned pound and lira evidently vanishes in 1992, although the lira weakens again from 1995.

Table 2.3. Expected objective function values ('the costs to go') under four basic decision schemes, 1990–6 inclusive

Country	Reference solution (Simulation A)	Domain solution (Simulation B)		Preference transfer (Simulation C)		Domain solution under German preferences (Simulation E)	
		National prefer-ences	% im-prove-ment	National prefer-ences	% im-prove-ment	National prefer-ences	% im-prove-ment
USA	11.07	10.91	+1.4	11.06	0	10.96	+0.1
Japan	10.12	10.28	−1.6	9.89	+2.3	10.21	+0.1
Canada	28.92	28.48	+1.5	28.78	+0.5	28.54	+1.5
Germany	57.23	87.92	−53.4	54.73	+4.4	70.16	−22.6
UK	160.08	124.34	+22.3	182.84	−14.2	133.15	+16.8
France	48.09	18.28	+62.0	52.08	−8.3	26.96	+43.9
Italy	104.53	72.11	+31.0	113.97	−9.0	81.65	+21.9

Notes:
1 Objective function values at this baseline are: 22.09 (USA), 23.02 (Japan), 60.55 (Canada), 63.06 (Germany), 232.06 (UK), 66.83 (France) and 135.39 (Italy).
2 The German objective function value for the domain solution using *either* average European preferences *or* the average of the non-German preferences was 31.89 (compare column 4) or 18.86 (compare column 1), respectively.
3 Improvements are all relative to the reference (non-cooperative) solution.

This completes the baseline and reference solution ERM specification; the remaining currencies are free to float. Finally, all the simulations are 'open loop' in that they use the initial information set. Our policy projections are therefore not revised again, although in practice they would be revised as often as new information became available. That is because we wish to compare decision strategies *ex ante*, as they would appear when policy makers had to make a choice between them. Such comparisons must be made with one fixed, but plausible, information set.[6]

4   Empirical results: the three alternative decision rules

The results of our three basic decision procedures are given in tables 2.3 and 2.4. They cover:

(a) *Our reference solution*: standard optimal non-cooperative (Nash equilibrium) policies under national preferences and ideal values (simulation A).

Table 2.4. The mean and variance outcomes of the optimized policies: the basic decision procedures, 1990–6 inclusive

Country		Baseline (Historical projections)		Reference solution (Simulation A)		Domain solution (Simulation B)		Preference transfer (Simulation C)		Domain solution (Simulation E)	
		Mean	Variance	Mean	Variance	Mean	Variance	Mean	Variance	Mean	Variance
USA	$G\dot{N}P$	2.19	1.55	2.28	0.85	2.28	0.82	2.27	0.85	2.28	0.83
	$\dot{P}$	3.38	1.05	3.42	1.19	3.39	1.21	3.41	1.19	3.38	1.22
	G/Y	18.53	0.74	18.90	1.39	18.91	1.39	18.92	1.39	18.92	1.40
	RS	4.19	1.56	4.45	0.00	4.45	0.00	4.45	0.00	4.44	0.00
Japan	$G\dot{N}P$	2.20	2.03	2.49	0.90	2.50	0.92	2.49	0.89	2.50	0.91
	$\dot{P}$	1.79	1.11	1.89	0.43	1.89	0.44	1.87	0.42	1.88	0.44
	G/Y	15.21	0.31	15.33	2.27	15.32	2.31	15.34	2.21	15.32	2.29
	RS	4.41	1.43	3.89	0.05	3.89	0.05	3.89	0.04	3.89	0.04
Canada	$G\dot{N}P$	1.67	2.18	2.26	1.77	2.28	1.66	2.26	1.85	2.28	1.70
	$\dot{P}$	2.65	1.83	3.41	4.68	3.41	4.69	3.39	4.64	3.40	4.70
	G/Y	22.61	0.67	22.68	0.87	22.67	0.85	22.69	0.87	22.67	0.86
	RS	6.23	2.78	5.24	0.08	5.24	0.08	5.23	0.07	5.24	0.08
Germany	$G\dot{N}P$	1.71	1.52	1.47	1.34	2.17	1.05	1.47	1.28	1.86	0.94
	$\dot{P}$	3.23	0.70	3.05	0.58	3.79	1.53	3.04	0.48	3.53	1.27
	G/Y	21.70	0.73	21.14	1.88	21.54	1.44	21.19	1.71	21.11	1.90
	RS	7.73	1.93	7.48	1.22	6.08	0.18	7.42	1.84	6.41	0.32
UK	$G\dot{N}P$	1.20	2.70	1.53	1.24	1.82	0.77	1.32	1.91	1.77	0.87
	$\dot{P}$	4.48	2.55	4.92	6.08	5.21	6.19	4.67	3.95	5.13	6.10
	G/Y	24.00	0.63	24.81	1.49	24.94	1.10	24.67	3.86	24.96	1.12
	RS	7.93	3.17	7.72	16.74	7.08	13.16	8.10	19.83	7.21	13.95

France	$G\dot{N}P$	1.64	1.35	2.00	0.67	2.37	0.50	1.66	0.64	2.31	0.50
	$\dot{P}$	2.85	0.59	2.86	0.23	3.20	0.28	2.54	0.20	3.14	0.26
	G/Y	21.40	0.28	21.65	0.52	21.79	0.38	21.20	0.78	21.81	0.39
	RS	7.50	3.21	6.95	6.56	6.02	2.47	7.25	6.47	6.16	2.88
Italy	$G\dot{N}P$	1.71	1.25	2.21	0.66	2.63	0.44	1.70	1.20	2.57	0.46
	$\dot{P}$	4.80	1.19	5.34	1.10	5.71	1.23	4.79	0.76	5.65	1.18
	G/Y	19.89	0.21	19.82	0.45	20.07	0.33	19.16	1.49	20.09	0.34
	RS	9.23	3.10	8.01	13.94	7.40	10.00	8.44	14.08	7.52	10.42
European average	$\dot{P}$	3.65	0.84	3.91	0.60	4.37	0.68	3.67	0.45	4.24	0.60

(b) *The domain solution*: as in the reference solution except that the German policy makers are required to target the average European inflation rate, and the remaining European countries target deviations of their inflation rate from the European average with their own inflation priority weights. Two versions are given. Simulation B has Germany policy makers targeting European inflation using average European penalties. This solution is evaluated either at European average preferences – the social welfare solution – or through the original national preference functions. Simulation E, by contrast, has German policy makers targeting European inflation with German penalties. In the rest of the ERM, policy makers target their deviations from average European inflation as before, and the outcomes are all evaluated through the national preferences as before. This is the Maastricht-consistent domain solution.

(c) *The preference transfer solution*: as in the reference solution except that France, Italy, and the UK are obliged to use German priority weights in their objective functions, in place of their national preferences (simulation C).

Table 2.4 summarizes the outcomes, in terms of mean values and variances over the period 1990–6, for the underlying target variables and policy instruments, for each country under each decision procedure. The corresponding mean and variance figures for the baseline/historical policy choices are also given for comparison.[7] Table 2.3 gives the expected objective function values under each of these strategies.

4.1   Non-cooperative policy-making

The reference solution shows that, even on a non-cooperative basis, optimization would produce significant improvements over the baseline/ historical policies. In objective function terms, the non-European countries register improvements of a little over 50 per cent, while the four European economies are better off by between 27 per cent and 33 per cent. In the non-European economies, these improvements come largely from reducing the volatility of the target variables and from stabilizing monetary policy. That implies a more active use of fiscal policy to absorb external shocks, but no more than marginal upward adjustments to average output growth and inflation.

In the European economies we see a different picture. Like the USA and Japan, Germany does not change its policies much in the reference solution. There is some tightening of German fiscal policy (a less ambitious reunification programme, in other words), which allows a small relaxation in interest rates and monetary policy. Again that leads to more active fiscal interventions, but not to much stabilization of monetary policy. The result is a fall in the already low growth rate and in inflation. France, on the other hand, is able to reduce interest rates a little and expand fiscally, to produce slightly higher growth for no extra inflation. However, both fiscal and monetary policies have had to become more active to achieve that outcome.

The UK and Italy meanwhile enjoy more significant gains on the real side, but at the cost of much greater volatility on the monetary side. The result is some small relaxation of monetary policy, for the same or slightly expanded fiscal policy. That yields gains in average growth rates for only minor increases in trend inflation. So what we are observing is that attempts to stabilize the UK and Italian exchange rates, when realignments appear warranted, comes at the cost of stability in monetary policy; in short, there is a trade-off between exchange rate stability and interest rate stability. The same is true of France, but to a smaller extent.

4.2   The domain solution

4.2.1   The advantages for individual countries

Evaluating the domain solution at national preferences (columns 2 and 3 of table 2.3) shows that the three follower economies (France, Italy, and the UK) gain substantially over our non-cooperative reference solution. France gains disproportionately with a 62 per cent improvement; Italy is next best with a 31 per cent gain; while the UK gains by 22 per cent. Thus France gains by two or three times as much as the other two. That is to be expected because France is the only one of the three that is not allowed an exchange rate realignment in 1992/3. As a result, introducing more relaxed controls on individual price levels that reduce the deflationary pressure on France will be especially helpful because the resulting (larger) price rises in Germany can be balanced against small rises in France to leave stable European prices *on average*. By contrast, Italy and the UK realigned their currencies down in 1992 and that has its own inflationary consequences. They therefore offer less scope for improvements when the restraints on individual national price levels are relaxed. The domain solution would therefore show a more *even* distribution of the gains, but at a worse overall level, if the UK and Italy were not allowed their realignments (see table 2.5 below).

On the other hand, our theoretical results have been unable to show that the leading economy (Germany in this case) would also benefit from a domain solution. Obviously, if the domain solution improves the general performance of the follower economies, then some of those improvements will spill over and improve German performance too. But it matters where the improvements in France, Italy, and the UK appear. If, as here, they are in higher growth at the cost of somewhat higher inflation, then Germany will also enjoy faster growth (at higher prices) *both* from spillovers through the usual trade and monetary linkages *and* through the policy relaxation needed to generate those improvements elsewhere in Europe. But that has come by requiring Germany to accept a slightly higher inflation rate. If the penalties on the latter are large enough, then German preferences will register an overall loss even if the favourable spillovers on growth are quite large. And that is the case here. Inflation, per percentage point, is penalized at five times the rate for failing to achieve adequate rates of growth. The inflation consequences of relaxing German policies to suit European objectives therefore cause a 53 per cent deterioration in German objectives. That gives an idea of the magnitude of the *disincentive* that the Germans would have to face if they were to give up their national objectives for the sake of helping the rest of Europe. It would be a considerable commitment to the ideals of a united Europe for them to accept material losses on this scale.[8]

4.2.2   The effects on Europe

Europe, on the other hand, would clearly benefit as a whole, *even* under German preferences, unless participants think it necessary to put an implausibly high weight on satisfying German national objectives. The weighted average of the German and non-German national outcomes in column 2 of table 2.3 is less than that of column 1 so long as the German components are given 76 per cent or less of the total weight. A preference transfer solution is therefore unlikely to be helpful.

4.2.3   On the problem for incentive incompatibility

All this confirms the results of section 2.5. However the important point to note is the *power* of the domain solution in generating improvements in performance, *both* for Europe as a whole under any of the preference schemes under consideration *and* for three out of the four members on their own private preferences.

However, the domain solution could obviously do better if it were extended to output growth targets as well. Re-optimization would produce better outcomes for average growth and average inflation, and, since the former is under target and the latter over target in the restricted solution in table 2.4, this can only increase the gains already observed for Europe *and* the three follower economies (because they minimize their own deviations from the European averages). But that, by the same token, is going to make Germany even worse off in terms of its own preferences, unless the spillovers from better performances elsewhere in Europe are very substantial, because we are in effect adding extra targets to Germany's optimization problem without supplying extra instruments. In other words, unless the spillover benefits to Germany are large relative to these sacrifice losses in its own targets, the problem with the domain solution will always be a conflict between gains on average vs. incentive incompatibility for the policy leader. We have already seen that incentive incompatibility of the 'inflation only' solution in column 2 of table 2.3, and adding output targets into the problem would only make this trade-off worse. That would reinforce German fears that concessions to Europe would damage German domestic targets. Such concessions are therefore simply not politically feasible, at least as long as the Bundesbank remains an independent guardian of German interests.

4.2.4   An EMU (Maastricht) consistent domain solution

If the previous solution is politically infeasible, at least in terms of Germany's losses, then the obvious remedy is a domain solution with German preferences. That would minimize the incentive incompatibility problem, as well as represent a neat political bargain: the Germans would be allowed to retain their strong anti-inflation preferences so long as they take other (European) inflation rates into consideration when designing their policies.

Table 2.3, however, shows that this solution is still not incentive compatible. Germany loses out by 22 per cent compared with the reference solution; less than half of its losses in the domain solution in simulation B it is true, but still hard to justify in domestic political terms. The other European countries continue to make nice gains, albeit a little smaller than in the other solution. But the most important point is that the Bundesbank's worst fears of extending its domain of policy are realized: Germany itself will still be made worse off than without any form of cooperation. Put another way, in order to make EMU incentive compatible it is actually necessary to make the European central bank *tougher* than (not just as tough as) the Bundesbank in its anti-inflation preferences/credentials. But the consequences of that latter point are clear to see in table 2.4. Everybody gets significantly slower growth – particularly Germany – for only small reductions in the inflation rate. A large imbalance in the preferences would therefore have to be introduced in order to justify this, because incentive incompatibilities will otherwise remain. In other words, policy makers will have to do something *more* than just integrate their policy-making and economies if they are to generate Pareto improvements for all participants.

4.3   The preference transfer solution

Section 2.4 established that the preference transfer solution would generate worse outcomes for the follower economies and for Europe as a whole. Those results are borne out in table 2.3. France, Italy, and the UK suffer losses of between 8 per cent and 14 per cent, compared with the reference solution. Germany does adjust its policies in response to the changes that appear in France, Italy, and the UK as result of the higher (German) inflation penalties imposed on those countries, but those adjustments are pretty small. Indeed, forcing lower inflation in France, Italy, and the UK allows a small reduction in German interest rates given the smaller inflation spillovers from elsewhere. But any gains on that score are more than offset by the fact that the same tighter monetary (and fiscal) policies reduce growth everywhere. Consequently the changes in Germany amount to no more than a 4 per cent improvement over the reference solution, while Europe as a whole is left worse off.

Two other important points: first, the larger policy changes appear in going from the reference solution to the domain solution, rather than in moving from the reference to the preference transfer solution; second, the preference transfer solution is in fact remarkably similar to the baseline historical policies. Hence it appears that some preference transfers may already have taken place in Europe, but a domain solution would have had stronger coordinating effects.

4.4   The transatlantic interactions

Tables 2.3 and 2.4 show that the US and Japanese economies are virtually unaffected by the different policy solutions that might be adopted in Europe. The more expansionary domain solution produces marginal benefits for the USA, but losses to Japan where European monetary relaxation creates more competition for Japanese exports and growth. A very mild beggar-thy-neighbour regime therefore. In contrast, the spillovers onto growth are positive in the USA. But these changes are all very small, and amount to no more than 1.5 per cent in welfare terms. The more contractionary preference transfer solution works the other way round, producing no overall impact on the USA and a 2 per cent gain for Japan.

That is not to say that Europe does not have any impact on the USA and Japan, or vice versa. Simply recognizing their interdependence through non-cooperative policy choices produces 50 per cent improvements for the USA and Japan over the baseline policies, against 30 per cent improvements for the European economies. These gains are largely efficiency gains, i.e. they give higher output growth for (virtually) no increases in inflation. The imbalance in the gains is also a typical result, and reflects the greater market *flexibility* in the US and Japanese economies, which allows them to adjust their responses to the consequences of unfavourable foreign policy spillovers fairly rapidly. Recognizing that interdependence therefore permits significant domestic policy improvements, even in a non-cooperative world (Hughes Hallett, 1986).

These results suggest three conclusions:

(a) Coordination may be important, but mainly within Europe and as a G3 operation (i.e. between Europe on one side and the USA and Japan on the other).
(b) Market flexibility will be the key to further improvements in performance, and here the USA has an advantage. European policies should aim to enhance that flexibility (or recreate it where it fails). They also need to focus on stability on the real side, rather than exclusively on monetary stability.
(c) The policy regimes, which determine how the markets actually work, may have significant impacts on other countries, but the way in which people arrive at their policies does not. For the Europeans that means the regimes that they institute in their labour markets or for their exchange rates, or that govern their competition and fiscal policies, will have international as well as domestic effects, whereas the way they choose their policies (i.e. collectively or individually, with an independent central bank, German leadership, or via a *de facto* monetary union) may have domestic importance but will have few international spillovers.

5   Changes of regime: monetary policy

At the time of the 1992 currency crises, there were many who argued – in policy-making circles as well as in the academic literature – that currency realignments would be counterproductive and should be avoided. It therefore makes sense to examine what might have happened if no realignments had taken place in 1992 (tables 2.5 and 2.6). But it is also important because there is another side to this story. Consumers and investors are no less forward looking than agents in the financial markets – consumers because they base their expenditures (in part) on their wealth/asset holdings, whose value depends on expected future earnings

Table 2.5. Expected objective function values with no exchange rate realignments in Europe

Country	Reference solution		Domain solution	
	National preferences	% gain	National preferences	% gain
USA	12.16	−9.8	11.61	+4.6
Japan	10.57	−4.3	10.64	−0.8
Canada	29.41	+1.7	28.75	+2.2
Germany	126.6	−121.0	201.3	−60.0
UK	971.1	−507.0	777.9	+19.9
France	60.5	−25.0	30.45	+49.7
Italy	1772.4	−1026.0	1501.0	+15.3

Notes:
1 This table reports objective function values calculated using *national* preference weights in each case.
2 The domain solution's gains are those over the corresponding non-cooperative policy results (i.e. the reference solution in the previous two columns). The reference solution's gains are all calculated against the reference solution of table 2.3.

and interest rates, and investors because their investment plans depend on the current market values of firms (Tobin's Q), again a discounted sum of expected future earnings. Both effects are represented in this model. If consumers and investors see policy makers harden their monetary policies and exchange rate discipline in a recession or when the exchange rate is considered overvalued, they will anticipate higher interest rates and falling earnings and will therefore either reduce their expenditures or transfer them elsewhere – despite (or perhaps because of) the extra credibility that those policies might bring. The result would be further downward pressure on earnings and the exchange rate, and upward pressure on interest rates. That would reinforce the costs on the real side without relieving the pressure on the exchange rate.

5.1   No realignments in 1992

Against this background, tables 2.5 and 2.6 are relatively straightforward. The reference solution is as before except that the UK and Italy are not allowed to realign their currencies in 1992. They are obliged to hold to bands of DM 2.95±2.5 per cent for the pound and DM 1.33±2.5 per cent per 1000 lire, instead of 2.43±2.5 per cent and 0.993±2.5%, respectively. The result is disastrous for all four European

Table 2.6. Optimal policies with no exchange rate realignments in Europe

Country		Reference solution		Domain solution	
		Mean	Variance	Mean	Variance
USA	$G\dot{N}P$	2.35	1.01	2.33	0.97
	$\dot{P}$	3.83	0.63	3.73	0.73
	G/Y	18.77	1.61	18.80	1.58
	RS	4.53	0.01	4.51	0.01
Japan	$G\dot{N}P$	2.45	0.94	2.46	0.96
	$\dot{P}$	2.04	0.36	2.01	0.39
	G/Y	15.29	2.23	15.28	2.26
	RS	3.88	0.04	3.88	0.05
Canada	$G\dot{N}P$	2.12	1.63	2.15	1.54
	$\dot{P}$	3.69	3.74	3.63	3.89
	G/Y	22.67	0.84	22.65	0.82
	RS	5.25	0.65	5.26	0.07
Germany	$G\dot{N}P$	1.31	1.52	2.48	0.77
	$\dot{P}$	4.04	0.84	5.08	1.96
	G/Y	20.67	1.27	21.64	1.49
	RS	8.22	0.78	6.04	0.22
UK	$G\dot{N}P$	−0.25	0.41	−0.08	0.50
	$\dot{P}$	2.06	17.73	2.36	17.97
	G/Y	26.74	3.88	26.12	2.24
	RS	19.00	40.56	17.34	36.25
France	$G\dot{N}P$	1.82	1.07	2.18	0.76
	$\dot{P}$	3.51	0.06	3.74	0.03
	G/Y	21.55	0.53	21.64	0.34
	RS	7.18	7.00	6.17	2.23
Italy	$G\dot{N}P$	−1.01	7.14	−0.80	7.81
	$\dot{P}$	2.06	13.40	2.23	14.89
	G/Y	22.96	11.08	22.12	7.06
	RS	24.06	135.70	22.35	126.60
European	$\dot{P}$	3.03	1.99	3.55	1.99
German	$\dot{M}$	7.96	17.69	10.54	15.17

economies; not just for the two denied realignment. Compared with the realignment case, Germany is 120 per cent worse off, France 25 per cent, the UK 500 per cent, and Italy 1000 per cent worse off. These are very substantial losses. The size of the UK and Italian losses gives an idea of the damage that those economics were suffering through misaligned real exchange rates, and explains why their eventual decision to leave the European exchange rate system seems to have been unavoidable. No country can withstand losses on that scale. Similarly the size of the German losses explains why the German government was happy to recommend realignments; the cost of providing non-inflationary cred-ibility with locomotive power for the rest of Europe was simply too expensive domestically. Finally, the relatively small losses in France confirm why French policy makers thought they could get away with not realigning. The costs to France would not be huge if no one else realigned; but, relative to this case, gains would appear if others did realign and France did not have to. The French therefore attempted to free ride, believing they would gain from the (monetary) credibility of their existing policies, not realizing that that would leave them all the more exposed in terms of lost real credibility when everyone else had realigned but they had not – because the deflationary pressures would then become concentrated entirely within France.

One can see all these components appearing in table 2.6. The most dramatic changes (compared with simulation A) occur in the UK and Italy. There are massive increases in instability as recession, an over-valued exchange rate, and high interest rates, and hence losses in real credibility, drive things downward. There are no inflationary problems (prices fall by 2–3 per cent each year) but interest rates have to rise to levels not seen since the late 1970s in the USA. That generates a persistent recession (output falls 0.5–1 per cent each year, that is down 2–3 per cent on the realignment case). Fiscal policy expands sharply (as a percentage of GNP) to offset that, but to no avail. Germany meanwhile is left to counter the effects of that expansion on its own, so interest rates rise further. The net effect provides some countervailing growth in Europe, but also some local inflation. The increases in target variables (but decreases for the instruments) show the Germans beginning to lose control of the situation. France meanwhile sits by and does nothing – suffering only minor adjustments to its growth and inflation targets.

5.2   The transatlantic components

A final but important feature of this exercise is that this regime change is the first to have a significant impact on the rest of the world. The USA and Japan are made 10 per cent and 4 per cent worse off; not large numbers admittedly, but still five or six times larger than the disturbances in table 2.3. This is one piece of evidence that regime choices in Europe are important to the USA and elsewhere, but that the policy-making strategies adopted in Europe are not. In this case, the important factors are the higher inflation from a larger dollar depreciation implied by a harder exchange rate regime in Europe, and greater output instability transmitted directly from the greater instability in Europe. However, at no point is the \$/ECU exchange destabilized in any of these exercises. Its variance stays at the baseline figure of 0.007 ($\pm$0.002) in every case – including when there are no realignments.

6   Changes of regime on the real side: the labour market

6.1   Labour market inflexibility

The persistent and high levels of unemployment in Europe have triggered a debate about the performance of the labour market. The main issues are: the high level of wages relative to productivity; the apparent insensitivity of wages and of non-wage costs to market conditions in either the labour or the product markets; and the high level of non-wage costs.

On the one hand, the debate has been between those who believe in an 'American' model of more flexible labour markets, with minimal constraints for social protection and income distribution purposes and with strictly limited non-wage costs, and who argue that the costs in lost output, employment, and competitiveness are too high to be acceptable. On the other hand, there are those who argue that the goals of social protection and redistribution are too important and too vulnerable to be left to an unregulated market in labour, and that the inefficiencies and output losses created by imposing the (price) distortions of the current regime are only small anyway – the 'European' model.

It is therefore especially important to examine how large an impact the labour market regime has had on economic performance. There are two ways of doing this: one can define wage insensitivity in terms of developments in the *product* markets or in terms of conditions in the *factor* markets. MULTIMOD, in its current version (see Bartolini and Symanski, 1993), models wage inflation as follows:

$$\dot{w} = \gamma + \delta E\dot{p}_{+1} + (1 - \delta)\dot{p}_{-1} - \alpha(u - u^*) - \phi(w - p - pt)_{-1}, \quad (10)$$

where $E\dot{p}_{+1}$ and $\dot{p}_{-1}$ are the (expected) future and past inflation rates in consumption prices, pt is a long-run productivity trend, and u^* is the natural rate of unemployment. Increasing market insensitivity could be represented by reducing δ (insensitivity to predictable changes in demand and supply on the product market) or by reducing α or ϕ (insensitivity to disequilibria in the labour market itself). In fact a fall in δ would imply greater *real* wage rigidity; w is more closely linked to past price inflation, as real wages become more strongly influenced by an exogenous trend rather than by current market conditions or expected future prices. Likewise, a fall in α implies *nominal* wage rigidity: $\dot{w}$ is less sensitive to excess supply (positive or negative) in the labour markets. Finally, a fall in ϕ implies greater relative wage rigidity: $\dot{w}$ is less sensitive to the competitiveness of real wages compared with the 'datum' of an exogenous productivity trend. In all three cases the result is to make wage changes more dependent on the exogenous trend γ, and therefore too low in a boom or too high in recession. That could be the result of the institutional setting of the wage-bargaining process, or because labour market regulations are such that non-wage costs prevent prices from adjusting sufficiently.

6.2   The costs of labour market inflexibility in Europe

6.2.1   Relative wage rigidities (declining competitiveness)
Tables 2.7 and 2.8 show the impact of a regime of greater labour market inflexibility in Europe, when the wage inflation equations have their ϕ parameters cut by 10 per cent (a more persistent real wage gap). It is clear that this does significant damage everywhere, and that there are also significant spillovers to countries with no such problem (the USA, Japan, and Canada). The transatlantic spillovers cause performance losses of about 14 per cent, the biggest so far. Intriguingly these spillover effects are not much less than the performance losses within Europe itself (13 per cent for Germany, 16 per cent for the UK, and 22 per cent for Italy). And, once again, the effects within Europe are badly distributed, with France now the principal victim. France's 40 per cent loss is due to its relative lack of competitiveness, having not realigned in 1992/3, becoming more exaggerated by an across-the-board reduction in wage sensitivity, *plus* a comparative disadvantage in policy effectiveness (given the stronger German monetary policies, driven by German anti-inflation preferences) for dealing with the implications of fading competitiveness. One can see these movements quite clearly in table 2.8 where, compared with the reference solution (table 2.4), French output growth is unchanged on average but inflation increases. By contrast, its competitors (Germany, the UK, the USA) have unchanged output growth with falling inflation rates. Thus, in each case, France's relative losses come from expenditure

Table 2.7. Labour market inflexibility: objective function values

Country	Φ falls 10%	% gain	α falls 10%	% gain	δ falls 10%	% gain
USA	12.66	−14.4	11.88	−7.4	11.50	−3.9
Japan	11.13	−10.0	10.84	−7.2	10.51	−3.9
Canada	32.94	−12.2	30.20	−4.3	29.57	−2.3
Germany	60.80	−13.2	60.8	−6.2	59.6	−4.1
UK	185.03	−15.6	166.9	−4.3	163.5	−2.2
France	67.48	−40.3	54.5	−13.3	51.7	−7.4
Italy	127.49	−21.9	113.5	−8.5	109.7	−4.6

Notes:

1 ϕ falls implies increasing rigidities in relative wages,
   σ falls implies greater rigidity in nominal wages,
   ϕ falls implies greater rigidity in real wages.
2 Percentage gains are measured against the reference solution (simulation A).

switching effects being larger than the income/expenditure/wealth effects. That suggests that the 'franc fort' policy causes more problems than it solves because it denies France the income benefits of restoring French competitiveness for the sake of the smaller expenditure switching benefits that come from slower inflation and more stable monetary policies.

On a wider view, table 2.8 shows that labour market inflexibilities generally produce higher inflation in France and Italy (with output losses in Italy), higher interest rates (up by 0.5 per cent on average), and considerably more monetary policy volatility in Europe. These are all unwelcome developments. In the USA and Japan, the spillovers take the form of lost output and greater volatility on the real side. This is coming from fiscal contractions in the USA and Japan, which are necessary to prevent European inflation being transferred via ECU appreciations. Hence labour market inflexibilities in Europe have imposed a 'beggar-thy-neighbour' policy regime on the G7 that operates through real rather than monetary effects.

6.2.2 Nominal wage rigidities

Tables 2.7 and 2.8 also show the consequences of increasing nominal wage rigidities in Europe; the α parameters are cut by 10 per cent to reflect a greater insensitivity to conditions on the labour markets.

The result is a similar set of spillovers and performance losses as in the previous (sticky relative wages) case, except that the losses are on average *less* serious in absolute size but the spillovers are relatively *more* serious than before. That is, the spillovers and losses are still significant and

Table 2.8. Optimal policies with labour market inflexibility

Country		ϕ falls		α falls		δ falls	
		Mean	Variance	Mean	Variance	Mean	Variance
USA	$G\dot{N}P$	2.13	1.59	2.24	0.87	2.25	0.86
	$\dot{P}$	3.33	1.00	3.49	1.22	3.46	1.19
	G/Y	18.69	1.09	18.87	1.38	18.88	1.38
	RS	4.56	0.03	4.47	0.00	4.47	0.00
Japan	$G\dot{N}P$	2.32	1.57	2.45	0.87	2.47	0.89
	$\dot{P}$	1.81	0.09	1.94	0.47	1.92	0.44
	G/Y	15.09	2.05	15.29	2.27	15.30	2.27
	RS	3.89	0.04	3.88	0.04	3.89	0.04
Canada	$G\dot{N}P$	2.15	2.28	2.22	1.81	2.24	1.79
	$\dot{P}$	3.42	5.02	3.47	4.77	3.45	4.71
	G/Y	22.66	0.82	22.66	0.86	22.67	0.87
	RS	5.37	0.26	5.26	0.08	5.25	0.08
Germany	$G\dot{N}P$	1.45	1.16	1.33	1.38	1.40	1.35
	$\dot{P}$	2.93	0.83	3.07	0.58	3.07	0.59
	G/Y	21.77	1.88	21.04	1.86	21.09	1.88
	RS	7.99	2.52	7.69	1.16	7.58	1.20
UK	$G\dot{N}P$	1.68	0.89	1.45	1.33	1.48	1.29
	$\dot{P}$	4.93	7.26	4.98	6.04	4.95	6.04
	G/Y	24.81	1.92	24.80	1.54	24.80	1.51
	RS	8.29	14.97	7.78	17.11	7.76	16.92
France	$G\dot{N}P$	1.93	0.51	1.90	0.72	1.94	0.70
	$\dot{P}$	2.94	0.42	2.91	0.23	2.89	0.23
	G/Y	21.64	0.66	21.63	0.54	20.64	0.53
	RS	7.49	10.01	7.04	6.87	7.00	6.72
Italy	$G\dot{N}P$	1.96	0.66	2.04	0.69	2.09	0.68
	$\dot{P}$	5.53	1.66	5.32	1.17	5.31	1.15
	G/Y	19.75	0.54	19.88	0.56	19.88	0.54
	RS	8.58	15.68	8.30	13.68	8.23	13.70
European	$\dot{P}$	3.81	0.56	3.82	0.61	3.86	0.61
German	$\dot{M}$	7.61	16.70	7.75	17.04	7.87	16.74

France is (as always) the worst affected – followed now by Italy, the USA, and Japan. But their losses have been cut to half the size of the previous case. Similarly the spillovers to the USA and Japan are half as big; but, relative to the losses caused in Europe, the spillovers have increased quite a bit. Thus, protected labour markets with nominal wage rigidity would appear to carry the potential for greater tension between the USA and Europe, despite smaller losses in total, than would declining competitiveness.

To amplify those results, table 2.8 shows that nominal wage rigidities in Europe cause output losses and greater real volatility there, and a tendency to higher inflation, which has to be offset by monetary relaxation (lower and more stable interest rates). The last point means that the US and Japanese fiscal contractions of the previous case can be eased somewhat, which in turn produces higher output and greater stability on the real side but mildly worse inflation figures – so there are gains, but not by enough to match the monetary easing in Europe. Hence the absolute improvement but relative deterioration in the USA and Japan.

6.2.3   Real wage rigidities
The final columns of table 2.7 and 2.8 show the result of cutting the European δ parameters by 10 per cent to reflect greater real wage persistence. Unsurprisingly, this produces scaled-down results of the relative wage rigidity case: the losses are about half those for nominal wage rigidities, and a quarter of those for relative wage rigidities. France is still worst affected; but, unlike nominal wage rigidities, the spillover effects are now no larger than those in Europe and the losses are quite small in absolute value.

7   The need and scope for transatlantic coordination

Up to this point, our exercises have taken a European policy perspective, and have then looked to see if there were significant spillovers onto the USA or Japan. Our conclusion was that the different decision strategies that could be adopted in Europe would not, in themselves, have any particular consequences for the USA or Japan. However, the different policy regimes that might be imposed on European monetary policy, labour market behaviour, or fiscal control certainly can have important spillovers. The rule of thumb is that regimes have important transatlantic spillovers when their income or wealth effects are stronger than any expenditure switching (relative price) effects.

This implies that the US economy is not greatly affected by many of the current policy developments (as opposed to regime changes) in Europe, and is certainly not dependent on how they work out. The remaining question then is, does the same thing hold in reverse? Is Europe, integrated through its exchange rate mechanism, similarly not much affected by events in the USA – or is there still an asymmetric dependence as in the 1970s and 1980s?

7.1   *A reduction in the US budget deficit*

To examine this question, we simulated a substantial reduction in the US budget deficit – a major component in the Clinton administration's economic programme. We suppose the administration *aims* to reduce the deficit to GNP ratio from its historical value of 3.5 per cent in 1993 to 1 per cent four years later in 1996; that is, to halve its baseline value by the end of the administration. These are target values however; the US government doesn't necessarily achieve its aims, although we penalize it for not doing so. In fact, the simulation shows that it ends up with budget cuts that match these aims to within 0.1 percentage point of the required ratio.

The results are given in tables 2.9 and 2.10. In the short term, the main loser is the USA itself. Budget cuts of this size in a period of slow growth and low inflation are hard to sustain without compensation from elsewhere. In this case, government expenditures are cut back 0.2 per cent of GNP each year, which leads to a drop in the growth rate. Monetary policy is eased a bit and has to be more vigorous; but not too much in order not to generate inflation either domestically or via a dollar depreciation.

The spillover effects of the US fiscal contraction are moderate (except perhaps for Canada). Japan, Germany, and France are left about 5 per cent worse off than in the reference solution, and Britain and Italy about 2 per cent. These losses stem largely from a destabilization of monetary policy in each case (and of fiscal policy in Germany). The average levels of the targets and instruments, and the stability of prices and output, are not much affected.

7.2   *Trade restrictions*

Tables 2.9 and 2.10 also show the effect of imposing a sustained negative shock of 1 per cent in each of the transatlantic export equations, to give an idea of the potential impacts of the quantity restrictions of the kind threatened by the USA and EU during the Uruguay Round negotiations.

The USA loses significantly in this exercise, and Europe makes very small gains. That may seem counterintuitive,[9] but trade restrictions in this scenario would help Europe (Germany principally) by offsetting the

Table 2.9. The scope for transatlantic policy coordination (objective function values)

Country	US deficit reduction		Trade restrictions		Full cooperation						Policy bloc solutions			
					All G7		G3 only		G2 only		EU coalition		Tri-polar case	
	National prefs	% gain	National prefs	% gain	Weights	% gain	Weights	% gain	Weights	% gain	Weights	% gain	Weights	% gain
USA	16.42	−46.9	12.36	−11.6	0.59	+4.7	0.80	+0.76	0.90	−4.8	Nash	0.7	Nash	3.0
Japan	10.61	−4.8	10.07	+0.0	0.09	+15.8	0.10	+1.69	0.10	+0.4	Nash	3.6	Nash	3.6
Canada	31.71	−9.6	28.42	+1.7	0.02	+21.2	0	+2.81	0.	−2.5	Nash	14.7	Nash	16.5
Germany	60.52	−5.7	56.23	+1.7	0.09	+23.9	0.10	+9.91	0.70	−47.6	0.70	−23.6	0.25	−74.1
UK	163.01	−1.8	157.71	+1.5	0.08	+4.9	0	−0.01	0.10	−0.8	0.10	0.6	0.25	2.1
France	50.17	−4.3	47.32	+1.6	0.07	+24.1	0	+1.54	0.10	−8.6	0.10	9.1	0.25	28.3
Italy	107.38	−2.7	101.05	+3.3	0.06	+8.9	0	−12.11	0	−7.8	0.10	11.7	0.25	24.1

Note:
'Nash' denotes playing non-cooperatively against other countries or policy blocs.

Table 2.10. Optimal policies under transatlantic policy coordination

Country		US deficit reduction		Trade restrictions		Full cooperation				Policy bloc solutions			
						All G7		G3 only		EU coalition		Tri-polar	
		Mean	Variance	Mean	Variance	Mean	Variance	Mean	Variance	Mean	Variance	Mean	Variance
USA	$\dot{G}NP$	2.09	0.42	2.00	0.98	2.21	1.01	2.26	0.89	2.23	1.07	2.23	1.06
	$\dot{P}$	3.44	1.42	3.26	0.76	3.21	1.07	3.39	1.15	3.24	1.14	3.21	1.10
	G/Y	18.73	3.93	19.16	1.63	18.80	1.24	18.86	1.34	18.84	1.29	18.86	1.32
	RS	4.33	0.33	4.34	0.01	4.25	0.00	4.41	0.01	4.20	0.16	4.20	0.17
Japan	$\dot{G}NP$	2.49	0.90	2.49	0.92	2.48	0.85	2.49	0.90	2.49	0.94	2.49	0.95
	$\dot{P}$	1.87	0.46	1.89	0.40	1.79	0.40	1.88	0.41	1.78	0.40	1.77	0.40
	G/Y	15.35	2.42	15.31	2.27	15.38	2.29	15.33	2.34	15.37	2.09	15.38	2.08
	RS	3.89	0.05	3.89	0.04	4.00	0.00	3.94	0.04	3.88	0.04	3.88	0.04
Canada	$\dot{G}NP$	2.20	1.35	2.27	1.65	2.61	1.74	2.27	1.73	2.26	1.86	2.26	1.81
	$\dot{P}$	3.37	5.98	3.45	4.53	3.51	4.04	3.39	4.55	3.19	3.88	3.18	3.80
	G/Y	22.76	0.72	22.66	0.85	23.37	3.37	22.68	0.87	22.74	0.88	22.74	0.86
	RS	5.15	0.18	5.25	0.08	5.01	0.23	5.23	0.08	5.17	0.05	5.17	0.05
Germany	$\dot{G}NP$	1.47	1.34	1.20	1.52	1.76	0.94	1.47	1.20	1.69	0.94	1.70	0.89
	$\dot{P}$	3.04	0.71	3.00	0.57	3.29	1.44	3.00	0.47	3.26	1.66	3.36	1.95
	G/Y	21.17	2.15	21.29	1.74	20.48	4.16	21.06	2.86	20.39	3.89	20.01	5.85
	RS	7.45	1.63	7.33	1.06	5.70	3.22	7.40	1.26	5.74	3.05	5.33	4.68
UK	$\dot{G}NP$	1.53	1.29	1.25	1.43	1.72	1.40	1.83	0.79	1.56	1.75	1.79	1.16
	$\dot{P}$	4.89	6.15	4.85	5.65	4.93	6.66	5.24	6.64	4.77	6.65	4.92	6.58
	G/Y	24.82	1.50	24.99	1.49	24.33	0.93	24.90	1.08	24.22	0.94	24.39	0.91
	RS	7.45	17.27	7.56	15.81	6.17	4.66	6.91	10.39	6.43	7.21	6.10	4.18

France	$G\dot{N}P$	1.99	0.67	1.67	0.77	2.10	0.38	2.28	0.55	2.01	0.47	2.18	0.31
	$\dot{P}$	2.84	0.30	2.78	0.14	2.79	0.17	3.13	0.27	2.72	0.19	2.86	0.18
	G/Y	21.67	0.53	21.86	0.54	21.01	0.61	21.81	0.40	20.95	0.52	21.19	0.35
	RS	6.69	6.92	6.79	6.05	5.28	0.21	6.25	2.80	5.40	0.30	5.19	0.14
Italy	$G\dot{N}P$	2.19	0.64	1.89	0.79	2.48	0.60	2.57	0.46	2.33	0.65	2.52	0.42
	$\dot{P}$	5.32	1.28	5.20	0.78	5.28	0.77	5.67	1.19	5.14	0.83	5.30	0.81
	G/Y	19.85	0.50	20.05	0.44	19.16	0.47	20.06	0.31	19.20	0.44	19.35	0.25
	RS	8.02	14.40	7.83	13.40	6.64	3.23	7.47	9.23	6.91	5.03	6.70	3.17

demand expansion and inflation. That allows Germany to reduce its interest rates. Monetary policy eases everywhere therefore. So, although output is damaged by the trade restriction (it falls by an average of 1 per cent p.a.), inflation is also lower (by 0.5 per cent p.a.) and the monetary relaxation allows some countervailing expansion. These effects largely cancel out, to leave Europe marginally better off. But the individual spillovers are not in themselves negligible, witness the USA where there is no expansion to offset.

7.3   Outright cooperation

Although the transatlantic spillovers may not be particularly large in any of these exercises, they may have most of their impact on the target (rather than non-target) variables. In that case, coordination would yield important gains, despite modern spillovers, because of the 'policy sensitivity' of those variables in the preference functions being optimized. And there is still an issue of the *distribution* of the gains, over and above their size.

Tables 2.9 and 2.10 report several sets of cooperative policies. The first is for explicit cooperation involving all seven members of the G7 group, with bargaining weights chosen to ensure incentive compatibility and hence a politically feasible solution. The second is chosen so that only the G3 countries (the USA, Japan, and Germany as the EU's representative and dominant policy maker) take explicit part in the bargaining. The four excluded countries therefore play Nash (non-cooperation) against a self-interest coalition of the G3 countries. The idea here is to test the view that there will be little difference between the two solutions, at least as far as the G3 coalition members are concerned. In other words, are these gains from policy coordination largely driven by the G3 coalition – or do the remaining countries of the G7 group also make significant contributions of their own?

Inspection of the figures in tables 2.9 and 2.10 shows that such a proposition is only partly true – the differences between full G7 coordination and its G3 counterpart are small in average policy *levels*, but *not* in the variability of those policies. Generally the G3 policies have to be rather more vigorous, and the targets more volatile, than when the full G7 group coordinate – even if the policy stances are broadly similar. That shows up the policy sensitivity that drives the gains from coordination. Secondly, the G3 solution has been constructed to ensure incentive compatibility (i.e. gains over non-cooperation) for the three participants. But those gains are noticeably smaller – down to a third or a tenth of their G7 counterparts. Moreover the four non-participants get squeezed to the extent that any gains that they might have made under the G7 regime vanish or turn negative (i.e. losses compared with full non-cooperation). That shows that cooperation may well generate gains for the participants at the cost of making the outsiders worse off. Thirdly, the smaller gains for the insiders are distributed quite differently – away from the USA and Japan, and towards Germany. (Under a G7 regime the USA takes 11 per cent of the gains, Japan 35 per cent, and Germany 54 per cent; but in a G3 regime those figures change to 6 per cent, 14 per cent, and 80 per cent respectively.) Since the weaker economies are the ones that benefit most from the help of the stronger economies under cooperation, these last two results point to a degree of asymmetric dependence between the USA on the one hand and Germany (or Europe) on the other; and, then again, between Germany and the other countries within Europe.

These three points demonstrate that G7 cooperation and a G3-led regime are not equivalent, despite their similar policy settings, and suggest that to get Pareto improvements we need either to stick at G7 cooperation or go to a G2-led regime (other countries playing Nash). Unfortunately, when we tried the latter (table 2.9; for reasons of space we have not included the individual policy results from this solution in table 2.10), we found losses all round – very large for Germany and France, and also for the USA, whose preferences are given most weight in this solution. This says that ignoring the EU's locomotive power does significant damage to performance, not only within Europe but also to other members of the G7. This is because, given the earlier G3/G7 results, we found that the European economies are relatively weak or inflexible. As a result, coordination becomes an exercise in trading off the creation of efficiency gains all round against the degree to which EU countries can appropriate those gains for themselves. The big issue for transatlantic coordination is therefore whether the emergence of 'policy blocs' in and around the G7 would have significant effects and whether important performance gains would be lost in such bloc behaviour.

7.4   Policy blocs

There are two issues here: how would an EU policy bloc (playing non-cooperatively) affect the world economy; and how would a tri-polar world, consisting of EU, NAFTA, and East Asian policy blocs, affect things? Arguably the first is or is likely to become a reality, and the second might emerge from the tri-polar trading arrangements that have developed in recent years. We have simulated both, and the results are reported in tables 2.9 and 2.10. In each case policies are chosen cooperatively within each bloc but non-cooperatively between them.

Within the 'EU coalition', German preferences receive 70 per cent of the weight and the others 10 per cent. Then the EU plays non-cooperatively against the USA, Canada, and Japan, which do not cooperate. In the tripolar solution, the EU is again cooperative internally but with each country's objective function being weighted equally, and it plays non-cooperatively against the USA and Canada together (representing NAFTA) and against Japan (representing East Asia).

Both solutions are rather similar, although the EU coalition is uniformly inferior (especially for Germany). In fact, most of the differences between them are concentrated in Europe, and in the sharp losses for Germany in particular. This shows the immense amount of extra locomotive policy work that Germany has to undertake to make the European coalition competitive in policy terms. Evidently the effort of doing that is detrimental to Germany's own private objectives, while the benefits accrue largely to France and Italy. (Notice the destabilization of German monetary and fiscal variables. These effects do not transfer to French or Italian targets.) That is not likely to prove a stable or attractive option for Europe as a whole. Outside that, the USA and Japan make small gains whatever the internal arrangements within Europe, although those gains are much smaller than could have been achieved through full G7 cooperation. So bloc behaviour costs them quite a bit, even if it is still better than no cooperation at all. Thus, what matters to them is relations with Europe, not the arrangements within Europe.

7.5 Summary

The final point of interest is the great sensitivity of the gains from G7 cooperation to the distribution of bargaining weights. Smaller weights on the USA and UK *rapidly* worsen their objective function values and give them losses. France, Italy, and Canada, on the other hand, show no such sensitivities and record significant gains so long as Germany (for the first two) and the USA (for Canada) continue to do well. For example, changing the weights to 0.35 (for the USA), 0.25 (for Japan), 0.20 (for Germany), and 0.05 for the others gives a loss for the USA but a larger gain for Germany – and hence much stronger gains for France and Italy – than is reported in table 2.9. In other words: (a) the relationship of asymmetric dependence between the USA and Europe is still there; (b) a second relationship of asymmetric dependence exists within Europe, between Germany and its Romance partners; and (c) although the transatlantic spillovers appear fairly small, transatlantic policy coordination remains important because those spillovers touch policy-sensitive variables.

8 Conclusions

(a) Transatlantic policy spillovers under the new economic regimes in Europe and the USA are not large, but policy coordination is still important because of the policy sensitivity of those spillovers. Moreover, forming policy blocs is a poor substitute for full cooperation.

(b) The spillover regimes remain asymmetric between the USA and the EU, and equally between Germany and its EU partners.

(c) Spillovers and coordination are important where (real) income effects dominate expenditure switching effects.

(d) The decision strategies adopted in the 'New Europe' have very little impact on transatlantic economic relations. But the regimes imposed on specific markets (e.g. the labour market) may have considerable impacts.

(e) Exchange rate misalignments, not exchange rate volatility, caused the most difficulty here. The costs of that can be very large and come through the real side in the form of lost real credibility, rather than lost financial credibility.

(f) The domain solution is an attractive alternative to non-cooperative decision-making when preferences are very asymmetric between countries, but suffers from a severe incentive compatibility problem for the leading country. To fix that incentive problem requires either a greater commitment to economic integration *or* a new set of union-wide institutions stronger than any in the existing member countries.

Appendix: Incorporating a unified Germany into MULTIMOD

Output in eastern Germany is represented by a CES production function.

$$YE_t = A(\beta KE_{t-1}^{-\rho} + (1 - \beta)LE_t^{-\rho})^{-\frac{1}{\rho}}, \tag{A1}$$

where ρ is calibrated from data on YE, KE, and LE for 1991–3. The remaining parameters are taken from the West German counterpart; 'E' denotes an eastern variable, 'O' a western one.

Given projections on KE, the real wage SE would provide a solution for efficient employment LE^* – that is, employment that would have resulted from profit maximization. We solve for LE^* and YE^* (efficient output) from:

$$YE_t^* = A[\beta KE_{t-1}^{-\rho} + (1 - \beta)LE_t^{*-\rho}]^{-\frac{1}{\rho}} \tag{A2}$$

$$LE_t^* = YE_t^*[(1 - \beta)/(\rho SE_t A)]^{\frac{1}{(1+\rho)}} \tag{A3}$$

Equation (A3) follows by setting the marginal product of labour equal to the real wage. Not surprisingly, the LE^* figures fall far short of actual employment. The difference between real wages SE and the marginal product of $(LE-LE^*)$ indicates an implicit or 'shadow' subsidy to labour,

$$SE_t(LE_t - LE_t^*) = YE_t - YE_t^* + SUB_t. \tag{A4}$$

This subsidy, less fiscal transfers, is treated as a 'shadow' transfer from capital to labour. With respect to investment, we assume identical behaviour east and west, based on Tobin's Q:

$$GYKE_t = YE_t - SE_t LE_t \tag{A5}$$
$$YKE_t = (1 - t_{KE})GYKE \tag{A6}$$
$$KE_t^0 = \int_t^\infty YKE_t e^{-\gamma t} dt \tag{A7}$$
$$KE_t = K(KE_t^0/KE_{t-1}) \tag{A8}$$
$$IE_t = \Delta KE_t + dKE_{t-1}, \tag{A9}$$

where $GYKE$ is pre-tax capital income in East Germany, YKE is the post-tax level of this income, and d is the rate of depreciation. The tax rate on capital income in the east, t_{KE}, stands below the one in the west, t_{KO}, because of tax concessions in the east. We infer t_{KE} as a residual given the tax yields in MULTIMOD and have it converge on to t_{KO} over twenty years.

Migration and commuting are treated separately. Let

$$L^sO = L^sO^* + L2 + L3 \tag{A10}$$
$$L^sE = L^sE^* - L2 - L3, \tag{A11}$$

where L^sO^* and L^sE^* are exogenous values based on demography and labour participation rates, based on United Nations and other official projections. We include German immigrants from the former USSR and Eastern Europe and assume eastern participation rates fall linearly to those in the west by the year 2000. The number of commuters,

$$L3_t = L3_{t-1} - L3O_t + L3E_t, \tag{A12}$$

depends on the number commuting the year before, less those who now decide to settle in the west, plus those who subsequently return to the east. Then,

$$\begin{cases} L3O_t = yL3_{t-1} & \text{if } L3E \geq 0 \\ L3O_t = y(L3_{t-1} + L3E_t) & \text{if } L3E_t < 0 \end{cases} \tag{A13}$$

So a fraction of commuters, each year, eventually settle in the west, but some return east if $L3E < 0$. Survey data suggest $y = 0.05$. The choice between working in the east or commuting to the west depends on changes in employment in the east:

$$L3E_t = \begin{cases} -z\Delta LE_t & \text{for } \Delta LE_t < 0 \text{ (new commuters), } z=0.1 \\ -\left(\frac{uO}{uE}\right)_t \left(\frac{L3}{UE+L3}\right)_{t-1} \Delta LE_t & \text{for } \Delta LE_t > 0 \begin{smallmatrix}\text{(old commuters who return}\\\text{to work in the east)}\end{smallmatrix} \end{cases} \tag{A14}$$

where U refers to the number of unemployed, and u to the unemployment rate. The decision to migrate and settle is taken to depend on both unemployment and wage differentials:

$$\Delta L2 - L3O_t = \begin{cases} L^s E_t^* \Omega (0.9 - WGAP_{t-1}) & \text{if } WGAP \le 0.9 \\ 0 & \text{if } WGAP > 0.9 \end{cases} \quad \text{(A15)}$$

where $WGAP_t = [WHE_t/(L^S E_t^* + L3_t)]/[WHO_t/(L^S O_t - L3_t)]$, $L2$ is the stock of settlers in the west, and $\Omega = 0.1$
Then:

$$WHO_t = \int_t^\infty YHO_t \exp(-rt)dt \quad \text{(A16)}$$

$$WHE_t = \int_t^\infty YHE_t \exp(-rt)dt \quad \text{(A17)}$$

$$YHO_t = (1-t_{HO})SO_t(LO_t - L3_t + 0.45UO_t - L3_t \quad \text{(A18)}$$

$$YHE_t = (1-t_{HE})SE_t(LE_t + 0.45UE_t + 0.35UE3_t) + (1-t_{HO})SO_t L3_t \quad \text{(A19)}$$

$$t_{HE} = \begin{cases} t_{HO} - \epsilon YGAP_{t-1} & \text{if } YGAP_{t-1} \ge 0 \\ t_{HO} & \text{if } YGAP_{t-1} < 0 \end{cases} \quad \text{(A20)}$$

where $YGAP = 0.9 - [YE/(L^s E + L3)]/[YO/(L^s E - L3)]$

$$UE3 = \begin{cases} [0.15 + 1.3(uE - 0.06)](UE - UE3) & \text{if } uE \ge 0.06 \\ 0.15(UE - UE3) & \text{if } uE < 0.06 \end{cases} \quad \text{(A21)}$$

Equation (A15) says that labour will move westward so long as human wealth per worker living in the east ($L^s E + L3$) falls below 90 per cent of the comparable level in the west (for $L^s O - L3$). The 90 per cent ratio is meant to capture the costs of movement – social, psychological, and material. Human wealth (WHO or WHE) depends upon post-tax wage income and unemployment compensation. We obtained the critical parameter by calibrating (A15) on data for 1990–3; γ likewise, where t_{HE} are the household tax rate parameters. These equations have fiscal implications. German unemployment compensation replaces 63 per cent of lost wages, but the federal labour office estimates only 65 per cent of western unemployed and 80 per cent of easterners qualify. Hence the coefficients in (A18) and (A19). $UE3$ refers to those unemployed easterners on retraining programmes and is derived from data supplied by the federal labour office. But to get the full fiscal implications, we need to sum up the eastern and western tax revenues and government expenditures. The former is straightforward; the latter implies

$$G = G^* + TR + 0.45[SE(UE - UE3 + 2.5UE3) + SOUO] + rB_{-1}/P, \quad \text{(A22)}$$

where G^* and TR are exogenous (discussed in section 3), but the unemployment compensation and the interest on the debt, rB_{-1}, are endogenous. The 2.5 coefficient on this equation reflects the fact that the government spends about 2.5 as much on each person in the training programme ($UE3$) than per person otherwise unemployed ($UE - UE3$).

One of the distinctive features of the European economies is stickiness in the labour markets. Germany contributes to this, with eastern wages catching up to 90 per cent of their western counterparts by the year 2000:

$$SE_t = 0.9SO_t + e^{-\mu t}(SE_{t-1} - 0.9SO_{t-1}),$$ (A23)

where μ is fitted to provide SE equal to $0.9SO$ by 2000.

Data appendix

Table 2.A1. Database used for the reference simulation A (Nash solution)

	1990	1991	1992	1993	1994	1995	1996
USA							
GDP	0.8	−0.7	2.6	2.9	3.6	3.0	3.141
P	5.4	4.2	3.0	2.9	2.7	2.42	3.03
Def/GDP	2.5	3.4	4.8	3.5	3.0	2.5	2.0
Debt/GDP	56.2	59.8	63.2	65.1	65.9	66.2364	66.985
$/ECU	1.269	1.236	1.29366	1.17647	1.13122	1.0989	1.075
G/GDP	19.0651	19.5186	19.1708	18.4852	18.0317	17.8097	17.620
RS	7.5	3.5	3.0	3.0	3.8	4.0	4.5
Japan							
GDP	5.2	4.4	1.1	0.1	0.2	1.4	3.0
P	3.1	3.3	1.7	1.3	0.6	0.5	2.0
G/GDP	14.8520	14.7846	15.3589	15.6845	15.3670	15.1812	15.126
RS	7.1	5.4	4.5	3.0	3.3	3.6	4.0
Canada							
GDP	−0.5	−1.7	0.7	2.5	3.3	3.6	3.8
P	4.9	5.6	1.5	1.8	0.9	1.6	2.3
G/GDP	22.5820	23.4359	23.3859	22.8470	22.3796	21.9673	21.649
RS	11.7	7.3	7.1	4.0	4.0	4.5	5.0
Germany							
GDP	3.3	1.5	2.1	−1.3	1.2	2.2	3.0
P	2.7	3.5	4.0	4.2	3.2	2.5	2.5
Euro_P	5.00530	4.55651	3.83249	3.18172	2.94456	2.84265	3.293
M	11.94526	6.43661	14.53194	6.62252	6.2	6.2	6.2
G/GDP	20.5808	22.5688	22.3537	22.0525	21.6754	21.4043	21.197
RS	9.2	9.6	9.0	6.0	5.2	5.6	6.0
UK							
GDP	0.6	−2.4	−0.5	1.9	2.8	3.0	3.0
P	9.5	5.8	3.7	1.6	2.8	4.0	4.0
Pdiff	4.49470	1.24349	−0.13249	−1.58172	−0.14456	1.15735	0.706
DM/£	2.9	2.92	2.45	2.5	2.516	2.5	2.5
G/GDP	22.7882	23.5742	24.4628	24.6260	24.3735	24.1740	24.026
RS	14.0	10.5	7.0	5.5	5.5	6.5	6.5

Table 2.A1 (*cont.*)

	1990	1991	1992	1993	1994	1995	1996
France							
GDP	2.7	1.1	1.2	−0.7	1.2	3.0	3.0
P	3.4	3.1	2.4	2.1	1.8	2.0	2.6
Pdiff	−1.60530	−1.45651	−1.43249	−1.08172	−1.14456	−0.84265	−0.693
DM/FFr	0.2976	0.295	0.296	0.29672	0.29414	0.29583	0.296
G/GDP	21.3434	21.7893	21.6537	21.5101	21.3637	21.1804	20.979
RS	10.1	10.3	12.0	6.3	4.2	4.6	5.0
Italy							
GDP	2.2	1.4	0.9	−0.4	1.7	3.2	3.0
P	6.1	6.5	5.2	4.2	3.9	3.2	4.5
Pdiff	1.09470	1.94349	1.36751	1.01828	0.95544	0.35735	1.206
DM/lira	1.35135	1.33651	1.19048	1.02	1.02284	1.02284	1.022
G/GDP	20.0563	20.0870	20.0528	19.9471	19.8243	19.6864	19.557
RS	12.1	12.3	12.9	8.3	7.0	6.0	6.0

Notes:

GDP	= growth rate;
P	= inflation rate;
Euro_P	= European weighted inflation rate;
Pdiff	= domestic inflation rate minus European inflation rate;
Def/GDP	= government deficit/GDP ratio;
Debt/GDP	= public debt/GDP ratio;
G/GDP	= government current expenditure/GDP ratio;
RS	= nominal short-term interest rate;
M	= nominal money growth rate.

NOTES

We have benefited from comments from Peter Kenen, Maria Demertzis, Matt Canzoneri, Alberto Giovannini, Noriel Roubini, and Jacques Mélitz on different aspects. We gratefully acknowledge financial support from the Leverhulme Trust.

1   Rational expectations models can be accommodated by incorporating the 'non-causal' multipliers, or anticipations effects, in the 'above-diagonal' submatrices of R_{AA} and R_{AB}. The terminal conditions, y_∞, then join the initial conditions of y_0 as components of s^A; see Fisher and Hughes Hallett (1988).

2   The extension to any number of interdependent countries is summarized in Hughes Hallett (1987a).

3   The generalization for economies of unequal size is to define y in (7) as $y = ay^A + (1 - a)y^B$ with $0 < a < 1$. Then

$$w^D = ay^A[aC]y^A + (1 - a)y^{B'}[(1 - a)C]y^B + 2a(1 - a)y^{A'}Cy^B$$
$$= w - 2a(1 - a)y^{A'}Cy^B$$

where w is (5) evaluated at $\alpha = a$; $C^A = aC$; and $C^B = (1 - a)C$. The remaining requirement for w^D to represent an improvement on average is that $2a(1 - a)\mathbf{y}^{A'}C\mathbf{y}^B \leq \frac{1}{2}(w^A_{NC} + w^B_{NC})$ should hold for some $\mathbf{y}^A$ and $\mathbf{y}^B$ in the incentive-compatible range for C^A and C^B.

4   Interest rates are included to reflect the central bankers' concern for continuity in monetary policy and their dislike of large or sudden changes. Penalizing interest rate movements prevents such changes. It also prevents interest rates turning negative. None of these characteristics can be captured by the model, so we use the objective function to generate them. The non-negativity constraints excepted, the numerical results are not sensitive to the penalty values placed on RS.

5   To that end, note that the IMF estimates the total cost of unification to the year 2001 will be DM 1700 bn (McDonald and Thumann, 1990). We suppose that half of that will be paid for by central and local government, spread as a declining balance over fifteen years to cover fiscal transfers, social security, infrastructure, and private investment support. Accordingly we add DM 850 bn to the exogenous government spending, spread as DM 56 bn, 160 bn, 120 bn, and 70 bn in 1990, 1991, 1992, and 1993, respectively, and then DM 36 bn each year until 2005. That corresponds to a fiscal shock of 7.9% of GDP at its peak, but of 1.5% or less after 1994. These figures run a little below the actual peak expenditures, estimated at DM 180 bn, but include the operating deficits of the Treuhand agency from 1991 and its debt of DM 325 bn. The migration figures are taken from Hughes Hallet et al. (1994), as explained in the appendix.

6   This has the effect of tying policy makers into the rules of a regime, and therefore excludes any time inconsistency in policy decisions until the moment comes for renegotiating or redesigning the regime as a whole (see Walsh, 1995).

7   The complete year-by-year paths may be obtained from the authors.

8   These results underline the importance of Garrett's (1993) analysis of why the Germans may support monetary union in Europe even when it may not be in their economic interest to do so.

9   These results support Johnson's (1953) theoretical finding that, in a tariff war with retaliation, some countries will always lose even if there are others that gain.

REFERENCES

Bartolini, L. and S. Symanski (1993), 'Notes on Unemployment and Wage Determination in MULTIMOD', IMF Working Paper, Washington DC.

Bryant, R., P. Hooper and C. Mann (1993), 'Evaluating Policy Regimes: New Research in Empirical Macroeconomics', Brookings Institution, Washington DC.

Fisher, P. G. and A. Hughes Hallett (1988), 'Efficient Solution Techniques for Linear and Nonlinear Rational Expectations Models', *Journal of Economic Dynamics and Control* 12, 635–57.

Garrett, G. (1993), 'International and Domestic Institutions in the EMU Process', *Economics and Politics* 5, 125–44.

Hughes Hallett, A. (1986), 'International Policy Design and the Sustainability of Policy Bargains', *Journal of Economic Dynamics and Control* 10, 457–94.

(1987a), 'The Impact of Interdependence on Economic Policy Design: The case of the US, EEC and Japan', *Economic Modelling* 4, 377–96.

(1987b), 'How Robust Are the Gains to Policy Coordination to Variants in the Model and Objectives', *Ricerche Economiche* 41, 341–72.

Hughes Hallett, A. and Y. Ma (1994), 'Real Adjustment in a Union of Incompletely Converged Economies: An Example from East and West Germany', *European Economic Review* 38, 1731–61.

Hughes Hallett, A., Y. Ma and J. Melitz (1994), 'Unification and the Policy Predicament in Germany', Centre for Economic Policy Research Discussion Paper No. 956.

Johnson, H. G. (1953), 'Optimal Tariffs and Retaliation', *Review of Economic Studies* 21, 142–53.

Kenen, P. B. (1992), 'EMU after Maastricht', Group of Thirty, Washington DC.

McDonald, D. and G. Thumann (1990), 'Investment Needs in East Germany', in L. Lipschitz and D. McDonald (eds.), *German Unification: Economic Issues*, IMF Occasional Paper 75, Washington DC.

Masson, P. and G. Meredith (1990), 'Economic Implications of German Unification for the Federal Republic and the Rest of the World', IMF Working Paper WP90/85, Washington DC.

Masson, P., S. Symanski and G. Meredith (1990), *MULTIMOD Mark II: A revised and extended model*, IMF Occasional Paper 70, Washington DC.

Oudiz, G. and J. Sachs (1984), 'Policy Coordination in Industrial Countries', *Brookings Papers on Economic Activity* 1, 1–64.

Walsh, C. E. (1995), 'Optimal Contracts for Central Bankers', *American Economics Review* 85, 150–67.

Discussion

NOURIEL ROUBINI

This interesting and stimulating paper covers a lot of issues regarding the potential gains from macro policy coordination. Although the title of the paper refers to transatlantic coordination, the bulk of the analysis in the paper deals with the gains from policy coordination in the EMS area. The paper makes a number of interesting points and discusses quite systematically several important issues that are at the centre of the European debate about the future of European coordination. In my discussion I will concentrate on the more controversial points and issues rather than stress the aspects of the paper with which I agree.

The paper makes use of an amended version of a large macro-econometric model of the world economy (the MULTIMOD model) to study the implications of alternative policy rules, regimes, and solution concepts and the potential benefits from inter-European and trans-atlantic policy coordination. I have a number of methodological observations about the approach taken in the paper.

The first comment concerns the components of the loss function used in the analysis. In addition to final policy goals (inflation and growth), the authors include the policy instruments (interest rates and fiscal policy) directly in the loss function. I find this approach unusual and somewhat confusing. I always thought that instruments matter mostly in so far as they are tools for achieving final targets rather than being final targets themselves. Moreover, by giving the same weight to the instruments as to the final targets, the paper constrains the policy instrument set significantly.

This issue is important because in some experiments the significant improvement in welfare is due mostly to the lower variance of the instruments rather than to an improvement in the policy targets. For example, table 2.3 shows a significant increase in welfare in the USA, Japan, and Canada (around 50 per cent) when moving from the historical base to the non-cooperative Nash equilibrium. However, this increase in welfare is not due to improved performance on the inflation–growth dimension. It is all due to the lower variance of interest rates under Nash (i.e. interest rates are almost completely smoothed under Nash). I would therefore suggest that the results should be presented in a way that allows the reader to distinguish how much of the welfare gain is due to policy instrument smoothing compared with the actual performance of final targets.

The second observation regards the issue of what is the correct baseline to be used in the discussion of coordination gains. If we compare the historical baseline with the Nash non-cooperative equilibrium in table 2.3, we observe a significant increase in welfare both in Europe (by 30 per cent on average) and in the rest of the OECD (by 50 per cent on average). This result is a bit surprising and puzzling because it suggests that, even if policy makers do not cooperate at all, there would be a significant welfare gain just by playing Nash. In the Nash equilibrium, inflation and growth are lower for Germany than in the historical baseline, while they are higher for the rest of the EMS countries (table 2.4).

These results imply that actual historical policies were implicitly not optimal, i.e. policy makers were wrong or mistaken in their actual policy choices. I am uncomfortable with this implicit implication. Maybe the true world is such that the actual potential trade-off between inflation and growth is not as favourable as the one implied by the model estimated in the paper. If this is the case, Nash would imply that we could have done much better than actual history. But maybe the estimated model is incorrect and policy makers had a better idea of the actual trade-offs. So the potential gains may be mostly in the model estimates rather than in reality.

In this sense, I would be more comfortable if the non-cooperative equilibrium closely tracked the actual historical record, if the period under consideration was one where there was not much cooperation. The above point is also important because I believe that any discussion of the gains from cooperation should start from a comparison between a non-cooperative equilibrium and a fully cooperative one. A number of large macro-econometric models and simulation models (such as the MSG model on which I worked a while ago) suggest that the gains from coordination might be small and close to zero. The reason for that result is that the structural externalities and international spillovers of policies are estimated to be very small. Although I am not familiar with the details of the MULTIMOD model used in the paper, my guess would be that the coordination gains cannot be very large in that model either. If they are, it would be interesting to know what is in the model that leads to such large gains.

Some results on full cooperation are presented in tables 2.9 and 2.10 but the meaning and the source of the gains are not clear. First, are the percentage gains under cooperation relative to a Nash equilibrium or relative to some other equilibrium? Second, are Nash and full coopera-tion fully comparable (i.e. are the desired levels of targets and instruments the same in the two experiments)? Third, if they are comparable, why is full cooperation so much superior to Nash? The published figures in table 2.10 on the targets do not show a large difference in inflation rates or growth rates in the two equilibria. So it is not clear what the source is of such gains; is it all in the reduction in the variance of the policy instruments?

The next observation regards the concept of non-cooperative equili-brium used in the paper. If I understand the exercise, both in the historical baseline and in the Nash case it is assumed that exchange rates are fixed in the 2 per cent ERM band (with the caveat of a realignment for the British pound and the Italian lira in 1992). We however know that a fixed-rate regime must be by definition a cooperative one. Either it is symmetric, so that all countries intervene and change monetary policy to maintain the fixed parities, or it is asymmetric, with the leader country setting its monetary policy and the others following. In either case, maintaining fixed rates implies explicit cooperative rules about policies, intervention, and sterilization policies.

For example, a formally symmetric cooperative system such as the EMS, where unlimited marginal intervention should have been the norm, became in practice an asymmetric regime with German leadership because the interventions were mostly intra-marginal and, even when they were marginal, the Bundesbank would systematically sterilize their effects on the German money supply. So my question is: if parities are fixed in the baseline and in the Nash case, how can we speak of a non-cooperative equilibrium when fixed rates imply a set of explicit cooperative policies? In the ERM, the countries with parities tied to Germany have no monetary autonomy either in the baseline or in the Nash case. So, what is the non-cooperative equilibrium all about?

The next observation is on the implication for international spillover of policies deriving from the imposition of an asymmetric fixed exchange rate rule. As suggested in Roubini (1991), there is a significant difference between structural international spillovers and international spillovers induced by a policy regime. Suppose that the structural international spillovers of policies are small under floating exchange rates (because of small trade and financial links); then monetary policy transmission from one country to another is very small. Suppose now that we impose an asymmetric fixed exchange rate regime where the follower country has to peg its exchange rate and the leader sets the monetary policy for the union. Now, even if structural spillovers are small, actual spillovers of policy would appear to be large: if the leader contracts its money supply, the follower has to contract money as well in order to maintain the pegged parities; this reaction will then induce a large output and/or price effect in the follower country. However, this large spillover effect is completely due to the policy regime, not to any structural international link. This point suggests that a large part of the international spillovers and ensuing benefits from coordination in the paper might be driven by the asymmetric fixed-rate regime imposed on the system: under a pure float, the inter-European gains from coordination might be much smaller.

A final observation about fixed exchange rates. Although the model includes in its historical baseline the 1992 exit of the pound and the lira from the ERM and the significant depreciation of these two currencies, it is not clear how the non-cooperative Nash equilibrium results in Italian and British policies optimally leading to a devaluation of their currencies in 1992–3. It must be the case that these devaluations are imposed on the system *a priori* rather than derived from the optimal non-cooperative policy choices of these countries.

Another comment is on the two new solution concepts presented in the paper. The authors argue that, since full cooperation is hard to achieve because of political conflicts on goals and the possibility of errors and disagreements about the true model of the world, it might be better to consider two different solution concepts: the domain solution and the preference transfer solution. I have a few observations on these concepts. First, these solution concepts appear to be subject to implementation difficulties similar to those of a cooperative equilibrium. Second, they are operationally cumbersome and conceptually confusing. What is, for example, the practical meaning of France using the German preferences on output and inflation in setting its policies but then using its original relative weights in measuring the true welfare gains? Third, these solution concepts are qualitatively similar to a set of fully cooperative solutions where the relative weights of Germany and the rest of the EMS in the planner functions are completely skewed in favour of Germany in the case of the preference transfer solutions, or skewed in favour of the rest of the EMS countries in the domain solution case.

If the reason for using these complex solution concepts is to address the issues of incentive compatibility, political feasibility, and policy conflicts between countries, it would be much simpler and clearer to talk about the set of efficient cooperative solutions; then, rule out those that make one country worse off relative to Nash, to take care of incentive compatibility questions; and, finally, concentrate on the set of Pareto-improving equilibria for both countries.

The use of new complex solution concepts mostly clouds the discussion of trade-offs and conflicts rather than clarifies it. The discussion on the results of the domain solution and preference transfer solution can be summarized more simply in the following way. There are cooperative or efficient equilibria where sufficient weight is given by the planner to the growth concerns of non-German EMS countries that the resulting equilibrium implies a German inflation rate higher than that desired by Germany. In this case Germany is worse off because it cares a lot about inflation, even if its growth performance is better. This is qualitatively similar to the result in the domain solution. Alternatively, there are other efficient equilibria where most of the planner's weight is given to Germany's welfare; in this case the Bundesbank rules, inflation is low, and growth is low. Germany is much better off, while the rest of Europe is worse off. This is qualitatively similar to the result in the preference transfer solution.

Section 5 discusses changes in monetary regimes in Europe. I have two positive observations and one normative comment. First, I would argue that any realistic scenario for the future of Europe should start from the realization that the ERM is in effect dead and that the baseline is now a system of non-cooperative managed exchange rates. Second, given this new regime, one may then ask a number of interesting questions. For example, is it now in the non-cooperative interest of France to expand money and let the exchange rate depreciate (in the wider ERM band), as the UK and Italy did, in order to stimulate growth and reduce unemployment? And how would Germany respond non-cooperatively to such a French policy? Would a non-cooperative equilibrium with floating rates be very different from an ERM regime? The answer to this question is: not necessarily. In fact, if France or the other ERM countries care enough about inflation on their own, policies might not change very much under the current new wide-band/semi-float system, and the equilibrium might be similar to the old ERM with tight-band/semi-fixed exchange rates.

On the normative side, the EMS crisis has finally shattered the myth that you can gain credibility just by announcing a fixed exchange rate. That argument did not even make sense from a theoretical point of view: exchange rate target announcements are as time inconsistent as monetary target announcements. Credibility is something you gain the hard way, following monetary, fiscal, and other policies that are consistent with fixed parities. Moreover, we have now learned that being too tough in the short run and using the nominal exchange rate as a nominal anchor might lead to significant real exchange rate misalignments (if there is sluggish adjustment of wages and prices), increasing current account imbalances, persistent fiscal deficit and debt accumulation if seigniorage is reduced, increased unemployment rates, and much less credibility down the line. By being too tough in terms of monetary credibility, the EMS countries and the three Nordic ones ended up losing a lot of real credibility: major devaluations eventually occurred with a vengeance and the system collapsed. In this regard, the discussion in the paper is quite correct in suggesting that there is some trade-off between monetary and real-side credibility.

The discussion in the paper on labour market inflexibility and its effects is quite interesting and relevant for Europe. However, the lesson that I get is somewhat different from the one presented in the paper. Rigidities on the supply side and in the labour markets suggest that there is relatively little room for traditional macro policies in Europe. Monetary policy will have to remain relatively conservative in order to maintain inflation credibility (more so now that the EU is in effect under a semi-floating exchange rate regime). Fiscal policy is also very constrained because of the large deficits and high public debt to GDP ratios in most of Europe. Therefore, there is little room for gains from cooperative or non-cooperative macro policies. The real and tough choices have to be made on the real/supply side, starting with more flexibility in the labour markets.

Finally, a comment on the relative gains from transatlantic versus inter-European cooperation. My prior belief has been that the gains from transatlantic coordination are likely to be very small given the actual size of international spillovers. The results in the paper mostly suggest that this is the case if we concentrate on the possibility of achieving better performance on the final policy goals through cooperation. The paper also suggests that these coordination gains might be significantly larger in the inter-European area. For the reasons discussed above, I am somewhat more sceptical than the paper's authors about the possibility of achieving significant gains from traditional macro-policy coordination in the European context.

REFERENCES

Roubini, Nouriel (1991), 'Leadership and Cooperation in the European Monetary System: A simulation approach', *Journal of Policy Modeling*, April.

3 Foreign exchange intervention and international policy coordination: comparing the G3 and EMS experience

AXEL A. WEBER

1 Introduction

The present paper deals with some key issues in the literature on central banks' foreign exchange intervention and international policy coordination. The aim of the paper is to question the validity of commonly held views about international policy coordination within the framework of the Group of Three (G3) consultations (between the United States, Japan, and Germany) and the European Monetary System (EMS), and to provide new empirical evidence on how these systems have worked and why they may have failed.

The first set of issues to be discussed in the present paper regards international, in particular transatlantic and EMS, policy coordination. After a period of benign neglect for the exchange rate prior to 1985, the United States reportedly changed its attitude towards exchange rate policies with the Plaza–Louvre agreements in 1985. Following an initial period aimed at driving down the value of the dollar, the G3 countries reportedly switched towards a policy of targeting their dollar exchange rates within wide unofficial bands of ± 12 per cent (see Funabashi, 1988, or McKinnon, 1993). The collapse of the narrow exchange rate target zones of the EMS in August 1993 has also resulted in a system of wide exchange rate bands of ± 15 per cent around the unchanged old parities. Both systems may therefore currently operate in a quite similar fashion, and it is thus interesting to analyse whether the past experience of G3 countries with policy coordination, exchange rate management, and central bank intervention in the framework of wide exchange rate bands holds any lessons for the future of the EMS. In order to pass such judgement, a quantitative evaluation and comparison of both the G3 and the EMS experience is in order.

The most important issue discussed in the present paper is whether the G3 and EMS countries have primarily relied on policy coordination and

54

convergence or on central bank intervention in stabilizing exchange rates, and whether such intervention was sterilized, coordinated, and effective. It is found that G3 intervention during the Plaza–Louvre period appears to have displayed three main characteristics: first, as postulated by McKinnon (1993), G3 intervention was apparently sterilized, both in its immediate impact and in its long-run consequences; second, intervention was coordinated between the Bundesbank and the Federal Reserve, but there is much less evidence of coordination between these two central banks and the Bank of Japan; third, intervention by G3 countries was ineffective in the long run in the sense that it did not significantly reverse the trend of bilateral exchange rates. Similar evidence is obtained for the EMS countries. The present study thus confirms results reported previously by Obstfeld (1988), Bordo and Schwartz (1991), Klein and Rosengren (1991), Ghosh (1992), Kaminsky and Lewis (1992), and Lewis (1992) that sterilized intervention, whether coordinated or not, has had no lasting exchange rate effects.

The main difference between the EMS and the G3 system is found to lie in the degree to which policy coordination other than intervention has been implemented. Long-term or even short-term policy coordination is virtually absent in the G3 context, irrespective of whether interest rate or money growth policy coordination is concerned. For the EMS, on the other hand, there exists strong evidence of short-term policy coordination, in particular with respect to interest rate policies.

The remainder of the paper is organized as follows: section 2 presents a brief summary of commonly held views about the G3 intervention, exchange rate management, and policy coordination process, and confronts these views with the data; section 3 provides similar evidence for the EMS; section 4 concludes the paper with a summary and comparison of the paper's main findings and an outlook onto the future of European monetary and economic integration.

2   G3 policy coordination and exchange rate management

In order to analyse the common features and dissimilarities between the process of international policy coordination in the G3 context and the working of the European Monetary System (EMS) it is essential first to establish the rules that governed both processes in the past and to examine whether any changes have occurred in recent years. But the post-1973 process of international G3 policy coordination, unlike the international monetary orders of Bretton Woods, the European currency snake, or the EMS, is extremely hard to characterize in a few words. In a recent attempt McKinnon (1993) summarizes a number of distinctive

---

BOX 1
Testable propositions adapted from McKinnon's (1993) rules of the 'Floating-Rate Dollar Standard, 1973–1984'

The United States

I   Remains passive in the foreign exchanges and pursues no exchange rate target. Does not hold significant official reserves of foreign exchange.

II   Pursues monetary policies independent of a foreign exchange value of the dollar and of the rate of money growth in other industrial countries – without trying to anchor any common price level.

Germany and Japan (plus other industrial countries)

III   Use the dollar as the intervention currency (except for some transactions to stabilize intra-European exchange rates), and keep official reserves mainly in US treasury bills.

IV   Smooth near-term fluctuations in dollar exchange rates without committing to a par value or to long-term exchange rate stability.

V   Partially adjust short-run growth of national money supplies to support major exchange interventions: reduce when the national money is weak against the dollar and expand when it is strong.

VI   Set long-run growth in national money supplies (and price level) independently of the United States, and allow corresponding secular adjustments in dollar exchange rate.

---

characteristics of the international monetary order. McKinnon's (1993) view of the 'rules of the game' is derived from an economist's interpretation of G3, G5, or G7 declarations and Funabashi's (1988) transcripts of interviews with policy makers involved in these events. However, this account of the *de facto* rules of the G3 international monetary order is not based on own empirical evidence and only a few references to the empirical literature evaluating the various propositions are made. The purpose of the present study is to re-examine some of McKinnon's claims about the G3 policy coordination process by confronting them with the facts in an empirical study.

2.1   The rules of the G3 policy coordination process

In describing the process of international policy coordination between the major industrialized countries within the context of the G3, G5, or G7 framework,[1] McKinnon (1993) differentiates between the pre-1985 'floating-rate dollar standard' and the post-1985 'Plaza–Louvre intervention accords for the dollar exchange rate', primarily on the basis of issues related to exchange rate management and foreign exchange intervention. The various rules describing each of these international monetary orders

---

BOX 2
Testable propositions adapted from McKinnon's (1993) rules of the 'Plaza–Louvre Intervention Accords for the Dollar Exchange Rate, 1985–1992'

Germany, Japan, and the United States

I   Hold foreign exchange reserves symmetrically in each other's currencies: US government has to begin building up reserves in Deutschmarks and yen, and possibly other convertible currencies.

II   Set broad target zones for the DM/dollar and yen/dollar exchange rate of ± 12 per cent. Do not announce the agreed-on central rates, and leave zonal boundaries flexible.

III If disparities in economic fundamentals among the G3 change substantially, adjust the implicit central rates.

IV Intervene in concert, but infrequently, to reverse short-run trends in the dollar exchange rate that threaten to pierce zonal boundaries. Signal the collective intent by not disguising these concerted interventions.

V   Sterilize the immediate monetary impact of intervention by not adjusting short-term interest rates.

VI In the long run, aim each country's monetary policy towards stabilizing the national price level in traded goods – thus indirectly anchoring the world price level and limiting drift in the position of the (unannounced) target zone.

Other industrial countries

VII Support, or do not oppose, interventions by G3 to keep the dollar within designated DM and yen zones.

---

are displayed in Boxes 1 and 2, and will be the focus of the empirical analysis below.

An interesting point about the post-1985 G3 international monetary order is that it closely resembles the new post-1993 wide-band EMS regime. It is therefore appropriate to ask whether the past experience in the G3 policy coordination process holds any lessons for the future of European monetary integration. In answering this question, two sets of related issues need to be analysed: (i) intervention policy and foreign exchange reserve management, and (ii) monetary policy coordination. The first set of issues is by far the more complex. Special attention will be paid below to the conduct of intervention policies, the objectives governing such foreign exchange intervention, their effectiveness, as well as their degree of domestic sterilization and international coordination.

2.2   G3 intervention policies and exchange rate management

Catte *et al.* (1992) argue that the commitment of the G3 (G5, G7) in the area of foreign exchange intervention has been much more specific than

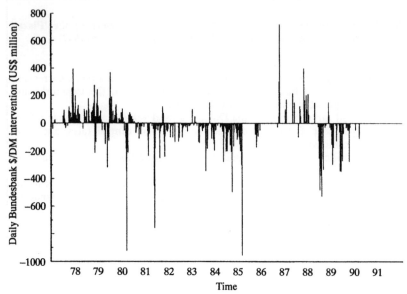

(a) Bundesbank intervention, sales (−) and purchases (+) of dollars for DM, 1977–92

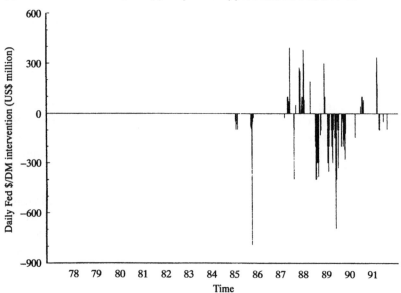

(b) Fed intervention, sales (−) and purchases (+) of dollars for DM, 1985–92

Figure 3.1   Bundesbank and Fed interventions (US$ billion)

in the domain of macro or structural policies. In particular, since 1985 coordinated efforts have been undertaken initially to revue (after the Plaza agreement) and later to stabilize (after the Louvre accord) the value of the dollar. So, does the year 1985 mark a regime shift from almost complete exchange rate flexibility to a managed float? Little formal empirical evidence has been reported to support such a drastic regime change hypothesis.[2] This paper aims at filling this gap.

2.2.1 Stylized facts about G3 intervention

Rare intervention?   Catte *et al.* (1992) report that G3 intervention was rare and concentrated in time: during 1985–92 each of the G3 central banks was on the market for less than one out of six trading days. Figure 3.1, which displays the US \$/DM market interventions by the Bundesbank and the Federal Reserve (Fed), shows that this fact holds only for the post-1985 intervention. Unilateral intervention by the Bundesbank in the pre-1985 period occurred regularly and not sporadically: the Bundesbank was on the market for a majority of trading days, and frequently with substantial amounts.

Coordinated and consistent intervention?   Catte *et al.* (1992) also report that the G3 countries never pursued conflicting intervention, but their time-series plots fail to demonstrate this fact to any great extent. Panel (a) of figure 3.2 clearly supports their statement for the US \$/DM market. When the Federal Reserve was on the market to support the dollar, the Bundesbank was either absent from the market or was doing the same thing, and vice versa. Panel (b) of figure 3.2 further shows that the Fed never pursued inconsistent intervention. When the Federal Reserve was on the US \$/yen market to support the dollar, it was either absent from the US \$/DM market or was also intervening in support of the dollar there, and vice versa. Catte *et al.* (1992) also report that the timing of G3 intervention clusters almost always coincides for at least two of the three countries, which strongly suggests that the bulk of the post-1985 intervention was coordinated amongst pairs of G3 central banks.[3]

Effective intervention?   Catte *et al.* (1992) identify nineteen non-sporadic, prolonged, and concerted intervention episodes between 1985 and 1992, eighteen of which they classify as aimed at countering the trend of the dollar ('leaning-against-the-wind'). The authors judge these periods as being either transitorily or permanently successful (i.e. the trend was reversed) or unsuccessful (trend continued), and report the following stylized facts about coordinated central bank intervention:

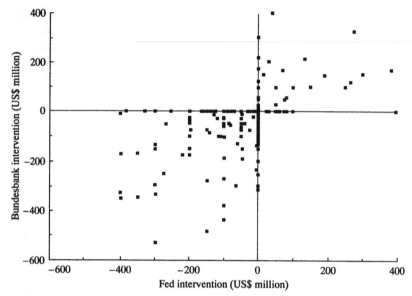

(a) Coordination between the Bundesbank's and the Fed's $/DM interventions

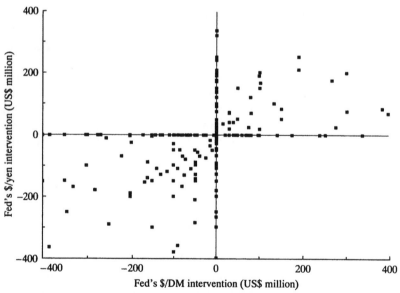

(b) Coordination between the Fed's $/DM and $/yen interventions

Figure 3.2   Bundesbank and Fed intervention coordination, 1985–92

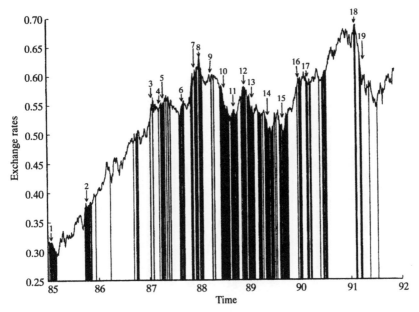

Source: Own calculations, with intervention episodes taken from Catte *et al.* (1992).

Figure 3.3 Coordinated daily central bank intervention and the US $/DM exchange rate, second sub-sample (01/01/1985 – 31/12/1991)

(a) the bulk of operations was concerted intervention by two central banks; only in 66 out of 461 intervention days did all G3 central banks intervene in a coordinated fashion;

(b) all episodes were successful in the sense of temporarily inverting the trend of the dollar, and in nine out of nineteen cases intervention was definitely successful in the sense that the next concerted intervention took place in the opposite direction;

(c) all major turning points of the dollar coincided with concerted intervention;

(d) in the majority of the intervention episodes the very short-term interest rate differentials moved according to the exchange rate objective pursued by the authorities, that is, helped the intervention.

The problem with this evidence is that it is purely descriptive and not based on any formal testing. Also, as Truman (1992) points out, adopting a slightly different criterion for the evaluation of the effectiveness of intervention leads to the conclusion that at the best five out of nineteen episodes were partially successful. Figure 3.3 reproduces the graphical

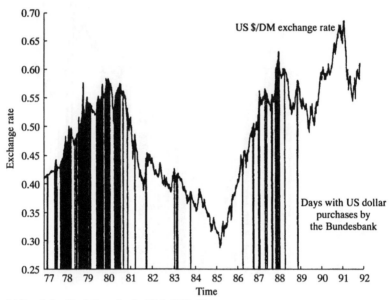

(a) Bundesbank's dollar sales for DM, 1977–92

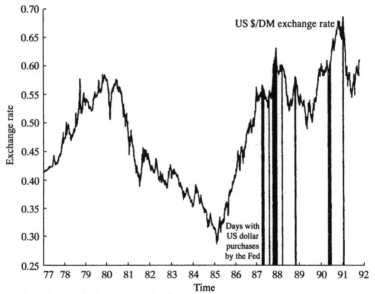

(b) Fed's dollar sales for DM, 1985–92

Figure 3.4   US $/DM exchange rate and Bundesbank's and Fed's interventions

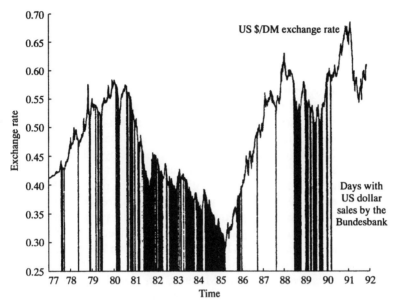

(c) Bundesbank's dollar purchases for DM, 1977–92

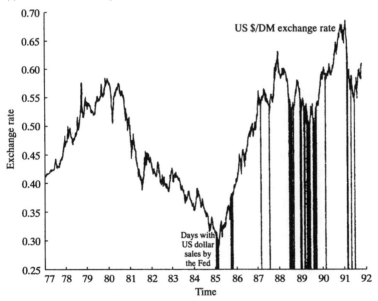

(d) Fed's dollar purchases for DM, 1985–92

Figure 3.4 (continued)

evidence from Catte *et al.* (1992) for the US \$/DM exchange rate. Although it is true that intervention occurred at many turning points of the exchange rate, there also exist many turning points at which no intervention at all occurred. This strongly supports Truman's (1992) scepticism with respect to the claim of Catte *et al.* (1992) that coordinated intervention was definitely effective in the short run.

A more differentiated picture of central bank intervention is suggested by figure 3.4, which displays the US \$/DM exchange rate jointly with a coding of foreign exchange trading days with sales (panels (a) and (b)) and purchases (panels (c) and (d)) of foreign exchange by the Bundesbank and the Federal Reserve. The most obvious fact from figure 3.4 is the difference in the Bundesbank's intervention behaviour prior to 1985 and thereafter. Prior to 1985, the Bundesbank pursued frequent unilateral leaning-against-the-wind intervention by selling dollars when the \$/DM rate rose (1977–81) and buying dollars when it declined (1981–5). After 1985, the Bundesbank appears to have intervened much less frequently by buying dollars when the exchange rate was relatively high and selling dollars when it was relatively low. Much of this post-1985 Bundesbank intervention was obviously coordinated with the Federal Reserve.

The noticeable change in the Bundesbank's intervention pattern raises the question of what objectives govern central bank intervention. Figure 3.5 looks at a number of potential arguments that are frequently referred to in studies of central bank reaction functions. Panel (a) of figure 3.5 reveals that for the post-1977 period the Bundesbank on average bought dollars when the exchange rate was below a value of 0.45 \$/DM and sold dollars when it was above. Furthermore, massive intervention occurred when the exchange rate took extreme values. In terms of a level target this would suggest that, during the post-1977 sample period, the Bundesbank aimed at a target zone with a 0.45 \$/DM (= 2.22 DM/\$) parity and fluctuation bands of ±33 per cent on either side of the parity. Such a level target is, however, only a poor description of the Bundesbank's intervention pattern in the \$/DM market. Similar poor representations of a Bundesbank intervention objective are obtained when average intervention is displayed against short-term and medium-term interest rate differentials (panels (b) and (d)) or expected exchange rate movements, as reflected by the forward premium (panel (c)).

The best explanation of Bundesbank and Federal Reserve intervention in the \$/DM market is obtained when short-term leaning-against-the-wind behaviour is postulated, as is shown in figure 3.6. Panel (a) displays the Bundesbank's average intervention against the change of the \$/DM exchange rate over an eight-week period. The Bundesbank purchased dollars when the \$/DM rate was falling and sold dollars when the DM/\$

rate was rising. The average intervention amounts increased as the short-term drift in the exchange rate accelerated, suggesting that leaning-against-the-wind intervention was stronger the more exchange rates changed. The same intervention pattern is revealed in panel (c) for the Federal Reserve in the post-1985 period. Both results strongly suggest that interventions by G3 central banks were governed by attempts to smooth near-term fluctuations in the dollar exchange rate without committing to a par value or long-term exchange rate stability.

2.2.2 Empirical evidence about G3 intervention

The objectives governing foreign exchange intervention, their effectiveness, as well as their degree of domestic sterilization and international coordination may also be analysed more formally by using econometric methods. This section provides such evidence and compares these results to the stylized facts derived above from the publicly available intervention data. The present study subsequently extends this analysis to ERM countries for which intervention data are not made publicly available. For all central banks, intervention is thereby approximated by the monthly change in the net foreign asset component of the monetary base. For the United States and Germany, where daily intervention data are available, this approximation works quite well, as figure 3.7 shows: changes in net foreign assets pick up the intervention activities of both central banks quite well. Thus, in order to obtain comparative international evidence, the remainder of the study is based on the monthly proxy of intervention.

Sterilization. The problem with an econometric analysis of central bank intervention is that the degrees of sterilization, coordination, and effectiveness of intervention must not be viewed as separate issues. One potential link exists between the sterilization of intervention and its effectiveness. For example, the Jurgensen report did not view sterilized intervention as an effective policy instrument. According to the Jurgensen (1983) report, the effect of unsterilized intervention, which directly affected a country's monetary base, was considered to be much larger than that of sterilized intervention. Funabashi (1988) also reports that the Bank of Japan at times conducted unsterilized intervention in order to maximize its effectiveness. The Bundesbank has repeatedly portrayed intervention and monetary policy as a *whole strategy*, which suggests that the Bundesbank's intervention may at times not have been fully sterilized. However, other than in the case of Japan and Germany, intervention by the Federal Reserve was generally considered to be completely sterilized (Funabashi, 1988).

The sterilization issue has been estimated in a large number of studies.

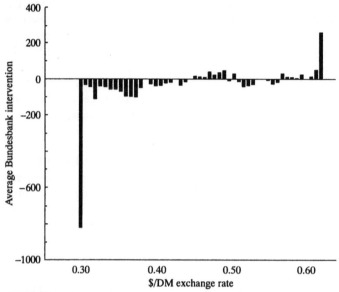

(a) US $/DM exchange rates

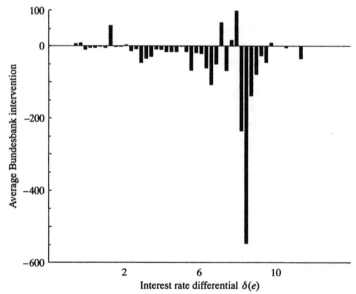

(b) 1-month interest rate differentials

Figure 3.5   The relationship between Bundesbank interventions and exchange rates, interest rate differentials, and forward premia/discounts, 1977–92

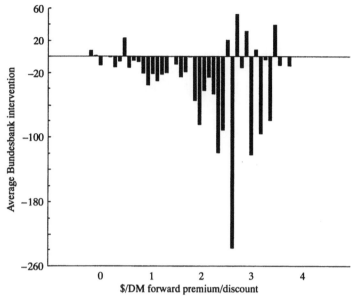

(c) 3-month forward premia

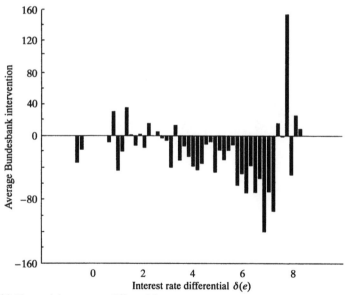

(d) 12-month interest rate differentials

Figure 3.5   (continued)

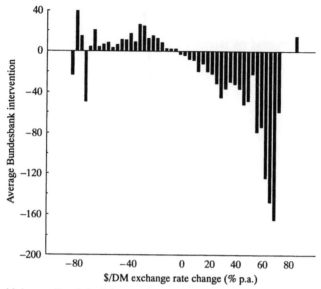

(a) Average Bundesbank intervention, 1977–92

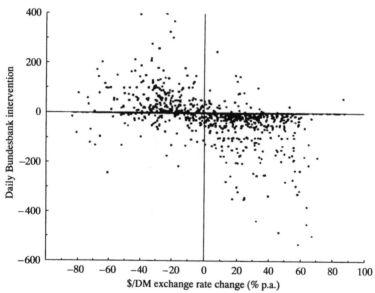

(b) Daily Bundesbank intervention, 1977–92

Figure 3.6   The relationship between Bundesbank and Fed interventions and US $/DM exchange rate changes (over an eight-week interval, % p.a.)

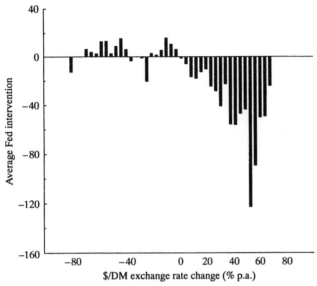

(c) Average Fed intervention, 1985–92

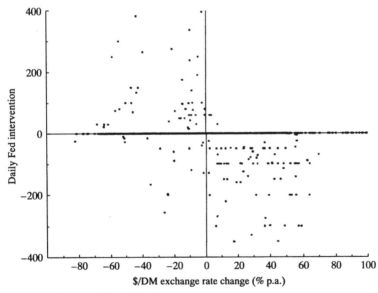

(d) Daily Fed intervention, 1985–92

Figure 3.6   (continued)

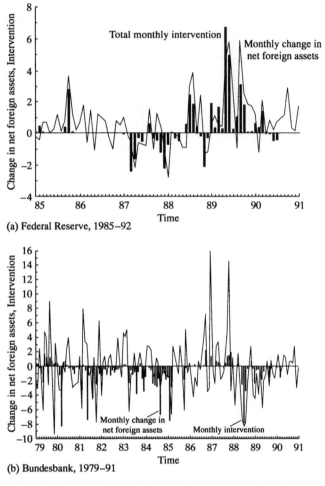

Figure 3.7   Monthly sums of daily interventions and monthly changes in the net foreign assets of the Federal Reserve and the Bundesbank

The evidence from these studies is somewhat mixed. Some early studies find that the Bundesbank completely sterilized its interventions (Herring and Marston, 1977a,b; Obstfeld, 1983; Mastropasqua *et al.*, 1988), whilst others find that sterilization was less than complete (Neumann, 1984; Gaiotti *et al.*, 1989), in particular its long-run effects on base money growth (von Hagen, 1989; Neumann and von Hagen, 1991). Empirical studies for Japanese data, on the other hand, largely reveal complete sterilization (Gaiotti *et al.*, 1989; Takagi, 1991).

Formally, the sterilization issue may be studied by relating base money creation to changes in the foreign component. To the extent that monetary base growth is determined exclusively by domestic policy objectives, changes in the foreign component (Δf) caused by intervention should be offset by equal and opposite changes in the domestic component (Δb) and thus imply no changes in the monetary base (Δm). This is the case of complete immediate sterilization of foreign exchange intervention:

$$\Delta m_t = \lambda_{mf}\Delta f_t + \ldots + \varepsilon_t, \tag{1}$$

with a sterilization coefficient $\lambda_{mf} = 0$. Estimation of equation (1) is complicated by two facts. First, sterilization may not be completed contemporaneously. In practice it therefore makes sense to distinguish between immediate and long-run sterilization by using the dynamic specification:

$$\Delta m_t = \lambda_{mf}\Delta f_t + \ldots + \sum_{j=1}^{p} \alpha_{mm}^{j}\,\Delta m_{t-j} + \sum_{j=1}^{p}\alpha_{mf}^{j}\Delta f_{t-j} + \varepsilon_t, \tag{2}$$

which allows the concept of long-run versus short-run sterilization to be implemented empirically. A second important complication in the estimation of equations (1) or (2) arises from the fact that the foreign component f_t cannot be safely considered an exogenous variable. For example, if the central bank aims at holding a constant fraction of its total assets in international reserves, the latter would grow in line with the monetary base (Scholl, 1983). In the single-equation framework above, such reversed causation between international reserve growth and monetary base growth would mislead researchers into wrongly interfering in a less than complete sterilization.

The above endogeneity problem is explicitly taken into account only in the study by Mastropasqua et al. (1988). They estimate a recursive two-equation system:

$$\Delta m_t = \lambda_{mf}\Delta f_t + \ldots + \varepsilon_t^{m}, \tag{3a}$$

$$\Delta f_t = \sum_{j=1}^{p}\alpha_{ff}^{j}\Delta f_{t-j} + \ldots + \sum_{j=1}^{p}\alpha_{fm}^{j}\,\Delta m_{t-j} + \varepsilon_t^{\eta}, \tag{3b}$$

by OLS, 2SLS, and Zellner's seemingly unrelated regression (SUR) techniques. The present paper aims at estimating the simultaneous two-equation system:

Table 3.1. The long-run sterilization of foreign exchange interventions in G3 countries, overall period (1973 M1–1992 M12) and two sub-periods (1973 M1–1984 M12, 1985 M1–1992 M12)

Country	Period	VAR estimates			Structural model estimates			$\gamma_{mf} = 0$ in 95% confidence interval			Estimates imposing $\gamma_{mf} = 0$		
		σ_m^2	σ_f^2	cor_{mf}	σ_m^2	σ_f^2	cor_{mf}	λ_{fm}	λ_{mf}	γ_{fm}	λ_{fm}	λ_{mf}	γ_{fm}
Germany	73:1–92:12	72.42	41.77	**0.01**	67.67	15.64	**0.35**	>0.2	<−0.06	>−0.47	**0.83 (0.43)**	**−0.27 (0.14)**	1.50 (0.95)
USA	73:1–92:12	41.90	17.65	**−0.22**	43.59	7.52	**−0.27**	<0.0	>−0.09	<1.18	**−0.88 (0.41)**	0.07 (0.08)	−1.55 (1.16)
Japan	73:1–92:12	78.66	58.92	**0.12**	2.03	22.88	**0.02**	>−0.6, <0.8	>−0.4, <0.3	>−2.6, <3.4	0.05 (0.26)	0.06 (0.14)	0.11 (1.04)
Germany	73:1–84:12	38.10	38.72	**0.13**	26.64	16.78	**0.63**	>0.4	<−0.29	>0.72	**0.65 (0.20)**	**−0.59 (0.20)**	**0.99 (0.27)**
USA	73:1–84:12	17.93	12.71	**−0.00**	27.71	5.83	**−0.07**	>−1.2, <0.4	>−0.2, <0.4	>−3.5, <2.9	−0.28 (0.29)	0.14 (0.13)	−0.32 (1.10)
Japan	73:1–84:12	65.55	59.75	**0.10**	84.28	25.99	**−0.42**	<0.4	>−0.25	<0.99	−0.17 (0.26)	0.23 (0.20)	−1.35 (0.87)
Germany	85:1–92:12	101.90	42.56	**−0.04**	146.10	12.39	**0.27**	–	–	–	1.06 (1.56)	−0.20 (0.26)	3.20 (6.38)
USA	85:1–92:12	58.54	21.07	**−0.27**	68.64	9.72	**−0.46**	<0.6	>−0.14	<5.43	−1.49 (0.93)	0.11 (0.14)	−3.25 (2.53)
Japan	85:1–92:12	89.55	54.19	**0.20**	122.00	19.35	**0.59**	>−0.2	<0.19	>0.53	0.55 (0.46)	−0.09 (0.17)	**3.71 (1.82)**

Notes: All results for the second moments are based on VARs with six lags. σ_i^2 denotes the variance estimate for variable i, cor_{ij} indicates the correlation between variables i and j. Variances and correlations are calculated for the residuals of the unrestricted VARs and the shocks implied by the long-run covariance matrix of the estimated VAR (the spectral density matrix of the variables at frequency zero). The coefficient ranges in columns 9–11 are those for which the long-run sterilization proposition cannot be rejected at the 95% level. The point estimates of the coefficients and their standard errors (in parentheses) implied by long-run sterilization are reported in the last three columns. Estimates that are significant at the 95 per cent level are in bold type.

$$\Delta m_t = \lambda_{mf} \Delta f_t + \sum_{j=1}^{p} \alpha^j_{mm} \Delta m_{t-j} + \sum_{j=1}^{p} \alpha^j_{mf} \Delta f_{t-j} + \varepsilon^m_t, \qquad (4a)$$

$$\Delta f_t = \lambda_{fm} \Delta m_t + \sum_{j=1}^{p} \alpha^j_{ff} \Delta f_{t-j} + \sum_{j=1}^{p} \alpha^j_{fm} \Delta m_{t-j} + \varepsilon^\eta_t, \qquad (4b)$$

by using the 2SLS instrumental variable techniques developed in King and Watson (1992) and discussed in more detail in Weber (1995). This simultaneous equation approach has two major advantages over the previous empirical literature. First, the estimates explicitly allow international reserve growth to be both predetermined ($\lambda_{fm} = 0$) and/or exogenous in the long run [$\gamma_{fm} = \alpha_{fm}(1)/\alpha_{ff}(1) = 0$ with $\alpha_{fm}(L) = \lambda_{fm} + \sum_{j=1}^{p} \alpha^j_{fm} + L^j$ and $\alpha_{ff}(L) = 1 - \sum_{j=1}^{p} \alpha^j_{ff} L^j$], without necessarily imposing these restrictions onto the data. Second, equations (4a) and (4b) provide a natural framework within which the concept of immediate sterilization ($\lambda_{mf} = 0$) versus long-run sterilization [$\gamma_{mf} = \alpha_{mf}(1)/\alpha_{mm}(1) = 0$ with $\alpha_{mf}(L) = \lambda_{mf} + \sum_{j=1}^{p} \alpha^j_{mf} L^j$ and $\alpha_{mm}(L) = 1 - \sum_{j=1}^{p} \alpha^j_{mm} L^j$] can be formalized and tested empirically without having to resort to the essentially arbitrary definition of permanent and transitory components of base money growth adopted in the studies by von Hagen (1989) and Neumann and von Hagen (1991).

As noted by King and Watson (1992), the simultaneous equation system (4a,b) is econometrically unidentified. In the current context this implies that the sterilization restriction is no longer testable when the net foreign assets component is endogenous. Thus, even if the hypothesis that the shocks ε^m_t and ε^η_t are uncorrelated is maintained, one additional restriction is required in order to identify the linear simultaneous equation model. In the literature, various identifying restrictions are to be found. It is common practice in the older literature on sterilization to assume that the foreign assets component of base money is exogenous, so that $\gamma_{fm} = (\lambda_{fm} + \sum_{j=1}^{p} \alpha^j_{fm})/(1 - \sum_{j=1}^{p} \alpha^j_{ff}) = 0$ which holds, for instance, if $\lambda_{fm} = \alpha^1_{fm} = \alpha^2_{fm} = \ldots = \alpha^p_{fm} = 0$. Another approach is to assume that the model is recursive, so that either $\lambda_{mf} = 0$ or $\lambda_{fm} = 0$, as in the paper by Mastropasqua et al. (1988). Finally, long-run sterilization of intervention with $\gamma_{mf} = (\lambda_{mf} + \sum_{j=1}^{p} \alpha^j_{mf})/(1 - \sum_{j=1}^{p} \alpha^j_{mm}) = 0$ may be assumed in order to identify the system and estimate the remaining parameters. In principle it is possible to identify the above simultaneous equation model by specifying a value of any one of the four parameters $\lambda_{mf}, \lambda_{fm}, \gamma_{mf}$, or γ_{fm} and then finding the implied estimates for the other three parameters. This is in fact the approach taken by King and Watson (1992), but, rather than focusing on a single identifying restriction, the authors report results for a wide range of identifying restrictions by

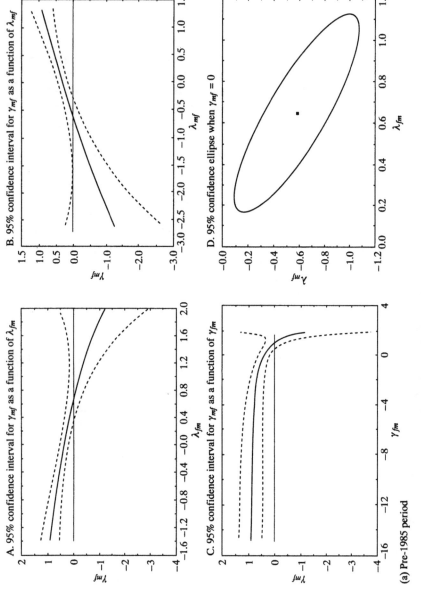

(a) Pre-1985 period

Figure 3.8   The long-run sterilization of Bundesbank interventions

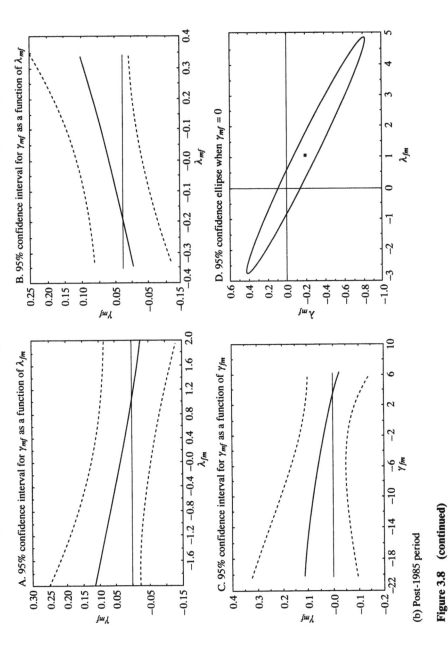

(b) Post-1985 period

Figure 3.8 (continued)

iterating each of the four reaction coefficients ($\lambda_{mf}, \lambda_{fm}, \gamma_{mf}$, and γ_{fm}) within a reasonable range, each time obtaining estimates of the remaining three parameters and their standard errors.

The empirical evidence about the degree of sterilization of G3 intervention uncovered by this approach may be best discussed by referring to figure 3.8, which displays the estimates for the Bundesbank's sterilization attempts for the pre-1985 period (panel (a)) and the post-1985 period (panel (b)). Long-term sterilization of Bundesbank intervention is consistent with the pre-1985 data only within a narrow range of identifying parameter restrictions, while it cannot be rejected over the entire range of possible identifications in the post-1985 sample. For the case of predetermined ($\lambda_{fm} = 0$) or long-run exogenous ($\gamma_{fm} = 0$) intervention, which is typically analysed in the literature, the data reject long-run sterilization in the pre-1985 period but not in the post-1985 sample. Also, short-run sterilization ($\lambda_{mf} = 0$) does not guarantee long-run sterilization ($\gamma_{fm} = 0$) in the first sub-sample. Rather, the estimates suggest that in order to achieve long-term sterilization the Bundesbank would have had to overcompensate the effects of intervention by a more than proportional reduction of the domestic credit component. I view this as evidence against the long-run sterilization hypothesis for Bundesbank intervention prior to 1985. Given its very frequent and in part substantial daily intervention activities in the first sub-sample, it is scarcely surprising that the Bundesbank was unable to safeguard the domestic money supply completely from the long-run consequences of its foreign exchange operations, even if sterilization of any immediate impact was possible at times.

Table 3.1, which displays the results for the entire post-1973 period and the two sub-periods postulated in McKinnon (1993), further reveals that for the United States and Japan both predetermined and long-run exogenous intervention is compatible with long-run sterilization in both sub-samples. The point estimates under long-run sterilization of intervention suggest that the Federal Reserve in both sub-samples has tended to reduce the foreign component when the monetary base increased ($\lambda_{fm} < 0$), while for Japan and Germany positive but insignificant coefficients ($\lambda_{fm} > 0$) are found for the post-1985 period. Unlike the Bundesbank in the pre-1985 period, the Bank of Japan and the Federal Reserve throughout the sample do not appear to have aimed at maintaining a certain proportionality in domestic credit and net foreign asset growth.

To summarize, the above findings of long-term non-sterilized intervention by Germany in the pre-1985 period and sterilized intervention otherwise are broadly consistent with the results reported in the previous literature. As in the papers by Gaiotti *et al.* (1989) and Takagi (1991), the data suggest complete sterilization for Japan. The pre-1985 result for Germany further explains why long-run sterilization ($\gamma_{mf} = 0$) is frequently rejected in single-equation studies, such as von Hagen (1989) and Neumann and von Hagen (1991), which imply $\gamma_{fm} = 0$. Finally, the present study also shows that failure to sterilize the long-run impact of intervention does not rule out that the immediate impact of intervention may have been sterilized, as has been suggested by Herring and Marston (1977a,b) and Obstfeld (1983).

Coordination.   In order to study the degree to which intervention by G3 central banks was coordinated, I have estimated the simultaneous two-equation system:

$$\Delta f_t^* = \lambda_{f^*f}\Delta f_t + \sum_{j=1}^{p}\alpha_{f^*f^*}^j\,\Delta f_{t-j}^* + \sum_{j=1}^{P}\alpha_{f^*f}^j\Delta f_{t-j} + \varepsilon_t^\nu, \quad (5a)$$

$$\Delta f_t = \lambda_{ff^*}\,\Delta f_t^* + \sum_{j=1}^{p}\alpha_{ff}^j\Delta f_{t-j} + \sum_{j=1}^{p}\alpha_{ff^*}^j\,\Delta f_{t-j}^* + \varepsilon_t^\eta, \quad (5b)$$

whereby Δf^* and Δf represent the changes in the net foreign assets component of the monetary base in the foreign and home country, respectively. If the home country intervenes on its own account ($\lambda_{ff^*} = 0, \gamma_{ff^*} = 0$) and the foreign country coordinates its intervention in the bilateral exchange market accordingly, this should result in negative short-run ($\lambda_{f^*f} < 0$) and long-run ($\gamma_{f^*f} < 0$) coefficient estimates. If in addition the intervention shares are equally distributed between both central banks, coefficients of minus one should emerge. However, coordinated intervention in third currencies should result in positive coefficient estimates. Such intervention is likely to be a rare exception within the G3 context, but in order to allow for both alternatives the presence of coordinated intervention is tested by evaluating the null-hypothesis $\gamma_{f^*f} = 0$.

Table 3.2 summarizes the results for the hypothesis that intervention of G3 central banks was not subject to a long-run coordinated strategy. The short-run and long-run correlations of intervention activities (in columns 5 and 8 respectively)[4] are low for all combinations of central banks except the post-1985 Bundesbank (BBK) and Federal Reserve (FED) intervention. For these two central banks the degree of coordination is substantial, in both the short run (-0.64) and the long run (-0.73). A much lower degree of coordination is found between the United States and Japan (BOJ) (-0.22, -0.28), and coordination appears to be absent

Table 3.2. The long-run independence of foreign exchange interventions in G3 countries, two sub-periods (1973 M1–1984 M12, 1985 M1–1992 M12)

Central banks	Period	VAR estimates			Structural model estimates			$\gamma_{ij} = 0$ in 95% confidence interval			Estimates imposing $\gamma_{ij} = 0$		
		σ_i^{2*}	σ_j^2	cor_{ij}	σ_i^2	σ_j^2	cor_{ij}	λ_{ij}	λ_{ji}	γ_{ij}	λ_{ij}	λ_{ji}	γ_{ij}
BBK,FED	73:1–84:12	18.07	57.91	**−0.16**	28.47	53.80	**−0.45**	<0.00	>0.77	>0.04	**−0.14 (0.07)**	1.05 (0.69)	**−0.24 (0.12)**
FED,BBK	73:1–84:12	57.91	18.07	**−0.16**	53.80	28.47	**−0.45**	<0.64	>−0.10	>0.06	−0.54 (0.58)	0.00 (0.05)	**−0.85 (0.44)**
BOJ,FED	73:1–84:12	18.39	79.32	**−0.16**	29.72	116.00	**0.28**	>−0.06	<0.48	>−0.5, <−0.1	−0.00 (0.05)	−0.69 (0.77)	0.07 (0.08)
FED,BOJ	73:1–84:12	79.32	18.39	**−0.16**	116.00	29.72	**0.28**	no	no	no	0.55 (1.10)	−0.07 (0.05)	1.09 (1.16)
BOJ,BBK	73:1–84:12	59.95	79.09	**0.29**	56.95	122.70	**−0.30**	<0.29	>0.04	>0.3, <0.6	−0.18 (0.18)	**0.64 (0.23)**	−0.14 (0.15)
BBK,BOJ	73:1–84:12	79.09	59.95	**0.29**	122.70	56.95	**−0.30**	<1.16	>−0.52	–	0.26 (0.32)	0.08 (0.18)	−0.65 (0.68)
BBK,FED	85:1–92:12	55.60	114.00	**−0.64**	81.39	153.40	**−0.73**	<0.18	>−1.67	<0.01	**−0.23 (0.12)**	−0.50 (0.57)	**−0.39 (0.20)**
FED,BBK	85:1–92:12	114.00	55.60	**−0.64**	153.40	81.39	**−0.73**	no	no	no	−1.87 (0.54)	0.32 (0.41)	**−1.37 (0.69)**
BOJ,FED	85:1–92:12	50.16	97.37	**−0.22**	62.06	126.60	**−0.28**	<0.81	>−2.22	–	0.01 (0.17)	−0.48 (0.55)	−0.14 (0.19)
FED,BOJ	85:1–92:12	97.37	50.16	**−0.22**	126.60	62.06	**−0.28**	<0.31	>−0.18	–	−1.03 (0.55)	0.18 (0.17)	−0.57 (0.79)
BOJ,BBK	85:1–92:12	106.40	101.60	**0.31**	137.90	136.10	**0.21**	–	–	–	0.47 (0.39)	−0.15 (0.42)	0.21 (0.48)
BBK,BOJ	85:1–92:12	101.60	106.40	**0.31**	136.10	137.90	**0.21**	–	–	–	0.07 (0.31)	0.25 (0.31)	0.21 (0.46)

Notes: All results for the second moments are based on VARs with six lags. σ_i^2 denotes the variance estimate for variable i, cor_{ij} indicates the correlation between variables i and j. Variances and correlations are calculated for the residuals of the unrestricted VARs and the shocks implied by the estimated VAR (the spectral density matrix of the variables at frequency zero). The coefficient ranges in columns 9–11 are those for which the long-run independence proposition cannot be rejected at the 95% level. The point estimates of the coefficients and their standard errors (in parentheses) implied by long-run independence are reported in the last three columns. Estimates that are significant at the 95 per cent level are in bold type.

between Germany and Japan, where the positive correlations (0.31, 0.21) suggest simultaneous intervention with respect to the third currency, the US dollar. Thus, the data are primarily consistent with long-run coordination between Bundesbank and Federal Reserve intervention in the \$/DM market. Note that this finding is in line with the informal evidence from the daily data reported above. However, an identifying assumption is required to determine whether this high correlation arises from a long-run causal relationship running from Federal Reserve intervention to Bundesbank intervention or vice versa. Columns 9–11 of table 3.2 suggest a significant degree of long-run coordination ($\gamma_{f^*f} < 0$) across the entire range of identifying restrictions on both the short-run (λ_{f^*f} and λ_{ff^*}) and long-run (γ_{f^*f}) reaction coefficients if the causal link is postulated to run from the Bundesbank to the Federal Reserve, whereas for the case of reversed causation long-run coordination holds only for a restricted range of $\lambda_{f^*f}, \lambda_{ff^*}$, and γ_{f^*f} coefficients. In particular, the case of predetermined ($\lambda_{f^*f} = 0$) or exogenous ($\gamma_{f^*f} = 0$) Federal Reserve intervention is incompatible with long-run coordination ($\gamma_{f^*f} < 0$). This suggests that the Federal Reserve engaged primarily in coordinated intervention, whereas for the Bundesbank both coordinated and exogenous unilateral intervention are compatible with the post-1985 data. This finding again is consistent with the evidence from the daily intervention data reported above.

Effectiveness.   In the theoretical literature, the effectiveness of unsterilized central bank intervention is unquestioned, but there exists considerable controversy over the effectiveness of sterilized intervention. Two channels have been identified through which sterilized intervention may affect the exchange rate: the expectations or signalling channel and the portfolio channel.

Mussa (1981) points out that, under uncovered interest rate parity, sterilized intervention, which leaves interest rates unaltered, can have an indirect effect on the spot exchange rate by changing the expected future exchange rate. This may be the case if current intervention is perceived by market participants as a signal of future changes in monetary policy. However, the empirical evidence in support of this expectations or signalling channel is weak, and most empirical studies, such as Klein and Rosengren (1991), Ghosh (1992), Kaminsky and Lewis (1992), and Lewis (1992), provide rather unfavourable results.

The literature on the portfolio channel postulates that, owing to foreign exchange risks, domestic and foreign assets are imperfect substitutes, and risk-averse agents have to be compensated for the higher risk of holding foreign bonds by being paid a risk premium. Sterilized intervention (that

Table 3.3. The long-run ineffectiveness of foreign exchange interventions in G3 countries, two sub-periods (1973 M1–1984 M12, 1985 M1–1992 M12)

Bank, rate	Period	VAR estimates			Structural model estimates			$\gamma_{ef}=0$ in 95% confidence interval			Estimates imposing $\gamma_{ef}=0$		
		σ_e^2	σ_f^2	cor_{ef}	σ_e^2	σ_f^2	cor_{ef}	λ_{fe}	λ_{ef}	γ_{fe}	λ_{fe}	λ_{ef}	γ_{fe}
BBK,$/DM	73:1–84:12	37.91	32.28	**0.35**	26.23	38.06	**0.33**	>−0.1	<0.35	>−0.09	0.19 (0.20)	0.17 (0.13)	0.23 (0.17)
FED,DM/$	73:1–84:12	17.92	31.45	**0.02**	28.46	37.92	**0.52**	>0.2	<−0.59	>0.08	**0.27 (0.13)**	**0.82 (0.36)**	**−0.39 (0.17)**
BOJ,$/¥	73:1–84:12	62.23	29.26	**0.29**	74.65	38.46	**0.55**	>−1, <−0.1	<0.1, >3.5	—	**1.18 (0.49)**	−0.15 (0.13)	**1.06 (0.48)**
FED,¥/$	73:1–84:12	18.20	29.04	**−0.03**	27.76	39.55	**0.06**	>0.4	<0.04	>−0.04	0.04 (0.12)	0.15 (0.28)	−0.04 (0.20)
BOJ,DM/¥	73:1–84:12	65.27	27.47	**0.13**	89.39	52.36	**0.77**	>0.45	<−0.06	<0.84	**1.29 (0.54)**	**0.19 (0.10)**	**−1.31 (0.36)**
BBK,¥/DM	73:1–84:12	38.75	27.09	**0.24**	25.40	48.72	**0.03**	>−0.1, <1.3	<0.86	—	0.46 (0.25)	−0.07 (0.12)	0.01 (0.16)
BBK,$/DM	85:1–92:12	99.04	32.36	**0.17**	189.10	46.21	**−0.03**	—	—	—	−0.33 (2.59)	0.09 (0.26)	−0.13 (3.47)
FED,DM/$	85:1–92:12	56.58	31.72	**−0.15**	71.65	46.98	**−0.33**	<0.4, >1	>−0.4, <−0.1	—	−1.48 (0.95)	0.43 (0.37)	−0.50 (0.66)
BOJ,$/¥	85:1–92:12	57.18	31.74	**−0.08**	74.50	46.27	**0.20**	—	—	—	−0.09 (0.67)	−0.02 (0.20)	0.33 (0.73)
FED,¥/$	85:1–92:12	87.01	31.85	**0.19**	127.40	44.72	**0.04**	—	—	—	−0.34 (1.08)	0.11 (0.13)	0.11 (1.28)
BOJ,DM/¥	85:1–92:12	98.94	25.78	**0.00**	121.10	36.33	**−0.23**	—	—	—	−3.16 (2.91)	0.21 (0.19)	−0.76 (1.76)
BBK,¥/DM	85:1–92:12	92.34	26.36	**−0.02**	129.40	37.21	**−0.16**	—	—	—	0.30 (1.19)	−0.03 (0.09)	−0.55 (1.49)

Notes: All results for the second moments are based on VARs with six lags. σ_i^2 denotes the variance estimate for variable i, cor_{ij} indicates the correlation between variables i and j. Variances and correlations are calculated for the residuals of the unrestricted VARs and the shocks implied by the long-run covariance matrix of the estimated VAR (the spectral density matrix of the variables at frequency zero). The coefficient ranges in columns 9–11 are those for which the long-run ineffectiveness proposition cannot be rejected at the 95% level. The point estimates of the coefficients and their standard errors (in parentheses) implied by long-run ineffectiveness are reported in the last three columns. Estimates that are significant at the 95 per cent level are in bold type.

is, a change in the supply of domestic relative to foreign assets) then requires a change in the risk premium for portfolio investors to maintain equilibrium. This risk premium is typically measured as the deviation from uncovered interest rate parity. Thus, for given exchange rate expectations and a given interest rate differential, the change in the risk premium requires a corresponding change in the spot exchange rate. The effectiveness of sterilized intervention in influencing the exchange rate thus depends critically on the assumption of imperfect substitutability of domestic and foreign assets. Although Dominguez and Frankel (1993) report some empirical evidence in favour of the portfolio channel by using survey data on exchange rate expectations, most of the empirical literature finds little or no evidence in its support, as Rogoff (1984), Obstfeld (1988), and Bordo and Schwartz (1991) point out.

The discussion in the previous section of the paper revealed that most of the G3 intervention appears to have been sterilized. In view of the literature discussed above, its effectiveness thus appears to be questionable. The problem thereby is that, in order to judge formally the effectiveness of intervention, it is necessary to relate central bank intervention to its ultimate objective. To be more precise, the discussion of the daily intervention data above has revealed that intervention by the Bundesbank and the Federal Reserve may best be explained in terms of a leaning-against-the-wind objective. For example, in the event that the Bundesbank buys US dollars through sales of Deutschmarks ($\Delta f > 0$) in order to support the dollar, such stabilizing intervention should be negatively correlated with present or past changes in the \$/DM exchange rate ($\Delta e < 0$). If the intervention ($\Delta f > 0$) is effective, it should further cause current and/or future exchange rate changes in the opposite direction ($\Delta e > 0$). Thus, in order to capture both aspects of intervention, the present paper reports empirical results obtained by estimating the simultaneous two-equation system:

$$\Delta e_t = \lambda_{e,f}\Delta f_t + \sum_{j=1}^{p}\alpha_{e,e}^{j}\Delta e_{t-j} + \sum_{j=1}^{p}\alpha_{e,f}^{j}\Delta f_{t-j} + \varepsilon_f^{\nu}, \qquad (6a)$$

$$\Delta f_t = \lambda_{f,e}\Delta e_t + \sum_{j=1}^{p}\alpha_{f,f}^{j}\Delta f_{t-j} + \sum_{j=1}^{p}\alpha_{f,e}^{j}\Delta e_{t-j} + \varepsilon_t^{\eta}, \qquad (6b)$$

whereby Δf and Δe represent the changes in the net foreign assets component of the monetary base and changes in the exchange rate (measured as the ratio of foreign to domestic money), respectively. Exogenous or predetermined intervention ($\lambda_{f,e} = 0, \gamma_{f,e} = 0$) is effective in stabilizing the exchange rate only if it gives rise to significant negative

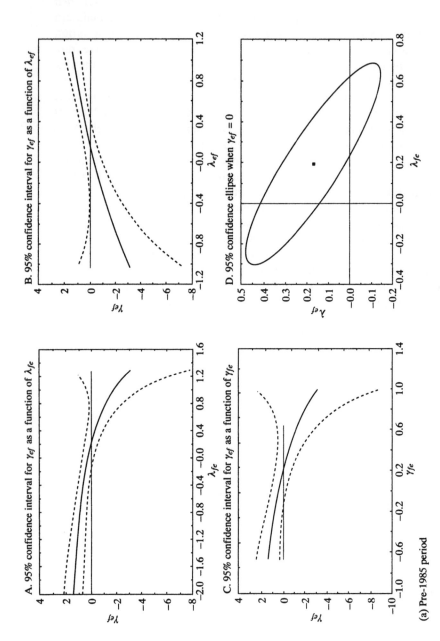

A. 95% confidence interval for γ_{ef} as a function of λ_{fe}

B. 95% confidence interval for γ_{ef} as a function of λ_{ef}

C. 95% confidence interval for γ_{ef} as a function of γ_{fe}

D. 95% confidence ellipse when $\gamma_{ef} = 0$

(a) Pre-1985 period

Figure 3.9   The long-run ineffectiveness of the Bundesbank's $/DM interventions

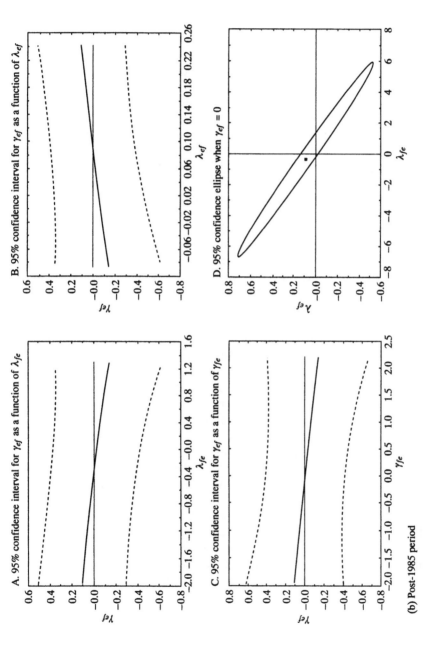

A. 95% confidence interval for γ_{ef} as a function of λ_{fe}

B. 95% confidence interval for γ_{ef} as a function of λ_{ef}

C. 95% confidence interval for γ_{ef} as a function of γ_{fe}

D. 95% confidence ellipse when $\gamma_{ef} = 0$

(b) Post-1985 period

Figure 3.9 (continued)

short-run ($\lambda_{e,f} < 0$) and/or long-run ($\gamma_{e,f} < 0$) coefficient estimates. This simultaneity problem between the causes and the effects of intervention, which has been completely disregarded in the previous literature, is the prime focus of the analysis below.

The results for the Bundesbank's intervention in the \$/DM market are displayed in figure 3.9. Bundesbank intervention in the post-1985 period has clearly been ineffective in altering the dollar exchange rate in the long run, irrespective of the possible identifying restrictions on the coefficients $\lambda_{f,e}, \gamma_{f,e}$, and $\lambda_{e,f}$. Imposing long-run ineffectiveness ($\gamma_{e,f} = 0$), reveals no significant short-run effects ($\lambda_{e,f} \neq 0$) of predetermined intervention ($\lambda_{f,e} = 0$), as is indicated by the fact that the origin lies within the 95% confidence ellipse for the long-run ineffectiveness hypothesis. A rather different result is obtained for the pre-1985 period. Although, as above, predetermined and long-run exogenous intervention ($\lambda_{f,e} = 0, \gamma_{f,e} = 0$) is found to be ineffective in the long run, modestly leaning-against-the-wind intervention ($\lambda_{f,e} < -0.1$ and $\gamma_{f,e} < 0.09$) is found to have significant long-run exchange rate effects. Moreover, imposing long-run ineffectiveness ($\gamma_{e,f} = 0$) reveals significant short-run effects ($\lambda_{e,f} > 0$) of predetermined foreign exchange intervention ($\lambda_{f,e} = 0$) because the origin lies outside the 95% confidence ellipse for parameters satisfying the long-run ineffectiveness hypothesis.

Table 3.3 shows the results for all combinations of G3 exchange rates and intervention policies. The long-run effectiveness of intervention is rejected by all the data for the post-1985 period, and imposing long-run exchange rate neutrality of intervention reveals no significant short-run effects. For the pre-1985 period, the long-run effectiveness of intervention is not rejected over such a wide range of identifying restrictions. Predetermined ($\lambda_{f,e} = 0$) or leaning-against-the-wind intervention ($\lambda_{f,e} < 0$) typically has significant positive long-run effects ($\gamma_{e,f} > 0$). Furthermore, intervention by the Bank of Japan in the DM/¥ market and by the Federal Reserve in the DM/\$ market has significant short-run effects even if long-run ineffectiveness is imposed upon the data.

To summarize, G3 intervention during the Plaza–Louvre period appears to have displayed the following three characteristics. First, as postulated by McKinnon (1993), G3 intervention was apparently sterilized, both in its immediate impact and in its long-run consequences. Second, intervention was coordinated between the Bundesbank and the Federal Reserve, but there is much less evidence of coordination between these two central banks and the Bank of Japan. Third, intervention by G3 countries was ineffective in the long run in the sense that it did not significantly reverse the trend of bilateral exchange rates. A major finding of the present paper therefore is that sterilized G3 intervention, whether coordinated or not, has had no lasting exchange rate effects. The evidence on the effectiveness of central bank intervention obtained by the simultaneous equation approach of the present paper is therefore largely consistent with previous results reported in Obstfeld (1988), Bordo and Schwartz (1991), Klein and Rosengren (1991), Ghosh (1992), Kaminsky and Lewis (1992), and Lewis (1992) for the post-1985 period.

2.3   G3 policy coordination

Given that G3 intervention appears to have been an ineffective tool for stabilizing exchange rates, might it be that international policy coordination has helped in stabilizing exchange rates? To answer this question, two forms of economic policy coordination are examined. First, interest rate policy coordination may have fostered interest rate convergence, which in turn may have stabilized expected and actual exchange rates. Second, monetary policy coordination may have worked towards inflation convergence, which also may have helped in stabilizing exchange rates.

2.3.1   Interest rate policy coordination
Some non-formal evidence about the degree of interest rate policy coordination amongst G3 countries is provided in figure 3.10. Discount rate policies appear to be relatively closely coordinated between Germany and Japan prior to 1990, but after German unification this close link between both rates breaks down. After 1990 the Japanese discount rate policies switch from following the German discount rate to closely following the United States' discount rate. A similar switch is found in overnight money market rates and short-term treasury bill rates, but it is less apparent in long-term government bond yields. To summarize, the time-paths of interest rates in G3 countries suggest some degree of coordination between Germany and Japan prior to 1990, with Japanese rates typically following German rates with some time-lag.

In order to obtain formal evidence on the degree of international interest rate policy coordination the present study estimates the simultaneous two-equation system:

$$\Delta i_t^* = \lambda_{i^*,i} \, \Delta i_t + \sum_{j=1}^{p} \alpha_{i^*,i^*}^j \, \Delta i_{t-j}^* + \sum_{j=1}^{p} \alpha_{i^*,i}^j \, \Delta i_{t-j} + \varepsilon_t^{\nu}, \tag{7a}$$

$$\Delta i_t = \lambda_{i,i^*} \, \Delta i_t^* + \sum_{j=1}^{p} \alpha_{i,i}^j \Delta i_{t-j} + \sum_{j=1}^{p} \alpha_{i,i^*}^j \Delta i_{t-j}^* + \varepsilon_t^{\eta}, \tag{7b}$$

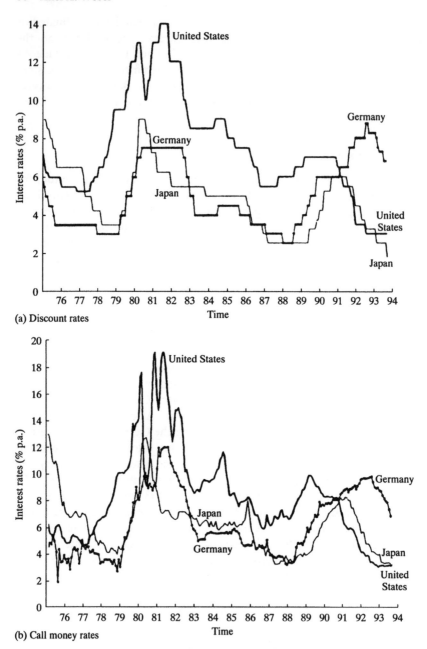

(a) Discount rates

(b) Call money rates

Figure 3.10   Official and market interest rates in G3 countries

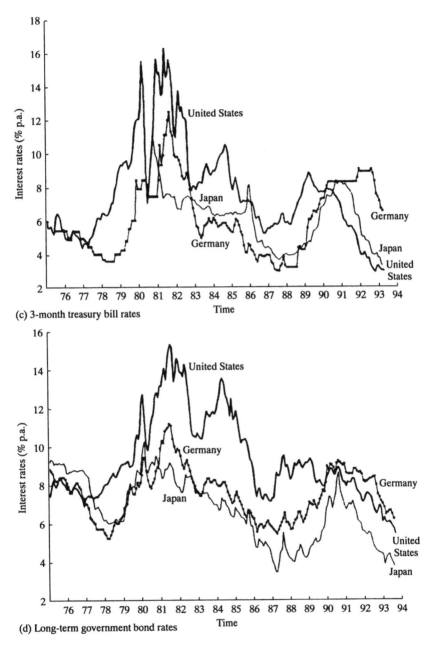

(c) 3-month treasury bill rates

(d) Long-term government bond rates

Figure 3.10 (continued)

Table 3.4. The long-run independence of interest rate policies in G3 countries, two sub-periods (1973 M1–1984 M12, 1985 M1–1992 M12)

Central banks	Period	VAR estimates			Structural model estimates			$\gamma_{i,i^*}=0$ in 95% confidence interval			Estimates imposing $\gamma_{i,i^*}=0$		
		$\sigma^2_{i^*}$	σ^2_i	$cor_{i^*,i}$	$\sigma^2_{i^*}$	σ^2_i	$cor_{i^*,i}$	$\lambda_{i^*,i}$	λ_{i,i^*}	$\gamma_{i^*,i}$	$\lambda_{i^*,i}$	λ_{i,i^*}	$\gamma_{i^*,i}$
BBK,FED	73:1–84:12	0.89	1.21	**0.10**	1.09	0.99	**0.83**	>0.33	<−0.48	>0.74	**0.46 (0.14)**	**−0.75 (0.24)**	**0.92 (0.17)**
FED,BBK	73:1–84:12	1.21	0.89	**0.10**	0.99	1.09	**0.83**	>0.33	<−0.17	>0.58	**0.71 (0.26)**	**−0.33 (0.14)**	**0.75 (0.14)**
BOJ,FED	73:1–84:12	0.89	0.41	**0.10**	0.86	1.27	**0.42**	>0.66	<−0.13	>−0.48	**1.66 (0.53)**	**−0.34 (0.12)**	0.28 (0.24)
FED,BOJ	73:1–84:12	0.41	0.89	**0.10**	1.27	0.86	**0.42**	>−0.66	<2.44	>−1.02	−0.08 (0.16)	0.56 (0.67)	0.62 (0.52)
BOJ,BBK	73:1–84:12	1.27	0.41	**0.17**	0.82	1.14	**0.45**	>0.66	<0.00	>−0.25	**1.91 (0.73)**	**−0.16 (0.08)**	0.33 (0.23)
BBK,BOJ	73:1–84:12	0.41	1.27	**0.17**	1.14	0.82	**0.45**	>−0.22	<1.50	>−0.20	0.01 (0.09)	0.39 (0.85)	0.62 (0.45)
BBK,FED	85:1–92:12	0.24	0.24	**0.10**	0.42	0.37	**0.11**	–	–	–	−0.51 (0.42)	0.57 (0.35)	−1.27 (1.19)
FED,BBK	85:1–92:12	0.24	0.24	**0.10**	0.37	0.42	**0.11**	–	–	–	−0.25 (0.37)	0.35 (0.34)	0.10 (0.37)
BOJ,FED	85:1–92:12	0.24	0.30	**0.19**	0.45	0.58	**0.42**	>−0.22	<0.39	–	0.28 (0.22)	−0.22 (0.34)	0.33 (0.30)
FED,BOJ	85:1–92:12	0.30	0.24	**0.19**	0.58	0.45	**0.42**	>−0.66	<0.47	–	0.33 (0.40)	−0.07 (0.27)	0.54 (0.50)
BOJ,BBK	85:1–92:12	0.29	0.24	**0.17**	0.62	0.44	**0.67**	>0.00	<0.21	>0.00	0.37 (0.36)	−0.12 (0.25)	0.96 (0.53)
BBK,BOJ	85:1–92:12	0.24	0.29	**0.17**	0.44	0.62	**0.67**	>−0.33	<0.35	>−0.18	0.52 (0.30)	−0.61 (0.51)	0.47 (0.26)

Notes: All results for the second moments are based on VARs with six lags. σ^2_i denotes the variance estimate for variable i, cor_{ij} indicates the correlation between variables i and j. Variances and correlations are calculated for the residuals of the unrestricted VARs and the shocks implied by the long-run independence proposition (in parentheses) implied by long-run independence are reported in the last three columns. Estimates that are significant at the 95 per cent level are in bold type.
at frequency zero). The coefficient ranges in columns 9–11 are those for which the long-run independence proposition cannot be rejected at the 95% level. The point estimates of the coefficients and their standard errors (in parentheses) implied by long-run independence are reported in the last three columns. Estimates that are significant at the 95 per cent level are in bold type.

whereby $\Delta i*$ and Δi represent the changes in the interest rate in the foreign and home country, respectively. Note that equations such as (7a) are typically estimated in the context of Granger causality tests, and have been applied by De Grauwe (1988), Fratianni and von Hagen (1990a,b), Cohen and Wyplosz (1989), and Weber (1990b) in order to test the hypothesis of EMS asymmetry. The empirical evidence from this literature suggests a quite symmetrical working of the EMS, with causality typically running both ways. But Wyplosz (1989) argues that this finding is hardly surprising, given that the policy-game literature suggests that it is suboptimal for policy makers to follow a predetermined or long-run exogenous policy without taking the other central bank's past or current reaction to its policy into account. Equation (7b) captures precisely this fact. The two-equation system estimated here may thus be viewed as a more consistent approach towards testing for asymmetry in the conduct of monetary policy if policy makers are known to behave strategically and to care about each other's policy settings.

Table 3.4 reports the evidence on the hypothesis that interest rate policies in G3 countries are independent in the long run. The correlations between interest rate innovations are all positive and higher in the long run (column 8) than in the short run (column 5). Predetermined ($\lambda_{i*,i} = 0$) and long-run exogenous ($\gamma_{i*,i} = 0$) interest rate policy of the foreign country has significant long-run effects on domestic interest rates in the case of Germany and the United States, with causation running both ways. But for Japan, predetermined interest rate policy ($\lambda_{i*,i} = 0$) has significant long-run effects only if causation is assumed to run from Germany or the United States to Japan, and not vice versa. Furthermore, imposing long-run independence reveals significant short-run effects ($\lambda_{i,i*} = 0$) in these four cases, and each time a significant positive short-term feedback coefficient ($\lambda_{i*,i} > 0$) is found.

For the post-1985 sample, interest rate policies are largely found to be uncoordinated in the long run. Furthermore, imposing long-run independence upon the estimates reveals no significant short-run coordination ($\lambda_{i,i*} \neq 0$) or feedback ($\lambda_{i*,i} \neq 0$), as is reflected by the fact that in panel (b) of figure 3.11 the origin lies within all 95% confidence ellipses for the long-run independence hypothesis. In panel (a) of figure 3.11, the significant short-run effects for the case of bi-directional causation between Germany or the United States, as well as for the two cases with causation running from Germany and the United States to Japan, are obvious.

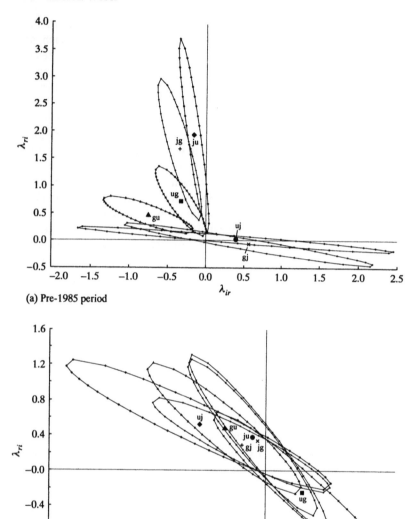

(a) Pre-1985 period

(b) Post-1985 period

Figure 3.11   The long-run independence of interest rate policies in G3 countries

2.3.2   Monetary policy coordination

In order to obtain evidence on the degree of international monetary policy coordination, the present study estimates the simultaneous two-equation system:

$$\Delta m_t^* = \lambda_{m^*,m} \Delta m_t + \sum_{j=1}^{p} \alpha_{m^*,m^*}^{j} \Delta m_{t-j}^* + \sum_{j=1}^{p} \alpha_{m^*,m}^{j} \Delta m_{t-j} + \varepsilon_t^{\nu}, \quad (8a)$$

$$\Delta m_t = \lambda_{m,m^*} \Delta m_t^* + \sum_{j=1}^{p} \alpha_{m,m}^{j} \Delta m_{t-j} + \sum_{j=1}^{p} \alpha_{m,m^*}^{j} \Delta m_{t-j}^* + \varepsilon_t^{\eta}, \quad (8b)$$

whereby Δm^* and Δm represent the changes in high-powered money in the foreign and home country, respectively. Equations such as (8a) have also been estimated in the context of the EMS asymmetry, and the results of this literature with respect to money growth rates are reviewed in Weber (1990a). The evidence obtained from estimating the simultaneous equation system (8a,b) for the G3 countries is summarized in table 3.5.

Table 3.5 suggests that monetary policy has typically not been coordinated between G3 countries. The only exception is the post-1985 link between the United States and Japan. In the case where causality runs from the Federal Reserve to the Bank of Japan, significant long-run coordination is detected if US monetary policy is assumed to be predetermined ($\lambda_{m^*,m} = 0$). Moreover, imposing long-run independence reveals a significant positive short-term feedback coefficient ($\lambda_{i^*,i} > 0$).

To summarize, significant short-run or long-run policy coordination in areas other than foreign exchange intervention was not found to have been a feature of the post-1985 G3 consultation process. This confirms results previously reported in Catte *et al.* (1992). G3 central banks have failed in significantly coordinating both their interest rate and money growth policies, and appear to have relied primarily on concerted intervention in managing the dollar. But the fact that coordinated intervention was typically sterilized seems to have greatly reduced its effectiveness in stabilizing the dollar, at least as far as long-run stabilization is concerned.

3   European policy coordination and exchange rate management

The previous section has reviewed and evaluated empirically some stylized facts about G3 policy coordination and foreign exchange intervention over the past two decades. This section aims at providing similar evidence for the process of policy coordination and intervention within the European Monetary System (EMS).

Table 3.5. The long-run independence of monetary policies in G3 countries, two sub-periods (1973 M1–1984 M12, 1985 M1–1992 M12)

Countries	Period	VAR estimates			Structural model estimates			$\gamma_{m,m'} = 0$ in 95% confidence interval			Estimates imposing $\gamma_{m,m'} = 0$		
		$\sigma^2_{m'}$	σ^2_m	$cor_{m',m}$	$\sigma^2_{m'}*$	σ^2_m	$cor_{m',m}$	$\lambda_{m',m}$	$\lambda_{m,m'}$	$\gamma_{m',m}$	$\lambda_{m',m}$	$\lambda_{m,m'}$	$\gamma_{m',m}$
DEU,USA	73:1–84:12	12.39	38.95	**-0.08**	5.88	17.49	**0.03**	>0.1,<0.7	>-7.0,<-1.3	>0.2,<0.5	-0.02 (0.05)	-0.07 (0.39)	0.01 (0.07)
USA,DEU	73:1–84:12	38.95	12.39	**-0.08**	17.49	5.88	**0.03**	-	>-0.13	-	0.03 (0.56)	-0.03 (0.05)	0.10 (0.64)
JAP,USA	73:1–84:12	12.35	55.41	**0.25**	6.00	25.73	**0.26**	>0.11	<-1.30	>-0.02	**0.10 (0.03)**	-0.97 (0.70)	0.06 (0.05)
USA,JAP	73:1–84:12	55.41	12.35	**0.25**	25.73	6.00	**0.26**	-	-	-	0.29 (0.89)	0.04 (0.04)	1.10 (0.99)
JAP,DEU	73:1–84:12	38.65	56.17	**0.17**	17.23	25.03	**0.02**	>-0.5,<0.2	>-0.8,<0.2	>-0.47	**0.21 (0.12)**	-0.20 (0.25)	0.01 (0.17)
DEU,JAP	73:1–84:12	56.17	38.65	**0.17**	25.03	17.23	**0.02**	<0.55	>-0.11	-	-0.17 (0.30)	0.19 (0.12)	0.03 (0.36)
DEU,USA	85:1–92:12	20.11	42.42	**0.01**	10.42	13.78	**0.16**	>-0.15	>-2.1,<0.7	-	0.06 (0.12)	-0.28 (0.49)	0.12 (0.23)
USA,DEU	85:1–92:12	42.42	20.11	**0.01**	13.78	10.42	**0.16**	-	-	-	0.06 (0.44)	-0.01 (0.09)	0.21 (0.40)
JAP,USA	85:1–92:12	18.48	53.37	**0.47**	7.99	17.10	**-0.15**	>0.1,<0.4	>-3.6,<0.5	>0.3,>0.8	**0.19 (0.06)**	-0.29 (0.63)	-0.07 (0.13)
USA,JAP	85:1–92:12	53.37	18.48	**0.47**	17.10	7.99	**-0.15**	<0.64	>0.12	<1.28	-0.89 (0.92)	**0.24 (0.06)**	-0.32 (0.58)
JAP,DEU	85:1–92:12	43.18	51.69	**0.17**	12.69	19.06	**-0.11**	<0.29	<0.06	<1.14	0.27 (0.16)	-0.19 (0.21)	-0.07 (0.18)
DEU,JAP	85:1–92:12	51.69	43.18	**0.17**	19.06	12.69	**-0.11**	>-0.1,<0.7	>-0.8,<-0.2	<0.48	-0.34 (0.30)	**0.36 (0.16)**	-0.16 (0.40)

Notes: All results for the second moments are based on VARs with six lags. σ^2_i denotes the variance estimate for variable i, cor_{ij} indicates the correlation between variables i and j. Variances and correlations are calculated for the residuals of the unrestricted VARs and the shocks implied by the long-run covariance matrix of the estimated VAR (the spectral density matrix of the variables at frequency zero). The coefficient ranges in columns 9–11 are those for which the long-run independence proposition cannot be rejected at the 95% level. The point estimates of the coefficients and their standard errors (in parentheses) implied by long-run independence are reported in the last three columns. Estimates that are significant at the 95 per cent level are in bold type.

BOX 3
Testable propositions adapted from McKinnon's (1993) rules of the 'European Monetary System as a greater Deutschmark area, 1979–1992'

All member countries

I   Work symmetrically towards convergence of national macroeconomic policies and unchanging long-run par values for exchange rates.

Member countries except Germany

II   Intervene intramarginally, within formal bilateral limits of ±2.25 per cent around central parities, to stabilize the national exchange rate *vis-à-vis* the DM.

III   Adjust short-term national money growth and/or short-term interest rates to support exchange market interventions – whether intramarginally or at the bilateral parity limit.

IX   Keep adjusting long-term money growth so that domestic price inflation converges to, or remains the same as, price inflation in Germany.

Germany

XI   Remains passive in foreign exchange markets with other EMS countries: does not pursue an intramarginal exchange rate target.

XII   Sterilizes (perhaps passively) the effects of German or other EMS countries' official intervention in the European foreign exchange markets on the German monetary base.

XIII Anchors the DM (EMS) price level for tradable goods by an independently chosen German monetary policy.

3.1   The rules of the EMS

McKinnon's (1993) account of the *de facto* rules for exchange rate management, foreign exchange intervention, and policy coordination in the EMS is summarized in Box 3. Except for the fact that in the EMS official and relatively narrow exchange rate target zones existed, the characterization of this system is quite similar in design to the post-1985 G3 regime. Both systems became even more similar with the collapse of the narrow target zones in August 1993. The key point is the apparent asymmetry between Germany as the centre country and the remaining EMS countries, which are assumed to have primarily targeted the bilateral exchange rate relative to the Deutschmark. The validity of this 'DM-zone' view of the EMS is analysed empirically below.

3.2   EMS intervention policy and exchange rate management

The empirical analysis above has revealed that Bundesbank intervention during 1985 to 1992 was sterilized in both its short-run impact and its long-run consequences for base money growth. Bundesbank and Federal

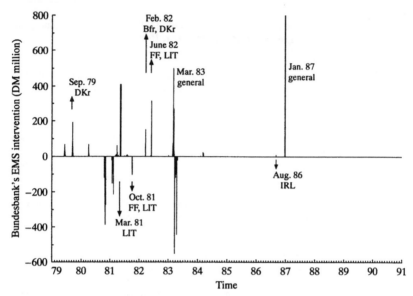

Figure 3.12 EMS realignments and foreign exchange intervention by the Bundesbank

Reserve interventions in the DM/$ market were also found to have been coordinated and governed by leaning-against-the-wind behaviour. Finally, intervention had no long-lasting effects on the exchange rate. The obviously strong orientation of the Bundesbank's intervention policy towards the US dollar raises the question of how committed the Bundesbank was towards intervention within the EMS.

In McKinnon's (1993) interpretation, the EMS as a 'greater Deutschmark area' or 'DM-zone' implies that the Bundesbank should not have pursued any intramarginal or unsterilized intervention. In addition, all obligatory marginal bilateral intervention should, by the rules of the EMS, have been coordinated and carried out jointly by the Bundesbank and the respective partner central bank, and intervention should have aimed at reverting the trend of the exchange rate. Intervention by the non-German central banks, on the other hand, should have been primarily intramarginal, non-sterilized, and aimed at stabilizing the exchange rate within the band. The remainder of this section examines the validity of these propositions.

3.2.1   Stylized facts about EMS intervention

Figure 3.12 displays the daily EMS intervention of the German Bundesbank during the EMS period.[5] Several stylized facts are obvious.

First, the Bundesbank intervened only rarely in the EMS, and intervention typically occurred prior to realignment dates, when exchange rates threatened to breach their bilateral limits. This suggests that the Bundesbank engaged only in marginal mandatory intervention. Figure 3.13, which displays the average daily Bundesbank intervention against the EMS exchange rate band positions of participating countries, strongly supports this view. In particular, figure 3.13 suggests that the Bundesbank's entire EMS intervention activities may be viewed as marginal intervention in support of a French franc target (panel (a)). The impression that marginal intervention occurred with respect to the Danish krona and Irish pound results from the fact that these currencies were weak against the Deutschmark when the French franc was weak, and strong when the French franc was strong.[6]

Another stylized fact about the Bundesbank's EMS intervention is displayed in figure 3.14. Unlike the Federal Reserve, which never pursued differential intervention with respect to the Deutschmark and the Japanese yen, the Bundesbank has at times implemented differential intervention with respect to the US dollar and EMS currencies. In particular, during 1981, when the Deutschmark was strong against the dollar and weak within the EMS, sales of EMS currencies occurred against purchases of US dollars. Since such simultaneous intervention in opposite directions does not change the foreign asset component of the monetary base, it does not even require subsequent sterilization.

3.2.2   Empirical evidence about EMS intervention

In order to compare the EMS and the G3 experience with policy coordination and foreign exchange intervention, the tests reported in the previous section were also conducted for the original EMS member countries – Germany, France, Italy, the Netherlands, Belgium, Denmark, and Ireland – and in addition for the United Kingdom.

Sterilization.   Table 3.6 reports the estimation results for the sterilization issue. As for the G3 countries, above, there is little evidence of long-run non-sterilized intervention in the post-1985 period. Except for Germany and France in the pre-1985 period and the Netherlands and Ireland in the post-1985 period, predetermined intervention ($\lambda_{fm} = 0$) and long-run exogenous intervention ($\gamma_{fm} = 0$) are found to have been non-sterilized in the long run ($\gamma_{mf} \neq 0$). Also, short-run sterilization ($\lambda_{mf} = 0$) does not guarantee long-run sterilization ($\gamma_{mf} = 0$) for France in either sub-sample. Finally, the point estimates under long-run sterilization of intervention suggest that most European central banks in the post-1985 period have tended to increase the foreign component

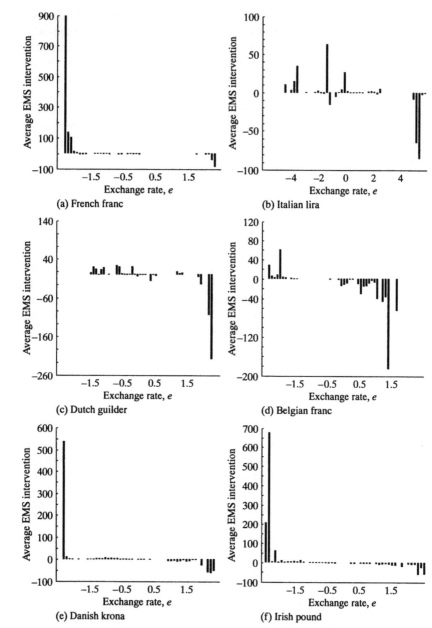

Figure 3.13   Daily DM exchange rate band positions and average daily EMS interventions by the Bundesbank, 21/03/1979–08/05/1990 (DM billion)

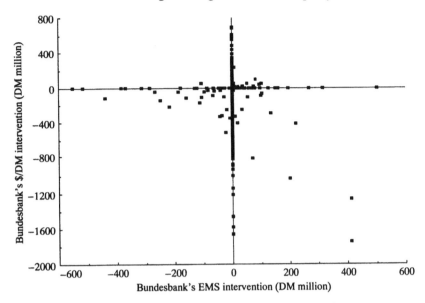

Figure 3.14   EMS and US dollar interventions by the Bundesbank

when the monetary base increased ($\lambda_{fm} > 0$), although the coefficient λ_{fm} is statistically significant only for Ireland.

To summarize, the finding of long-term sterilization of intervention for the recent EMS period is broadly consistent with the results reported above in the G3 context. The key point is that the predominant use of sterilized intervention by all EMS member countries may have strongly undermined any potential disciplinary effects arising from quasi-fixed exchange rates. The predominant use of sterilized intervention may also have greatly reduced the effectiveness of EMS intervention.

Coordination.   In order to study the degree to which intervention by EMS central banks was coordinated, the simultaneous two-equation system (5a,b) has been estimated. Table 3.7 summarizes the results under the hypothesis that EMS intervention was not subject to a long-run coordinated strategy. For Germany relative to Italy and France, the short-run (column 5) and long-run cross-country correlations (column 8) of changes in the net foreign asset component of the monetary base are negative and relatively high. This points towards a substantial degree of coordination of EMS intervention between the central banks of the three larger EMS economies. For the link between France and Germany, the estimates indicate significant long-run coordination ($\lambda_{ff} < 0$) of intervention

Table 3.6. The long-run sterilization of foreign exchange interventions in EMS countries, two sub-periods (1973 M1–1984 M12, 1985 M1–1992 M12)

Country	Period	VAR estimates			Structural model estimates			$\gamma_{mf}=0$ in 95% confidence interval			Estimates imposing $\gamma_{mf}=0$		
		σ_m^2	σ_f^2	cor_{mf}	σ_m^2	σ_f^2	cor_{mf}	λ_{fm}	λ_{mf}	γ_{fm}	λ_{fm}	λ_{mf}	γ_{fm}
Germany	73:1–84:12	38.10	38.72	**0.13**	26.64	16.78	**0.63**	>0.40	<−0.29	>0.72	**0.65 (0.20)**	**−0.59 (0.20)**	**0.99 (0.27)**
France	73:1–84:12	104.00	47.41	−0.08	135.90	36.64	**−0.70**	<−0.20	>0.05	<−0.99	**−1.04 (0.53)**	0.19 (0.11)	**−2.60 (0.86)**
Italy	73:1–84:12	45.80	24.92	0.01	102.10	12.49	−0.08	—	—	—	−0.39 (0.77)	0.12 (0.22)	−0.67 (3.65)
Netherlands	73:1–84:12	57.24	25.83	0.08	39.14	15.87	**−0.31**	>−0.4, <1.2	>−0.2, <0.1	<0.38	0.45 (0.37)	−0.06 (0.07)	−0.76 (0.52)
Belgium	73:1–84:12	50.57	20.87	0.01	46.59	16.74	0.15	>−0.8, <1.6	>−0.2, <0.1	—	0.12 (0.46)	−0.02 (0.07)	0.41 (0.80)
Denmark	73:1–84:12	491.50	65.56	0.02	286.40	53.52	**−0.53**	<1.80	>−0.2	—	−1.05 (1.41)	0.02 (0.02)	**−2.82 (1.29)**
Ireland	73:1–84:12	86.52	45.13	0.16	72.01	30.92	0.26	>−0.60	>−0.3, <0.2	—	0.20 (0.38)	0.03 (0.10)	0.62 (0.60)
UK	n.a.	n.a.	n.a.	n.a.	n.a.	n.a.	n.a.	n.a.	n.a.	n.a.	n.a.	n.a.	n.a.
Germany	85:1–92:12	101.90	42.56	−0.04	146.10	12.39	0.27	—	—	—	1.06 (1.56)	−0.20 (0.26)	3.20 (6.38)
France	85:1–92:12	113.10	50.00	−0.32	30.92	21.65	0.23	>−1.20	<−0.27	>−0.58	−0.32 (0.43)	−0.08 (0.07)	0.33 (0.39)
Italy	85:1–92:12	91.93	21.36	0.06	79.57	16.42	0.48	—	—	—	0.83 (1.13)	−0.03 (0.06)	2.34 (1.57)
Netherlands	85:1–92:12	47.46	72.17	0.11	30.69	33.16	0.63	>0.00	<0.16	>0.31	0.25 (0.15)	−0.43 (0.32)	**0.58 (0.25)**
Belgium	85:1–92:12	76.69	20.96	−0.06	65.55	11.45	0.18	>−0.60	<0.01	—	1.36 (1.03)	−0.12 (0.07)	1.02 (1.81)
Denmark	85:1–92:12	120.70	173.70	0.16	124.40	140.00	0.14	—	—	—	0.35 (0.23)	−0.53 (0.51)	0.12 (0.34)
Ireland	85:1–92:12	96.32	43.51	0.30	87.35	23.56	0.48	>0.40	<0.01	>−0.13	**1.34 (0.56)**	−0.17 (0.14)	1.77 (0.98)
UK	88:1–92:12	174.90	32.09	−0.05	138.80	7.99	0.40	—	—	—	0.34 (1.60)	−0.02 (0.05)	6.89 (5.84)

Notes: All results for the second moments are based on VARs with six lags. σ_i^2 denotes the variance estimate for variable i, cor_{ij} indicates the correlation between variables i and j. Variances and correlations are calculated for the residuals of the unrestricted VARs and the shocks implied by the long-run VAR (the spectral density matrix of the variables at frequency zero). The coefficient ranges in columns 9–11 are those for which the long-run sterilization proposition cannot be rejected at the 95% level. The point estimates of the coefficients and their standard errors (in parentheses) implied by long-run sterilization are reported in the last three columns. Estimates that are significant at the 95 per cent level are in bold type.

Table 3.7. The long-run independence of foreign exchange interventions in EMS countries, second sub-period (1985 M1–1992 M12)

Countries	Period	VAR estimates			Structural model estimates			$\gamma_{ff} = 0$ in 95% confidence interval			Estimates imposing $\gamma_{ff} = 0$		
		σ^2_ε	σ^2_f	$cor_{\varepsilon f}$	σ^2_ε	σ^2_f	$cor_{\varepsilon f}$	$\lambda_{\varepsilon f}$	λ_{ff}	γ_{ff}	$\lambda_{\varepsilon f}$	λ_{ff}	$\gamma_{\varepsilon f}$
DEU,FRA	85:1–92:12	114.40	101.60	**−0.85**	45.75	132.50	**−0.84**	no	no	< −0.13	**−0.84 (0.13)**	−0.23 (0.19)	**−0.29 (0.10)**
FRA,DEU	85:1–92:12	101.60	114.40	**−0.85**	132.50	45.75	**−0.84**	no	no	no	**−0.83 (0.15)**	0.48 (1.16)	**−2.43 (0.83)**
DEU,ITA	85:1–92:12	94.83	99.16	**−0.77**	93.98	121.80	**−0.81**	no	no	< −0.85	**−0.89 (0.15)**	0.56 (0.75)	**−0.62 (0.24)**
ITA,DEU	85:1–92:12	99.16	94.83	**−0.77**	121.80	93.98	**−0.81**	< −0.15	> −0.68	< −0.38	**−0.69 (0.23)**	−0.22 (0.33)	**−1.05 (0.40)**
DEU,NDL	85:1–92:12	49.25	101.80	0.40	35.78	133.10	0.77	> −0.06	< 1.04	> 0.06	0.12 (0.10)	0.34 (0.37)	**0.21 (0.09)**
NDL,DEU	85:1–92:12	101.80	49.25	0.40	133.10	35.78	0.77	> 0.81	< 0.00	> 0.76	**2.20 (0.95)**	−0.56 (0.54)	**2.87 (1.25)**
DEU,BEL	85:1–92:12	77.79	98.60	−0.01	70.08	167.90	0.24	–	–	–	−0.12 (0.20)	0.18 (0.30)	0.10 (0.27)
BEL,DEU	85:1–92:12	98.60	77.79	−0.01	167.90	70.08	0.24	–	–	–	0.51 (0.90)	−0.33 (0.55)	0.58 (1.57)
DEU,DNK	85:1–92:12	113.60	101.60	−0.28	146.40	146.20	0.58	–	–	–	−0.36 (0.31)	0.05 (0.26)	0.58 (0.49)
DNK,DEU	85:1–92:12	101.60	113.60	−0.28	146.20	146.40	0.58	–	–	–	0.94 (1.16)	−1.15 (0.78)	0.58 (0.49)
DEU,IRE	85:1–92:12	97.63	100.20	−0.42	96.93	129.30	−0.30	–	–	–	−0.23 (0.23)	−0.21 (0.23)	−0.23 (0.38)
IRE,DEU	85:1–92:12	100.20	97.63	−0.42	129.30	96.93	−0.30	–	–	–	−0.50 (0.43)	0.08 (0.52)	−0.40 (0.67)
DEU,GBR	88:1–92:12	176.70	92.67	0.58	136.10	133.60	0.22	–	–	–	−1.23 (1.51)	0.47 (0.13)	0.23 (0.69)
GBR,DEU	88:1–92:12	92.67	176.70	0.58	133.60	136.10	0.22	–	–	–	0.59 (0.38)	−3.01 (7.40)	0.22 (0.67)

Notes: All results for the second moments are based on VARs with six lags. σ^2_i denotes the variance estimate for variable i, cor_{ij} indicates the correlation between variables i and j. Variances and correlations are calculated for the residuals of the unrestricted VARs and the shocks implied by the long-run covariance matrix of the estimated VAR (the spectral density matrix of the variables at frequency zero). The coefficient ranges in columns 9–11 are those for which the long-run independence proposition cannot be rejected at the 95% level. The point estimates of the coefficients and their standard errors (in parentheses) implied by long-run independence are reported in the last three columns. Estimates that are significant at the 95 per cent level are in bold type.

across the entire range of identifying restrictions on the reaction coefficients $\lambda_{f,f^*}, \lambda_{f^*,f}$, and γ_{f,f^*}, regardless of the postulated direction of causality. Italian intervention is also found to have been coordinated with the Bundesbank, irrespective of the identifying restrictions on $\lambda_{f,f^*}, \lambda_{f^*,f}$, and γ_{f,f^*}, but for the case of reversed causation the data are consistent with long-run coordination only within a much narrower range. In all four bilateral combinations the reference cases of predetermined ($\lambda_{f,f^*} = 0$) and long-run exogenous intervention ($\gamma_{f,f^*} = 0$) are consistent with significant long-run coordination. On the other hand, imposing long-run independence, which for these four bilateral combinations is clearly an inadequate restriction, is consistent with the data only if one postulates a significant negative feedback of foreign intervention on domestic intervention, either contemporaneously ($\lambda_{f,f^*} < 0$) or in the long run ($\gamma_{f,f^*} < 0$). I view this as strong evidence in support of significant coordination of intervention between the three larger EMS economies.

Relatively high positive correlations are found for Germany and the Netherlands. Such positive correlations point towards simultaneous intervention in third currencies. The fact that the relatively stable exchange rate of the Dutch guilder (Hfl) relative to the Deutschmark underwent only two minor realignments during the EMS period is consistent with the view that coordinated intervention between Germany and the Netherlands may have been aimed not at stabilizing the bilateral rate but rather at stabilizing their exchange rates *vis-à-vis* weak third EMS currencies. Finally, for the remaining EMS currencies no significant long-run or short-run coordination of intervention activities is found in the data.

Effectiveness.   The evidence about the effectiveness of intervention in EMS foreign exchange markets is displayed in table 3.8. EMS intervention during the post-1985 period is found to have been ineffective in stabilizing DM exchange rates in the long run, regardless of the possible identifying restrictions on the coefficients $\lambda_{f,e}, \gamma_{f,e}$, and $\lambda_{e,f}$. The only exception is the Bundesbank's intervention with respect to the Italian lira exchange rate, where significant positive long-run effects are obtained no matter what identifying restrictions were placed on $\lambda_{f,e}, \gamma_{f,e}$, and $\lambda_{e,f}$. The positive sign thereby suggests that Bundesbank intervention has without doubt been unsuccessful, as it appears to have destabilized ($\lambda_{e,f} > 0$) rather than stabilized ($\lambda_{e,f} < 0$) the lira exchange rate.

To summarize, central bank intervention in the EMS exhibited the following three characteristics. First, intervention by all EMS countries, and not only German intervention as postulated by McKinnon (1993),

Table 3.8. The long-run ineffectiveness of foreign exchange interventions in EMS countries, second sub-period (1985 M1–1992 M12)

Countries	Period	VAR estimates σ^2_e	σ^2_f	cor_{ef}	Structural model estimates σ^2_e	σ^2_f	cor_{ef}	$\gamma_{ef}=0$ in 95% confidence interval λ_{fe}	λ_{ef}	γ_{fe}	Estimates imposing $\gamma_{ef}=0$ λ_{fe}	λ_{ef}	γ_{fe}
DEU,FRA	85:1–92:12	114.10	5.45	**0.08**	32.76	9.06	**−0.31**	–	–	–	−0.70 (4.21)	0.01 (0.01)	−1.12 (1.26)
FRA,DEU	85:1–92:12	100.10	5.42	**0.10**	134.90	8.95	**0.07**	–	–	–	0.23 (9.11)	0.00 (0.03)	1.10 (8.69)
DEU,ITA	85:1–92:12	87.70	10.10	**0.47**	68.97	18.09	**0.76**	no	no	–	**11.8 (3.31)**	**−0.28 (0.23)**	**2.88 (1.19)**
ITA,DEU	85:1–92:12	101.80	10.64	**0.51**	97.27	23.19	**0.80**	> −1.50	> −0.09	–	**13.3 (4.67)**	**−0.32 (0.43)**	**3.37 (1.48)**
DEU,NDL	85:1–92:12	48.31	1.35	**0.20**	26.80	0.82	**0.29**	–	–	–	3.04 (8.35)	0.00 (0.01)	9.58 (9.20)
NDL,DEU	85:1–92:12	101.80	1.32	**−0.23**	138.20	1.09	**−0.73**	–	–	–	−73.9 (43.1)	0.01 (0.01)	**−92.3 (46.3)**
DEU,BEL	85:1–92:12	77.22	2.78	**0.23**	68.66	3.39	**0.16**	–	–	–	3.96 (6.90)	0.00 (0.01)	3.33 (7.01)
BEL,DEU	85:1–92:12	101.70	2.88	**0.05**	155.40	3.52	**−0.03**	–	–	–	−3.73 (20.7)	0.00 (0.02)	−1.47 (27.7)
DEU,DNK	85:1–92:12	121.40	3.97	**0.42**	102.70	4.43	**0.21**	–	–	–	−10.2 (12.2)	0.02 (0.01)	4.75 (7.35)
DNK,DEU	85:1–92:12	100.90	3.88	**0.12**	147.40	5.68	**−0.09**	–	–	–	−5.76 (15.8)	0.01 (0.02)	−2.43 (15.6)
DEU,IRE	85:1–92:12	97.48	11.89	**0.03**	89.43	15.06	**0.12**	–	–	–	0.77 (2.03)	−0.01 (0.03)	0.71 (2.33)
IRE,DEU	85:1–92:12	102.10	12.16	**0.22**	127.80	14.70	**−0.21**	–	–	–	−3.76 (5.76)	0.07 (0.06)	−1.79 (5.02)
DEU,GBR	88:1–92:12	185.40	17.81	**−0.29**	140.00	29.12	**0.38**	–	–	–	2.00 (3.80)	−0.04 (0.03)	1.83 (2.35)
GBR,DEU	85:1–92:12	101.50	21.18	**0.25**	145.30	30.92	**0.32**	–	–	–	1.01 (2.35)	0.01 (0.10)	1.49 (2.59)

Notes: All results for the second moments are based on VARs with six lags. σ^2_i denotes the variance estimate for variable i, cor_{ij} indicates the correlation between variables i and j. Variances and correlations are calculated for the residuals of the unrestricted VARs and the shocks implied by the long-run covariance matrix of the estimated VAR (the spectral density matrix of the variables at frequency zero). The coefficient ranges in columns 9–11 are those for which the long-run independence proposition cannot be rejected at the 95% level. The point estimates of the coefficients and their standard errors (in parentheses) implied by long-run independence are reported in the last three columns. Estimates that are significant at the 95 per cent level are in bold type.

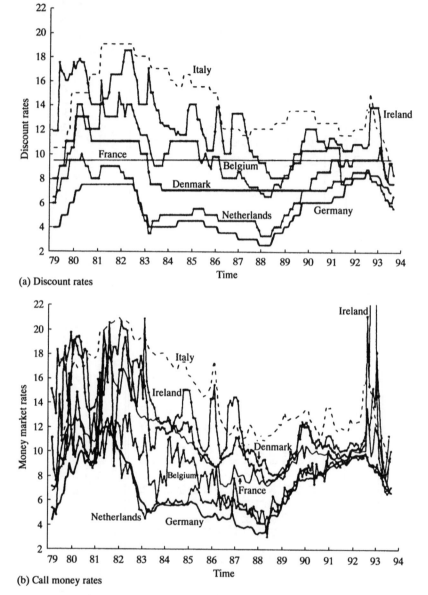

(a) Discount rates

(b) Call money rates

Figure 3.15 Official interest rates, market interest rates, and inflation rates in EMS countries (% p.a.)

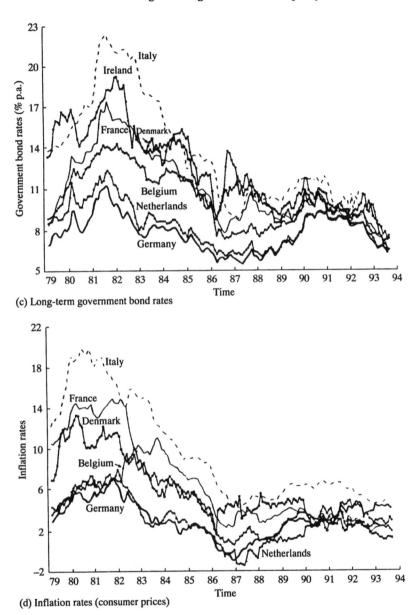

(c) Long-term government bond rates

(d) Inflation rates (consumer prices)

Figure 3.15   (continued)

has been sterilized in both its immediate impact and its long-run consequences for national money supplies. Second, intervention was coordinated between the Bundesbank, the Banque de France, and the Banca d'Italia only. Evidence on the coordination of bilateral intervention between the Bundesbank and the remaining EMS central banks was not found in the data. Third, intervention by EMS central banks was ineffective in the long run in the sense that it did not significantly stabilize bilateral exchange rates. This finding is consistent with the non-formal evidence from the daily EMS intervention data, which suggest that the Bundesbank participated in mandatory intervention only at the margins of the bands. The fact that such marginal intervention typically occurred prior to EMS realignments in itself suggests that it was unsuccessful in defending the pre-realignment exchange rate target zone. The long-run ineffectiveness result for the EMS is also consistent with the evidence reported for intervention in the G3 context: sterilized intervention is unlikely to be an effective means of stabilizing exchange rates.

3.3   EMS policy coordination

The fact that EMS intervention has not been an effective tool for stabilizing exchange rates raises the question of whether or not monetary policy coordination and convergence have helped in stabilizing exchange rates. To answer this question two forms of economic policy coordination – short-run interest rate policy coordination and long-run money growth policy coordination – are examined.

3.3.1   Interest rate policy coordination

Some non-formal evidence about the degree of interest rate policy coordination amongst G3 countries is provided in figure 3.15. Discount rate policies appear to be relatively closely coordinated between Germany, the Netherlands, and to a slightly lesser extent Belgium (panel (a)). The same three countries display close co-movements of short-term money market rates (panel (b)), long-term government bond rates (panel (c)), and inflation rates (panel (d)) between 1985 and 1992. Figure 3.15 also shows the destabilizing effects of the speculative attacks between September 1992 and August 1993 on short-term EMS interest rates, in particular for Italy, Ireland, and Denmark. The overall impression from figure 3.15 is that interest rate policies within the EMS were substantially more coordinated than were those between the G3 countries.

In order to obtain evidence on the degree of interest rate policy coordination and asymmetry in the EMS, the present study estimates the simultaneous two-equation system (7a,b), where – unlike in the Granger

Table 3.9. The long-run independence of interest rate policies in EMS countries, second sub-period (1985 M1–1992 M12)

Countries	Period	VAR estimates			Structural model estimates			$\gamma_{i,r}=0$ in 95% confidence interval			Estimates imposing $\gamma_{i,r}=0$		
		σ_r^2	σ_i^2	$cor_{r,i}$	σ_r^2	σ_i^2	$cor_{r,i}$	$\lambda_{r,i}$	$\lambda_{i,r}$	$\gamma_{r,i}$	$\lambda_{r,i}$	$\lambda_{i,r}$	$\gamma_{r,i}$
FRA,DEU	85:1–92:12	0.23	0.52	−0.03	0.41	0.36	**0.74**	>0.40	<−1.99	>0.37	1.05 (0.83)	−4.87 (3.28)	**0.85 (0.32)**
DEU,FRA	85:1–92:12	0.52	0.23	−0.03	0.36	0.41	**0.74**	–	–	–	−0.77 (0.52)	0.14 (0.10)	**0.64 (0.24)**
ITA,DEU	85:1–92:12	0.24	0.64	0.13	0.41	0.51	**0.32**	>0.00	<0.35	–	0.20 (0.15)	−1.23 (1.25)	0.26 (0.31)
DEU,ITA	85:1–92:12	0.64	0.24	0.13	0.51	0.41	**0.32**	–	–	–	−0.20 (0.63)	0.07 (0.07)	0.41 (0.49)
NDL,DEU	85:1–92:12	0.23	0.33	0.34	0.39	0.38	**0.94**	>1.20	<−4.30	>0.83	2.14 (1.32)	256 (9644)	**0.97 (0.14)**
DEU,NDL	85:1–92:12	0.33	0.23	0.34	0.38	0.39	**0.94**	–	–	–	−0.00 (0.28)	**0.25 (0.11)**	**0.91 (0.13)**
BEL,DEU	85:1–92:12	0.24	0.53	−0.15	0.41	0.49	**0.89**	>0.40	<−1.95	>0.58	0.80 (0.52)	**−3.26 (1.40)**	**0.75 (0.16)**
DEU,BEL	85:1–92:12	0.53	0.24	−0.15	0.49	0.41	**0.89**	–	–	–	0.01 (0.49)	−0.07 (0.09)	**1.05 (0.23)**
DNK,DEU	85:1–92:12	0.24	0.46	0.05	0.47	0.86	−0.14	–	–	–	0.10 (0.23)	−0.26 (0.81)	−0.08 (0.34)
DEU,DNK	85:1–92:12	0.46	0.24	0.05	0.86	0.47	−0.14	–	–	–	−0.54 (0.97)	0.17 (0.25)	−0.26 (1.16)
IRE,DEU	85:1–92:12	0.24	1.92	−0.04	0.44	2.78	−0.40	–	–	–	−0.05 (0.05)	2.59 (3.25)	−0.06 (0.11)
DEU,IRE	85:1–92:12	1.92	0.24	−0.04	2.78	0.44	−0.40	–	–	–	−0.77 (4.72)	0.01 (0.07)	−2.49 (4.51)
GBR,DEU	85:1–92:12	0.24	1.01	**0.16**	0.42	0.71	**0.47**	–	–	–	**0.15 (0.10)**	−2.28 (2.10)	0.28 (0.22)
DEU,GBR	85:1–92:12	1.01	0.24	**0.16**	0.71	0.42	**0.47**	–	–	–	0.12 (1.03)	0.03 (0.05)	0.80 (0.65)

Notes: All results for the second moments are based on VARs with six lags. σ_i^2 denotes the variance estimate for variable i, cor_{ij} indicates the correlation between variables i and j. Variances and correlations are calculated for the residuals of the unrestricted VARs and the shocks implied by the long-run covariance matrix of the estimated VAR (the spectral density matrix of the variables at frequency zero). The coefficient ranges in columns 9–11 are those for which the long-run independence proposition cannot be rejected at the 95% level. The point estimates of the coefficients and their standard errors (in parentheses) implied by long-run independence are reported in the last three columns. Estimates that are significant at the 95 per cent level are in bold type.

Table 3.10. The long-run independence of monetary policies in EMS countries, second sub-period (1985 M1–1992 M12)

Countries	Period	VAR estimates $\sigma^2_{m^*}$	σ^2_m	$cor_{m^*,m}$	Structural model estimates $\sigma^2_{m^*}$	σ^2_m	$cor_{m^*,m}$	$\gamma_{m,m^*}=0$ in 95% confidence interval $\lambda_{m^*,m}$	λ_{m,m^*}	$\gamma_{m^*,m}$	Estimates imposing $\gamma_{m,m^*}=0$ $\lambda_{m^*,m}$	λ_{m,m^*}	$\gamma_{m^*,m}$
DEU,FRA	85:1–92:12	43.80	47.41	−0.02	14.79	23.41	**−0.54**	<0.18	<−0.15	<−0.08	−0.23 (0.19)	0.25 (0.19)	**−0.34 (0.16)**
FRA,DEU	85:1–92:12	47.41	43.80	−0.02	23.41	14.79	**−0.54**	<0.11	<−0.11	>0.06	−0.38 (0.26)	0.31 (0.20)	**−0.85 (0.40)**
DEU,ITA	85:1–92:12	20.29	41.50	−0.05	14.26	12.88	**−0.17**	>0.22	>−0.56	<0.82	−0.11 (0.11)	0.38 (0.43)	−0.19 (0.30)
ITA,DEU	85:1–92:12	41.50	20.29	−0.05	12.88	14.26	**−0.17**	<0.99	>−0.21	–	0.02 (0.39)	−0.03 (0.08)	−0.16 (0.25)
DEU,NDL	85:1–92:12	71.95	44.56	0.04	30.06	12.99	**0.08**	–	>−0.40	–	0.11 (0.42)	−0.02 (0.15)	0.19 (0.70)
NDL,DEU	85:1–92:12	44.56	71.95	0.04	12.99	30.06	**0.08**	<0.44	>−0.70	–	0.04 (0.12)	−0.03 (0.26)	0.04 (0.13)
DEU,BEL	85:1–92:12	20.86	44.53	−0.18	11.72	14.37	**−0.27**	<0.22	>−0.86	<0.47	−0.11 (0.11)	0.10 (0.46)	−0.22 (0.24)
BEL,DEU	85:1–92:12	44.53	20.86	−0.18	14.37	11.72	**−0.27**	<0.55	>−0.16	<0.63	−0.49 (0.44)	0.02 (0.09)	−0.34 (0.35)
DEU,DNK	85:1–92:12	45.64	178.10	−0.03	12.96	144.20	**−0.06**	–	–	–	−0.01 (0.05)	0.04 (0.63)	−0.01 (0.03)
DNK,DEU	85:1–92:12	178.10	45.64	−0.03	144.20	12.96	**−0.06**	–	–	–	−0.19 (1.04)	0.00 (0.06)	−0.64 (3.46)
DEU,IRE	85:1–92:12	45.84	43.89	0.08	25.06	12.88	**0.14**	<0.99	>−0.78	–	0.21 (0.23)	−0.11 (0.19)	0.26 (0.52)
IRE,DEU	85:1–92:12	43.89	45.84	0.08	12.88	25.06	**0.14**	<0.55	>−0.43	–	0.02 (0.18)	0.06 (0.17)	0.07 (0.14)
DEU,GBR	88:1–92:12	29.97	41.37	0.01	8.23	14.11	**0.24**	–	–	–	0.09 (0.19)	−0.16 (0.31)	0.14 (0.20)
GBR,DEU	88:1–92:12	41.37	29.97	0.01	14.11	8.23	**0.24**	–	–	–	0.17 (0.37)	−0.08 (0.17)	0.40 (0.57)

Notes: All results for the second moments are based on VARs with six lags. σ^2_i denotes the variance estimate for variable i; cor_{ij} indicates the correlation between variables i and j. Variances and correlations are calculated for the residuals of the unrestricted VARs and the shocks implied by the long-run covariance matrix of the estimated VAR (the spectral density matrix of the variables at frequency zero). The coefficient ranges in columns 9–11 are those for which the long-run independence proposition cannot be rejected at the 95% level. The point estimates of the coefficients and their standard errors (in parentheses) implied by long-run independence are reported in the last three columns. Estimates that are significant at the 95 per cent level are in bold type.

causality testing approach – the central bank's interest rate policy may incorporate an endogenous reaction with respect to interest rate policy abroad, rather than being predetermined or exogenous.

Table 3.9 reports the empirical evidence on the hypothesis that interest rate policies in the EMS countries were uncoordinated in the long run. Except for Denmark and Ireland, the long-run correlations (column 8) between interest rate innovations are all positive and fairly high for France (0.74), Belgium (0.89), and the Netherlands (0.94). Only with respect to these three EMS countries has predetermined ($\lambda_{i^*,i} = 0$) and long-run exogenous ($\gamma_{i^*,i} = 0$) German interest rate policy shown significant long-run effects. Column 10 of table 3.9 further reveals that, even if German interest rate policy has no immediate impact ($\lambda_{i,i^*} = 0$) on interest rates in France, Belgium, and the Netherlands, it nevertheless has significant long-run effects ($\gamma_{i,i^*} > 0$). However, for the case of reversed causation no significant long-run effects onto German interest rates are to be found across the entire range of possible identifying restrictions for these countries. This provides strong evidence in favour of an asymmetrical working of the EMS, with the Bundesbank as the dominant central bank. This result is consistent with the evidence from Granger causality tests for interest rates provided in Weber (1990b), who finds substantially more asymmetry in the EMS than do De Grauwe (1988), Cohen and Wyplosz (1989), and Fratianni and von Hagen (1990a,b). Finally, the data for Italy, Denmark, Ireland, and the United Kingdom reject such significant long-run effects of German interest rate policy with respect to these countries for the 1985–92 sample period. However, this result strongly depends on the choice of sample period. To be more precise, if the post-1991 speculative attacks are excluded from the sample period, results much closer in line with those discussed above are obtained.

3.3.2   Monetary policy coordination

The final empirical issue to be considered regards the coordination of monetary policy. The evidence obtained from estimating equations (8a,b) for the EMS is summarized in table 3.10. The short-term and long-term correlations between base money growth in Germany and the remaining EMS countries are relatively low and vary in sign. The highest long-run correlation is found for the link between France and Germany (-0.54), suggesting that monetary policy coordination within the EMS primarily involved Germany and France. In all cases, predetermined ($\lambda_{m^*,m} = 0$) and long-run exogenous ($\gamma_{m^*,m} = 0$) monetary policy had no long-run effects on foreign money growth, regardless of the direction of causality. The data also suggest that, if long-run independence of monetary policy is imposed upon the estimates, this is then consistent with the data only if significant long-run feedback ($\gamma_{m^*,m} = 0$) between France and Germany is assumed. The required feedback is thereby substantially larger if causality runs from German to French money growth, which implies that German monetary policy is likely to have had larger long-run effects on French money growth than vice versa.

To summarize, the post-1985 EMS appears to have worked as an asymmetrical system, with clear evidence in favour of German dominance, at least prior to the speculative attacks of 1992–3. The 'DM-zone' characteristics of the EMS are thereby quite pronounced for short-term interest rate policies compared with long-run money growth policies. Long-run coordination of monetary policy is found to have played a significant role only between Germany and France. This finding is consistent with the fact that EMS intervention by the Bundesbank was found to have been primarily oriented towards defending the FF/DM exchange rate target zone.

4   Summary and policy conclusions with respect to the future of economic and monetary union

In this paper I have examined the degree to which international policy coordination and exchange rate management differ between G3 countries and the EMS. McKinnon (1993) shows that, except for the width of the exchange rate band, the 'rules of the game' of international policy coordination are quite similar between the post-1985 'G3 Plaza–Louvre intervention accords' and the 'EMS as a DM zone'. The recent collapse of the EMS and its transformation to a system with wide exchange rate bands (of ± 15 per cent) have made both systems qualitatively even more similar. Is the EMS therefore obsolete? To answer this question the present paper has conducted an empirical evaluation of the quantitative differences between the EMS and the G3 policy coordination and exchange rate management process.

Foreign exchange intervention activities are found to have been very similar within the G3 and the EMS context. Three sets of issues have been discussed. First, intervention was shown to have typically been sterilized in its immediate impact and its long-run consequences for the domestic monetary base. Second, this sterilized intervention was found not to have had significant long-run exchange rate stabilization effects. This is not surprising, given that sterilization aims at delaying or avoiding precisely those domestic monetary policy adjustments that would be necessary for guaranteeing long-run exchange rate stability. Third, little empirical difference was detected in the degree to which intervention has been coordinated between G3 or EMS countries because in both cases the evidence is somewhat mixed.

The main difference between the EMS and the G3 system is found to lie in the degree to which policy coordination other than intervention has been implemented. Long-term or even short-term policy coordination is virtually absent in the G3 context, irrespective of whether interest rate or money growth policy coordination is involved. For the EMS there exists strong evidence of short-term policy coordination with respect to interest rates, but there is less evidence to support long-term coordination of money growth policies. Policy coordination is thereby particularly strong if Germany is assumed to set its policy instruments independently and the remaining EMS countries adjust their interest rates consistently with the degree of desired exchange rate stability. The problem is that all managed exchange rate systems, whether adjustable pegs such as the EMS or managed floats such as the post-1985 G3 regime, allow each participating central bank to choose its particular trade-off between monetary autonomy and exchange rate fixity in a discretionary manner. Such discretionary policy choices are well known to result in inherently unstable policy settings because policy makers have multiple objectives and a 'crisis mentality': they typically devote a lion's share of their attention to the most violated objective (Bernake and Mishkin, 1992), which may be considered to be exchange rate stability only at the edges of the band. Exchange rate bands may thus be destabilizing in the sense of delaying necessary policy adjustments until the edges of the bands are reached. But at that point speculative attacks on currencies may make it impossible for the central bank to defend the parity, in particular if sterilized intervention is used. A similar result is suggested by the recent exchange rate target zone literature if a central bank's commitment to defending the band is not credible *ex ante*. The current wide bands of the EMS may thus eliminate speculative attacks without necessarily disabling exchange rate targeting within narrower margins. The experience of the Netherlands, which never fully utilized even the narrow band, is encouraging in this respect.

In my view, the key to successful exchange rate targeting lies in international policy coordination alone, which needs to be reinforced in the EMS. Economic and monetary union (EMU) differs from the current EMS primarily in the degree to which monetary policy is coordinated and subject to joint decision-making. Stage 2 of the transition to EMU should therefore strengthen the policy coordination and consultation process within the EMS. Putting the new European Union institutions, such as the European Monetary Institute, into operation will also greatly enhance this process. Past EMS experience appears to have placed too much emphasis on exchange rate stability as a means for enforcing policy coordination and convergence. But exchange rate stability must be viewed as the outcome of a process of policy coordination and convergence in Europe, and not vice versa. In my view, the current wide-band EMS exemplifies the need for increased policy coordination much more clearly than the old EMS system ever did.

Appendix: Time-series and data sources

The paper uses both daily and monthly data. The econometric evidence is based on monthly data. Whenever original data were not seasonally adjusted, seasonal adjustment was carried out using the multiplicative adjustment procedure in Micro TSP 7.0. The time-series and data sources used were as follows.

Monthly data

Interest rates:
   Money market rates: International Monetary Fund (IMF), *International Financial Statistics*, various issues, line 60b.
   Discount rates: IMF, *International Financial Statistics*, various issues, line 60.
   Treasury bill rates: IMF, *International Financial Statistics*, various issues, line 60c.
   Government bond rates: IMF, *International Financial Statistics*, various issues, line 61.
Consumer prices: IMF, *International Financial Statistics*, various issues, line 64.
Base money: IMF, *International Financial Statistics*, various issues, line 14.
Net foreign assets: IMF, *International Financial Statistics*, various issues, calculated as the difference between foreign assets (line 11) and foreign liabilities (line 16c).
Term structure of interest rates: Umlaufrenditen festverzinslicher Wertpapiere, Deutsche Bundesbank, *Monatsberichte, Beiheft 2: Kapitalmarkt*, various issues.

Daily data

Intervention:
   Bundesbank intervention in the DM/$ market and in the EMS: Deutsche Bundesbank, unpublished data.
   Federal Reserve intervention in the DM/$ and yen/$ market: Federal Reserve Board of Governors, unpublished data.
Interest rates: Bank for International Settlements, unpublished data.
Exchange rates: Bank for International Settlements, unpublished data.
Forward premia: Bank for International Settlements, unpublished data.

NOTES

This work is also part of a research network on Macroeconomic Policy and Monetary Integration in Europe (grant no. SPES–0016–NL(a)) and of a CEPR research programme on Financial and Monetary Integration in Europe (grant no. SPES E89300205/RES). Financial support by the Commission of the European Communities and by the Deutsche Forschungsgemeinschaft, Sonderforschungsbereich 303, is gratefully acknowledged. I should like to thank Joseph Gagnon, Christian Bordes, and Matthew Canzoneri for detailed comments, and participants in seminars at the University of Bonn, the University of Mannheim, the University of Siegen, the PIES/CEPR Conference on 'The New Transatlantic Economy' at Georgetown University and the LARE Conference on 'European Currency Crisis and After' at Université Bordeaux I for useful discussions. The usual disclaimer applies. All programmes and data (except the confidential daily intervention data) used in this paper are available on request.

1 The G3 countries are the United States, Japan, and Germany, the G5 countries consist of the G3 plus the United Kingdom and France, and the G7 additionally includes Canada and Italy.
2 The major reason for this is that only in rare exceptions have central banks made intervention data available to outside academic researchers on a confidential basis. Also, most of the studies using confidential data tend to be more descriptive than econometrical. Noticeable exceptions are the studies by Obstfeld (1983, 1988, 1990), Rogoff (1984), Mastropasqua, Micossi, and Rinaldi (1988), Dominguez (1990, 1992), Dominguez and Frankel (1992, 1993), Kaminsky and Lewis (1992), and Lewis (1992).
3 Owing to the lack of Japanese intervention data this proposition cannot be re-confirmed here and is merely reported as it stands.
4 The term 'short-run correlations' thereby refers to the fact that these correlations are calculated for the residuals of the unrestricted vector-autoregressions (VARs) while the 'long-run correlations' are calculated for the shocks implied by the long-run variance-covariance matrix of the estimated VAR, that is, the spectral density matrix of the variables at frequency zero.
5 Intervention data from other EMS countries are not made publicly available. Thus, unlike the case of the DM/$ market, it is difficult to discuss issues such as the degree of coordination and the distribution of responsibilities for obligatory marginal and mandatory intramarginal intervention without a formal econometric evaluation.
6 This finding is consistent with the view expressed in Weber (1991) that the EMS initially worked as a bi-polar system: the Bundesbank and the Banque de France have managed the bilateral DM/FF exchange rate, and the remaining EMS countries have chosen either to level peg to the German hard currency standard, or to implement a crawling peg by pegging to the Deutschmark just slightly more than the French franc. As reported in Weber (1991), this behaviour has created the impression of a *de facto* French franc peg of the smaller EMS economies, Belgium, Denmark, and Ireland.

REFERENCES

Bernake, Ben and Frederic Mishkin (1992), 'Central Bank Behavior and the Strategy of Monetary Policy: Observations from Six Industrialized Countries', *National Bureau of Economic Research Macroeconomic Annual*.
Bordo, Michael D. and Anna J. Schwartz (1991), 'What Has Foreign Exchange Market Intervention Since Plaza Agreement Accomplished?' *Open Economies Review* 2, 39–64.

Catte, Pietro, Giampaolo Galli and Salvatore Rebecchini (1992), 'Concerted Intervention and the Dollar: An Analysis of Daily Data', mimeo.

Cohen, Daniel and Charles Wyplosz (1989), 'The European Monetary Union: An Agnostic Evaluation', Centre for Economic Policy Research Discussion Paper No. 306.

De Grauwe, Paul (1988), 'Is the European Monetary System a DM-zone?' Centre for European Policy Studies Working Document No. 39.

(1990), 'The Cost of Disinflation and the European Monetary System', *Open Economies Review* **1**(2), 147–73.

Dominguez, Kathryn M. (1990), 'Market Response to Coordinated Central Bank Intervention', in Allan H. Meltzer and Charles Plosser (eds.), *Carnegie Rochester Conference Series on Public Policy* **32**, 121–63.

(1992), 'Does Central Bank Intervention Increase the Volatility of Foreign Exchange Rates?' Harvard University, mimeo.

Dominguez, Kathryn M. and Jeffrey Frankel (1992), 'Does Foreign Exchange Intervention Matter? Disentangling the Portfolio and Expectations Effect for the Mark', University of California at Berkeley, mimeo.

(1993), 'Does Foreign Exchange Intervention Matter? The Portfolio Effect', *American Economic Review* **83**, S.1356–69.

Fratianni, Michele and Jürgen von Hagen (1990a), 'German Dominance in the EMS: Evidence from Interest Rates', *Journal of International Money and Finance* **9**(4), 358–75.

(1990b), 'The European Monetary System: Ten Years After', in Allan H. Meltzer and Charles Plosser (eds.), *Carnegie Rochester Conference Series on Public Policy* **32**.

Funabashi, Yoichi (1988), *Managing the Dollar: From Plaza to the Louvre*, Washington DC: Institute for International Economics.

Gaiotti, E., P. Giucca and S. Micossi (1989), 'Cooperation in Managing the Dollar (1985–1987): Interventions in Foreign Exchange Markets and Interest Rates', Banca d'Italia Discussion Paper No. 119.

Ghosh, Atish R. (1992), 'Is It Signaling? Exchange Intervention and the Dollar–Deutschemark Rate', *Journal of International Economics* **32**, 201–20.

Hagen, Jürgen von (1989), 'Monetary Targeting with Exchange Rate Constraints: The Bundesbank in the 1980s', *Federal Reserve Bank of St. Louis Review*, September/October.

Herring, R. J. and R. Marston (1977a), *National Monetary Policies and International Financial Markets*, Amsterdam: North-Holland.

(1977b), 'Sterilization Policy: The Trade-off Between Monetary Autonomy and Control Over Foreign Exchange Reserves', *European Economic Review* **21**, 455–74.

Jurgensen, Philippe, Chairman (1983), 'Report of the Working Group on Exchange Market Intervention', mimeo.

Kaminsky, Graciela L. and Karen K. Lewis (1992), 'Does Foreign Exchange Intervention Signal Future Monetary Policy?', Division of International Finance, Board of Governors of the Federal Reserve System, mimeo.

King, Robert G. and Mark W. Watson (1992), 'Testing Long Run Neutrality', National Bureau of Economic Research Working Paper No. 4156.

Klein, Michael and Eric Rosengren (1991), 'Foreign Exchange Intervention as a Signal of Monetary Policy', *New England Economic Review* (May/June), 39–50.

Lewis, Karen K. (1992), 'Are Foreign Exchange Intervention and Monetary Policy Related and Does It Really Matter?' National Bureau of Economic Research Discussion Paper No. 4377.

McKinnon, Ronald I. (1993), 'The Rules of the Game: International Money from a Historical Perspective', *Journal of Economic Literature* 31, 1–44.

Mastropasqua, Christina, Stefano Micossi and Roberto Rinaldi (1988), 'Interventions, Sterilization and Monetary Policy in the European Monetary System Countries, 1979–87', in F. Giavazzi, S. Micossi and M. Miller (eds.), *The European Monetary System*, Cambridge: Cambridge University Press, pp. 252–87.

Mussa, Michael (1981), *The Role of Official Intervention*, Group of Thirty Occasional Paper No. 6, New York: Group of Thirty.

Neumann, Manfred J. M. (1984), 'Intervention in the Mark/Dollar Market: The Authorities' Reaction Function', *Journal of International Money and Finance* 3, 223–39.

Neumann, Manfred J. M. and Jürgen von Hagen (1991), 'Monetary Policy in Germany', in Michelle Fratianni and Dominik Salvatore (eds.), *Monetary Policy in Developed Economies*, Handbook of Comparative Economic Policies vol. 3, Westport, Conn.: Greenwood Press, pp. 299–334.

Obstfeld, Maurice (1983), 'Exchange Rates, Inflation and the Sterilization Problem: Germany 1975–1981', *European Economic Review* 21, 161–89.

(1988), 'The Effectiveness of Foreign Exchange Intervention: Recent Experience', National Bureau of Economic Research Discussion Paper No. 2796.

(1990), 'The Effectiveness of Foreign Exchange Intervention: Recent Experience: 1985–1988', in William Branson, Jacob Frenkel and Morris Goldstein (eds.), *International Policy Coordination and Exchange Rate Fluctuations*, NBER Conference Volume, Chicago: Chicago University Press.

Rogoff, Kenneth (1984), 'On the Effects of Sterilized Intervention: An Analysis of Weekly Data', *Journal of Monetary Economics* 14, S.133–50.

Scholl, Franz (1983), 'Implications of Monetary Targeting for Exchange Rate Policy', in Paul Meek (ed.), *Central Bank Views on Monetary Targeting*, Federal Reserve Bank of New York.

Takagi, Shinji (1991), 'Foreign Exchange Market Intervention and Domestic Monetary Control in Japan, 1973–89', *Japan and the World Economy* 90, 147–80.

Truman, Edwin M. (1992), 'Comments on Paper Entitled: "Concerted Intervention and the Dollar: An Analysis of Daily Data" ', mimeo.

Weber, Axel A. (1990a), 'The Credibility of Monetary Target Announcements: An Empirical Evaluation', Center of Economic Research Discussion Paper No. 9031.

(1990b), 'European Economic and Monetary Union and Asymmetries and Adjustment Problems in the European Monetary System: Some Empirical Evidence', Centre for Economic Policy Research Discussion Paper No. 448.

(1991), 'Credibility, Reputation and the European Monetary System', *Economic Policy* 12, 57–102.

(1995), 'Testing Long-run Neutrality: Empirical Evidence from the G7-Countries with Special Emphasis on Germany', in Allan H. Meltzer and Charles Plosser (eds.), *Carnegie Rochester Conference Series on Public Policy* 41, 67–117.

Wyplosz, Charles (1989), 'EMS Puzzles', *Revista Espanola de Economia* 7, 33–66.

Discussion

JOSEPH GAGNON

This paper contains an enormous amount of information on intervention and policy coordination both among G3 countries and within the exchange rate mechanism (ERM) of the European Monetary System (EMS). I found most of the graphical presentations of intervention data to be quite convincing and easy to understand, so I will focus my remarks on the econometric technique that is used in most of the paper and on the plausibility of the conclusions drawn from that analysis.

The approach that is taken over and over again throughout the paper is to run a simple two-variable vector autoregression (VAR) on different variables of interest. In all cases the coefficients on lagged values of each variable are unrestricted so that we are letting the data tell us what has been the typical response of each variable to its own lags and to the other variable's lags. The difficulty is that we normally think that the variables being considered should affect each other contemporaneously as well. Since the contemporaneous effect can run in both directions, we are faced with a simultaneity problem. Using equations (4a) and (4b) for example, any given value of λ_{mf} will be associated with a value of λ_{fm} that fits the data equally well.

The approach taken by this paper is to see how various values of these parameters are related to each other. Although graphs are presented in a limited number of cases that show the relationship between these parameters over a wide range of values, most of the results focus on two types of restrictions: (1) a zero short-run effect in one direction, so that either λ_{mf} or λ_{fm} is zero; and (2) a zero long-run effect, so that $\lambda_{mf} = -\sum \alpha_{mf}$ or $\lambda_{fm} = -\sum \alpha_{fm}$. These long-run restrictions correspond to γ_{mf} or γ_{fm} equal to zero. To interpret the paper's statistical results, consider the following example. Suppose that we wish to find out whether intervention is sterilized in the long run. Try setting the coefficient on intervention in the money growth equation to the value needed to ensure complete long-run sterilization ($\lambda_{mf} = -\sum \alpha_{mf}$). If the short-run sterilization, λ_{mf}, implied by this restriction is either negative or greater than one, then the long-run restriction is implausible.

Before proceeding to assess the plausibility of the paper's specific results, a couple of caveats are in order. First, the two-variable VARs are obviously part of a much larger system in the real world. Omitted variables may be influencing both of the variables under study through some third channel that is not under consideration and that may induce a spurious correlation relative to the issues that are being considered. The importance of such effects can be assessed only judgementally on a case-by-case basis. I do not believe that this concern is so strong as to render the analysis completely useless, but perhaps I am being overconfident about my ability as an economist to bring knowledge about the rest of the economy to bear on the interpretation of the regression results. The second caveat is that six months may or may not be long enough to capture all the lagged effects. The problem is that longer lags use up many degrees of freedom, leading to more imprecise estimates and potentially spurious results.

Moving to the empirical results, let me start with those results that I find to be credible. The G3 results are consistent with complete short-run sterilization of intervention but some long-run effect of intervention on the monetary base, particularly for Germany prior to 1985. This result would be consistent with ineffective intervention that subsequently forces central banks to change the monetary base to achieve the desired exchange rate. It would also be consistent with signalling stories of intervention, in which sterilized intervention is effective because it signals future monetary developments. The G3 results are also consistent with significant coordination of intervention, especially after 1985, and with essentially no effectiveness of intervention.

The ERM results show significant coordination for the large countries but not for the small countries. I think this result is due to the fact that the data do not distinguish the currency composition of the central bank's foreign assets (except between EMS and non-EMS). If most of the Bundesbank's EMS intervention is in French francs, it will not be highly correlated with the Bank of Ireland's intervention unless the Irish pound and the French franc are highly correlated.

Probably the strongest results of the paper are for interest rate coordination in the ERM. I wondered if the exceptions to this result were due to strange behaviour at the beginning and end of the sample, and the author confirmed my conjecture. I was puzzled at first by the author's statement that there is no reverse causation from other ERM countries' interest rates to the German interest rate, because the estimated long-run effects often seem larger going toward Germany than coming from Germany. Then I realized that these estimates assumed that causality could go in only one direction, and the short-run coefficients look much more plausible when the long-run effect comes from Germany.

I have two major concerns with the interpretation of the remaining results. First, using money stocks as measures of monetary policy

confuses money demand shocks with policy shocks unless more information is added to the system. I am much more comfortable with the
interest rate results. Second, given how strongly interest rates have been
coordinated in the ERM, I am not certain how one should define
sterilization of intervention, or perhaps it would be more appropriate to
ask how intervention could ever be non-sterilized when interest rates are
tied so strongly together?

Finally, I would like to make a few comments on the collapse of the
ERM. An earlier version of the paper discussed this topic and I think it is
clearly relevant to the paper's objective. A common view, at least in the
United States, is that the shock that cracked the ERM was German
unification. In the face of massive government expenditures and
increased consumption and investment demand in eastern Germany,
ERM pressure contributed to looser monetary policy than the Bundesbank would have desired – Germany overheated and got inflation. The
other central banks were tighter than they wanted to be – they got slow
growth and disinflation. Policy coordination worked to the extent that
governments made compromises for the sake of a common goal.
However, the markets bet that the domestic political price was too high
to be sustained and the markets were right.

As an aside I would note that, if central banks had been determined to
maintain their parities and match German interest rates permanently,
sterilized intervention could have worked, provided that it was on a
massive scale. I don't think anyone would doubt that, if the Bank of
England had bought up the entire UK national debt by borrowing in
DM, the pound would not have fallen. In fact, the existence of interest
rate differentials in the ERM (at least under tight bands) seems to me to
be *prima facie* evidence that countries are not serious about maintaining
their parities. Whether this price is worth paying for the opportunity to
devalue is an interesting question, but any country that is willing to forgo
future devaluations should immediately take an asset position large
enough to drive the interest rate down to the German level.

I would like to end with the question of whether it is worthwhile
returning to a narrow-band ERM. The benefits of floating exchange
rates are that monetary policy is free to react optimally to shocks. The
benefits of a common currency are that exchange rate uncertainty is
eliminated and transactions costs are reduced. It is not implausible that
for Europe these respective benefits are both in the order of 1 per cent of
GDP. An ERM with narrow bands eliminates the benefits of independent monetary policy, and yet it does not eliminate the transactions costs
of different currencies. Moreover, as long as countries cannot credibly
commit to a permanent parity, realignments and currency crises will

continue and exchange rate uncertainty will not be effectively reduced. Thus, a narrow-band ERM represents the worst combination of these alternative monetary regimes. Until governments are ready to adopt a common currency, a wide-band ERM – or no ERM – would appear to be the best option.

4 Trading blocs and the sustainability of interregional cooperation

ERIC BOND and
CONSTANTINOS SYROPOULOS

1 Introduction

Recently, there has been a substantial increase in the number of regional trading arrangements, as well as reactivation or further expansion of existing integration schemes. In Europe, the European Union has both deepened market integration through its 1992 initiative and expanded its membership. In the Western hemisphere, the North American Free Trade Agreement (NAFTA) and MERCOSUR (Argentina, Brazil, Paraguay, and Uruguay) were formed, and the Andean Pact was revitalized. The free trade arrangement of the Association of South East Asian Nations (ASEAN) was formed in East Asia, and discussions are under way concerning regional arrangements in Africa, the Middle East, and Eastern Europe.

One of the implications of regional trading arrangements is that GATT (General Agreement on Tariffs and Trade) negotiations may increasingly be conducted between a small number of regional trading blocs, rather than between a large number of individual countries. The role of regional trading blocs as bargaining units was clearly evident in the recently concluded Uruguay Round of negotiations, where the fact that the European Union as a whole supported agricultural interests (concentrated primarily in France) was a significant factor in shaping agreements on agricultural trade. The potential for increased power in trade negotiations has frequently been advanced as an argument in favour of the formation of regional trading arrangements. For example, the Treaty of Asunción, which establishes MERCOSUR, cites as an objective 'the importance of securing their countries a proper place in the international economy'.

The view has sometimes been expressed, as in the concern over the formation of a 'Fortress Europe' under the European Communities, that large trading blocs would exercise their increased bargaining power by

118

raising their trade barriers on goods from non-member countries.[1] Under this view, regional trading arrangements might result in increased concentration of trade in regional markets. This contrasts with the view that regional trading arrangements might be stepping-stones to global free trade. The purpose of this paper is to present a theoretical model of the interactions between trading blocs and multilateral tariff negotiations that is capable of addressing how the structure and size of regional blocs are likely to increase or reduce tariffs on inter-bloc trade.

We assume that multilateral trading agreements are made between countries that interact repeatedly over time, but that there are no international enforcement mechanisms that can commit countries to tariff cuts made under the GATT. In the absence of these external enforcement mechanisms, countries are limited to multilateral trade agreements that are self-enforcing. However, the fact that countries interact repeatedly is important because it allows them to sustain explicit or tacit cooperation in trade policies along the lines suggested by Dixit (1987). Specifically, countries can use the (credible) threat of future punishments to sustain trade agreements that yield higher welfare levels for all countries involved than would be the case if tariffs are set to maximize welfare in a one-shot tariff-setting game. In our view, the GATT serves as a coordination mechanism under which countries determine which of the incentive-compatible trade agreements will be chosen as the object for coordination.

In contrast to multilateral trade agreements, we treat trading blocs as being able to commit to eliminating tariffs on intra-bloc trade. Thus, the trading blocs we have in mind are ones in which the elimination of trade barriers is part of a larger regional integration between the countries that allows them to enforce the elimination of barriers to intra-bloc trade. These enforcement mechanisms may come about as the result of specific side agreements between the countries regarding settlement of trade disputes, or as the result of the development of a broader range of institutions that involve joint decisions on public goods and policy coordination among members, as in the European Union.

Given this dichotomy between tariff-setting between blocs and tariff-setting within blocs, we analyse the question of how changes in the size of trading blocs affect which agreements are chosen for tacit coordination, and also how the change in the market power of blocs affects the incentive compatibility constraints for supporting these agreements.[2] One point that arises from our analysis is the importance of distinguishing between an absolute increase in the size of all trading blocs and an increase in the relative size of the trading blocs. The case of the increase in absolute size of trading blocs corresponds to the observed trend toward larger regional alliances, which reduce the number of negotiating units in the GATT. We show that there are two potentially conflicting effects of bloc size on the incentive constraints in this case. First, an increase in the size of trading blocs alters their incentive to defect from trade agreements. In general, larger trading blocs have more to gain from deviating from a free trade agreement, because their market power is greater. Second, an increase in the size of trading blocs affects the welfare level in the trade war that would ensue if the agreement were to break down. In general, trade wars lead to lower world welfare when blocs are larger. We use simulation analysis to show that, in our model, the former effect normally dominates, making free trade agreements more difficult to support as blocs increase in size. Similarly, we show that the lowest tariff that can be supported in inter-bloc tariff negotiations will rise as the absolute size of trading blocs increases.

We also examine the effect of a change in the relative size of trading blocs on the sustainability of cooperation in the case where there are only two trading blocs, under the assumption that the cooperative tariff rate is chosen using the Nash bargaining solution. The primary effect for the asymmetric case is that the larger bloc has greater bargaining power because it fares better in the tariff war that would result if an agreement broke down. Simulations indicate that it is the larger bloc that provides the constraint on the sustainability of the agreement, since it finds defection relatively more attractive. Simulation results also indicate that, if lump sum transfers are feasible, a Pareto-optimal agreement is less likely to be sustainable as the relative size of the larger bloc increases. If lump sum transfers are not available, the relationship between bloc size and the desire of the large blocs to cooperate is ambiguous.

Section 2 presents the basic trading model, which is a generalization of the endowment model used by Krugman (1991). Our model provides intuitive characterization of the size of trading blocs and the degree of comparative advantage (i.e. the magnitude of gains from trade) in terms of parameters that can be used in comparative statics analysis. Following Friedman (1971), trading blocs are allowed to utilize trigger strategies to support inter-bloc trade agreements. Section 3 explores the effect of increases in bloc size when the world is divided into blocs of equal size. The increase in bloc size in this case is absolute, i.e. it results in an increase in the absolute size of all blocs, with no change in relative size. The symmetry of the trading blocs in this case allows us to focus on free trade agreements as the obvious candidates in multilateral negotiations. Section 4 analyses the effect of relative bloc size in a two-bloc model, which captures the effect of changes in the 'market power' of blocs. Section 5 offers some concluding remarks.

2 The model

In this section we present an endowment model in which there are M countries, which are divided into N ($\leq M$) trading blocs, and examine the conditions under which a trade agreement between blocs can be supported in an infinitely repeated tariff-setting game. A trading bloc is defined here to be a coalition of countries that has written an agreement that binds members to a policy of zero tariffs on intra-bloc trade and a common external tariff on imports from the rest of the world. It is assumed that it is impossible to write binding free trade agreements between countries that are not members of the same trading bloc, so that tariffs set by trading blocs will be best responses to the tariffs set by the rest of the world (ROW) blocs. Therefore, zero tariffs on inter-bloc trade will emerge only if they are a subgame perfect equilibrium of the repeated tariff-setting game that is played between trading blocs.

2.1 The endowment model

We will utilize the simple endowment model of trade presented in Bond and Syropoulos (1992), which highlights the role played by bloc size. We assume that there are M countries and M goods. Preferences over goods at a point in time are identical in all countries and are represented by the Cobb–Douglas utility function, $U^i = \prod_j (c_j^i)^{1/M}$, where c_j^i is the consumption of good j in country i and U^i is utility in country i. Letting Y_i denote income of country i at domestic prices and p_j^i the domestic price of good j in country i, these preferences imply the demand functions

$$c_j^i = \frac{Y_i}{Mp_j^i}. \tag{1}$$

Country i $(i = 1, \ldots, M)$ is assumed to have an endowment of $x + z$ of good i and an endowment of x of all other goods $j \neq i$ (where x, $z > 0$). Since x and z are the same for all goods, the world supply of each good will be $K = Mx + z$ in each period.

The symmetry of endowments and preferences ensures that prices of all goods will be identical in the free trade equilibrium, with each country consuming K/M units of each good and $U^F = K/M$. Each country will export the good with the same index. The parameter z thus serves as a measure of the degree of comparative advantage, since it determines the volume of trade in the free trade equilibrium.[3] In the presence of tariffs, the domestic prices will be $p_j^i = q_j(1 + \tau_j^i)$, where τ_j^i is the *ad valorem* tariff levied by country i on imports of good j and q_j is the world price of good j. We assume that there are no export taxes. The simple trading pattern in this model will then yield the following pattern of tariffs in the presence of trading blocs: $\tau_j^i = 0$ if countries i and j are members of the same bloc and τ_j^i is the common external tariff imposed by country i's bloc on imports of good j if they are members of different blocs.

2.2   Supporting free trade in the infinitely repeated tariff game

Now suppose that we have an exogenously given partition of countries into N trading blocs, with B_j denoting the number of countries in bloc j ($j = 1, \ldots, N$). Owing to the symmetry of the model, the identity of the bloc members is inconsequential and equilibria can be characterized in terms of the number of countries contained in each bloc. In the absence of binding agreements between blocs, the external tariffs set by blocs must be self-enforcing (i.e. they maximize the welfare of a representative member, given the tariffs set by ROW blocs). We will assume that countries interact in an infinitely repeated tariff-setting game, which allows a bloc's external tariff strategy to depend on the past strategies of other blocs. We adopt this approach because it captures the repeated interactions between countries over tariff policy (e.g. GATT negotiating rounds) that seem to characterize inter-bloc trade relations. It is well known that in infinitely repeated games of this type, it will in general be possible to support allocations that Pareto dominate the Nash equilibria of a one-shot tariff-setting game if there is more than one trading bloc. In the one-shot game, any bloc (even if it is a single country) will have a non-zero optimal tariff in light of its monopoly power in the market for its export goods.

More specifically, we will study trade agreements that can be supported using trigger strategy equilibria as studied in Friedman (1971).[4] With these strategies, deviation by one of the trading blocs triggers a punishment phase in which all blocs revert permanently to their strategies in the Nash equilibrium of the single-period game. The assumption of a permanent breakdown of the agreement following a deviation is made for simplicity, and the analysis can easily be modified to incorporate finite punishment periods. The choice of the single-period Nash equilibrium for punishment ensures that the equilibrium of the repeated game is subgame perfect. Let U_j^{CH} denote the utility level obtained by bloc j when it cheats on the trade agreement and imposes its optimal tariff, and U_j^{A} the utility level obtained by bloc j under the agreement. The gain to a representative bloc j member from bloc j's defection in the current period is $U_j^{\text{CH}} - U_j^{\text{A}}$. The cost of deviating is that the bloc loses $U_j^{\text{A}} - U_j^{\text{NE}}$ in every subsequent period, where U_j^{NE} is the payoff to country j in the single-period Nash equilibrium. Letting δ denote the discount factor (assumed common to all countries), the present value of the utility loss to country j from deviating from the agreement is $\delta(U_j^A - U_j^{NE})/(1 - \delta)$. It then follows that country j will not deviate from the trade agreement if

$$U_j^{CH} - U_j^A \leq \delta(U_j^{CH} - U_j^{NE}). \tag{2}$$

The minimum discount factor for bloc j, denoted $\underline{\delta}^i$, is the value for which (2) is satisfied with equality. A trade agreement can be supported as a subgame perfect equilibrium utilizing this trigger strategy if $\delta \geq \max \underline{\delta}^i$.

It is well known that trigger strategies can support multiple agreements, and that any trade agreement that is Pareto superior to the Nash equilibrium is a candidate for tacit coordination. In the case where the blocs are all of equal size, however, a free trade agreement (with no transfers between countries) is a logical candidate to attempt to support with trigger strategies in this model. First, free trade is a Pareto-optimal allocation. If countries attempt to coordinate on an equilibrium, it seems natural that they would choose among the Pareto-optimal allocations. Second, given the assumed symmetry between countries and blocs, one would expect equilibrium outcomes to be such that all countries receive the same utility level. If trading blocs are asymmetric, then the case for a free trade agreement is less compelling. A larger bloc may receive a greater payoff in the non-cooperative tariff war if there is no agreement, and is likely to be able to bargain for a better payoff than a smaller bloc. We capture this element by assuming that the agreement is chosen using the Nash bargaining solution.[5] The Nash bargaining solution yields the free trade agreement in the symmetric case, and in the asymmetric case it gives a larger payout to the bloc with the better disagreement (i.e. trade war) payoff.

To analyse the relationship between bloc structure and tacit coordination in inter-bloc trade relations we will study the effects of changes in the size of trading blocs on the minimum discount factor associated with a free trade agreement. In particular, we will say that a particular bloc structure makes cooperation easier if it results in a reduction in the minimum discount factor associated with a free trade agreement. Of course, this definition is not the only one. Alternatively, we can hold δ fixed and determine the best agreement (i.e. maximal value of U^A) that it is possible to support. In this case, a particular bloc structure would make cooperation easier if it allows countries to obtain a higher value of U^A. We show below that the results of the paper extend naturally under this alternative definition.

3   Cooperation with symmetric blocs

In order to restrict the range of cases to be considered, we concentrate on two ways of changing the coalition structure. In this section we consider the case where there are N blocs of equal size, with $B_j = B \equiv M/N$ for all j. Comparative statics results for the effects of changes in B capture the effect of increasing the absolute size of trading blocs while holding their relative size constant. The effects of changes in relative bloc size will be considered in section 4.

It is clear from (2) that free trade will be easier to support (i.e. $\underline{\delta} = \underline{\delta}^i$ is lower) the lower are U^{CH} and U^{NE}. Therefore, we will consider the effect of bloc size on the incentives to cheat and on the punishment for cheating, in turn.

3.1   Bloc size and incentives to cheat

Suppose that bloc 1 defects from an initial free trade equilibrium, and chooses external tariff rates τ_i^1 $(i = 2, \ldots, N)$ to maximize the welfare of a representative member country. Owing to the symmetry of the model, all countries will agree on the level of the external tariff. We show in Bond and Syropoulos (1992) that there is no loss of generality in assuming that bloc 1 imposes a uniform tariff on all imports because of our assumption of symmetry in preferences and endowments. Symmetry ensures that the price elasticity of export supply of each good associated with a ROW bloc will be the same, which implies that the optimal tariff on each ROW good will be the same. Similarly, the world price of each ROW good will be the same, so that if good 1 is the numéraire then $q_i = q$ $(i = 2, \ldots, M)$.[6] Defining $\beta = B/M$ to be the fraction of countries contained in bloc 1, the utility function of a bloc i country can be written as $U^i = (c_1^i)^\beta (c_2^i)^{1-\beta}$, where $c_1^i (c_2^i)$ is the consumption by a bloc i country of a representative bloc 1 (ROW bloc) good.

The budget constraint for a bloc 1 country requires that $(M - B) q(c_2^1 - x) + B(c_1^1 - x) - z = 0$. The market-clearing condition for a bloc 1 good requires $B(c_1^1 - x) - z = (M - B)(x - c_1^2)$. Substituting this condition in the bloc 1 country budget constraint yields the trade balance condition $q(c_2^1 - x) = (c_1^2 - x)$. The trade balance condition and the bloc 1 country budget constraint can be substituted into the bloc 1 utility function to yield an expression for bloc 1 welfare as a function of q, $U^1 = [x + z/B + (M - B)m_2(q)/B]^\beta [x + m_2(q)/q]^{1-\beta}$, where $m_2(q) \equiv (c_1^2 - x)$ is the ROW import demand function. Choosing q to maximize home utility yields the familiar optimal tariff formula:

$$\tau^1 = \frac{1}{\varepsilon_2 - 1}, \tag{3}$$

where $\quad \varepsilon_2 = \dfrac{\partial m_2}{\partial q}\dfrac{q}{m_2}$

is the elasticity of a ROW country's import demand function.

The elasticity of the ROW import demand function can be derived using (1) and an expression for income of a ROW country. Each ROW country has an endowment x of each of the B goods associated with bloc 1, an endowment x of each of the $(M - B)$ ROW goods, and an additional endowment z of its own good. Since there are no tariffs in ROW countries under the agreement, national income will equal the value of their endowment at world prices, $Y_2^* = Bx + q[z + (M - B)x]$. Using (1), imports of bloc 1 goods by a ROW country will be $c_1^2 - x = (Y_2^* - Mx)/M$. Defining $\alpha = z/(xM)$, the elasticity of ROW import demand will be $\varepsilon_2 = q(1 - \beta + \alpha)/[q(1 - \beta + \alpha) - (1 - \beta)]$. Substituting this elasticity into the optimal tariff formula (3) and omitting superscripts yields

$$\tau = \left(1 + \frac{\alpha}{1 - \beta}\right)q - 1. \tag{4}$$

The parameter $\alpha \in (0, \infty)$ is a measure of the degree of comparative advantage, because an increase in α (holding the world endowment, K, of each good constant) is associated with a greater volume of trade at the free trade equilibrium. From (4), the optimal tariff will be higher (at given q) the greater is the degree of comparative advantage because the foreign offer curve becomes less elastic. Equation (4) also indicates that the larger is the deviating bloc (i.e. larger β), given q, the greater will be the optimal tariff. Finally, increases in q will raise the optimal tariff.

In order to determine the optimal tariff, we must solve for the equilibrium value of q. The value of q can be obtained by solving the market-clearing condition for a ROW good, $Bc_2^1 + (M - B)c_2^2 = Mx + z$. Using (1) and the fact that there are no tariffs in ROW countries, $c_2^2 = [Bx + q(z + (M - B)x)]/(Mq)$. For bloc 1 countries, income equals the value of the endowment at domestic prices plus tariff revenue, $Y^1 = Bx + z + (M - B)[px + q\tau(c_2^1 - x)]$. Substituting for c_2^1 using (1), this expression can be solved for domestic income as

$$Y_1 = Y_1^*\left(\frac{1 + \tau}{1 + \beta\tau}\right), \tag{5}$$

where $Y_1^* \equiv Bx + z + q(M - B)x$ is the value of the bloc 1 endowment at world prices. Income at domestic prices is a multiple $(1+\tau)/(1+\beta\tau)$ of income at world prices, owing to the fact that increases in income generate increases in tariff revenue. Substituting (5) into the market-clearing condition for good 2 yields the equilibrium value of q:

$$q = \frac{1 + \alpha + (1-\beta)\beta\tau}{1 + \alpha + (2-\beta+\alpha)\beta\tau}. \tag{6}$$

For $\tau > 0$, the equilibrium price of ROW goods will be less than 1, the free trade price.

Substituting (6) into (4) yields the following quadratic equation for the optimal tariff: $(2-\beta+\alpha)\beta\tau^2 + (1+\beta+\alpha)\tau - \alpha(1+\alpha)/(1-\beta) = 0.$[7] The effect of bloc size on the return to cheating is obtained by solving this equation for the optimal tariffs, and then substituting the values for the optimal tariffs and corresponding equilibrium prices into the indirect utility function,

$$U^{CH} = \left[\left(\beta x + \frac{z}{M} + q(1-\beta)x\right)\left(\frac{1+\tau}{1+\beta\tau}\right)\right][q(1+\tau)]^{(\beta-1)}. \tag{7}$$

The relationship between bloc size, comparative advantage, and U^{CH} is illustrated in figure 4.1. The benefits of defecting are increasing in α (given β), because the market power of the defecting bloc is increasing in α. Note that, as β approaches 0, U^{CH} approaches the free trade level of welfare. Although very small blocs are still able to improve their terms of trade using tariffs, the significance of the exported good in the consumption bundle shrinks to 0 as β approaches 0. Similarly, U^{CH} approaches the free trade level as β approaches 1. Thus, the benefits of cheating on the free trade agreement are greatest for blocs that have an intermediate share of world trade. Figure 4.1 also indicates that the relationship between bloc size and the gain from cheating is single-peaked, and that the value of β at which U^{CH} is maximized is decreasing in α. For $\alpha > 2.92$, this peak occurred at $\beta < 0.5$.

3.2   Bloc size and punishment with symmetric blocs

The previous section analysed the benefits of cheating on the free trade agreement, which was shown to be independent of the ROW bloc structure. Once a bloc has defected, the trigger strategies considered specify reversion to the single-period Nash equilibrium in all future periods.[8] In this section we derive the Nash equilibrium tariffs for the symmetric bloc case, and then substitute these tariffs into the indirect utility function to obtain the utility level in the single-period Nash

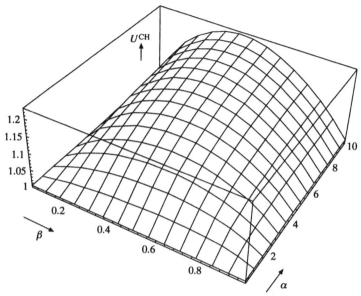

Figure 4.1   The relationship between average welfare in a defecting bloc, absolute bloc size, and comparative advantage

equilibrium, U^{NE}. These values of U^{NE}, combined with the values of U^{CH} obtained in the previous section, will then be substituted back into (2) to solve for the minimum discount factors in the symmetric bloc case.

We begin by establishing that a Nash equilibrium exists in which all blocs impose identical tariffs on imports from other blocs. First, it can be shown that if ROW blocs $2, \dots, N$ each choose the same tariff, τ^{ROW}, on their trade with other blocs, bloc 1 will choose a common tariff τ^1 on all imports from other blocs. A common tariff is optimal because bloc 1 will face identical offer curves from each of the other blocs. The resulting reaction function for bloc 1, $\phi(\tau^{ROW})$, will be functionally identical to the reaction functions of all other blocs because of the symmetry of the trading blocs. Therefore, the fixed point of ϕ, $\tau = \phi(\tau)$ will be a symmetric Nash equilibrium in which all blocs levy the same tariff.

To derive the optimal tariff for bloc 1, note that the assumption of a common tariff τ^1 by bloc 1 and a common tariff τ^{ROW} by ROW blocs, combined with the symmetry of preferences and endowments, guarantees that $q_2 = q_3 = \dots = q_N$. We will denote the common world price of ROW bloc goods by q. The argument then proceeds as in the previous section to show that the optimal tariff for bloc 1 will be given by the optimal tariff formula (3).[9] The only difference between the optimal tariff formula for this case and that derived above for the cheating case is that ε_2 now must reflect the presence of ROW tariffs, τ^{ROW}. Therefore, we must take into account the effect of tariff revenue in determining the income level of ROW bloc countries, Y_2, to substitute in (1). Income of a representative ROW country will be the sum of endowment income and tariff revenue, $Y_2 = Bx + q[z + (N-1)Bx] + B(N-1)\tau^{\text{ROW}}q(c_1^2 - x)$. Substituting from (1) for the consumption levels yields $Y_2 = [Bx + q(z + (N-1)Bx)](1 + \tau^{\text{ROW}})/(1 + \beta\tau^{\text{ROW}})$. Substituting this expression for income into (1) yields the demand function $c_1^2 = [\beta x + q(1 - \beta)x + qz/M]/(1 + \beta\tau^{\text{ROW}})$. Differentiating this expression and defining the comparative advantage parameter $\alpha = z/(Mx)$ as before, the elasticity of ROW import demand is $\varepsilon_2 = (1 - \beta + \alpha)q/[(1 - \beta + \alpha)q - (1 - \beta + \beta\tau^{\text{ROW}})]$. The optimal tariff formula (3) then yields

$$\tau^1 = q\frac{(1 - \beta + \alpha)}{(1 - \beta + \beta\tau^{\text{ROW}})} - 1. \tag{8}$$

(8) implicitly defines the tariff reaction function for bloc 1. Comparing with (4), it can be seen that the presence of ROW tariffs tends to make the ROW offer curve more elastic, leading to a lower bloc 1 tariff (given q, α, and β). Increases in the degree of comparative advantage (α) will raise the tariff imposed by bloc 1. The effect of an increase in β on τ^1 is ambiguous, because an increase in β has two conflicting effects on the elasticity of the ROW import demand curve, c_1^2. The first effect is to reduce the slope of the ROW import demand function (i.e. $\partial^2 c_1^2/(\partial q \partial \beta) < 0$), because bloc 1 now exports a wider variety of goods. The second effect is generally to reduce the level of import demand for bloc 1 goods, because tariff revenue is lost, which reduces c_1^2 at a given Y_2^* (i.e. Y_2/Y_2^* falls). Differentiation of (8) establishes that τ^1 is increasing in β iff $\alpha/(1 + \alpha) > \tau^{\text{ROW}}$.

In a Nash equilibrium, all blocs will set tariffs according to (8), which ensures that $\tau^1 = \tau^{\text{ROW}} = \tau$ and $q = 1$. Utilizing these conditions in (8) yields a quadratic formula for the optimal tariff, $\beta\tau^2 + \tau - \alpha = 0$. Differentiation of this condition establishes that the tariff rate in the non-cooperative Nash equilibrium is increasing in α and decreasing in β. The result that a greater degree of comparative advantage leads to higher Nash equilibrium tariffs is consistent with the result obtained from (8) that each bloc sets higher tariffs (given ROW tariffs) as α increases. It is also similar to the result obtained for the case of a deviating bloc, because a higher α reduces the elasticity of the ROW offer curve. The result that an increase in β reduces Nash equilibrium tariffs may seem surprising. However, it was noted in the discussion of the bloc's reaction function that an increase in size would reduce tariffs only if ROW tariffs were sufficiently low. In the Nash equilibrium, tariffs exceed this critical value, so $\partial \tau / \partial \beta < 0$. It should be noted that autarky is also a Nash equilibrium for the single-period tariff game. We consider below the effects of using autarky in the punishment phase.

The equilibrium tariffs can now be utilized to capture the effects of an increase in the number of trading blocs on world welfare. Substituting the expression for domestic income (5) and the Nash equilibrium condition $q = 1$ into the indirect utility function yields

$$U^{\text{NE}} = \left(\frac{Y^*}{M(1 + \tau\beta)} \right) (1 + \tau)^{\beta}. \tag{9}$$

When trading blocs are arbitrarily small ($\beta = 0$), we obtain the free trade welfare level $Y^*/M = K/M$. An increase in β (holding τ fixed) has two effects in (9). The first is that there will be increased trade with the new bloc members, because the domestic price for products involved in intra-bloc trade falls from $1 + \tau$ to 1. However, this also results in decreased consumption of all other commodities, because Y falls owing to the decrease in tariff revenue. In addition to these effects at fixed τ, there is also the effect of the change in bloc size on Nash equilibrium tariffs. As noted above, an increase in β will lead to lower tariffs. Since (9) is decreasing in τ and τ is increasing in β, this strategic effect will tend to raise U^{NE} as β increases.

The overall effect of β on U^{NE} is illustrated in figure 4.2 for a value of $\alpha = 0.5$. Since all blocs are of equal size in this case, the largest possible value of β is 0.5. The graph in figure 4.2 treats β as a continuous variable on [0,0.5], abstracting from the constraints imposed on $\beta = 1/N$ by the fact that N must take integer values. At $\beta = 0$, the Nash equilibrium welfare level equals the free trade level. As bloc size increases, welfare in the single-period Nash equilibrium initially declines. If the integer constraint on N is taken into account, punishment is most severe when there are three blocs ($\beta = 0.33$).[10]

The U-shaped relationship between bloc size and welfare in the Nash equilibrium is similar to that obtained by Krugman (1991), who suggested that world welfare might be adversely affected by the presence of a small number of trading blocs. In the present setting, this low level of welfare has a more favourable interpretation, because the severe punishment imposed in the single-period Nash equilibrium makes it more costly to deviate from the free trade equilibrium. Therefore, to obtain the overall effect of bloc size on the sustainability of free trade, it

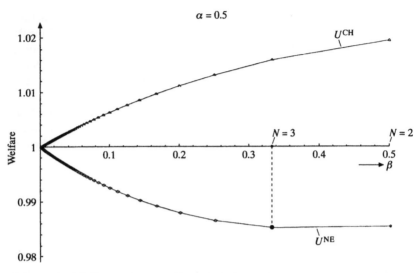

Figure 4.2   Welfare under cheating and in the punishment phase as a function of absolute bloc size

will be necessary to substitute the values of both U^{NE} and U^{CH} derived above into (2) to obtain the relationship between minimum discount factors and bloc size.

The relationship between absolute bloc size (captured by β) and U^{CH} for $\alpha = 0.5$ is also shown in figure 4.2, to facilitate the comparison of the costs and benefits of deviating from the free trade agreement. Note that, as the number of trading blocs decreases from 3 to 2, both U^{CH} and U^{NE} increase. From (2), the minimum discount factor is increasing in both U^{CH} and U^{NE}. Therefore, a decrease from 3 to 2 blocs must make supporting a free trade agreement more difficult. For $\beta < 0.33$, the benefits of cheating are also increasing as β increases. However, the punishment is also becoming more severe in this region, because U^{NE} is decreasing in β. Calculation of the minimum discount parameters for this case indicates that the former effect dominates over the entire interval [0,0.5]. It becomes more difficult to sustain free trade as blocs increase in absolute size or, equivalently, as the number of trading blocs decreases.

We found the positive relationship between $\underline{\delta}$ and β throughout the entire range of β to be quite surprising. In particular, we did not anticipate that the benefits of higher income in the cheating phase, $(\partial U^{CH}/\partial \beta)$, would always dominate the effects of increased punishment over the region $(\partial U^{NE}/\partial \beta)$ where the two effects conflicted. Therefore, we examined whether this conclusion was robust to variations in the parameters of the model. The first parameter we examined was the measure of comparative advantage, α. Increases in α lead to higher tariffs in the single-period Nash equilibrium as noted above, and thus raise the welfare losses associated with retaliation. Since $U^{NE} = U^F$ at $\beta = 0$ for all α, the welfare in the punishment phase will fall more rapidly with β (on average) up to the point where world welfare is minimized. Other things constant, this would tend to make free trade easier to support as bloc size increases. On the other hand, increases in α will raise U^{CH}, as illustrated in figure 4.1. Since $U^{CH} = U^F$ at $\beta = 0$, welfare in the cheating phase rises more rapidly (on average) up to the point where world welfare is maximized. This effect tends to make free trade harder to support as bloc size increases. Simulations for values of α on the interval [0.1,10] yielded two conclusions. First, increases in α make free trade easier to support. Increases in α increase the punishment by relatively more than they increase the gains to cheating, so $\underline{\delta}$ falls. Second, increases in β make free trade more difficult to support for all the values of α considered. Thus, the conclusion that free trade is easier to support when there is a large number of small trading units is robust to variations in the degree of comparative advantage.

A second question is whether the conclusion regarding the effect of bloc size is robust to variations in the intertemporal elasticity of substitution. Since increases in β involve gains in income in the high-income cheating state and losses in the low-income punishment, the relationship between $\underline{\delta}$ and β might be sensitive to the assumption that the marginal utility of income is independent of income. We calculated the minimum discount factors from (2) using transformations of the utility function of the form $V = U^\gamma$. As expected, a higher value of $\gamma > 0$ makes it more difficult to support free trade. With higher values of γ, the utility of income in the cheating phase is raised relative to that in the punishment phase, making it more attractive to defect from the free trade agreement. Results indicated that $\underline{\delta}$ is increasing in β. Thus, the conclusion that larger trading blocs make it more difficult to support free trade is also robust to transformations of the utility function of the type considered here.

These results establish a presumption that an increase in the size of symmetric trading blocs will make free trade harder to support, because they hold over a wide range of values of α and γ. It is possible to construct utility functions for which an increase in β will make free trade easier to support over some range.[11] However, the fact that such instances were not found using the transformation $V = U^\gamma$ suggests that these examples are relatively uncommon.

3.3   *Alternative criteria for cooperative agreements*

The above results indicate that increases in bloc size raise the minimum discount factor required to support free trade when the interior Nash equilibrium is used as the punishment for deviating blocs. Our criterion for the ability to sustain cooperative agreements has been a comparison of the minimum discount factors, which can be thought of as a comparison of the likelihood that the free trade equilibrium can be supported using trigger strategies. An alternative criterion would be to fix the discount parameter, and ask what is the lowest tariff rate that can be supported in equilibrium using the trigger strategies described earlier. Thus, if the incentives to deviate from the free trade agreement are too large to sustain the free trade agreement, it may be possible to sustain an agreement with tariffs that are positive but lower than the Nash equilibrium tariffs. Define $\tilde{\tau}(\beta, \delta)$ to be the minimum tariff rate that can be supported with bloc size β and discount parameter δ. This tariff rate is the solution to $\delta = [U^{CH}(\tau) - U^{A}(\tau)]/[U^{CH}(\tau) - U^{NE}]$, where $U^{CH}(\tau)$ is the utility obtained by the deviating bloc when all other countries levy tariffs at rate τ. Using this criterion, a change in bloc structure facilitates cooperation if it reduces the minimum tariff rate that can be supported. We have constructed a simulation analysis that suggests that, for values of the discount parameter where free trade cannot be supported, $\tilde{\tau}$ is increasing in β. This criterion also yields the conclusion that increases in bloc size make the sustainability of cooperative trade agreements more difficult.

A second variation that could be considered is to use the autarky equilibrium in which there is no inter-bloc trade as punishment for deviations from the agreement. Since the autarky equilibrium results in lower utility levels in the punishment phase, it makes cooperation easier to support relative to the case with the interior Nash equilibrium. Furthermore, since autarky still allows for intra-bloc trade, the level of utility is increasing in the size of trading blocs. Therefore, punishment is less severe as bloc size increases, and we continue to obtain the conclusion that cooperation is harder to support with large trading blocs.

4   The effect of relative bloc size with two trading blocs

The previous section examined the effect of increasing the absolute size of blocs on the minimum discount factor, while holding the relative size of trading blocs constant. An alternative way of considering changes in bloc size is to hold the number of blocs constant but to change their relative size. In this section we examine this question in the simplest case, which occurs when there are only two trading blocs.[12] As in the previous section, we can characterize the size of bloc 1 by the fraction of the world's regions it contains, $\beta_1 = B_1/M$. The additional consideration introduced arises from the fact that the model is no longer symmetric, since $\beta_2 = 1 - \beta_1$. We choose bloc 1 exports to be the numéraire, and let q denote the world price of bloc 2 exports.

In the asymmetric case, the free trade equilibrium is no longer the natural agreement for the blocs to choose among the Pareto-efficient trade agreements. For example, the larger bloc might actually prefer the non-cooperative Nash equilibrium to the free trade outcome (i.e. it wins the trade war, as in Kennan and Riezman, 1988). The preference of the large country for the trade war means that it would be impossible for the two countries to support the free trade equilibrium using trigger strategies. However, trigger strategies could potentially be used to support an agreement that is Pareto superior to the outcome of the trade war.

The utility levels resulting from the feasible and individually rational trade agreements for the asymmetric case are illustrated in figure 4.3. If lump sum transfers are allowed between countries, then the Pareto-efficient frontier is a straight line through the free trade point ($U_1^F = U_2^F = K/M$) with slope $-\beta_1/(1 - \beta_1)$.[13] The efficient frontier becomes steeper as β_1 increases because a larger transfer is required per country in bloc 2 to raise the utility of a bloc 1 country. An increase in β_1 thus raises the cost of increasing utility in bloc 1.

We will assume that the outcome is chosen using the Nash bargaining solution, which is equivalent to assuming that the agreement chosen is the one that maximizes the product of the difference between the payoff in the event of an agreement and the payoff if no agreement is reached. We take the disagreement payoff to be the non-cooperative Nash equilibrium, so that the agreement chosen will be the one that maximizes $W = (U_1 - U_1^{NE})(U_2 - U_2^{NE})$ over the set of efficient agreements (U_1, U_2). The necessary condition for optimization is then

$$\frac{U_2^{NB} - U_2^{NE}}{U_1^{NB} - U_1^{NE}} = \frac{\beta_1}{1 - \beta_1}, \tag{10}$$

where U_i^{NB} denotes the utility level of bloc i in the Nash bargaining solution. Point A$'$ in figure 4.3 illustrates the disagreement point for the case of symmetric blocs. The chosen agreement is illustrated by the tangency between the efficient frontier and the indifference curves, which represent level contours of W. For the symmetric case with $\beta_1 = 0.5$, this tangency will occur at the free trade point where welfare in each bloc is U^F.

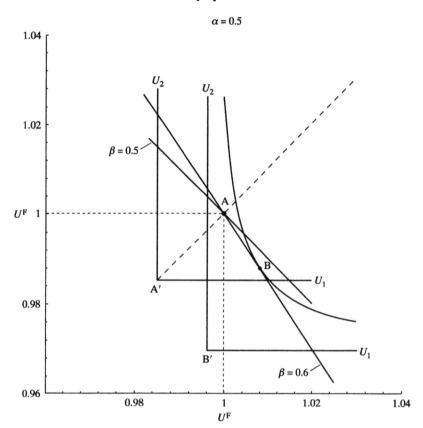

Figure 4.3   Nash bargaining outcomes and relative bloc size

An increase in the size of bloc 1 has two effects on the agreement. First, an increase in bloc size will alter the disagreement points. Point B' illustrates the case in which an increase in β_1 raises bloc 1's payoff and reduces bloc 2's payoff in the non-cooperative Nash equilibrium, which increases the bargaining power of bloc 1. The second effect is due to the shift in the efficient frontier, which raises the relative cost of transferring income to bloc 1. Whether bloc 1 receives a higher or lower payoff in the optimal agreement will depend on which of these effects dominates. We will use simulation analysis to evaluate the importance of these two effects.

The first step in the simulation is to calculate the effect of a change in bloc size on U_i^{NE}. The optimal tariff for each country can be derived using (3), although the solutions for the world price and optimal tariffs are slightly more complicated in the asymmetric case because the Nash

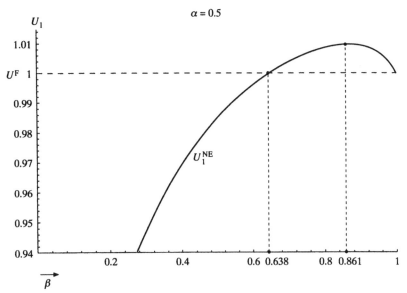

Figure 4.4   Average welfare in bloc 1 in the two-bloc Nash equilibrium

equilibrium tariffs for the two blocs will differ. The Nash equilibrium welfare levels are obtained by substituting these solutions for optimal tariff rates and prices into the indirect utility function. Figure 4.4 illustrates the relationship between the size of bloc 1 and U_1^{NE} in the case where $\alpha = 0.5$. Since $\beta_2 = 1 - \beta_1$, figure 4.4 illustrates that the larger bloc always obtains a higher welfare level than the smaller bloc in the tariff war. For $\beta_1 > 0.638$, U_1^{NE} exceeds U^F and country 1 'wins' the tariff war. The welfare of bloc 1 is maximized at $\beta_1 = 0.861$. As the size of bloc 1 increases beyond that point, the benefits obtained from the optimal tariff are lower because of the reduction in the volume of external trade.

The results on Nash equilibrium can be used to illustrate how the disagreement point shifts as the size of bloc 1 increases. For $\beta_1 < 0.861$, the disagreement point shifts downward and to the right as indicated by the movement from point A' to B' in figure 4.3. For $\beta_1 > 0.861$, the disagreement point shifts toward the origin as β_1 increases, because the welfare of both blocs is falling. This result on the shift in the disagreement point can be combined with the shift in the Pareto-efficient frontier to derive the changes in the agreements under the Nash bargaining solution. The payoffs to the two countries in the Nash bargaining solution as the size of bloc 1 increases are illustrated in figure 4.5. Starting at $\beta_1 = 0.5$, increases in the size of bloc 1 will initially increase the welfare of bloc 1

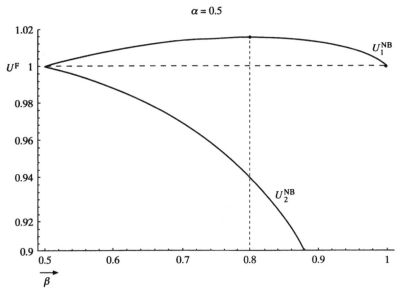

Figure 4.5   Average welfare at Nash-bargained outcomes and relative bloc size

and reduce the welfare of bloc 2. Over this region, the improvement in the disagreement point leads to an improvement in the U_1^{NB}. For values of $\beta_1 > 0.797$, the welfare of bloc 1 diminishes as it expands. Note that for $\beta_1 \in [0.797, 0.861]$, the improvement in the disagreement point (illustrated in figure 4.4) is dominated by the inward shift of the frontier.

The above results illustrate how the point chosen on the efficient frontier varies as bloc size changes. It remains to determine the range of discount factors for which the chosen point on the efficient frontier can be supported using trigger strategies. The minimum discount factors for each bloc are calculated using (2). In the asymmetric case, the minimum discount factors will differ across blocs. The minimum discount factors for each bloc when $\alpha = 0.5$ are shown in figure 4.6. Note that the minimum discount factor for the larger bloc always exceeds that for the smaller bloc. This results from the fact that the payoff from the non-cooperative Nash equilibrium is higher for the larger bloc, making the punishment less onerous and requiring a greater valuation on future payoffs to make cooperation attractive. As the size of the larger bloc increases, the minimum discount factor becomes larger, indicating that the agreement on the efficient frontier will be harder to support. This reflects the fact that deviating is becoming more attractive relative to the payment received under the agreement as bloc size increases.

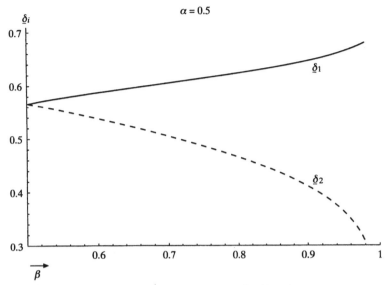

Figure 4.6   Minimum discount factors and relative bloc size

We conclude the analysis of the asymmetric case by noting how the results are modified if the countries are constrained to non-negative taxes on imports. The constrained efficient frontier satisfying the non-negativity of trade taxes condition will lie inside the efficient frontier in figure 4.3, with a tangency between the two frontiers occurring at the free trade point. Simulations for the utilities in the Nash bargaining solution and the minimum discount factors yield two conclusions regarding the constrained efficient case with no transfers between countries. First, the conclusion regarding the relationship between the size of the larger bloc and its payoff under the agreement is virtually unaffected by the constraint on transfers. The second conclusion is that the relationship between bloc size and the sustainability of the agreement on the frontier is ambiguous when transfers between countries are ruled out. Simulations for various degrees of comparative advantage indicated that the minimum discount factors for the large bloc may have an increasing, decreasing, or U-shaped relationship to bloc size. In all of these cases, however, the minimum discount factor of the large bloc exceeds that of the smaller bloc, indicating that the large bloc provides the effective constraint on supporting the cooperative agreement.

5   Concluding remarks

This analysis provides some indications of how changes in the size of trading blocs affect the sustainability of tacit coordination in tariffs and the types of cooperative agreements that may be obtained. Our results indicate that, in the symmetric case, increases in the size of trading blocs make cooperative agreements more difficult to sustain. Although the increase in the size of trading blocs generally makes the punishment for deviating from trade agreements more severe, this effect is more than offset by the fact that deviations from trade agreements are more attractive when trading blocs are large. There was also some evidence of an unfavourable effect of a relatively large trading bloc on inter-bloc trade relations in the two-bloc case with transfers between countries, where it was found that efficient agreements were more difficult to support with large blocs.

In interpreting these results, it should be noted that we have assumed that there are no explicit resource costs of arriving at the trigger strategies that are to be played. We have considered only the costs and benefits of deviation from a given trigger strategy. If the costs of agreeing on the trigger strategy to be used and the agreement to be supported are increasing in the number of blocs, then there may be some benefits of reducing the number of trading blocs. Still, however, our analysis suggests that there exist additional forces that affect the stability of trade agreements on interregional trade. The larger the number of trading blocs and the more symmetric in size are the blocs, the more likely it is that tariff agreements will be supportable.

This analysis has also taken the structure of trading blocs as exogenous, and examined how welfare is affected by bloc structure. An interesting issue for future research would be to examine the incentives for countries to form trading blocs, which would allow for some dynamics of the bloc-formation process.

NOTES

1 Winters (1993) notes that, although the representation of EC trade policy as a 'Fortress Europe' is an exaggeration, there had been a fivefold increase in the coverage of non-tariff barriers in the EC between 1966 and 1986.
2 Bagwell and Staiger (1993a,b), in work developed simultaneously with ours, analyse the dynamic effect of customs unions and free trade areas on the incentive constraints present in multilateral tariff negotiations. They focus on the difference between the incentive constraints prevailing during the negotiating period, when the negotiations for a regional agreement are under way but not complete, and those present when the agreement has actually

been completed. We deal exclusively with the impact of customs unions on multilateral agreements once the agreement has actually been completed, and focus on how the effect of the formation of customs unions is related to the size of the trading blocs involved and the magnitude of gains from trade attainable under the agreements.

3 This model is similar in spirit to that of Krugman (1991), who considered an endowment model with as many countries as goods. Krugman assumes a CES utility function with an elasticity of substitution exceeding 1, and an endowment structure with $x = 0$. Our specification has the advantage of yielding closed form solutions for tariffs in the symmetric equilibrium below, and allows for considering the role played by the degree of comparative advantage through variations in z. If $z < 0$, then each country has a comparative disadvantage in a single good and exports all others at the free trade equilibrium. All conclusions in this paper regarding the effects of comparative advantage and bloc size will carry through if $z \in (-K/M, 0)$. Therefore, we limit discussion in the paper to the case of $z > 0$.

4 Canzoneri and Henderson (1991) use a similar approach for modelling international policy coordination on monetary policy. Alternatively, one can use Abreu's (1986) optimal punishments. Unfortunately, the use of 'stick and carrot' punishment complicates our analysis considerably and makes the prospect of obtaining further results unclear.

5 This approach of using the Nash bargaining solution to choose among the agreements to be supported in a repeated game has been used in a different context by Harrington (1991) to analyse the allocation of output levels in a price-setting cartel when firms differ in their marginal costs.

6 The supply of imports of a bloc j good to bloc 1 will be

$$(M - B_1)x + z - \sum_{i \neq 1} B_i c_j^i.$$

Since the remaining blocs are following a free trade policy for $i = 2, \ldots, N$, we have $\tau_j^i = 0$ and $p_j^i = q_j$ and

$$Y^i = \left(B_1 + \sum_{k \neq 1} B_k q_k \right) x + q_i z.$$

Substituting these conditions into the demand function (1), it can be seen that the import supply schedules for goods associated with all ROW blocs will have the same elasticity.

7 Simulation results indicated that the optimal tariff rates were increasing in α, and that there is a U-shaped relationship between β and the optimal tariffs.

8 We assume that, in the event of a deviation, the entire agreement breaks down and all countries revert to the one-shot Nash equilibrium. An alternative is to allow countries to use discriminatory strategies to punish only defecting trading blocs. We have not adopted this approach for several reasons. First, it is much more complex computationally, because it requires considering incentive compatibility constraints for all previous possible defections (e.g. when one bloc has deviated, two blocs have deviated, etc.). Second, the intuitive appeal of discriminatory punishments is that they allow countries to 'gang up' on a defector, since $N - 1$ blocs can punish a defector. We suspect

that this benefit of discriminatory punishments would make it relatively easier to support trade when there are a large number of blocs, because the payoff to the bloc being punished will decline as the number of punishing blocs increases (figure 4.4 below). In light of our findings below, this would only strengthen the results concerning bloc size and cooperation. Finally, note that discriminatory punishments can do no better than the reversion to autarky punishments that we consider below.

9   Since each bloc now consists of $\beta = 1/N$ of all countries, the utility of a bloc 1 country can be written as $U^1 = (c_1^1)^\beta (c_2^1)^{(1-\beta)}$. The argument used to derive (3) will apply if it can be shown that the trade balance condition $q(c_2^1 - x) = c_1^2 - x$ holds. Market clearing for a ROW good requires $B[c_2^1 + c_2^2 + (N-2) c_2^3] = Mx + z$, where c_2^3 denotes demand for good 2 by blocs $j \neq 1, 2$. Multiplying this market-clearing condition by q and rewriting yields $q B(c_2^1 - x) = q [z - B(c_2^2 - x) - B(N-2)(c_2^3 - x)] = q [z - B(c_2^2 - x) - B(N-2)(c_2^3 - x)]$, where the second equality follows from symmetry of blocs $2, \ldots, N$. Substitution of this condition in the budget constraint for country 2 at world prices, $B[c_1^2 + qc_2^2 + q(N-2)c_3^2] = B[x + q(N-1)x] + z$, yields the trade balance condition.

10 In Bond and Syropoulos (1992) we explore more fully the relationship between comparative advantage and the value of β for which world welfare is minimized.

11 For example, suppose the utility function takes the form

$$V(U) = \begin{cases} U & \text{if } U \leq A \\ A & \text{if } U > A \end{cases}$$

where U is the value of the Cobb–Douglas utility function defined in the text. Choose a value of β, denoted $\tilde{\beta}$, such that $\partial u^{NE}/\partial \beta < 0$, and let $A = u^{CH}(\tilde{\beta})$. Increases in β in the neighbourhood of this point must reduce $\underline{\delta} = (V^{CH} - V^F)/(V^{CH} - V^{NE})$, since the numerator is unaffected by β and the denominator is increasing in β.

12 In Bond et al. (1993), we consider the effect of the formation of a union between two countries in a three-country model. This case involves mixing both relative size and absolute size effects.

13 The internal relative price of bloc 2 goods is equal to unity in each bloc for points on the efficient frontier. National income in the respective countries can then be written as $Y_1 = K + (M - B_1)T$ and $Y_2 = K - B_1 T$, where $K \equiv Mx + z$ and $T = \tau^1 q(c_2^1 - x) = -\tau^2(c_1^2 - x)$ is the transfer paid to bloc 1 countries on each bloc 2 good through trade taxes. Since consumption of each good in country i will be Y_i/M from (2), we can use these expressions for national income to solve for the efficient frontier.

REFERENCES

Abreu, Dilip (1986), 'Extremal Equilibria of Oligopolistic Supergames', *Journal of Economic Theory* 39, 191–225.

Bagwell, Kyle and Robert W. Staiger (1993a), 'Multilateral Tariff Cooperation During the Formation of Regional Free Trade Areas', NBER Working Paper No. 4364.

(1993b), 'Multilateral Tariff Cooperation During the Formation of Customs Unions', Working Paper.
Bond, Eric W. and Costas Syropoulos (1992), 'Optimality and Stability of Regional Trading Blocs', Penn State Working Paper.
Bond, Eric W., Costas Syropoulos and Alan Winters (1993), 'Implications of European Integration for Transatlantic Cooperation in Trade', Penn State Working Paper.
Canzoneri, Matthew and Dale Henderson (1991), *Monetary Policy in Interdependent Economies*, Cambridge, Mass.: MIT Press.
Dixit, Avinash (1987), 'Strategic Aspects of Trade Policy', in Truman Bewley (ed.), *Advances in Economic Theory*, Cambridge: Cambridge University Press.
Friedman, James (1971), 'A Non-cooperative Equilibrium for Supergames', *Review of Economic Studies* 38, 1–12.
Harrington, Joseph (1991), 'The Determination of Price and Output Quotas in a Heterogeneous Cartel', *International Economic Review* 32 (November), 767–92.
Kennan, John and Raymond Riezman (1988), 'Do Big Countries Win Tariff Wars?' *International Economic Review* 29, 81–5.
Krugman, Paul (1991), 'Is Bilateralism Bad?' in Elhanan Helpman and Assaf Razin (eds.), *International Trade and Trade Policy*, Cambridge, Mass.: MIT Press.
Winters, L. Alan (1993), 'The European Community: A Case of Successful Integration?' Centre for Economic Policy Research Discussion Paper No. 755.

Discussion

KONSTANTINE GATSIOS

Just as the initial interest of economists back in the 1950s and 1960s in customs union theory seems to have been inspired by the creation of the European Common Market, similarly the current resurgence of interest seems to be caused by renewed efforts to create the European Union as well as the establishment of the North American Free Trade Agreement.

In the face of such developments in the world economy, the question of how world welfare is affected by the formation of trading blocs assumes new importance. This is the question addressed by the paper by Bond and Syropoulos. In particular, they seek to investigate how changes in the size of symmetrical trading blocs affect world welfare and to examine, in this context, the possibility of supporting a free trade regime through tacit coordination.

Their work is an extension of that by Krugman (1991) which, in turn, draws heavily on Gros (1987). The main difference is that the present paper employs a repeated game framework while Krugman's is of a static nature. So it might be interesting to recapitulate the main result of Krugman's paper, which relates world welfare to the number of symmetrical trading blocs into which the world is organized.

Krugman considers N countries being allocated into B symmetrical trading blocs consisting, thus, of N/B countries. Each country has a CES utility function of the form

$$U = \left[\sum_{i=1}^{N} C_i^{\theta}\right]^{1/\theta} \qquad \text{with } 0 < \theta < 1.$$

Hence, the elasticity of substitution is $\sigma = 1/(\theta - 1)$. It is immaterial whether one thinks of this model as being one of a pure exchange economy or of the usual monopolistically competitive type. This is because in either case the only effect of an *ad valorem* tariff is to affect the relative amount consumed in each country of the representative good produced in the bloc and outside the bloc.

Furthermore, in this model there are no 'small countries', i.e. price takers. Even if one considers the case of one-country blocs and then takes $N \to \infty$ (or, equivalently, the share of countries in each bloc $\beta = 1/B \to 0$), the tariff is positive, $(1 - \theta)/\theta$ or $1/(\sigma - 1)$.

Krugman then executes some numerical examples to see the impact of the number of symmetrical blocs on world welfare. Figure 4D.1 reproduces the main diagram of his paper.

Clearly, if $\beta = 1$, i.e. all countries are in one bloc, then by definition $U = U^F$, the free trade welfare level. On the other hand, if $\beta \to 0$ then $t = 1/(\sigma - 1)$, which in turn implies that as $\sigma \to \infty$ then $t \to 0$ and $U \to U^F$. This explains why $U_1 > U_2$ when $\sigma_1 > \sigma_2$ and $\beta = 0$ in the diagram. Furthermore, we know from Gros (1987) that, in this model, a country can benefit from a trade war only if is almost three times as big as ROW. Since here we are examining symmetrical trading blocs, it follows that, as we move away from free trade ($\beta = 1$), world welfare decreases. Finally, the different functions $U(\beta; \sigma)$ never cross one another, because if they did it would have to be that for given β their underlying tariff should have been the same. This, in turn, contradicts the fact that t is a one-to-one decreasing function of σ. Hence, U_2 must lie entirely below U_1.

This is a good example of situations in which the intuition derived from non-strategic general equilibrium models does not apply in strategic situations. Since free trade, i.e. one trading bloc, is the optimum in this model, one might have suggested that the fewer the trading blocs the

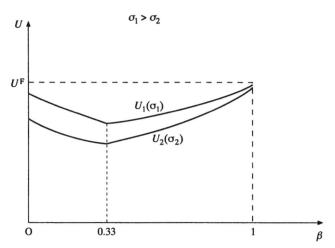

Figure 4D.1

better. Not so! In fact, the world attains its minimum level of welfare if the number of trading blocs is three! Furthermore, starting from a non-cooperative world consisting of more than three trading blocs, things are bound to get worse as the world moves towards free trade, before they start getting better.

All these counterintuitive results are rooted in the second-best nature of the problem and therefore should not be entirely surprising. Put differently, different degrees of cooperation induce different games. A comparison of the equilibria of these different games is, in general, ambiguous.

There are very similar counterintuitive results in the industrial organization literature. One such result has been provided by Salant *et al.* (1983). Think of three identical firms being engaged in a Cournot–Nash game. The equilibrium represents a Prisoner's Dilemma, the worst possible outcome for them. The most favourable joint outcome is to merge and attain monopoly profits. Now imagine two of them merging and choosing output in a Cournot–Nash fashion *vis-à-vis* the third firm. Surprisingly, the two merged firms may not be better off compared with the non-cooperative equilibrium. In a model with linear demands they will in fact be worse off!

Gatsios and Karp (1992) have extended this result in a trade model of the Brander and Spencer (1985) type, involving *n* countries/firms. They show that, if a subset *m* of these countries form a union and coordinate their trade policies, then it is possible that their welfare may be lower than that of the non-cooperative equilibrium. The reasons are essentially the same as those in Salant *et al.*

Notice how similar in flavour the results of these two models are to those of Krugman. Notice also that they too involve the formation of coalitions that are in fact asymmetric. In Gatsios and Karp, in particular, there are $(n - m)$ coalitions, each consisting of one country, and one coalition consisting of $m < n$ countries. Even though the formation of the m-member coalition is followed, in their paper, by a reaction by the rest of the countries that is the most favourable to the coalition, in the sense that each one of them pursues a non-cooperative strategy on its own, none the less the members of the union may be worse off.

This would lead us to an even more pessimistic view than that provided by Krugman. The road from non-cooperation to free trade may, in fact, be more difficult than suggested by the symmetric case example.

We are now ready to turn to the present paper by Bond and Syropoulos. The endowment structure they assume is as follows:

	Country			
Commodity	1	2	....	M
1	$z + x$	x	....	x
2	x	$z + x$		
$\vdots$	$\vdots$		$\ddots$	
M	x			$z + x$

Each country's utility function is Cobb–Douglas, $U = \Pi \, c_i^{1/M}$, i.e., with a constant elasticity of substitution, $\varepsilon \geq 1$. This implies that the countries are small, in the sense that if we think of one-country blocs then, as $M \to \infty$, the optimal tariff $t \to 0$, i.e. the free trade level.

As I said before, the paper differs methodologically from that of Krugman in that the game played between trading blocs is infinitely repeated. Hence, the authors employ trigger strategies to support free trade as an implicitly coordinated equilibrium. In the presence of multiple equilibria with trigger strategies, the choice of free trade equilibrium as the one to focus on seems reasonable because it represents the only symmetrical equilibrium that is Pareto optimal. Free trade can be supported as a subgame perfect equilibrium of the game by the use of trigger strategies if $\delta \geq (U_j^{CH} - U_j^{F})/(U_j^{CH} - U_j^{NE})$, where δ is the discount factor of each country and U_j^{CH} the utility obtained by bloc j when it deviates from the free trade equilibrium, while U_j^{F} and U_j^{NE} represent its utility at the free trade and non-cooperative equilibrium, respectively.

What should be stressed is that the partition of countries into trading blocs is prior to the commencing of the game. Hence if the M countries are organized in N symmetrical trading blocs, each one containing

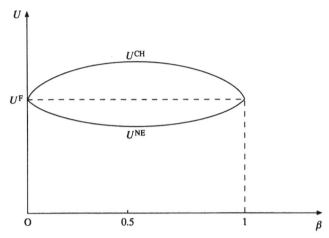

Figure 4D.2

$B = M/N$ of them, then if one bloc deviates from free trade the trigger strategies require that the rest $(N-1)$ of the blocs break away from free trade and a non-cooperative equilibrium among the N players/blocs ensues. This in turn raises some doubts as to whether trigger strategies are conceptually the best way to think of implicit threats in real world situations. For instance, why should it be that if a bloc deviates from free trade the rest do likewise instead of coordinating their strategies *vis-à-vis* the deviant?

If one accepts this assumption, what happens then is easy to see. As with Krugman, everything hinges on the size of the symmetrical blocs, or, put differently, on the fraction of countries contained in each bloc, $\beta = B/M$. Figure 4D.2 gives a flavour of the main result and is similar to figure 4.2 of the paper. We can understand this figure as follows. Look first at the graph of U^{CH}, the utility of cheating on a free trade arrangement. If $\beta = 1$, that is, if the deviating bloc consists of all M countries, then $U^{CH} = U^F$; one cannot deviate from oneself. For $\beta \to 0$, on the other hand, it has to be that $M \to \infty$ and $t \to 0$. In other words, if there are infinitely many countries then the dominant strategy of any finite bloc will be free trade. Hence, again $U^{CH} = U^F$. Finally, for $0 < \beta < 1$, consider the simple case in which all blocs but one follow a free trade policy, setting $t = 0$. Then clearly the best response of the deviant bloc is to set $t > 0$ and increase its welfare. This explains the concavity of the U^{CH} function.

Now turn to the graph of U^{NE}, the utility of a symmetric Nash equilibrium outcome. If $\beta = 1$ then $U^{NE} = U^F$ by definition. If $\beta \to 0$

then, for the same reasons as those given above, $U^{\text{NE}} = U^{\text{F}}$. Finally, for $0 < \beta < 1$, the non-cooperative equilibrium represents a Prisoner's Dilemma so it must be that $U^{\text{NE}} < U^{\text{F}}$. This explains the convexity of the U^{NE} function.

On the basis of numerical simulations associated with figure 4.2 the authors come to an interesting conclusion; namely, that it becomes more difficult to sustain free trade as the number of trading blocs decreases, while the opposite is true when there is a large number of small trading blocs. Furthermore, this result is robust both to variations of comparative advantage and to monotonic transformations of the utility functions.

The spirit of this result is close to that of Krugman and complements it. It is also close in flavour to the industrial organization literature discussed earlier. That is, moving from a completely non-cooperative world towards free trade through the successive creation of ever-larger trading blocs may not be a very promising procedure.

Finally, the authors turn to the case of two asymmetric trading blocs. This is a natural and interesting extension of their previous discussion on symmetric blocs, because it tries to capture the effect of changes in the market power of blocs on their ability to support cooperative agreements on the Pareto-efficient frontier. The bargaining process envisaged here is of the Nash type. The simulation results are less clear-cut than those of the symmetric bloc case. If inter-bloc transfers are allowed, then the ability to support cooperation is inversely related to the asymmetry between the two blocs. Since the larger bloc wins a tariff war, it is the one to generate constraints on the set of cooperative solutions. If inter-bloc transfers are not allowed, then the possibility of sustaining a cooperative agreement may be positively or negatively related to the asymmetry of bloc sizes and depends on the degree of comparative advantage.

REFERENCES

Brander, J. and B. Spencer (1985), 'Export Subsidies and International Market Share Rivalry', *Journal of International Economics* 18, 83–100.
Gatsios, K. and L. Karp (1992), 'The Welfare Effects of Incomplete Harmonisation of Trade and Industrial Policy', *Economic Journal* 102, 107–19.
Gros, D. (1987), 'A Note on the Optimal Tariff, Retaliation, and the Welfare Loss from Tariff Wars in a Model with Intra-Industry Trade', *Journal of International Economics* 23, 357–67.
Krugman, P. (1991), 'Is Bilateralism Bad?' in E. Helpman and A. Razin (eds.), *International Trade and Trade Policy*, Cambridge, Mass.: MIT Press.
Salant, S., S. Switzer and R. J. Reynolds (1983), 'Losses from Horizontal Merger: The Effects of an Exogenous Change in Industry Structure on Cournot–Nash Equilibrium', *Quarterly Journal of Economics* 98, 185–99.

5   The effects of trade liberalization on the members of a trading bloc: a lumpy country analysis

ALAN V. DEARDORFF

1   Introduction

The completion of the Uruguay Round will cause a number of changes in world markets, including a move somewhat closer to free trade for most of the countries of the world. The effects of such a move have long been the subject of economic analysis in the pure theory of international trade. Therefore one would think that we would already have a very clear idea of who will gain, who will lose, and what adjustments will take place as trade barriers fall. In fact, however, while we do indeed have several important insights into this issue, these have focused primarily on the effects on particular industries and the effects on particular factors as they will be affected by trade. In today's world it is increasingly important to ask also about the effects on individual countries within trading blocs.

The need for this is apparent throughout the transatlantic economy, in considering both Europe and North America. In Europe, the completion of the single European market in 1992 has meant that, from an economic standpoint, Europe should be treated more as a single country than as a group of countries in international trade. But in practice the several countries of Europe do retain their separate identities, and they will naturally be concerned with the effects of trade liberalization on themselves individually. Further, although great strides have indeed been made within Europe toward removing barriers to the movement of goods and factors, there also remain significant differences across countries that could matter for the patterns of production and trade. Therefore it is useful to ask how the separate countries of Europe may be affected by the Uruguay Round trade liberalization.

Similarly, in North America, it has long been true that the sheer size of the United States economy has meant that there could be significant differences across its regions in the effects of any economic policy. This becomes even more true now, however, with the implementation of the North American Free Trade Area (NAFTA), in which all of North America will form a single trading bloc. As in the European Union, the effects of multilateral trade liberalization are best understood not by considering the countries individually as though that bloc did not exist, or by considering the entire bloc as a monolithic whole. Rather, what is needed in North America, as in Europe, is an analysis of trade liberalization that can identify effects on countries that are also linked in such a bloc.

I will address this question in purely theoretical terms. I will use the model of a lumpy country that Paul Courant and I have developed elsewhere for other purposes (Courant and Deardorff, 1992, 1993). In this model, the 'lumpy country' – which I here call a trading bloc and identify either with the European Union as a whole or with NAFTA as a whole – consists of two regions between which, for one reason or another, factor prices fail to be equalized. In its simplest version, factor price equalization (FPE) between regions fails because they have different exogenous factor endowments, and I will begin with that case below. Because the regions in that case also have different patterns of specialization, the welfare effects of trade liberalization are likely to differ between them substantially. Identifying the regions of the lumpy country as the separate countries within a trading bloc, this suggests that some countries may gain and others may lose from at least some aspects of the Uruguay Round.

However, mobility of factors within a bloc, and especially the completion of the single market in the case of Europe, makes the assumption of exogenous factor endowments suspect. I therefore turn next to another case that we have also considered before, where factor prices remain unequal in equilibrium *because of* labour mobility, owing to a difference in consumer amenities across regions.

Finally, in order to capture an additional feature of the transatlantic economy that might also account for factor price differences and specialization, and that would in any case be a cause of concern in the context of the Uruguay Round, I introduce subsidies to agriculture. By allowing one country to provide a production subsidy that the other does not, I get an alternative scenario in which wages are equalized after all, but land rents are not. The essential feature of lumpiness is still present in the form of necessary differences in patterns of specialization across regions. In this situation, again, the effects of trade liberalization on the separate countries can be quite different.

1.1   Lessons from traditional models

Before beginning the lumpy country analysis, it is useful to review what traditional models of trade theory would have to say about the effects of trade liberalization on the countries of a trading bloc. Trade liberalization removes trade barriers at home and abroad, and the main impact of that on a competitive economy is through a change in relative prices. Reduction of the bloc's tariffs or other trade barriers will lower the relative price, within the bloc, of the goods that it imports from outside.[1] Reduction in trade barriers abroad could in principle have the opposite effect, to the extent that other countries reduce barriers on the same imported good, but on average the rest of the world must import different goods, and one therefore expects trade liberalization abroad to increase demands for, and raise the world prices of, the goods that the trading bloc exports. Thus the primary effect of trade liberalization for the trading bloc, as it is for a single country, is to lower the relative prices inside the bloc of its import goods relative to its exports. There are also additional effects that arise from the lost tariff revenue but, without any presumption as to who shares in these revenues, these effects are impossible to identify and I will ignore them. I will focus therefore only on the effects of this relative price change. These effects depend, of course, on the assumptions made.

Suppose first that the countries of the bloc are characterized by an extreme specific factors model, in which all factors are specific to their respective industries. In that case all factors gain or lose in proportion to the changes in the prices of the goods they help to produce. Trade liberalization will therefore benefit or harm individual countries within the bloc depending on whether each shares or does not share the trade pattern of the bloc as a whole. Thus, in a two-good model in which the bloc as a whole exports good M and imports good A (which is the configuration I will assume throughout the paper), each country within the bloc that also exports good M will be a net gainer from trade liberalization, and each country (if any) that imports good M will lose. Of course in this case it is really the factors that are employed in producing good M that gain, wherever they may live, and the factors that are employed in producing good A that lose. But when you add up the incomes of the factors in any geographic entity, such as a country, the answer will depend on how many of each are present, and that will in turn be reflected in the country's trade pattern.

In the more conventional and less extreme version of the specific factors model, known also as the Ricardo–Viner model, in which, say, land is specific in each sector but labour is mobile throughout, only the owners of land necessarily gain and lose along with the fortunes of their industries of employment. Workers, now assumed mobile both between industries and throughout the trading bloc, are all affected the same and in an ambiguous direction, depending on their preferences for consuming the two goods. If labour's preferences are representative of the trading bloc as a whole, then all labour will tend to share in the fortunes of the bloc as a whole, and will therefore gain from trade liberalization unless adverse terms of trade effects bias the outcome unduly.[2] Thus, in this model, countries within the trading bloc will all tend to gain, through their mobile workers, and will differ among themselves only to the extent that their specific factors, land, are employed in different industries. Thus a country that is a net exporter of the bloc's import, good A, may lose from liberalization, as in the extreme specific factors model, but it need not. If labour is a sufficiently important input or if the country has a substantial presence in the other industry (good M) as well, then the gains to labour and to M-industry land can outweigh the losses to A-industry land. Still, the primary determinant of each country's gain or loss from trade liberalization is its pattern of trade relative to the trade of the trading bloc as a whole.

Finally, consider the Heckscher–Ohlin model. Here, with both factors mobile among sectors, and assuming FPE across countries within the bloc, it is the ownership of factors, not the industry of employment, that determines who gains and loses from trade. Assume that the A-good is land intensive and the M-good is labour intensive, and also as before that the bloc as a whole is a net exporter of the M-good. Then, from the Stolper–Samuelson Theorem, labour will gain and land will lose, in real terms, from trade liberalization. The distribution of these gains across the countries of the trading bloc therefore depends only on the distribution of the factors among the countries. However, the distribution of factors also determines the outputs of the countries, and it is again true that each country in the aggregate will gain or lose from trade liberalization depending on whether it is a net exporter or a net importer of good M, the export of the trading bloc as a whole.[3]

Thus, in all of these traditional models the main determinant of a country's stake in trade liberalization is its pattern of trade relative to that of the trading bloc. One thing to watch for in the lumpy country analysis below is whether this continues to be true there.

Another thing to watch for is the effect of trade liberalization on the flows of factors (labour) among countries of the trading bloc, if such flows are permitted to occur.[4] In the case of a common market, the defining characteristic is that these flows can occur, yet in two of the three models just considered they do not. In the extreme specific factors model, labour in the same sector is paid the same in all countries, and therefore has no incentive to move. Likewise, in the Heckscher–Ohlin model, FPE assures that outcome as well.[5] In the Ricardo–Viner model, labour may move across countries in response to trade liberalization, but the movements do not appear to be large or easily described. Starting with the same wage in two countries, for example, a drop in the price of the A-good will cause a somewhat smaller drop in the wage in both countries. Which country will experience the greater wage decline depends on various shares and elasticities of the production functions. As I will observe below, in a lumpy country the changes can be more systematic and more pronounced.

2   A lumpy country with immobile factors

To begin the lumpy country analysis, assume that the trading bloc (which plays the role of the lumpy country) produces two goods, A = agriculture and M = manufactures, using two factors, L = labour and T = land, in two countries, F = France and G = Germany (which play the role of the regions in the lumpy country). The names are for mnemonic convenience and are not intended to represent the realities of the actual goods, factors, and countries of these names. Without loss of generality I assume that agriculture is relatively land intensive and that France is relatively land abundant.

I also assume, with considerable loss of generality, that the two countries together face exogenous prices, that the bloc as a whole is a net exporter of manufactures, and that when, in later sections, one factor becomes mobile across countries of the bloc, it is labour that moves. In the tradition of the Heckscher–Ohlin model, I assume henceforth that both factors are perfectly mobile within each country between sectors. All markets are perfectly competitive; production functions are neoclassical with constant returns to scale; there are no factor intensity reversals; and where necessary preferences are identical and homothetic.

As explained in Courant and Deardorff (1992), the various possible patterns of specialization and trade for the two countries can be mapped out as in the box diagram of figure 5.1. The dimensions of the box are the endowments of labour and land of the trading bloc as a whole. Factors located in France are measured from the lower left corner, factors in Germany from the upper right. Assuming that France has relatively more land than Germany, I will restrict attention to the portion of the box above the upward-sloping diagonal (not shown).

Given the prices for A and M faced by producers within the bloc and determined by exogenous world prices and trade barriers, production of

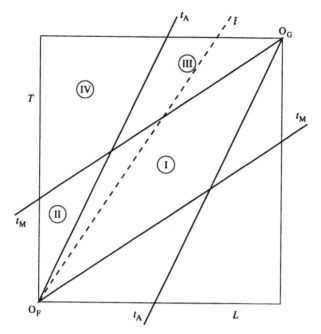

Figure 5.1   Regions of specialization in a lumpy common market

both goods within a single country will be possible only if certain unique factor prices prevail, and the factors will then be employed in the ratios t_A and t_M respectively, the determination of which will be explained below in figure 5.2. This will in turn be possible only if the factor endowments of the country lie between these two ratios. These ratios therefore delimit several regions of specialization in the box, denoted by Roman numerals.

In region I, endowments of both France and Germany lie between these ratios, and there is therefore FPE between them and incomplete specialization.[6] In region II, France has too much land to be kept fully employed at these factor ratios, and it therefore specializes instead in good A. Germany here continues to produce both goods and to have the factor prices of region I, but in France wages are higher and rents are lower than in Germany. In region III, this situation is reversed, with France producing both goods and Germany specialized in M. Now France has the factor prices of region I, while Germany has both a higher rent and a lower wage. Finally, in region IV, both countries specialize – France in A and Germany in M – and their factor prices both depart from region I but in opposite directions. Note that, throughout regions II, III, and IV, the wage in France is above that in Germany.

Patterns of trade of the bloc as a whole are somewhat indeterminate, because in all regions both goods are being produced in at least one of the countries. I therefore simply assume that preferences and prices are such that the bloc as a whole exports good M.[7] This is represented in the figure by defining $\hat{t}$ as the ratio of land to labour that would lead, at the prevailing prices, to outputs of A and M in the same ratio as they are demanded. It follows that a ray with the slope $\hat{t}$ must be steeper than the diagonal of the box but flatter than t_A (since along t_A only A is produced).

More interesting and important for the current purpose, however, are the patterns of trade of the separate countries within the trading bloc. These can be inferred from the patterns of specialization. In regions II and IV, for example, because France produces only good A, it must export it. And because by assumption the bloc as a whole imports good A, France in these regions must export it to Germany. Germany in turn must export even more of good M, both to France and to the rest of the world. In region III, France produces both goods, and its trade pattern depends on whether it produces more or less of good A than it demands. To the left of $\hat{t}$, therefore, it exports good A (to Germany) while to the right of $\hat{t}$ it imports A (from the rest of world).

Now consider the effects of a trade liberalization that lowers the domestic relative price of good A. This changes everything. The new goods price will lead to a new set of factor prices consistent with incomplete specialization, new factor input ratios corresponding to those factor prices, and therefore a new set of regions in the box diagram. For my purposes here, however, it is sufficient to look only at where the countries start out in the box, and then use familiar results from the Heckscher–Ohlin model to infer the effects on their respective factor markets. To help recall these familiar results, figure 5.2 illustrates the effects of a price change using the Lerner–Pearce diagram.

The solid curves represent the initial situation, in which unit value isoquants for goods A and M imply a common tangent that is the unit isocost line consistent with producing both goods. Rays from the origin through the two tangencies indicate the factor input ratios t_A and t_M of figure 5.1, while the intercepts of the isocost line measure the (reciprocals of) the initial FPE factor prices. A country with endowments between t_A and t_M will have these factor prices. A country with more land per labour than t_A, on the other hand, will produce only A, as at point a, and will have factor prices given by the isocost line tangent at that point. Likewise, a country with less land per labour than

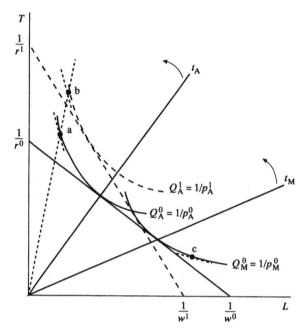

Figure 5.2 The effects of a drop in price of good A on factor prices with and without specialization

t_M will produce at a point such as c and have the factor prices indicated there.

When trade liberalization causes the domestic relative price of A, p_A, to fall, this will shift the unit value isoquant for A proportionally outward to the dashed curve shown as $Q_A^1 = 1/p_A^1$ (taking good M as numéraire). The common tangent rotates to the dashed line shown, with intercepts measuring a rise in wages, w, and a fall in rents, r (which is more than proportional to the price change – the Stolper–Samuelson result of a real decline). The factor input rays also rotate counter-clockwise to pass through the new tangencies, but I omit them from the figure to reduce clutter.

What happens to factor prices clearly depends on a country's factor endowments and its resulting pattern of specialization. If it produces both goods, then the Stolper–Samuelson results obtain, the wage rising and the rent falling more than in proportion to the price change. If it produces only good M, as at point c, then there is no change in its factor prices in units of the numéraire good M, but both factor prices increase in real terms owing to the fall in p_A. And if it produces only good A, then it moves from a point such as a proportionally outward to b, and both the wage and the rent fall by the fall in p_A, thus falling also in real terms. All of these changes are strictly correct only if the patterns of specialization remain unchanged. Since the cone of diversification rotates, this may not be the case – a country specialized in A may come to produce both goods and a country producing both goods may come to specialize in M. I ignore these possibilities because they are really just hybrids of the other cases.

Returning to figure 5.1, I can now report what happens to factor prices, both absolutely and comparatively across countries, for each region of the box.[8] In region II, where France specializes and Germany does not, both factor prices fall in France, while in Germany the rent also falls (by even more) and the wage rises. We are so far holding factor locations fixed, but there is apparently an incentive for labour to leave France. In region III, with the opposite pattern of specialization, real factor prices both rise in Germany, while French labour gains even more than German labour and French land loses. Here the incentive is for labour to move into France. Finally, in region IV, both factors lose in France and both gain in Germany, and once again the incentive is for labour to leave France. I will have more to say about how these incentives translate into actual labour movement in subsequent sections of the paper.

First, however, consider what happens to the aggregate welfare of the two countries. In region IV it is easy, because both factors either gain or lose in both countries: France loses and Germany gains, unambiguously, from the trade liberalization. In regions II and III the same unambiguous conclusions follow for the one country that specializes. What about the country that does not?

In region II, Germany, with a land–labour ratio less than that for the trading bloc as a whole, must be producing a higher ratio of M to A than the bloc demands and is therefore a net exporter of M. The rise in its relative price is therefore a terms of trade improvement, and we can be sure that Germany as a whole gains. That is, while German workers gain and landowners lose, the total gain for the former must be larger than the loss to the latter.

In region III it is France that produces both goods and French workers who gain while French landowners lose. Which of these changes is larger will again depend on the French net trade. To the left of $\hat{t}$ France exports A and the fall in p_A is a worsening of the French terms of trade. France as a country therefore loses, its landowners losing more than its workers gain. To the right of $\hat{t}$, on the other hand, the reverse is true.

Thus we see that trade liberalization can have quite different effects on the welfare of the countries of a trading bloc depending on the pattern of specialization. For each factor, there exist patterns of specialization for which they gain and others for which they lose in particular countries. And even for the countries as a whole, in the case of France even national welfare can go either way depending on how France individually (not the bloc as a whole) trades. The only change that is unambiguous is the national welfare of Germany, which, because it is assumed to share the comparative advantage of the bloc as a whole, always rises.

3   Mobile labour with amenities

An obvious problem with the above analysis is that it assumes that factors are immobile across countries. In the context of the European Union, where barriers to factor mobility have supposedly been removed, this is inappropriate. Even in the NAFTA, there is considerable mobility of at least some factors among the member countries.[9] And it is also troubling, because the 'lumpy country' cases that I have considered – regions II–IV of figure 5.1 as opposed to region I – are precisely those where factor prices differ across countries and one might expect factors to move if permitted to. Indeed, if I now allow labour to be mobile across countries and do nothing else, then labour will move out of Germany and into France as long as the wage is higher in France, as it is throughout regions II–IV, and the equilibrium labour allocation will be found only in region I. There, with FPE, both countries produce both goods and most of the interesting cases of section 2 of the paper disappear.

In Courant and Deardorff (1992), and more fully in Courant and Deardorff (1993), we addressed this problem by replacing the exogenous difference in factor endowments with an exogenous difference in something else that would matter for the location of labour, and thus were able to maintain lumpiness in the factor allocation as an equilibrium result rather than as an exogenous assumption. One such difference was in consumer amenities, which I now consider in this section.[10] Then in the next section I instead allow lumpiness to arise endogenously from a cause that we have not considered before, a difference in production subsidies.

Suppose then that labour is mobile between countries but that workers care not only about the wage but also about the levels of consumer amenities, which differ across countries. Specifically, assume that, say, the climate in Germany is more pleasant than that in France (*pardonnez-moi, mesdames et messieurs*), and that workers will therefore migrate into Germany until a sufficient wage premium is paid in France to compensate those who remain in France for staying there.[11]

Equilibrium is now found, within a box diagram like figure 5.1, only within regions II–IV, along a locus where the appropriate wage differential occurs. Since factor prices in a country are constant both throughout the diversification cone and also along any ray from the origin outside that cone, this equilibrium locus must consist of rays from the respective origins in regions II and III, connected by a curve in region IV. This is shown as the solid curve, $O_F A B O_G$, in figure 5.3.

Trade liberalization now causes the same changes shown in figure 5.2 and requires redrawing both the regions of specialization and this labour market equilibrium locus in figure 5.3. I omit the former to reduce clutter; they would be derived from steeper rays for both t_A and t_M, and thus lead to a revised region I that is skewed somewhat toward the sides of the box and away from its top and bottom. The revised labour market equilibrium locus is shown as the broken curve, $O_F A' B' O_G$. A' is its intersection with the new (undrawn) t'_M ray from O_G, and B' is its intersection with the new (undrawn) t'_A ray from O_F. Note that it lies to the left of the old locus throughout region II and to the right of it throughout region III, crossing it in region IV somewhere near its upper end.[12]

This pattern reflects the incentives for labour movement that were noted in the previous section. For example, if the land is mostly German, so that we start in region II of the box, with Germany producing both goods and France only good A, then trade liberalization causes a decline in the French wage and a rise in the German wage. Since the wage differential favouring France initially just compensated for its poorer climate, the new wages no longer will, and labour will migrate out of France. The new equilibrium will be found to the left of the old, with less labour in France and a wage differential equal to the old. In contrast, if France has more of the land, so that the initial equilibrium is in region III, with France producing both goods and Germany only good M, then the Stolper–Samuelson effect on the French wage instead increases the wage differential relative to Germany and causes labour to migrate in the other direction to restore the equilibrium wage differential. Finally, through most of region IV, where both countries specialize, trade liberalization also causes labour to migrate out of France, except for a small range of land allocations where the liberalization is sufficient to cause France to begin producing both goods.

What are the final effects on the factor prices and country welfare? Welfare has to be somewhat problematic now, because it is not obvious with which country a migrating worker should be included. I will focus on the effects on the countries' initial populations, which obviously could already include people who are citizens of the other.

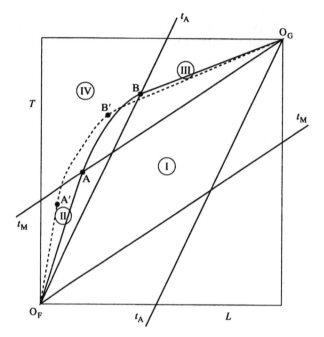

Figure 5.3   The effects of trade liberalization on labour market equilibrium

Start again with region II, where only France specializes. Trade liberalization initially harms both French landowners and French workers, but now the migration of labour brings the wage of French workers back up to the equilibrium premium above the German wage. Not only that, because the price change has caused a Stolper–Samuelson increase in the real wage in Germany, the new French wage must be even higher than at the start. So French workers clearly gain from the liberalization in this case. French landowners, on the other hand, lose even more than they did when labour was immobile, because the loss of workers has lowered the marginal product of land.

What happens to the welfare of France as a whole? Certainly its national income goes down, because it suffers not only a fall in its terms of trade but also a loss of population. Allowing for the increased incomes of the departing workers, however, it seems possible that the real income of the entire French initial population might rise. In Germany, too, landowners lose and workers gain, but here the country as a whole surely gains, because the terms of trade improve for the initial population and factor prices remain unchanged (owing to FPE) during the inflow of workers from France.

Consider next region III, where only Germany specializes. Here French workers gain and landowners lose owing to Stolper–Samuelson effects, and these factor prices remain fixed by FPE as migration occurs, this time from Germany into France. The French initial population now either gains or loses, depending on its pattern of trade and thus its initial position relative to the $\hat{t}$ ray of figure 5.1. Of course, French national income may rise with the immigration.

In Germany, both factors initially gain owing to the cheapening of the A-good, which they do not produce. The emigration of labour to France, however, causes the wage to rise further and the rent to fall, and it is not clear whether landowners end up better off or worse off. And although national income must fall with the departure of labour, I do not think one can determine necessarily the final effect on the overall real income of the aggregate initial German population.

Finally, consider region IV, where both countries completely specialize, and assume that both continue to specialize after the price change (thus ignoring the hybrid case of the slight possibility that labour flows into France). Here the initial decline in the rent in France and the rise in the rent in Germany are both enhanced by the effects of the labour flows from France to Germany. For workers, on the other hand, the labour flow restores the original wage differential in favour of France, undoing part or all of the harm to French workers and part or all of the gain to German workers. The net effect on both is ambiguous, in much the same way that the effect of a price change on labour in the Ricardo–Viner model is ambiguous. There would seem to be a presumption that the initial population of France loses in the aggregate from all of this, and that the initial population of Germany gains, but again I have not been able to verify this for sure.

The conclusion from this analysis is not any simple general rule, unfortunately. Rather, what lumpiness seems to mean is that the effects of liberalization, especially on factor owners, cannot be known without reference to the particular pattern of specialization that obtains among the countries of the trading bloc and how this pattern may interact with factor mobility.

4   Mobile labour with a production subsidy

There are many possible reasons for factor prices to differ across countries in the presence of factor mobility. Consumer amenities were chosen above largely because of their simplicity. In Courant and Deardorff (1993) we have also considered producer amenities and differences in the availability of non-traded goods, and undoubtedly many other causes are possible as well. In the context of the Uruguay Round, however, one such cause may be of particular interest: subsidies to production in agriculture. Agricultural subsidies were especially contentious in the Uruguay Round, and in the end very little was done to remove them. The discussion drew attention to their presence, however. It is interesting therefore that a production subsidy to a single sector in a single country of a trading bloc can have very similar effects on patterns of specialization and the effects of trade liberalization as other causes of lumpiness.

In this section, then, I will examine such a case, in which one country of the trading bloc provides a production subsidy to one sector, agriculture. I continue to assume identical technologies across countries of the bloc, so it is not the case that the subsidy is being used to compensate for differences in productivity. As such, although I will continue to call the countries France and Germany, the model really does not address the reality of the Common Agricultural Policy in the European Union. For this section especially, then, it is probably best to think of the analysis as applying with changed names of countries and factors to the NAFTA.

Suppose, then, that France subsidizes production of the A-good with a simple, fixed, *ad valorem* subsidy of size s and that Germany does not. Consumer amenities are now excluded, so that the mobile factor (labour) will again move to equalize wages across countries. The presence of the subsidy, however, will prevent that from happening without at least one country specializing, as before.

This may be seen in figure 5.4, which shows the effects of such a production subsidy in the Lerner–Pearce diagram. Here the solid curves represent unit value isoquants for Germany and the dashed curves represent them for France. The subsidy s on A-good output pulls the unit value isoquant for that good in France toward the origin by s per cent. Unit isocost lines indicate the factor prices that are consistent with incomplete specialization in both countries, and they are evidently different. If wages are equalized by labour mobility, then at least one country must specialize. For example, if Germany produces both goods, so that the wage is w_G^0, then this same wage must also prevail in France, requiring a unit isocost line (not shown) with the same labour intercept as in Germany. But this will be tangent only to the Q_A^F isoquant, at some factor ratio between t_A^F and t_A^G. Alternatively, if both goods are produced in France, then w_F^0 will prevail in both countries and Germany will use factor ratio t_M^F to produce only good M. Of course it is also possible that both countries will specialize completely.

These possibilities give rise to the configuration in figure 5.5, a box diagram that once again maps out patterns of specialization and shows

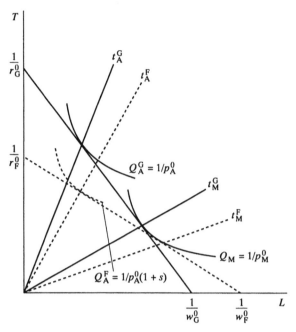

Figure 5.4   Comparison of factor prices with and without an agricultural subsidy

the labour market equilibrium locus. It is very similar to figures 5.1 and 5.3. The only qualitative difference in appearance is that region I is no longer a parallelogram, because the factor rays are different in the two countries. A more important difference underlies the picture, however: factor prices are not equalized in region I; rather the wage is lower and the rent higher in France than in Germany throughout this region, as determined in figure 5.4. Equality of wages is now found only on the labour market equilibrium locus, which is again drawn as O_FABO_G. As before it is composed of straight segments in regions II and III and a curve in region IV. In this case, the straight segment in region II, O_FA, is known from figure 5.4 to be intermediate in slope between t_A^F and t_A^G, while the segment BO_G is parallel to t_M^F.

None of this matters very much for the way the model behaves, however. Indeed, the situation is so similar to what was seen before that I have chosen not to complete the analysis by drawing additional curves in figure 5.5. Instead I merely note that trade liberalization will affect both countries individually, exactly as it did in figure 5.2, and the labour market equilibrium locus of figure 5.5 will therefore shift in exactly the same manner as that of figure 5.3. Thus figure 5.3 can be applied directly

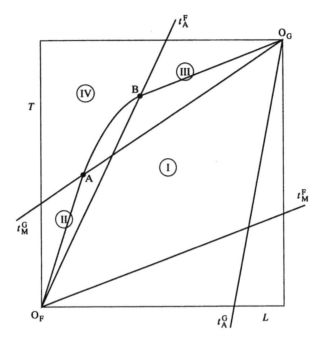

Figure 5.5   Labour market equilibrium with a French subsidy to agriculture

to the case of an agricultural production subsidy in France instead of to an amenity, the only difference being the unimportant shape of region I.

The conclusions therefore are also the same, and I will not repeat them in detail. When patterns of specialization differ across countries owing to a production subsidy, the effects of trade liberalization will once again be very different for the factors in the two countries. Exactly how they differ, however, will depend on which of the two countries specializes completely, and trade liberalization may cause the mobile factor to flow either into or out of the subsidizing country.

4.1   Subsidy reduction

In addition to trade liberalization and many other issues that I do not touch on here, the Uruguay Round also included negotiations over farm subsidies. Not a great deal was achieved in that area, but because some slight reduction in subsidies was agreed upon (and greater reductions were contemplated), it is interesting to examine how a reduction in the subsidy would affect the economies in this lumpy country analysis.

In figure 5.4, a reduction in the subsidy to, say, half the value shown would shift the French unit value isoquant for the A-good to a position halfway between Q_A^F and Q_A^G. This will rotate the French factor input rays counter-clockwise toward, but not all the way to, the German ones. The ratios of factors that would be used in each country at the other country's wage will also rotate in this direction. Together, these observations mean that the reduction in subsidy will have the following effects on figure 5.5: the top and right sides of region I will remain unchanged, but the bottom and left sides will rotate counter-clockwise, thus shifting up and to the left respectively; the labour market equilibrium locus will shift throughout its length, becoming steeper in both of regions II and III. Thus the shift of the locus (not shown) due to a cut in the subsidy is qualitatively similar to the shift found for trade liberalization in figure 5.3.

The effects on factors in the two countries are not quite the same, however. First, because I have assumed no subsidy in Germany and fixed prices, the cut in the French subsidy will have no effect on factors in Germany except possibly as a result of labour migration. In region II, where German factor prices are fixed by FPE, both German land and labour are unaffected even when the cut in the French subsidy causes workers to migrate to Germany. In region III, however, where Germany produces only good M, migration out of Germany causes the German wage to rise and its rent to fall.

In France, the effects are somewhat more similar to what happened with trade liberalization. In region II, producing only good A, the cut in subsidy causes an initial drop in both the wage and the rent, but the induced flow of workers to Germany returns the wage to its initial level and forces the rent even lower. In region III, producing both goods, the cut in subsidy causes a Stolper–Samuelson drop in the rent and a rise in the wage. The rise in the wage attracts labour from Germany but causes no further change in factor prices. Finally, in region IV, where both countries specialize and assuming that they continue to do so in the new equilibrium, French rents and wages both fall initially. The resulting labour flow from France to Germany partially reverses the wage decline while causing the rent to fall even further. In Germany, the labour inflow causes wages to fall and rents to rise.

These changes, especially in region IV, might seem to make France as a country unambiguously worse off, because both the wage and the rent have fallen. However this ignores the cost of providing the subsidy itself. No doubt one could show that the French government gains more than the factors lose when the subsidy is reduced. But this too would not tell the whole story if one allows for any possibility that the subsidy was motivated by some legitimate distortion or non-economic objective. I therefore decline to judge the net effect of the subsidy reduction on France as a whole.

In Germany, one might have expected a loss to follow from a reduction in the French subsidy, to the extent that Germans would now have to pay more for food. But the fixity of world prices in this model prevents that effect. Instead, either Germany is unaffected, if by producing both goods its factor prices are fixed by FPE, or it gains. The gain occurs if Germany specializes in M and labour flows in either direction. If workers migrate into Germany (as in the part of region IV considered above), their average product exceeds their marginal product for which they are paid, and the initial German population pockets the difference. If German workers migrate to France (as in the rest of region IV and all of region III), they earn a wage that exceeds their marginal product in Germany, and again the initial German population, including the migrants, gains.

5   Conclusion

Results from the previous sections are summarized in table 5.1. Signs indicate the effects I have derived above on real incomes of the factors. The main conclusion from this analysis is not any simple rule for the effects of the policy changes on the countries or their individual factors. Rather it is that, in a lumpy country, one really needs to know the patterns of specialization before one can infer what most of these effects will be. To the extent that the countries of the transatlantic economy, because of their participation in the trading blocs of the European Union and the NAFTA, are well represented by a lumpy country, this lesson would apply there as well. Notice in table 5.1, for example, that the effects on French labour and on German land are extremely mixed in this sense.

On the other hand, for the particular problems addressed here there is also one result that happens independently of patterns of specialization. French landowners lose both from trade liberalization and from the cut in subsidy in all cases. This is not surprising, and the adverse effect of cutting subsidies was obviously fully understood by French farmers during the Uruguay Round negotiations. What was perhaps less well understood was that trade liberalization would also hurt them. Note that this is true even if the Europeans themselves do not reduce trade barriers in agriculture. Trade liberalization in other countries of the world that are net exporters of agricultural goods will lower world agricultural prices and also have these effects.

I hesitate, however, to take the analysis here at all seriously as a

Table 5.1.   The effects of trade liberalization and subsidy reduction in a lumpy country model: effects on land (T) and labour (L) in France and Germany

	Specialization[1]	France			Germany		
		T	L	T+L	T	L	T+L
Trade liberalization[2]							
Immobile labour	II: F	−	−	−	−	+	+
	III: G	−	+	−[3]	+	+	+
	IV: F&G	−	−	−	+	+	+
Mobile labour	II: F	−	+	?	−	+	+
	III: G	−	+	−[3]	?	+	?
	IV: F&G	−	?	?	+	?	?
Cut in French subsidy	II: F	−	0		0	0	0
to agriculture[4]	III: G	−	+		−	+	+
	IV: F&G	−	−		+	−	+

[1] The results assume that patterns of specialization do not change as a result of the policy changes.
[2] The effects of trade liberalization ignore the distribution of tariff revenue.
[3] The sign assumes that France is a net exporter of good A.
[4] The effects of subsidy on France as a whole are not indicated, because these would have to include also the budgetary cost of the subsidy and its benefits in terms of correcting distortions or yielding non-economic benefits.

description of the actual effects that might occur from the Uruguay Round in Europe or in North America. As I said early on, the names of the countries were selected for mnemonic convenience, not because I was really trying to capture the reality of France and Germany. Whether the assumptions made here are even loosely accurate for these countries, I have no idea. The point is therefore not that these particular results will obtain. Rather it is that a more formal empirical analysis of what the effects of the Uruguay Round will be, in both Europe and North America, should acknowledge the fact that these countries are parts of trading blocs that therefore have some of the characteristics of lumpy countries. A proper analysis should take the effects of lumpiness into account.

NOTES

I have benefited from the comments and suggestions of Bill Ethier, Bob Stern, and Alan Winters. Partial financial support in writing this paper was provided by a grant from the Ford Foundation.

1 I ignore here, and in what follows, both the Metzler paradox and the Lerner paradox.
2 This is essentially the result of Ruffin and Jones (1977). Actually, the possibility of an adverse terms of trade effect should be ignored here since I am abstracting from the distribution of the tariff revenues. A tariff cut that lowers the domestic relative price of the imported good can benefit only workers who consume a preponderance of that good unless they also lose transfer income that would have been financed by tariff revenues.
3 Because of FPE, each country in the bloc can really be considered independently, because there will be no incentive for factors to move among countries even if they can. Therefore the welfare effect on each country depends only on its own terms of trade, which depend in turn only on its trade pattern compared with the internal price change for the bloc as a whole.
4 In the model, the factors are called labour and land, with labour the factor that is sometimes mobile among countries of the bloc. This is appropriate for the case of the European Union. For NAFTA, a better choice might be land and capital, with capital mobile across countries. The reader can supply that interpretation where appropriate.
5 Though in fact it may be necessary for some factors to move in order to maintain FPE. This will become clear in the lumpy country model.
6 Recalling that domestic prices are not necessarily the same as world prices, because of trade barriers, FPE here refers only to comparison of countries within the bloc and not to comparison with countries outside.
7 In Courant and Deardorff (1992) we assumed (with free trade) that prices happened to be such that the lumpy country would not trade at all in region I. This was done in order to isolate the effects of lumpiness on trade. Here I need an underlying pattern of trade to persist in order to focus on trade liberalization, and I therefore cannot map out the net trade pattern as we did there.
8 See table 5.1 on page 165 for a summary of these and later results.
9 Again, in NAFTA a more appropriate choice of factors might be land and capital, with capital mobile across countries.
10 In applying this analysis to NAFTA, if one replaces mobile labour with mobile capital, as suggested in previous notes, the consumer amenity no longer serves the purpose of creating lumpiness. However, similar results can be obtained with what in Courant and Deardorff (1993) we called production amenities, which are international differences in production functions or (immobile) factor productivities.
11 In Courant and Deardorff (1993) we also allowed for the possibility of congestion, so that equilibrium might in some cases be found within the FPE region. I will ignore that possibility here.
12 The crossing occurs at a point to the right of the new t'_A ray, which is not shown in the figure. It could be derived in figure 5.2 by constructing a straight line from the $(1/w^1)$ intercept tangent to the Q_A^0 isoquant, and noting the land–labour ratio at that tangency.

REFERENCES

Courant, Paul N. and Alan V. Deardorff (1992), 'International Trade with Lumpy Countries', *Journal of Political Economy* **100** (February), 198–210.

(1993), 'Amenities, Nontraded Goods, and the Trade of Lumpy Countries', *Journal of Urban Economics* **34**, 229–317.
Ruffin, Roy J. and Ronald W. Jones (1977), 'Protection and Real Wages: The Neoclassical Ambiguity', *Journal of Economic Theory* **14**, 337–48.

Discussion

L. ALAN WINTERS

This is a very stimulating paper and also a very readable one. Alan Deardorff takes a complex model and makes it accessible to a wide audience. In its focus on sub-national geographical entities (regions of a country, countries in a union), it is a close relation of the new economic geography, but it uses only neoclassical tools; in particular, it is rooted in the tradition of perfect competition. The basic idea is that, if at least one of two regions in a country lies outside the cone of diversification, national trade liberalization will have different effects in different regions. One of the nice features of the model is that lying outside the cone is not a matter of mere coincidence, but can actually be induced by distortions in the initial, pre-liberalization, conditions.

I have two sets of comments. The larger comprises a plea to Deardorff (and his co-author Courant) to return to this model and add back into the analysis the consideration of the revenue effects of their various policies. This will allow them to explore welfare effects more fully, and also to capture an important aspect of interregional economics and politics – transfers. For example, Deardorff assumes that the consumer amenity of France relative to Germany is a natural phenomenon, whereas one might equally well think of it as being due to local public goods. If some of these are funded centrally – as, for example, with EU Cohesion Funds – then transfers become immediately relevant and movements of population may have additional welfare effects on different regions. A second dimension where revenues matter is the consideration of simultaneous agricultural subsidies and tariffs. This requires second-best analysis, which is absent in this paper; one of the principal components of such analysis will be the effect of liberalization on the cost of the agricultural subsidy via its effects on agricultural output.

In fact, it would be nice to model the agricultural subsidy more pertinently. There are elements of the EU's agricultural policy that permit, but do not oblige, national authorities to subsidize local agriculture from local funds (as Deardorff has assumed), but in general the spending on the CAP emanates from the central authorities and population at large (in effect partly financed by a more or less uniform tax on consumers of food). Thus changes in the size of different members' agricultural sectors have transfer implications. More realistically still, the policy is supposed to be common across member countries. This poses more problems for Deardorff's model, for a uniform agricultural subsidy would not of itself guarantee that one country starts from outside the cone of diversification, although once one of them was outside and if there was no migration (Deardorff's first case) the subsidy would have non-uniform effects on factor prices in the two countries. In these circumstances and if the subsidy were the only policy, liberalization would essentially correspond to Deardorff's first case, except that in figure 5.1 liberalization would also shift the t-line, along which factor supplies just satisfy domestic demand. If there were both a subsidy and a tariff, the analysis of reducing the tariff would proceed more or less as in the paper, except that, by reducing French agricultural output, liberalization would reduce the transfer to the agriculture-intensive French economy.

Possibly a more fruitful approach to modelling common agricultural policies would be to let the policy be a price-floor, which may induce lumpiness, or to extend the model to include some specific factors.

My second comment is to observe that this model is essentially a three-country model in which two countries share the same trade policy, offer each other mutual preferences, and, possibly, have mutual factor flows. This raises the question of how that common trade policy is determined. Deardorff's model is ideally placed for analysing these sorts of issues. National governments are the ultimate players in the EU trade policy game and they are influenced by consideration of output, employment, and migration as well as by economic welfare simply interpreted. Deardorff makes starkly clear the divergence of interest in liberalization between different EU members. All that remains is to put some numbers to his model to generate some real predictions!

6 The increased importance of direct investment in North Atlantic economic relationships: a convergence hypothesis

JAMES R. MARKUSEN and ANTHONY J. VENABLES

1 Introduction

A number of researchers have noted the evolution of trade and investment among the developed economies. The increased importance of intra-industry trade relative to inter-industry trade has been noted, along with the fact that trade volumes have risen much faster than GNP levels. Somewhat less appreciated is the fact that direct foreign investment has similarly risen in importance, especially among the developed countries. Much recent trade theory has been devoted to trying to explain the rise of intra-industry trade and trade volumes relative to GNP, whereas there has been little effort to explain the rise in direct investment.[1]

Table 6.1 presents some data on bilateral trade and investment flows between the USA and Europe. These data are graphed in figures 6.1 and 6.2. Figure 6.1 graphs the outward trade flow and investment stock from the USA to Europe. The data reveal that both US exports to Europe and US direct investment in Europe have increased greatly over the twenty-four-year period shown, and indeed that direct investment stocks have grown slightly faster than the value of exports. Figure 6.2 gives the corresponding figures for European exports to and direct investment in the USA (data limitations unfortunately give us only eighteen years). Here we see dramatic evidence that direct investment from Europe has grown much faster than have exports from Europe. Whereas exports from Europe multiplied about 6.5 times in the eighteen-year period, European direct investment stocks in the USA multiplied about 24 times.

The most simple conceptual model of horizontal direct investment, the focus of this paper, seems to be an unlikely candidate for explaining these data.[2] Such a model envisions direct investment as primarily induced by tariff and transport-cost barriers. The savings in variable costs by 'jumping' the trade barriers outweigh any increase in fixed costs

169

Table 6.1.   US and European trade and direct foreign investment (US$m.)

Year	US exports[1]	US DFI[2]	European exports[1]	European DFI[2]
1966	9,100	16,390	7,410	–
1967	9,310	18,231	7,800	–
1968	10,480	19,851	9,830	–
1969	11,900	22,246	10,110	–
1970	13,060	25,255	10,988	–
1971	13,670	28,654	12,930	–
1972	14,806	31,696	15,412	11,087
1973	20,581	38,255	19,159	13,937
1974	27,626	44,782	22,994	16,756
1975	28,798	49,621	20,222	18,584
1976	31,410	55,139	22,440	20,162
1977	32,613	62,552	28,342	23,754
1978	37,940	70,647	36,008	27,895
1979	49,165	83,056	41,550	37,403
1980	65,817	96,287	44,040	45,731
1981	60,015	102,601	48,753	57,705
1982	55,934	99,525	48,755	83,193
1983	52,832	102,689	53,354	92,936
1984	53,773	103,663	66,962	106,567
1985	52,073	105,371	74,488	121,413
1986	55,879	123,183	84,710	144,181
1987	63,487	150,439	95,170	186,076
1988	79,633	156,932	97,288	216,418
1989	92,594	176,736	99,306	262,011

[1] Export data are taken from the United Nations *Yearbook of International Trade Statistics*, vol. 1 (various years), and list exports F.O.B. from the USA to the developed market economies of Europe, or vice versa.
[2] DFI data are taken from the *Survey of Current Business* (various years) in the August issue. The data show the foreign investment position of the United States in Europe (or vice versa) as a stock, including the reinvestment of equity capital in the respective foreign affiliates.

or loss of scale economies from serving both the domestic and foreign markets from separate plants. Although we should be suspicious of casual empiricism, our first guess would surely be that tariff and transport costs have fallen relative to other costs over the past several decades. Tariffs and other trade barriers have clearly fallen.

The purpose of this paper is to draw on both the modern industrial-organization approach to international trade and the related theory of the multinational, in order to investigate how the differences or similarities between two countries influence volumes of horizontal direct investment relative to trade. In particular, we seek to understand how

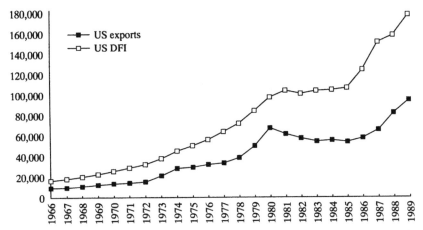

Figure 6.1 US exports to Europe, and US direct foreign investment position in Europe, 1966–89 (US$ m.)

Figure 6.2 European exports to the USA, and European direct foreign investment position in the USA, 1972–89 (US$ m.)

direct investment can grow in spite of constant or falling transport costs. This will give one conceptual framework in which to understand the changing nature of North Atlantic trade and investment shown in figures 6.1 and 6.2. We hope that more formal empirical work will follow.

There are two sectors in the two-country model. One sector (Y) produces a homogeneous commodity with constant returns to scale and perfect competition. The other sector (X) produces a homogeneous commodity with increasing returns to scale and imperfect competition.[3]

There is free entry and exit of firms, which are Cournot competitors. Markets are segmented. X sector firms produce with constant marginal cost, and incur two types of fixed costs. A firm-specific fixed cost, such as an R&D cost, is incurred independently of the number of plants operated by the firm. A plant-specific fixed cost is incurred for each plant.

There are three types of firms, each of which may or may not have active numbers in equilibrium. Home firms (type h) have only one plant in the home country, and may or may not serve the foreign country by exports. Foreign firms (type f) are similarly single-plant firms located in the foreign country. Multinational firms (type m) are two-plant firms, maintaining plants in both countries. In the case of multinational firms, the firm-specific fixed cost is divided between the two countries and we make no attempt in this paper to associate multinationals as being home or foreign owned.

Although some insights can be gained analytically, the dimensionality of the model and the fact that it contains many inequalities make the usual analytical techniques of limited value. We thus simulate the model using Rutherford's (1988) non-linear complementarity software MPS/GE, solving for the parameter values that support different regimes. A 'regime' is defined as a set of firm types active (producing positive outputs) in equilibrium. For example, type m and h firms active is one regime, while type m and f firms active is another regime.

The first sets of results illustrate some fairly obvious relationships. First, multinational firms exist when the level of plant-specific fixed costs is low relative to firm-specific fixed costs. Such a situation corresponds to multi-plant economies of scale that favour two-plant production. Second, multinational firms exist when the sizes of both countries are larger, given a fixed level of transport costs. Multinationals have higher total fixed costs but lower variable costs for serving two markets relative to national firms, and thus m-firms are more likely to be profitable the larger the two markets. Both of these results are found in Brainard (1992) and Horstmann and Markusen (1992). Third, the level of transport costs is important in its relationship to marginal costs of production, and falling transport costs do not move us away from multinational production if production costs are falling just as fast.

Less obvious is a set of results that we will collectively call the 'convergence hypothesis'. Multinational production will tend to displace national firms and trade as the two countries converge in (a) relative size, (b) relative factor endowments, and (c) relative production costs.[4] We emphasize in particular that this is not due to trade simply disappearing owing to the latter two effects. As is well understood in this type of industrial-organization model, the gross volume of two-way trade can increase as the countries converge in endowments and technologies. Although inter-industry trade may tend to disappear with convergence, two-way intra-industry trade rises and possibly rises faster than inter-industry trade falls if multinational production is not allowed.

Other interesting findings include some 'non-monotonicity' results. Beginning with countries of very different size, for example, growth of the smaller country may at some point give rise to the entry of national firms in the smaller country and subsequently to the disappearance of these firms as convergence proceeds.

We hope that these results shed some light on the statistics presented in table 6.1 and figures 6.1 and 6.2, and that they will help guide more formal empirical work on North Atlantic trade.

2   Specification of the model

As noted above, the model has two countries (h and f) producing two homogeneous goods, Y and X. There are two factors of production, L (labour) and R. L is mobile between industries but internationally immobile. R is a specific factor used only in the Y industry. R acts partly to 'convexify' the model. Expansion of the X sector draws labour from the Y sector, raising the R/L ratio in the Y sector, thereby raising the cost of labour measured in terms of Y. Y will be used as numéraire throughout the paper. Labour is used for both the fixed and the variable costs in producing X and in addition there are transport costs between countries, specified as units of labour per unit of X exported.

Subscripts (i,j) will be used to denote the countries (f,h). The output of Y in country i is a Cobb–Douglas function, where R_i is country i's endowment of R. The production function for Y is identical across countries throughout the analysis.

$$Y_i = L_{iy}^\alpha R_i^{1-\alpha}, \qquad i = h, f. \tag{1}$$

Superscripts (n,m) will be used to designate a variable as referring to national firms and multinational firms respectively. (m, n_i) will also be used to indicate the number of active m-firms and n-firms in country i. It is hoped that it will always be clear from the context what is being represented (e.g. n_i as a variable in an equation always refers to the number of national firms in country i).

X_i^m denotes the production and sales by a type-m firm in country i. X_{ii}^n denotes the production of a national firm in country i that is sold in country i, and X_{ij}^n denotes the production of a national firm in country i that is exported to country j. The labour used by one national firm in country i is given by

$$L_{ix}^n = c_i(X_{ii}^n + X_{ij}^n) + G_i + F_i, \qquad i,j = h,f, \qquad i \neq j. \qquad (2)$$

where c_i is the constant marginal cost in units of labour and G_i and F_i are the plant-specific and firm-specific fixed costs in units of labour, respectively. In one experiment later in the paper, we will let these costs vary across countries, but we rather arbitrarily assume throughout the paper that these costs are common across m- and n-firms within a country. The labour used by one multinational firm in country i is given by

$$L_{ix}^m = c_i X_i^m + G_i + F_i/2, \qquad i = h,f. \qquad (3)$$

As we noted above, we assume that technology is such that the firm-specific costs of a multinational firm are divided evenly between the two countries, and we make no attempt in this paper to associate multi-nationals with individual countries.[5]

τ will denote the amount of labour needed to transport one unit of X from country i to country j. We will vary this parameter, but we will always assume that costs are symmetric in both directions, hence τ is not subscripted by country.

$$L_{i\tau}^n = \tau X_{ij}^n, \qquad i,j = h,f. \qquad (4)$$

Let $\bar{L}_i$ denote the total labour endowment of country i. The adding-up constraint on labour supply is then

$$\begin{aligned} \bar{L}_i &= L_{iy} + L_{ix} + L_{i\tau}, & (5) \\ &= L_{iy} + n_i[c_i X_{ii}^n + (c_i + \tau)X_{ij}^n + G_i + F_i] + m(c_i X_i^m + G_i + F_i/2) \end{aligned}$$

Let p_i denote the price of X and w_i the wage in country i, both measured in terms of good Y. In equilibrium the X sector makes no profits so country i income, denoted M_i, is

$$M_i = Y_i + w_i(L_{ix} + L_{i\tau}), \qquad i = h,f. \qquad (6)$$

X_{ic} and Y_{ic} denote the consumption of X and Y in country i. Utility of the representative consumer in each country is Cobb–Douglas,

$$U_i = X_{ic}^\beta Y_{ic}^{1-\beta}, \qquad X_{ic} \equiv n_i X_{ii}^n + n_j X_{ji}^n + m X_i^m, \qquad (7)$$

giving demands

$$X_{ic} = \beta M_i/p_i, \qquad Y_{ic} = (1 - \beta)M_i. \qquad (8)$$

Since the consumer is on the budget constraint, trade is balanced.

Equilibrium in the X sector is determined by pricing equations (marginal revenue equals marginal cost) and free entry conditions. We denote proportional markups of price over marginal cost by e, so e_i^m is a multinational firm's markup in market i, and e_{ii}^n and e_{ij}^n are the markups of a national firm producing in market i and selling in i and j respectively. There are six pricing equations in the model, two for type-m firms (one for each market), two for type-h firms (for domestic and export sales), and two for type-f firms. These are written in complementary-slackness form with associated variables as follows:

$$p_i(1 - e_i^m) \leq w_i c_i \qquad (X_i^m) \tag{9}$$
$$p_i(1 - e_{ii}^n) \leq w_i c_i \qquad (X_{ii}^n) \tag{10}$$
$$p_j(1 - e_{ij}^n) \leq w_i(c_i + \tau) \qquad (X_{ij}^n) \tag{11}$$

There are three zero-profit conditions corresponding to the numbers of the three firm types. Given equations (9)–(11), zero profits can be written as the requirement that markup revenues equal fixed costs.

$$p_h e_h^m X_h^m + p_f e_f^m X_f^m \leq w_h(G_h + F_h/2) + w_f(G_f + F_f/2) \quad (m) \tag{12}$$
$$p_h e_{hh}^n X_{hh}^n + p_f e_{hf}^n X_{hf}^n \leq w_h(G_h + F_h) \qquad (n_h) \tag{13}$$
$$p_f e_{ff}^n X_{ff}^n + p_h e_{fh}^n X_{fh}^n \leq w_f(G_f + F_f) \qquad (n_f) \tag{14}$$

In a Cournot model with homogeneous products, the optimal markup formula is given by the firm's market share divided by the Marshallian price elasticity of demand in that market. In our model, the price elasticity is one (see equation (8)), reducing the firm's markup to its market share. This gives (also using demand equations (8)),

$$e_i^m = \frac{X_i^m}{X_{ic}} = \frac{p_i X_i^m}{\beta M_i}, \tag{15}$$
$$e_{ij}^n = \frac{X_{ij}^n}{X_{jc}} = \frac{p_j X_{ij}^n}{\beta M_j}, \tag{16}$$
$$e_{ii}^n = \frac{X_{ii}^n}{X_{ic}} = \frac{p_i X_{ii}^n}{\beta M_i}. \tag{17}$$

Using these expressions in pricing equations gives expressions for output in terms of price,

$$X_i^m \geq \beta M_i \frac{p_i - w_i c_i}{p_i^2}, \tag{18}$$

$$X_{ij}^n \geq \beta M_i \frac{p_j - w_i(c_i + \tau)}{p_j^2}, \tag{19}$$

$$X_{ii}^n \geq \beta M_i \frac{p_j - w_i c_i}{p_i^2}. \tag{20}$$

Each of these holds with equality if the right-hand side is positive, otherwise output equals zero. If the terms are positive then the free entry conditions (12)–(14) can be expressed as:

$$\beta \left[M_h \left(\frac{p_h - w_h c_h}{p_h} \right)^2 + M_f \left(\frac{p_f - w_f c_f}{p_f} \right)^2 \right] \leq w_h(G_h + F_h/2) + w_f(G_f + F_f/2), (m) \tag{21}$$

$$\beta \left[M_h \left(\frac{p_h - w_h c_h}{p_h} \right)^2 + M_f \left(\frac{p_f - w_h(c_h + \tau)}{p_f} \right)^2 \right] \leq w_h(G_h + F_h), \qquad (n_h) \tag{22}$$

$$\beta \left[M_h \left(\frac{p_h - w_f(c_f + \tau)}{p_h} \right)^2 + M_f \left(\frac{p_f - w_f c_f}{p_f} \right)^2 \right] \leq w_f(G_f + F_f), \qquad (n_f) \tag{23}$$

To summarize the X sector in the model, the six inequalities (18)–(20) are associated with the six output levels (two each for three firm types), and the three inequalities in (21)–(23) are associated with the number of firms of each type. Additionally goods prices are given by (8), income levels from (6), and factor prices from factor market-clearing equation (5) together with labour demand from the Y sector.

3   Preliminary results: symmetric countries

In order to understand the basic properties of this model, consider the case in which h and f are identical countries. Most of the basic results have been derived in Horstmann and Markusen (1992) and Brainard (1992), so we concentrate on relating the intuition rather than re-deriving the results.

A partial equilibrium variant of the model can be illustrated diagrammatically. Suppose that the Y sector uses labour alone, and has constant returns to scale ($\alpha = 1$). Wages then equal unity in each country, and income is simply the labour endowment, so:

$$w_h = w_f = 1, \quad M_h = \bar{L}_h, \quad M_f = \bar{L}_f. \tag{24}$$

The zero profit conditions (21)–(23) now contain only two endogenous variables, p_h and p_f, and are illustrated as the curves of figure 6.3, drawn for the case of symmetric economies. Thus the curve $\pi_m = 0$ is the zero-profit locus for type-m firms; above it type-m profits are positive and below negative. In the symmetric case its gradient on the 45° line is unity.

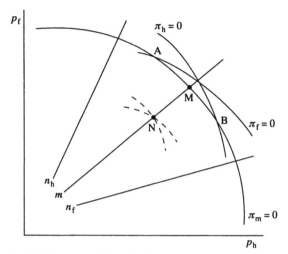

Figure 6.3   Equilibrium price determination

Curve $\pi_h = 0$ is the zero-profit locus for a national firm located in h; it is relatively steeply sloped, because, if $\tau > 0$, home profits are affected more by changes in p_h than in p_f. $\pi_f = 0$ is the analogous condition for a type-f firm.

In addition to zero-profit loci we need supply and demand information determining prices p_h and p_f. We include this on figure 6.3 as follows. Suppose that only type-m firms are active ($n_h = n_f = 0$). Then, setting the supply equal to demand for good X in each country gives,

$$mX_h^m = \beta M_h/p_h, \qquad mX_f^m = \beta M_f/p_f. \tag{25}$$

Eliminating m from these equations and using the supply equation (18) we derive,

$$p_h/(w_h c_h) = p_f/(w_f c_f). \tag{26}$$

Proceeding analogously for the case in which only n_h firms are active ($n_f = m = 0$) gives:

$$p_h/c_h = p_f/(c_h + \tau); \tag{27}$$

and for the case in which only n_f firms are active ($n_h = m = 0$):

$$p_f/c_f = p_h/(c_f + \tau). \tag{28}$$

These relationships are illustrated as the three straight lines, m, n_h, and n_f on figure 6.3. Thus, if type-m firms only are active, equilibrium prices must lie on m. If both type-m and n_h firms are active, prices lie between lines m and n_h, with proximity to these lines depending on the relative numbers of type-m and type-h firms.

From figure 6.3 we see that – in the symmetric case – two sorts of equilibrium are possible. If the zero-profit loci are as represented by the solid curves then the equilibrium is at point M. Only type-m firms are active, because M is below the $\pi_h = 0$ and $\pi_f = 0$ contours, meaning that prices are low enough that national firms would make a loss.[6] At M there is no intra-industry trade, as supply is met entirely by production by multinationals' plants in each country.

The other type of equilibrium occurs if the intersection of the $\pi_h = 0$ and $\pi_f = 0$ loci lies inside $\pi_m = 0$. This is illustrated by the broken curves, and equilibrium is at point N. There are no multinational firms, an equal number of national firms in each country (with symmetric economies), and all firms engage in trade, supplying both their domestic and export markets.

We have a number of results for the symmetric case. First, multinational and national firms do not coexist, except in the borderline case in which parameters are such that all three zero-profit loci intersect at the same point. This is clear from figure 6.3 for the partial equilibrium case, and is also true in general equilibrium. We can thus think of there being two firm types: high fixed-cost, low variable-cost firms (type m), and low fixed-cost, high variable-cost firms (types h and f). Except in borderline cases, one 'technology' will dominate, and free entry and exit will ensure that only multinational or national firms will survive.

The dividing line between cases is determined by magnitudes of transport costs, plant and firm economies of scale, and market size. Consider the role of transport costs. Reductions in transport costs have no effect on the zero-profit locus of multinationals (equation (21)), and shift the $\pi_h = 0$ and $\pi_f = 0$ loci inwards – with lower transport costs national firms can survive with lower consumer prices. Thus national firms exist when transport costs are low and multinationals when transport costs are high. This is, of course, simply the traditional tariff-jumping argument. It can also be noted that the relevant measure of transport costs is τ relative to marginal production costs, c_i. Equi-proportionate changes in transport costs and marginal production costs will not change the equilibrium configuration.

Next consider the role of firm-specific versus plant-specific fixed costs, and in particular consider the ratio of two-plant fixed costs to one-plant fixed costs:

$$1 \leq \frac{2G + F}{G + F} \leq 2. \tag{29}$$

Consider the extreme case where this ratio takes on the value of 2, implying that $F = 0$. In this case there are no multi-plant economies of scale and the multinationals have no cost advantage. Provided that transport costs are not prohibitive, national firms dominate. A national firm and a multinational firm earn the same markup revenues in the national firm's home market, but the national firm earns markup revenues on export sales with no additional fixed costs. Consider the opposite case where the ratio in (29) equals one, implying that all scale economies are at the firm level. In this case multinational firms must dominate unless shipping costs are zero. A type-h firm will earn the same markup revenues as a type-m firm in the home market, but the type-m firm will earn higher markup revenues in the foreign market. Yet both have the same fixed costs, so the type-m firm dominates.

Market size also plays a role. Larger markets support more firms, each firm having a smaller market share but, with Cournot competition, a larger output (note how this differs from monopolistic competition models with a constant output per firm). Since multinationals have larger total fixed costs than national firms they benefit more from larger market size than do national firms. In terms of figure 6.3, larger market size shifts all the zero-profit loci inwards, but relatively more for multinationals than for national firms. Maintaining our assumption of symmetry, it is then the case that large markets tend to support equilibrium with multinationals, and smaller markets equilibrium with national firms and trade.

From this discussion we see that falling transport costs do lead to a bias away from multinational production, but only *ceteris paribus*. If, at the same time, (a) both countries are growing, and/or (b) technology is changing, emphasizing firm-specific scale economies relative to plant scale economies, and/or (c) marginal production costs are falling as fast as transport costs, then there is no presumption that national firms should be displacing multinational firms. Whether or not any of these three can be said to characterize the developments in North Atlantic income levels, technologies, and costs is of course an empirical question.

4   Asymmetric countries and the convergence hypothesis

The questions of most interest for this paper have to do with asymmetric countries, and in particular what happens as countries converge in such characteristics as absolute income levels, relative factor endowments, and

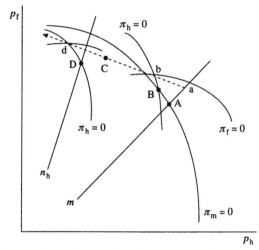

Figure 6.4   Country size, prices, and profits

relative technologies. The question of what regimes are supported as countries converge in these senses is the focus of this section.

It turns out that a rather rich set of outcomes is possible, and our main tool to describe them is numerical simulation. However, to give a flavour of the possibilities, consider figure 6.4. This is constructed in the same way as figure 6.3, and traces out the possible structure of equilibria as we change the relative sizes of the two economies. The thought experiment is the following. Starting from a situation in which both economies are the same size ($\bar{L}_h = \bar{L}_f$ in equations (24)), redistribute labour endowment (and hence market size, M_h and M_f) from the foreign country to home. What happens to the equilibrium? The main point to notice is that this redistribution shifts the $\pi_h = 0$ locus inwards and the $\pi_f = 0$ locus outwards. This can be derived from equations (22) and (23), and is as would be expected – firms gain or lose according to whether their domestic market expands or contracts.

The dashed line on figure 6.4 traces the intersections of $\pi_h = 0$ and $\pi_f = 0$ as endowment is redistributed. If the two economies are the same size, the intersection is at point a. This is exactly as in figure 6.3, so equilibrium is at A with multinational production only. An increase in the relative size of h shifts the zero-profit loci, and moves their intersection in the direction of the arrow, to a point such as b. Equilibrium is now at point B, involving production by firms of type-m and type-h. This is because the intersection of $\pi_h = 0$ with $\pi_m = 0$ lies inside $\pi_f = 0$ (so no type-f firms are active) and between the lines n_h

and m. The intuition is simply that increasing country h market size permits entry of national firms located in h.

Further redistribution of endowment to the home country shifts the intersection of $\pi_h = 0$ and $\pi_f = 0$ to a point such as C. Equilibrium is at C, with production by type-h and type-f firms, but no type-m. The intuition is that entry of home firms has reduced p_h, thus reducing multinational profits and necessitating a higher p_f if multinationals are to survive. But a high enough p_f induces entry of type-f firms, as we observe at point C. Increasing the size of h relative to f still further shifts the intersection of the profit loci to a point such as d. The equilibrium corresponding to this is at point D. Only type-h firms are active (hence the equilibrium must lie on n_h) and prices are too low to permit survival of either type-m or type-h firms.

Figure 6.4 illustrates one set of equilibrium configurations, but others are possible – for example, it need not be the case that point a lies above $\pi_m = 0$. To establish the full set of possibilities we use numerical simulation, and divide parameter space into regions of different equilibrium configurations. Numerical techniques also enable us to take into account general equilibrium considerations. In particular, changes in factor prices have the effect of shifting curves on figure 6.4, and this enriches the set of possible equilibria still further.

Figure 6.5 maps out equilibrium configurations as a function of relative country size and transport costs. Country f's size (factor endowment) as a proportion of country h's size is graphed on the vertical axis (country h's endowment is held constant). The ratio of two-plant to one-plant fixed costs is 1.6 in this simulation, and relative factor proportions are identical. Transport costs are on the horizontal axis. Examination of a column of figure 6.5 corresponds to the thought experiment we undertook on figure 6.4. Consider the case when $\tau = 0.06$, beginning at the bottom. When country f is extremely small, only type-h national firms are supported in equilibrium (as at point D in figure 6.4). Multinational firms cannot enter because the added plant-specific cost needed to open a plant in f is too large. National firms cannot enter in f because most of their sales would have to be export sales, and the transport costs create a competitive asymmetry with type-h firms.

As country f's size rises, national firms (type-f) can enter in country f (as at point C of figure 6.4). With only type-h firms, the price of X is higher in country f ($p_f > p_h$) and $w_h > w_f$ (no X is produced in f). Thus at some point national firms can enter in f even though their sales are substantially less than the total sales of a representative type-h firm. But type-m firms cannot enter. The intuition is that, although the type-m firm could more than cover fixed costs ($G + F/2$) in country f, these profits

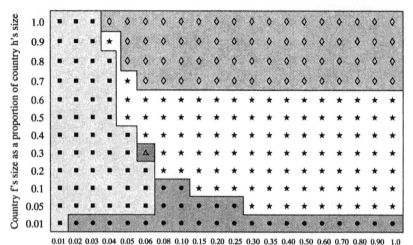

Figure 6.5   Foreign direct investment and country size

would be exceeded by losses in country h, where the type-h firms rely on exports to country f as an important source of earnings.

Figure 6.5 shows that further growth in country f, to 0.3 of country h's endowment level, leads to a regime that supports all three firm types (a case that does not arise if factor prices are fixed, as on figure 6.4). Type-h firms sell in both markets, and type-f firms sell only in country f. The somewhat counterintuitive result must follow that type-m firms earn profits in the small market f and suffer losses in the larger market h. Indeed, when the type-m firms first enter, they have larger sales in the smaller (but less competitive) market, country f. Commodity and factor prices remain unequal, allowing the smaller type-f firms to exist in equilibrium along with the larger type-h firms.

When country f's endowment is between 0.4 and 0.6 of country h's endowment (again, we are considering $\tau = 0.06$), the national firms in country f can no longer compete and disappear. The equilibrium regime has type-m and type-h firms (as at point B in figure 6.4). Commodity and factor prices are converging somewhat owing to the increased entry of type-m firms, and type-f firms can no longer survive. This is then an example of 'non-monotonicity': beginning at a very small size, growth in

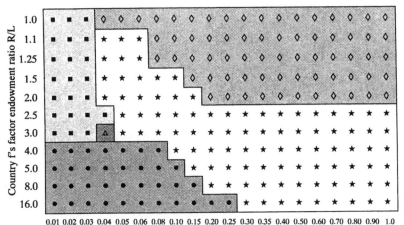

Figure 6.6   Foreign direct investment and factor endowments

country f at first leads to entry of type-f firms and subsequently to their disappearance.

Finally, as the endowments of the two countries are equalized in figure 6.5, only type-m firms can exist at this level of transport costs. In a rough sense, we see that multinational firms become dominant as the countries converge in size and that the growing dominance of multinationals is quite consistent with falling transport costs when the countries are converging in size.

Consider now figure 6.6. As in the case of figure 6.5, the countries are symmetric at the top of the vertical axis, and their initial R/L endowment ratios are indexed at 1.0. Then we perform an experiment in which R is transferred from country h to country f and L is transferred in the opposite direction from country f to country h in a way that roughly preserves their relative income levels. At the bottom of the vertical axis, the R/L ratio of country f is 16.0 times its initial ratio. In the bottom row of figure 6.6, country h is very well endowed with the factor used intensively in the X sector, and country f with the factor used intensively in the Y sector. The horizontal axis in figure 6.6 is identical to that in figure 6.5.

The pattern of the regimes in figure 6.6 is strikingly similar to that in figure 6.5. Consider the column corresponding to $\tau = 0.1$. At endowment ratio 5.0, labour is very expensive in country f and no type-f or type-m firms can enter, even though the price of X is high owing to transport costs from country h. As the endowment ratio R/L falls to 4.0, the price of labour falls enough to permit the entry of some type-m firms. Further falls in the endowment ratio R/L lead eventually to all production by multinational firms. We also have – for a small interval of trade costs, $\tau = 0.04$ – the same non-monotonicity result in figure 6.6 as we had in figure 6.5. Convergence of the endowment ratios moving up a column can at first lead to the entry of type-f firms and then to their exit.

The general result here is similar to that in figure 6.5. As the countries converge in relative factor endowments, total incomes roughly comparable, production is increasingly dominated by multinational firms.

Figure 6.7 graphs country f's 'cost disadvantage ratio' on the vertical axis. At the top of the axis, the value 1.0 indicates that the number of units of labour needed in variable and fixed costs to produce X is the same in both countries. As we move down the vertical axis, country f's value of c_f, G, and F are all increased by the multiple shown. Thus, as we move down the vertical axis, country f has an increasing Ricardian comparative disadvantage in X. The horizontal axis in figure 6.7 is identical to those in figures 6.5 and 6.6.

Figure 6.7 reveals a pattern of regime shifts quite similar to those in figures 6.5 and 6.6. If we move up the column corresponding to $\tau = 0.06$, we begin with only type-h firms, then get entry of type-f firms, and subsequently entry of type-m firms. The explanations run very similar to those in figures 6.5 and 6.6. When costs are very high in f, no firms can enter, despite the fact that the price of X is also high. As costs fall somewhat, type-f firms can enter, serving only the country f market. Type-m firms cannot enter because the losses they would suffer on their country h sales exceed their country f profits. Further reductions in costs generate the same regime shifts that we saw in figures 6.5 and 6.6, with type-m firms at first entering and then type-f firms exiting and finally type-h firms exiting. We therefore see the same examples of non-monotonicity with respect to type-f firms that we saw in figures 6.5 and 6.6.

Convergence in relative costs thus generates the same movement toward multinational production that we saw with convergence in terms of country size and relative factor endowments. Figure 6.8 displays figures 6.5, 6.6, and 6.7 together on the same page, and we can easily note the striking similarities.

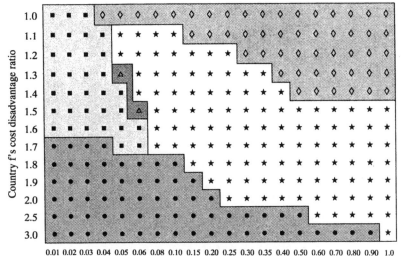

Figure 6.7   Foreign direct investment and cost differences

5   Summary and conclusions

The purpose of the conference was to improve our understanding of issues involving North Atlantic economic relationships, but we hope our findings will have broader implications. This paper focuses on one aspect of these relationships, the growing importance of direct investment along with trade. Indeed, data indicate that direct investment from Europe to the USA has grown substantially faster than have European exports to the USA.

As noted in the introduction, the most simple-minded model of direct investment, based on 'tariff jumping', seems to be an unlikely candidate to explain this growth in direct investment because casual empiricism suggests that tariff and transport-cost barriers between North America and Europe have surely fallen substantially over the past several decades. But, as we also noted, this is at best a *ceteris paribus* argument in a world in which other factors have also changed significantly.

Several of these possible 'other' factors that we have identified involve symmetric changes that are occurring across countries. If (a) two

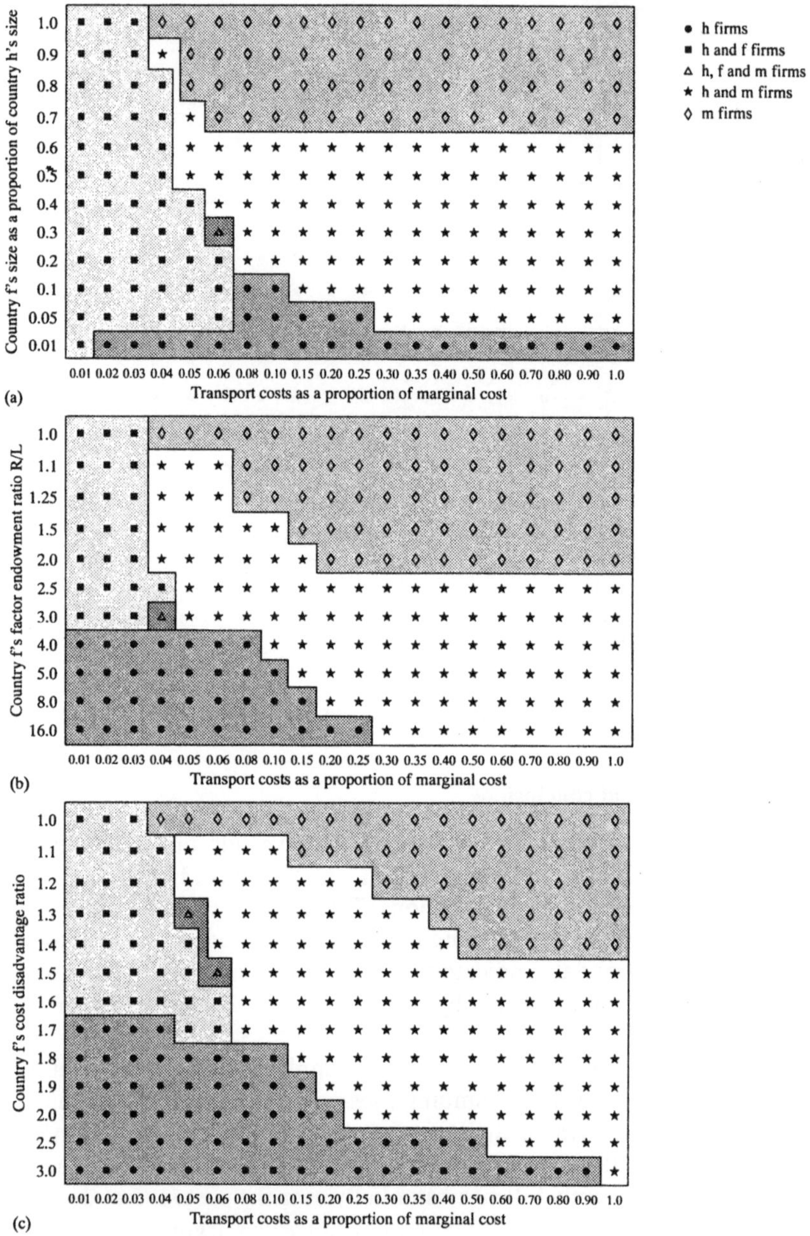

Figure 6.8 Comparison of results

economies are both growing in size, and/or (b) technology is shifting to emphasize firm-level as opposed to plant-level scale economies, and/or (c) marginal production costs have been falling as fast or faster than tariff and transport costs, then we expect to see a shift toward multinational production.

The other factors that we identify have to do with asymmetries between countries. Suppose that one country starts out much smaller in absolute endowments, smaller in the relative endowment of the factors used intensively in the increasing returns sector, and a higher-cost (measured in factor productivity) producer of the increasing returns good. Initially, there will be no production of the increasing returns goods at all in this poorer country. As convergence begins, we see entry of small national firms in the poorer country. Further convergence brings multinational firms into existence. Continued convergence leads to the disappearance of national firms in the (now relatively less) poor country, and complete convergence leaves all production in the hands of multinationals.

Casual empiricism suggests that more formal empirical work might reveal that Europe and North America have indeed converged over the decades since World War II in the three senses noted. The model would then present one conceptual framework for helping to understand the correlation between the convergence and the rising importance of multinationals in overall economic activity.[7]

Of course, other mechanisms not in the model involve causality running the other way. Multinationals can facilitate the transfers of both technology and physical factors from one country to another. In such cases, multinationals lead to convergence rather than (or in addition to) convergence leading to multinationals, as is the case in this paper.

NOTES

This paper began with a bar room discussion (which will not surprise the authors' friends) using napkins (aka serviettes) as the principal research tool. The authors thank the organizers and financers of the Conference on the Location of Economic Activity, Vigo, Spain, 17–19 December 1993, for their support and interest (we paid the bar tab). Markusen's portion of this research was financed under NSF grant SES-9022898.

1   Recent papers by Brainard (1993a,b) have provided cross-section evidence that greatly improves our understanding of the determinants of direct investment. The growing importance of direct investment is not addressed.

2   This paper will be exclusively concerned with horizontal direct investment. That is, direct investment in which the firm provides roughly the same products in both home and foreign markets. Vertical direct investment occurs when the production process is decomposed into stages; for example, capital-intensive phases of production are done in one country while labour-intensive

phases are done in another country. Vertical direct investment can obviously be encouraged by lower tariff and transport-cost barriers.

3   Similar results to ours occur in a differentiated-products model, and many of our results parallel those of Brainard (1992) who uses the differentiated products approach. It is certainly not surprising that the latter approach gives rise to intra-industry trade and direct foreign investment (Helpman and Krugman, 1985, provide a thorough treatment). It is somewhat more surprising that similar results can occur with homogeneous products, but this has been recognized since Brander and Krugman's (1983) model of reciprocal dumping. Brainard's results on direct investment are strikingly similar to those in Horstmann and Markusen's (1992) homogeneous goods model. We will not argue in favour of one approach or the other, but simply point out that the rich results obtained below demonstrate that product differentiation is not *required* to produce such results. We view that as a strength of our approach.

4   Some similar results are found in Brainard (1992) and, in a very different sort of model, Ethier (1986). In addition, the result that direct investment becomes more important as relative factor endowments converge is consistent with the empirical finding of Brainard (1993b).

5   We might also point out that multinational firms do not wish to serve one market from both plants. The firm's optimization condition for serving the home market from both plants is that the delivered marginal cost from f is equal to the marginal cost of production in h. But if this were true, the firm should shut its country h plant and serve both markets from f, turning the firm into a type-f firm.

6   Notice that points A and B are not equilibria. At A, multinationals and national firms in f make zero profits but, since A does not lie between lines n_f and m, no non-negative combination of n_f and m can give supplies consistent with prices at A; an analogous argument applies to point B.

7   We should note that some other models predict that multinationals will arise when countries are different from one another in relative factor endowments. Helpman (1984) has a model in which a multinational is a firm that locates its (single) production facility in a different country from its headquarters activities. Since these two phases of operation have different factor intensities, differences in endowments between countries give rise to multinationals. More generally, multinational production based on a vertical fragmentation of the production process is more likely to arise when countries are quite different, because it is partly or even largely motivated by international differences in factor prices.

REFERENCES

Brainard, S. Lael (1992), 'A Simple Theory of Multinational Corporations and Trade with a Trade-off between Proximity and Concentration', MIT and NBER Working Paper.

(1993a) 'An Empirical Assessment of the Proximity/Concentration Trade-off between Multinational Sales and Trade', MIT and NBER Working Paper.

(1993b) 'An Empirical Assessment of the Factor Proportions Explanation of Multinational Sales', MIT and NBER Working Paper.

Brander, James and Paul Krugman (1983), 'A "Reciprocal Dumping" Model of International Trade', *Journal of International Economics* 15, 313–23.

Ethier, W. J. (1986), 'The Multinational Firm', *Quarterly Journal of Economics* **101**, 805–34.

Helpman, Elhanan (1984), 'A Simple Theory of International Trade with Multinational Corporations', *Journal of Political Economy* **92**, 451–72.

Helpman, Elhanan and Paul Krugman (1985), *Market Structure and International Trade*, Cambridge, Mass.: MIT Press.

Horstmann, Ignatius and James R. Markusen (1992), 'Endogenous Market Structures in International Trade', *Journal of International Economics* **20**, 225–47.

Rutherford, Thomas F. (1988), 'General Equilibrium Modelling with MPS/GE', University of Western Ontario Working Paper.

Discussion

ALASDAIR SMITH

As one would expect from Markusen and Venables, even a paper written in a bar is a theoretically elegant exercise in free-entry oligopoly modelling and also a persuasive case for the use of numerical simulation modelling in theoretical analysis.

The objective is to explore reasons why foreign direct investment (FDI) might grow faster than trade. The model is one in which FDI is 'primarily induced by tariff and transport-cost barriers', this being the case where increased integration seems least likely to be accompanied by more FDI.

One inelegance in the model is the treatment of fixed costs: half are priced in the wages of the home country, half in the wages of the other country. This is not an attractive assumption because, technically, labour from each country is equally efficient, so it would be better to let the inputs to fixed costs be hired from whichever source is cheaper. This leads to a more general point about the role of factor endowments in the theory of foreign direct investment. The work of Helpman, to which the paper refers, allows the origins of foreign direct investment, like other activities with tradable outputs, to be determined by relative factor endowments. Given what we know about foreign direct investment in the real world, it is difficult not to attribute an important role to endowments of the particular factors of production that have a key role in the determination of firm-specific advantages. Even though the purpose of the paper seems to be to produce the simplest possible model consistent with some stylized facts, there is something to be gained by widening the model (or at least discussing the directions in which it could be widened) so as to explain more of the stylized facts.

The model shows investment growing as countries grow and as they become more similar, and we are expected to interpret figures 6.1 and 6.2 as showing these effects for the USA and Europe. But one would really like to see comparisons with what has happened in other countries. On the face of it, the strong position of Luxembourg as a host for FDI (in financial services) is not consistent with these predictions, not to mention less extreme cases such as Ireland. One might also wish to investigate the role of comparative advantage in the development of transatlantic FDI, by focusing on the growth of sectors in which FDI matters, or the growth of firms, rather than on the convergence of the economies themselves. How much of the growth shown in figures 6.1 and 6.2 is the result of the growth of sectors such as consumer electronics and financial services in which MNCs predominate, or the growth of firms such as Phillips and Ford that are different in kind from national firms, rather than the result of a given population of firms switching from exporting to direct investment?

Finally, two points about the presentation of the model. First, in section 4, something is made of the fact that three different types of convergence, in size, in relative factor endowments, and in relative costs, all give rise to the same pattern of results. This is really not too surprising, as in each case it is the relative size of the imperfectly competitive sectors in the two countries that is changing and that matters for the way the model works.

Second, some emphasis is also given to the non-monotonicity of structure: as the foreign country grows in size relative to the home country, the market structure may move from h to h&f to h&f&m to h&m to m, so foreign firms enter the market and then drop out. It would be good to have a sense of what is the dimension of discontinuity as we cross these boundaries. Do we have a relatively stable total population of firms, some of which are induced to open or close foreign plants as transport costs change? Or do we have a relatively stable total number of plants whose ownership changes?

7 Speculative attacks on pegged exchange rates: an empirical exploration with special reference to the European Monetary System

BARRY EICHENGREEN, ANDREW K. ROSE,
and CHARLES WYPLOSZ

1 Introduction

Epidemiologists study epidemics as a way of understanding the everyday transmission of infectious disease. In similar fashion, international economists can study currency crises as a way of understanding the determinants of exchange rates and international capital flows. It is surprising in this light that we do not possess a body of studies that establish stylized facts about the behaviour of macroeconomic variables around the time of speculative attacks. Our goal in this paper is to begin the process of identifying such regularities. We ask questions such as the following. Are there differences in the behaviour of key macroeconomic variables prior to speculative attacks on pegged exchange rates compared with other periods? Does the behaviour of these key variables change in the aftermath of speculative attacks? Do answers to these questions differ in the different times and places in which exchange rates are pegged? Do they differ for exchange rate mechanism (ERM) and non-ERM currencies, in particular?

Our findings are different for the ERM and non-ERM sub-samples. For the non-ERM sub-sample we find significant differences in the behaviour of budget deficits, inflation rates, rates of credit growth, and trade balances when comparing periods preceding speculative attacks and control-group observations. These differences are consistent with the predictions of early contributions to the speculative attack literature – what we call 'first-generation' models – such as those of Krugman (1979) and Flood and Garber (1984a).[1] For the ERM sub-sample, in contrast, there is a striking lack of differences. The behaviour of reserves and possibly also interest rates differs between periods of crisis and tranquillity; this is not surprising, however, because these are two of the variables on whose basis we categorize episodes as speculative crises. But the only other variables whose behaviour differs significantly between

191

crises and non-crises in the ERM sub-sample are money growth and inflation, and the direction of their effects is the opposite of those predicted by first-generation models. For the ERM sub-sample, then, key macroeconomic and financial variables to which first-generation crisis models direct attention do not behave as predicted.

An alternative interpretation of ERM crises is based on second-generation models of self-fulfilling speculative attacks and multiple equilibria in foreign exchange markets, in which policy shifts in a more expansionary direction in response to the attack (Flood and Garber, 1984b; Obstfeld, 1986). For the ERM sub-sample, we find little evidence of this pattern. Thus, although our findings cast doubt on the relevance of first-generation models for our ERM episodes of speculative crisis, they do not establish that second-generation models of self-fulfilling attacks necessarily fit the facts.

It is important here to note a problem of observational equivalence.[2] Although the absence of differences in monetary and fiscal variables in periods leading up to speculative attacks and other periods is consistent with models of multiple equilibria, it is also consistent with a restrictive class of models with unique equilibria. Models such as those of Flood and Garber (1984b) and Obstfeld (1986) generate multiple equilibria and self-fulfilling crises because they assume a contingent policy process in which policy shifts only in the event of an attack. One can also imagine a model in which policy is expected to shift in a more expansionary direction with certainty; the shift is not contingent. Anticipating that eventuality, speculators may attack the currency just before the policy shift is observed. This is a model with a unique equilibrium in which the speculative attack is motivated by imbalances in underlying fundamentals, but those imbalances become evident only after the attack. Thus, our results for the ERM, which fail to detect distinctive behaviour on the part of key macroeconomic variables in the period leading up to speculative attacks, are still consistent with first-generation models, but only with a restrictive sub-class in which no hint of future policy imbalances is contained in past and current policy. But the fact that we find little evidence of a shift in policy in more expansionary directions in the aftermath of speculative attacks is difficult to reconcile with this view.

A final important finding is that the behaviour of macroeconomic variables differs significantly around the time of speculative attacks on the one hand and realignments and changes in exchange rate regimes on the other. ERM countries undergoing realignments have significantly higher inflation rates, interest rates, rates of money and credit growth, and budget deficits, and their trade balances are significantly weaker. None of these statements is true about the events associated with realignments of non-ERM currencies or with the collapse of the Bretton Woods, Smithsonian, or Narrow Margin regimes of pegged exchange rates.

Our investigation has obvious relevance to current policy concerns. In 1992 and 1993 a series of speculative attacks on European currencies drove the Italian lira and the British pound out of the exchange rate mechanism (ERM) of the European Monetary System (EMS) and challenged the viability of the Maastricht blueprint for economic and monetary union (EMU). There remains considerable dispute over why these crises occurred. One view emphasizes the unsustainable policy stances of weak-currency countries (Dornbusch, 1993; Committee of Governors of the Central Banks of the Member States of the European Economic Community, 1993a,b; Williamson, 1993; Goldstein and Mussa, 1994). It blames EMS members whose currencies were attacked for courting danger by their pursuit of lax monetary and fiscal policies and by failing to adjust their exchange rates in timely fashion. Accommodating policies and excessive wage and price inflation are said to have led to a loss of international competitiveness, a current account deficit, and a profitability squeeze that left overvalued currencies 'ripe for the picking'. Another view observes that, for several countries concerned, the evidence of lax policies is far from compelling (Eichengreen and Wyplosz, 1993; Portes, 1993; Rose and Svensson, 1994; Obstfeld, 1994). Several ERM countries displayed little evidence of excessive inflation, accommodating policies, or mounting competitive difficulties prior to their currency crises. In this view, the speculative attacks that forced them to raise interest rates created incipient macroeconomic imbalances, rather than the other way around, and more generally increased the cost of defending the prevailing currency pegs. If the first view is correct, then it may be possible to complete Stage II of the transition to monetary union as sketched in the Maastricht Treaty by returning to the narrow bands of the pre-1993 EMS as soon as Europe's recession ends and policy convergence is restored. But if the second view is accurate, efforts to restore narrow bands may prove futile regardless of the current stance of macroeconomic policies.

In addition, the fiftieth anniversary of the Bretton Woods Agreement, combined with dissatisfaction about the performance of freely fluctuating exchange rates, has reinitiated discussion of international monetary reforms intended to enhance exchange rate stability. In periods when foreign exchange markets are tranquil, it has become customary to argue that exchange rates can be pegged within narrow bands if there is sufficient convergence of national macroeconomic policies. In turbulent periods, in contrast, observers display deep scepticism about whether policy makers will be able to resist market pressures regardless of the policies they are currently pursuing. In today's world of high capital mobility, in other words, it may not be possible to restore narrow exchange rate bands along the lines of the Bretton Woods System regardless of the stance of macroeconomic policies. Our attempt to understand whether speculative attacks on pegged exchange rates are necessarily prompted by the inadequate convergence of national policies or whether such attacks can occur even in the absence of policy imbalances has obvious relevance to transatlantic blueprints for international monetary reform.

The remainder of the paper is organized as follows. Section 2 elaborates the alternative theoretical models in more detail. Section 3 describes the data and procedures used to analyse the empirics of speculative attacks. Section 4 enumerates the speculative episodes generated by our procedures and contrasts them with informal discussions of balance-of-payments crises.[3] We make special reference to ERM members, because theirs is the experience around which much recent discussion revolves. Section 5 reports univariate characterizations of the behaviour of key variables around the time of speculative attacks, along with comparisons with control groups, and asks whether the attack and non-attack cases are drawn from the same underlying distributions. Section 6 draws out the implications of this empirical work for efforts to interpret speculative attacks in terms of theoretical models.

2   Theoretical models, empirical implications

2.1   A review of the literature

The first generation of balance-of-payments crisis models spawned a large literature that is difficult to catalogue comprehensively. Our selective survey focuses on contributions with empirical implications.

Krugman's seminal article (1979) assumed that an exogenous government budget deficit lay at the root of the balance-of-payments crisis. Excessively expansionary fiscal policy (or, equivalently, in Krugman's otherwise stationary economy, any budget deficit) is financed by issuing domestic credit. The authorities announce that they are prepared to peg the exchange rate until reserves reach a specified lower bound (for present purposes, zero), at which point they shift to floating. With the government pegging the relative rate of return on assets denominated in domestic and foreign currencies (in Krugman's model, the exchange rate), investors wish to hold domestic and foreign assets in fixed proportions. They rebalance their portfolios by exchanging some of the additional domestic assets for foreign exchange reserves of the central bank. Since they exchange only a portion of the incremental supply (portfolio proportions remaining constant), the shadow exchange rate, which will prevail in the event that the pegging policy is abandoned, depreciates gradually over time.[4] When it first equals the current exchange rate, investors attack the peg, depleting the authorities' remaining reserves, for to do otherwise would make available arbitrage profits and imply market inefficiency.

The empirical implication of the model, then, is that one should observe expansionary fiscal and monetary policies prior to speculative attacks. Those policies should be accompanied by a gradual decline in international reserves over an extended period.

Although Krugman assumes purchasing power parity, it is straightforward to extend his model to a semi-small country setting so that a shift to more expansionary fiscal policies increases the demand for domestic goods, driving up their price and leading to real exchange rate appreciation in the period leading up to the attack. Goldberg (1988), for example, relaxed the purchasing power parity assumption maintained by Krugman and Flood and Garber (1984a).[5] If it is assumed that domestic prices adjust only gradually in response to excess demand, they begin rising as soon as agents recognize that the exchange rate will be changed subsequently. The stickier are prices, the longer the period prior to the collapse over which real appreciation will be observed.

In models with forward-looking wage contracts (Willman, 1988), anticipated future price increases due to currency depreciation affect current wages. As a result, wages should start rising before the attack occurs. Although the real interest rate falls as the price level rises, stimulating output, the real exchange rate strengthens, shifting demand toward imports and depressing output. If output is demand determined – it depends positively on the real exchange rate but negatively on the real interest rate – then the behaviour of output in the period leading up to the crisis is theoretically ambiguous. If the trade balance depends negatively on the real exchange rate (as domestic prices rise, demand shifts toward foreign goods) and negatively on output, the deficit should grow in the period leading up to an attack unless a sufficiently large fall in output is observed.

Other research has focused on modifying Krugman's assumptions regarding the money supply process, the post-attack regime, and the degree of capital mobility. In many of the successful attacks we analyse below, countries did not permanently shift to floating but instead repegged the exchange rate at a depreciated level, sometimes following a limited period of floating. Wyplosz (1986) analyses devaluations in the presence of capital controls that limit the degree of capital mobility. The more stringent the controls, the longer the pre-attack period over which the standard correlates of speculative crises – fiscal deficits, domestic credit creation, real appreciation, and trade deficits – will persist. With sufficiently stringent controls, collapses of the peg can be averted; devaluations from one peg to another become possible. With permeable controls, crises are still possible: Obstfeld (1984) shows that crises occur earlier the larger the anticipated devaluation.

Flood and Garber (1984a) introduce uncertainty about the rate of domestic credit creation. In their discrete-time formulation, unanticipated increases in domestic credit can cause the shadow exchange rate to exceed the pegged rate temporarily. Now speculators attack the peg as soon as this situation makes arbitrage profits available. But, as domestic credit grows, an attack becomes increasingly likely, widening the differential between domestic and foreign interest rates. This should be accompanied by a growing forward discount on the domestic currency. Finally, the greater the uncertainty about the central bank's credit policy, the faster reserves should be depleted. The larger the variance of the process governing domestic credit creation, the greater the probability of a regime shift, so that reserve losses exceed increases in domestic credit (Claessens 1991).

To recapitulate, variants of the Krugman–Flood–Garber model have strong implications for the behaviour of macroeconomic and financial variables in the period leading up to a crisis. They predict that speculative attacks on pegged exchange rates should be preceded by growing budget deficits, accelerating rates of monetization or comparatively fast money growth, and rising wages and prices. Real exchange rates should become increasingly overvalued, and trade deficits should widen. International reserves should decline, domestic interest rates should rise, and forward exchange rates should weaken before the crisis occurs.

The second generation of speculative attack models has different empirical implications. Flood and Garber (1984b) and Obstfeld (1986) were the first to formalize the possibility of self-fulfilling speculative attacks. In their models, multiple equilibria exist in the foreign exchange market because of the contingent nature of the authorities' policy rule. In the absence of an attack, monetary and fiscal policies are in balance, and nothing prevents the indefinite maintenance of the currently prevailing currency peg. There is no reason to anticipate the empirical trends described in the preceding paragraph in the period leading up to the attack. If and only if attacked, however, the authorities switch to more accommodating policies consistent with a lower level for the exchange rate.[6] In this setting, speculative attacks can be self-fulfilling. But there is no reason to anticipate adverse trends in monetary and fiscal policies, wages and prices, reserves, or the trade balance prior to the attack. That this is more than a purely theoretical possibility is suggested by the following comment by a well-known market participant:

> A change in the exchange rate has the capacity to affect the so-called fundamentals which are supposed to determine exchange rates, such as the rate of inflation in the countries concerned; so that any divergence from a theoretical equilibrium has the capacity to validate itself. This self validating capacity encourages trend-following speculation, and trend-following speculation generates divergences from whatever may be considered the theoretical equilibrium. The circular reasoning is complete.[7]

Early second-generation models were predicated on the ad hoc assumption of a contingent policy rule. Subsequent contributions derived the policy process from the optimizing behaviour of governments. Ozkan and Sutherland (1994) postulated a trade-off between the interest rate and the level of unemployment, where the interest rate depended on the exogenously given foreign rate and the exchange rate regime. They showed that high and rising unemployment might lead the government to abandon the peg, anticipations of which could lead to an immediate attack. It is easy to see how this model can generate self-fulfilling attacks: if defence against an attack requires the authorities to raise interest rates relative to world levels and their action further exacerbates unemployment, multiple equilibria can arise.[8] This formulation implies rising unemployment in the period leading up to the attack, unlike the Willman version of Krugman's model, where the direction of pre-attack output and unemployment trends is ambiguous. Like the Krugman model augmented by risk premia, it predicts rising interest rates.

Thus, simple variants of alternative models generate rather different predictions for the period leading up to an attack. First-generation models predict expansionary fiscal policies and/or rapid growth of money and credit, increasingly overvalued exchange rates, and a steady drain of reserves. According to second-generation models, in contrast, none of these patterns will necessarily be visible in the period leading up to the attack. First-generation models do not predict any particular shift in the stance of monetary and fiscal policy following the attack. Most second-generation models, in contrast, suggest that rational self-fulfilling attacks should be followed by a shift in monetary and fiscal policies in a more expansionary direction (although there are exceptions, e.g. Bensaid and Jeanne, 1994).[9]

2.2   *Previous empirical studies*

Only a handful of studies seek to apply theoretical models of speculative attacks to actual experience with pegged exchange rates. Apparently the first such paper is Blanco and Garber (1986), who used a variant of the Krugman–Flood–Garber model to predict the timing and magnitude of devaluations forced by speculative attacks on the Mexican peso between 1973 and 1982.[10] Blanco and Garber examine whether the model explains the timing of the devaluations that took place in 1976 and 1982 using a standard money demand function and a first-order autoregressive function for the rate of growth of domestic credit.[11] International reserves decline as a function of the difference between money supply and money demand, until the critical level is reached at which the speculative attack occurs. They pick the value for that threshold that minimizes the residual sum of squares, subject to the constraint that the exchange rate that prevails following the attack is consistent with the post-attack level of domestic credit. Information from the forward market, in conjunction with the assumption of no risk premium, is used to proxy for the expected future exchange rate.

Cumby and van Wijnbergen (1989) take a similar approach to analysing attacks on the Argentine crawling peg of the early 1980s. Where Blanco and Garber combined all money supply and money demand factors into a single variable and fitted a stochastic process to it, Cumby and van Wijnbergen estimate different time-series processes for the money demand disturbance, the foreign interest rate, and domestic credit growth. They treat the level of reserves at which the central bank abandons its currency peg as a stochastic variable. They find that a sharp increase in the growth of domestic credit was the main factor triggering the attack on the currency.

These studies provide only limited information on the extent to which the predictions of the theoretical literature fit the facts. Typically, they are predicated on the predictions of the first-generation (Krugman) model and do not specify an alternative hypothesis or class of models against which those predictions might be contrasted. They focus on a particular country at a point in time, which raises questions – for those seeking to assess the general explanatory power of the models – about the representativeness of that episode. Further light on the explanatory power of these theories can be shed only by analysing a comprehensive set of crisis episodes and contrasting the behaviour of the relevant variables in these periods with their behaviour during non-crisis episodes.

Studies that do not build directly on the theoretical literature on speculative attacks come closest to what we have in mind. Klein and

Marion (1994) use panel data for sixteen Latin American countries and Jamaica during the period 1957–91 to study the determinants of the duration of exchange rate pegs. In their model, the timing of the peg's collapse is determined not by speculative anticipations but by the decisions of an optimizing government that trades off the economic costs of misalignment against the political costs of modifying the exchange rate. They justify this emphasis by referring to the prevalence of capital controls that limit the scope for adverse speculation in the countries in question. None the less, their results are broadly consistent with those of the speculative attack literature. They find that the probability of a pegged rate being abandoned increases with the extent of real over-valuation and that it declines with the level of foreign assets.[12] The limitations of this study are that it focuses on semi-industrialized economies rather than the industrial countries that are our concern here, and that capital controls were prevalent throughout the sample, in contrast to the situation in, say, Europe in the 1990s.

Similarly, Edwards (1993, 1989) examines devaluation episodes in developing countries between 1948 and 1971 and 1962 and 1982, respectively.[13] The behaviour of macroeconomic variables in cases where devaluation occurred is compared with that of a no-devaluation control group. Edwards finds that, in the period preceding a devaluation, the foreign assets of the central bank typically decline, the real exchange rate becomes overvalued, and fiscal policy becomes excessively expansionary. Besides the fact that Edwards is concerned with developing rather than industrial countries, a limitation of his studies for present purposes is that he compares devaluation and no-devaluation episodes, not attack and non-attack episodes.

3   The empirics of speculative attacks

3.1   Indicators of speculative pressure

A first step in any empirical analysis is identifying speculative attacks. We seek to do so in ways that minimize the danger of finding patterns purely as a consequence of the manner in which we generate the sample of attack episodes. Were we to limit our attention to successful speculative attacks in which the exchange rate peg or regime was altered (with the currency being devalued or floated), for example, our results would suffer from selectivity bias in so far as some attacks have been warded off by central banks and governments and successful and unsuccessful attacks differ from one another in non-random ways.

The obvious solution to this problem is to construct an index of speculative pressure that picks up both successful and unsuccessful attacks.[14] Ideally, such an index would derive the excess demand for foreign exchange from a model of exchange rate determination (from which the policy actions needed to maintain the exchange rate peg could also be derived). Unfortunately, much research (Meese and Rogoff, 1983, is a classic early reference) has underscored the inadequacy of models linking variables such as reserve flows and interest rates to the exchange rate. A particular set of weights and fundamentals is only as defensible as the theoretical model used to generate it.

Theory provides a way around this problem only if one is willing to adopt strong assumptions about linkages between exchange rates and macroeconomic fundamentals. To illustrate, consider the model underlying the Girton and Roper (1977) index of exchange market pressure. Assuming a textbook money demand function, Girton and Roper specify the percentage change in base money, h, as a function of the percentage change in the price level, p, the percentage change in real income, y, and the percentage change in interest rates, i. Since base money is the sum of domestic credit, D, and international reserves, R, we can define $r = ER/H$ and $d = D/H$, where E is the domestic price of a unit of foreign exchange and H is base money. Thus,

$$(r - r^*) + (d - d^*) = (p - p^*) + B(y - y^*) - a(i - i^*), \qquad (1)$$

where asterisks denote the foreign country, B is the income elasticity for money demand, and a is the interest rate semi-elasticity for money demand.

Using purchasing power parity to substitute the rate of depreciation for the inflation differential, and rearranging terms, we can derive:

$$e + (i - i^*) - (r - r^*) = (d - d^*) - B(y - y^*) + (1 + a)(i - i^*). \quad (2)$$

The left-hand side of (2) is an index of speculative pressure, which says that pressure increases as domestic reserves of foreign exchange decline, as interest rates rise, and as the exchange rate depreciates (e, the log of the exchange rate, rises). The theoretical underpinnings suggest that speculative pressure should be a parametric function of fundamentals such as the rate of growth of domestic credit, the level of income, and the interest rate differential.

There are obvious problems with this approach. First, even within the confines of the model, the weights attached to the three components of the index of speculative pressure are arbitrary, because terms can simply be added to both sides of (2). Thus, even imposing assumptions about what determines the value of the exchange rate does not pin down the weights attached to the components of the index or point to a specific list of fundamentals.

In addition, there is the fact that any such formulation is predicated on a model linking fundamentals to the exchange rate, and thereby to variables such as interest rates and international reserves that can be employed in its defence. We have utilized a monetary model to illustrate how indices of speculative pressure might be derived. So long as we are unable to build reasonable empirical models linking macroeconomic fundamentals to the exchange rate, however, we will be incapable of using such models to link the exchange rate to instruments such as interest rates and reserves that can be used to defend it or to derive weights to be attached to the components of an index of speculative pressure in a defensible way. To avoid predicating our analysis on a particular model of exchange rate determination, we consider a number of different weighting schemes in the analysis that follows.[15]

A further problem with measuring speculative pressure using linear combinations of exchange rate, reserve, and interest rate changes is created by the fact that, in our sample of countries and periods at least, the conditional volatility of percentage changes in reserves (scaled by the monetary base) is several times the conditional volatility of the percentage change in the exchange rate, which is several times the percentage change in the interest differential. Movements in an un-weighted average are therefore heavily driven by reserve movements rather than, say, actual realignments. An intuitive if arbitrary approach is therefore to weight the three components of the index so that their conditional volatilities are equal.[16] This is the measure we consider below. We conduct sensitivity analysis in order to gauge how much different weighting schemes matter.

3.2 Data

We assembled monthly data from 1967 through 1992 for twenty-two (mostly OECD) countries. The countries were chosen on the basis of data availability and are (in order of IMF country number) the USA, the UK, Austria, Belgium, Denmark, France, Italy, the Netherlands, Norway, Sweden, Switzerland, Canada, Japan, Finland, Greece, Ireland, Portugal, Spain, Australia, South Africa, India, and Korea, along with our centre country, Germany. The data are drawn from the CD-ROM version of *International Financial Statistics*. We compute changes in the exchange rate relative to the DM and changes in interest rates and international reserves relative to those of Germany.[17]

We use the following variables: short-term money market interest rates

(IFS line 60b), international reserves (line 11), corrected for international liabilities (line 16c) wherever possible, the ratio of the central government budget position (line 80) to nominal GDP (typically line 99a), the real effective exchange rate as measured by normalized unit labour costs (line reu, available since 1975 only), the ratio of exports (line 70) to imports (line 71) expressed as a seven-month centred moving average to eliminate excessive noise, domestic credit (line 32), narrow money (line 34i) normalized for the rate of growth of international reserves, and CPI inflation (line 64). The data have been checked for transcription and other errors and corrected. Virtually all of our variables are transformed by taking differences between domestic and German annualized first-differences of natural logarithms.

In interpreting our results, it is important to bear in mind the limitations of the data. First, published series on international reserves are a very imperfect guide to the magnitude of intervention in foreign exchange markets. Central banks sometimes report only the gross foreign assets of the monetary authorities. Since it is standard operating procedure to arrange for stand-by credits in foreign currency, this is a potentially serious problem. When the authorities intervene, they draw on their credit lines without having to sell any of their reported foreign assets. Even countries that provide data on foreign liabilities omit a number of operations that are typically undertaken during periods of speculative pressure, for example off-balance-sheet transactions such as swaps and forward market intervention.

Even when published data are accurate, intervention by foreign central banks can be hard to detect. In the ERM, interventions are compulsory at the margins of the currency grid. It is always the case that two (or more) currencies reach their margins simultaneously; thus, compulsory interventions are undertaken simultaneously by two (or more) central banks. Because we analyse changes in the reserves of each country relative to changes in German reserves and Germany has been the perennial strong-currency country, we are likely to pick up much of this foreign intervention. But intervention undertaken by third countries will not be detected. This would be the case if the Netherlands intervened to support the Italian lira, for example. There is also the problem of attributing Germany's interventions to a particular country. German intervention in support of the Italian lira could produce a large percentage rise in German reserves relative to those of the Netherlands, seemingly signalling an attack on the guilder in a period when Dutch reserves were rising.[18] Only detailed data on exchange-market intervention, which central banks rarely release, would solve this problem.

A further issue is that monthly observations may not be of a sufficiently fine periodicity to identify every speculative attack, especially unsuccessful ones. Pressure against pegged currencies can mount quickly and be repelled through interest-rate increases or foreign-exchange-market intervention within the month. If an attack is launched and repelled in a matter of days, the average behaviour of interest rates and international reserves over the month may not reveal the intensity of speculative pressures.[19]

In addition, changes in capital controls may affect the meaning of interest differentials and reserve changes. When controls are in place, the authorities may keep the interest rate on the domestic money market virtually unchanged while defending the parity with sterilized purchases on the foreign exchange market.[20] The problems this creates for our analysis could be circumvented through the use of offshore interest rates; in practice, these are available for only limited periods and countries, however. An alternative is to use the imperfect data that are available on capital controls to contrast the behaviour of interest rates, reserves, and other variables in periods when controls were present and absent; we pursue this in Eichengreen *et al.* (1994).

4   The attack episodes

We begin our analysis by selecting attack episodes (which we refer to as 'crises'). Initially, we weigh the components of our index so as to equalize the conditional volatilities of the exchange rate, the interest differential, and reserves; we then examine outliers that are two or more standard deviations above the sample mean for this index. Sometimes two (or more) outliers occur close together. To avoid measuring the same crisis twice (or more), we exclude second (and subsequent) observations that occur within given proximity to the first crisis (our window width is typically plus and minus six months).

A number of prominent pegged exchange rate crises, such as the September 1992 ERM attacks, show up in our initial list of crises. However, the list is dominated not by exchange rate realignments under the provisions of the EMS, the European Snake, or the Bretton Woods System but by large monthly movements in floating exchange rates. This points to an interesting fact about exchange rate behaviour: movements in exchange rates that take place in the wake of speculative attacks are often not significantly larger than the month-to-month movements that can occur in periods of floating. Unconditional exchange rate volatility varies systematically between floating and pegged-but-adjustable exchange rate regimes; in other words, pegged rates exhibit occasional spikes of volatility that do not compensate for the typical periods of tranquillity, because comparable spikes occur during floating regimes.[21]

One might argue that these large movements in exchange rates and interest differentials between countries with floating currencies should be classified as speculative attacks. If the governments concerned are engaged in a dirty float or are attempting to maintain a tacit crawling peg, a large movement in the rate beyond the limits of the implicit band might properly be regarded as a consequence of an attack.[22] For other periods and currencies, however, such as the dollar in the first half of the 1980s, when the exchange rate was essentially allowed to float freely, these episodes do not reflect speculative attacks in the sense implied by either the first or second generation of theoretical models.[23] Since most of the literature on speculative attacks and the interest of most observers have focused on attacks on pegged currencies, we limit our sample to countries and periods when currencies were pegged under the provisions of the Bretton Woods System, the Snake, the EMS, and other explicitly announced exchange rate bands.[24]

Even when we limit the sample in this way, several prominent realignments of pegged exchange rates do not appear in the list of 'crises'. This directs one to a second important fact: not all realignments involve speculative crises. It underscores our point that exchange rate changes and speculative attacks are not the same.

To assess the plausibility of the attack episodes or 'crises' generated by our procedure and their sensitivity to different weights, we limited the sample to 'ERM countries starting in 1979, because this pegged-rate regime has been the subject of intense study. The list of months and countries that we identify as 'crises' is arrayed in descending order of magnitude in table 7.1. For each, we report the value of the crisis index, the percentage change in the exchange rate (the domestic currency price of the DM), the percentage change in the interest differential, and the percentage change in relative reserves.

Three features of the table stand out. First, there is a correlation between the dates of ERM realignments and our list of speculative attacks on ERM currencies. At the head of the list are crises in a number of countries associated with the autumn 1992 ERM crisis. January 1987, which appears on the list for three countries, was the date of a major ERM alignment. We also identify episodes in which no realignment took place.[25] Most of these are readily interpretable; to cite two recent examples, they include pressure on the British pound in August 1992 and speculation against the French franc in the autumn of 1992 following the Scandinavian devaluations. Second, the most severe crises, as measured by our index, tend to be recent, underscoring the role of the growth of the foreign exchange market and the removal of capital controls in augmenting speculative capital flows.[26] Third, changes in exchange rates,

Table 7.1.   **ERM crises (ranked in order of magnitude of crisis)**

Country	Date	'Crisis'[1]	%Δe	%$\Delta(i - i^*)$	%$\Delta(r - r^*)$
Ireland	1992.11	18.7	−0.34	2.34	−33.58
Italy	1992.09	18.4	6.00	.24	−133.90
France	1992.09	14.9	.21	.33	−155.58
Spain	1992.09	10.6	4.68	.03	−71.33
Denmark	1992.09	8.7	.43	.15	−90.36
Ireland	1986.08	7.8	7.41	.04	−1.40
Belgium	1982.03	6.4	7.16	−0.13	−1.20
France	1987.01	5.1	1.46	.15	−31.58
Denmark	1979.06	4.8	2.03	.15	−21.91
Denmark	1987.01	4.7	.37	.12	−44.29
France	1982.06	4.7	3.83	−0.03	−12.87
Denmark	1981.03	4.7	1.77	.28	−11.63
Italy	1981.10	4.6	4.87	.07	9.18
UK	1992.08	4.6	1.69	−0.03	−38.87
Ireland	1986.01	4.6	1.13	.32	−14.63
France	1981.05	4.2	1.34	.27	−12.53
Belgium	1992.09	4.2	.19	.01	−49.18
Italy	1987.01	4.2	1.96	.11	−18.08
Ireland	1982.12	4.0	2.20	.28	1.41

[1] 'Crisis' is defined as Crisis $\equiv$ %$\Delta e_t + [7^* \%\Delta(i - i^*)_t] - [0.08^* \%\Delta(r - r^*)_t]$, where e denotes the price of a DM, i is the short interest rate, r is the level of international reserves, and an asterisk denotes German variables. A six-month exclusion window and a one-and-a-half-deviation episode delimiter are used to define crises.

interest rates, and reserves are correlated in the manner predicted by theory and intuition: interest rate increases and currency depreciation are positively correlated with one another, while both are negatively correlated with reserves.[27,28]

5   Results

5.1   Characteristics of speculative crises

We now compare the behaviour of macroeconomic and financial variables around the time of our 'crises' with a control group of non-crisis cases. We construct the control group as all observations that remain (with six-month exclusion windows on either side) once the crises are removed.[29]

The data are displayed in figures 7.1 and 7.2.[30] The four panels of figure

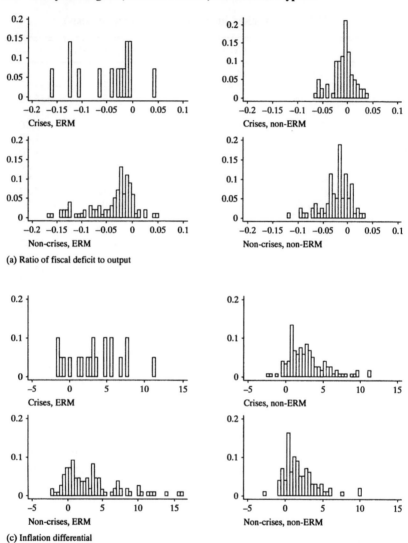

(a) Ratio of fiscal deficit to output

(c) Inflation differential

Figure 7.1   Comparisons of crises and non-crises: histograms of macroeconomic fundamentals (six-month window; 1.5 sigma crisis threshold)

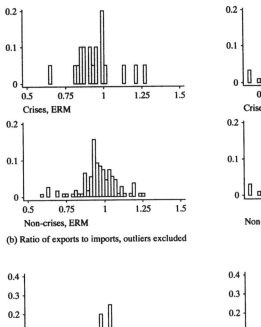

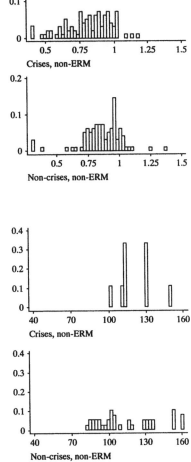

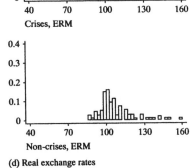

(b) Ratio of exports to imports, outliers excluded

(d) Real exchange rates

Figure 7.1   (continued)

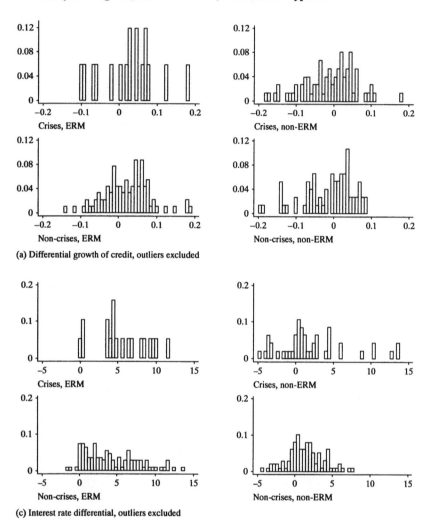

(a) Differential growth of credit, outliers excluded

(c) Interest rate differential, outliers excluded

Figure 7.2   Comparison of crises and non-crises: histograms of financial variables (six-month window; 1.5 sigma crisis threshold)

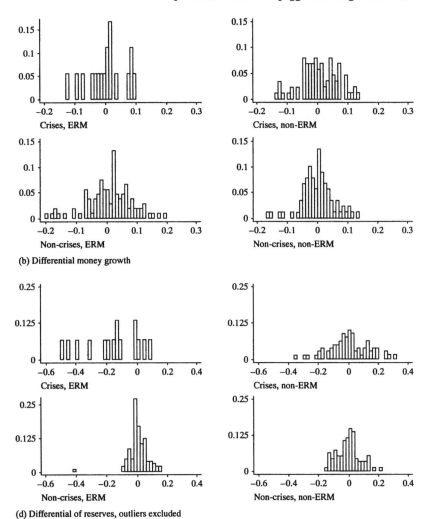

(b) Differential money growth

(d) Differential of reserves, outliers excluded

Figure 7.2   (continued)

7.1(a), for example, display the behaviour of fiscal deficits (as a percentage of GDP). They present histograms for ERM crises, ERM non-crises (tranquil periods), non-ERM crises, and non-ERM non-crises.[31] Figure 7.1 also presents histograms for the smoothed ratio of exports to imports (b), the inflation differential (c), and the real exchange rate relative to its 1985 level (d). Figure 7.2 contains comparable graphs for differential credit growth (a), differential money growth (b), the interest differential (c), and differential reserve growth (d).[32]

Differences are most apparent to the naked eye in the case of international reserves. This is not surprising, because their behaviour was one of the criteria used to differentiate crises from non-crises. Note, however, that a crisis can still take place without a loss of reserves (owing to a large change in the exchange rate or the interest differential), and that a large change in reserves can take place without necessarily classifying an observation as an event.[33] A number of other differences are also apparent in the histograms. Non-ERM trade ratios and interest differentials appear to have different distributions in crisis and non-crisis periods, for example.

The distributions displayed in figures 7.1 and 7.2 can be more systematically compared using statistical techniques. Comparisons between the crisis and non-crisis distributions are tabulated in table 7.2.[34] We report two non-parametric tests: the two-sample Kolmogorov–Smirnov test for equality of the distribution functions (which examines the entire distribution), and the Kruskal–Wallis test for the equality of populations (which focuses more on sample medians). We also report the traditional t-test for equality of first moments (without assuming equal variances).

In table 7.2 the null hypothesis is that there is no difference in the distributions of our variables in crisis and non-crisis periods. The statistics tabulated are probabilities computed under the null, so that small numbers lead one to reject the hypothesis of equality of distributions, i.e. to find evidence that the variables appear to behave differently in periods of crisis and tranquillity.

According to the Kolmogorov–Smirnov test, for the non-ERM sample we are able to reject the null of equality for the budget deficit, the inflation differential, the ratio of exports to imports, reserve growth, and possibly differential credit growth. Results are comparable for the Kruskal–Wallis test. Only for the real exchange rate, differential money growth, and the interest differential is it impossible to reject the null that the observations are drawn from a common underlying distribution.

The t-tests, in the third column, similarly reject the null of equal means for inflation, the trade balance, credit growth, and reserve growth. Most of the differences go in directions consistent with first-generation

Table 7.2.   Comparing crises with non-crises

Variable	Non-ERM			ERM		
	K–S	K–W	t	K–S	K–W	t
Fiscal ratio	.00	.01	−1.93	.75	.78	.12
Real exchange rate	.35	.53	−0.60	.45	.79	.37
Inflation	.02	.01	−2.28	.20	.08	2.78
X/M	.00	.00	3.14	.18	.13	−0.91
Credit growth	.09	.07	1.99	.35	.17	.79
Money growth	.12	.28	−1.19	.06	.03	2.65
Interest rate	.34	.37	−1.20	.05	.05	−1.92
Reserve growth	.00	.07	2.32	.00	.00	3.00

Notes:
'K–S' denotes probability computed under the null hypothesis (of equality of distribution across crises and non-crises), using the non-parametric Kolomogorov–Smirnov test; a low value is inconsistent with the null hypothesis. 'K–W' denotes probability computed under the null hypothesis (of equality of distribution across crises and non-crises), using the non-parametric Kruskal–Wallis test. 't' denotes a t-test of the null hypothesis of equality of first moments across crises and non-crises; a positive number indicates that the sample mean in the absence of crises is higher than the sample mean during crises.
   Throughout, a six-month exclusion window and a three-standard deviation event delimiter are used in defining crises.

speculative attack models. Inflation rates are lower, the ratio of exports to imports is higher, and reserve growth is faster in countries not suffering balance-of-payments crises.[35]

The results for the ERM are strikingly different. According to both the Kolmogorov–Smirnov and Kruskal–Wallis tests, we are unable to reject the null of equal distributions for the budget deficit, the real exchange rate, the inflation differential, the trade ratio, and differential credit growth. The results for differential money growth and the interest rate differential are more marginal, while reserves behave quite differently in attacks and non-attack periods – although, to repeat, reserves are one of the variables on the basis of which we categorized the observations.[36]

For the ERM sample we reject the null of equal means for relative rates of reserve growth, relative interest rates, money growth, and inflation. The first two results follow from our procedure for distinguishing crises from non-crises. But the signs on the t-statistics for inflation and money growth indicate that both variables are larger for non-crises than for crises, rather than smaller as predicted by first-generation models of balance-of-payments crises.

There is a danger of over-interpreting such results and, given the problem of observational equivalence emphasized in the introduction, of spuriously rejecting the predictions of the first-generation models. Nevertheless, the contrast between the ERM and non-ERM samples is striking. The results appear to corroborate some elements of standard first-generation theoretical attack models for non-ERM observations while apparently rejecting the model for the ERM.

As for why these contrasts are so pronounced, we can offer only conjectures. Not even ardent proponents of second-generation models of multiple equilibria and self-fulfilling speculative attacks would deny that policy imbalances and competitiveness problems have been at the root of some crises (in the final years of the Bretton Woods System, for example). But second-generation models suggest that the scope for self-fulfilling attacks is greatest in an environment of high capital mobility and abundant international liquidity. This characterizes the environment of the ERM to a greater extent than predecessors such as the Snake and the Bretton Woods System, which could possibly account for the different patterns we observe.

We undertook a number of experiments as sensitivity analyses; some of these are reported in table 7.3. We narrowed the exclusion window from (plus and minus) six to three months without changing our results (we also widened the window to twelve months and obtained similar results). We doubled the weight on reserves in our index of speculative pressure that is used to identify crises; again, the results did not vary greatly. Finally, we classified crises using a criterion of two (instead of three) standard deviations above the sample mean; again, the results proved relatively insensitive to the change.[37]

5.2   Analysis of realignments and changes in exchange rate regimes

In this subsection, instead of using our index of speculative pressure to identify crisis episodes, we look at actual realignments and changes in exchange rate regimes. We dub the latter 'events' to distinguish them from 'crises'.

It turns out that the results hinge critically on whether we compare events with non-events or crises with non-crises. Contrary to the results of section 5.1 on crises, the first-generation speculative attack models work relatively well for ERM events but not for non-ERM events. For the latter, there are few significant differences in the behaviour of key macroeconomic variables.

Figures 7.3 and 7.4 are histograms for event and non-event episodes that correspond to figures 7.1 and 7.2 for crises and non-crises. The histograms reveal substantial differences in the distributions of ERM

Table 7.3. Robustness checks for crises/non-crises comparison

Variable	Non-ERM		ERM	
	K–S	K–W	K–S	K–W
Three-month exclusion window				
Fiscal ratio	.00	.00	.94	.93
Real exchange rate	.25	.63	.61	.79
Inflation	.00	.00	.22	.09
X/M	.00	.00	.27	.14
Credit growth	.00	.00	.84	.52
Money growth	.01	.08	.07	.03
Interest rate	.33	.23	.04	.04
Reserve growth	.06	.01	.00	.00
Doubled weight on reserves				
Fiscal ratio	.00	.01	.23	.42
Real exchange rate	.38	.56	.29	.52
Inflation	.01	.00	.22	.14
X/M	.00	.00	.59	.66
Credit growth	.03	.04	.35	.17
Money growth	.15	.32	.53	.25
Interest rate	.40	.66	.03	.04
Reserve growth	.02	.18	.00	.00
A two-standard deviation event threshold				
Fiscal ratio	.00	.00	.30	.29
Real exchange rate	.30	.38	.22	.36
Inflation	.00	.00	.50	.42
X/M	.07	.07	.53	.89
Credit growth	.71	.73	.92	.89
Money growth	.04	.29	.11	.08
Interest rate	.55	.66	.05	.04
Reserve growth	.16	.58	.00	.00

Notes:
'K–S' denotes probability computed under the null hypothesis (of equality of distribution across crises and non-crises), using the non-parametric Kolomogorov–Smirnov test. 'K–W' denotes probability computed under the null hypothesis (of equality of distribution across crises and non-crises), using the non-parametric Kruskal–Wallis test.

fiscal ratios between events and non-events. ERM inflation and money growth differentials also appear to be noticeably different.

Table 7.4 is the analog to table 7.2 in that it shows the tests for equality of distributions and for equal means (now across events and non-events rather than crises and non-crises). None of the non-ERM statistics indicates significant differences at conventional significance levels. This is true not only of the non-parametric tests for equality of distributions and

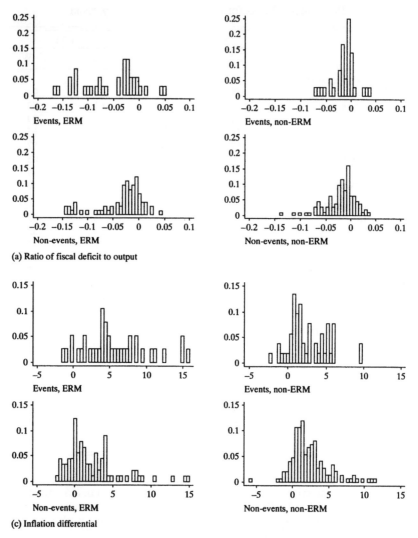

(a) Ratio of fiscal deficit to output

(c) Inflation differential

Figure 7.3 Comparisons of events and non-events: histograms of macroeconomic fundamentals (six-month window)

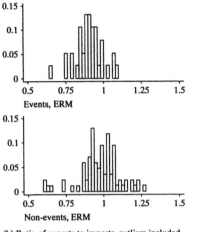

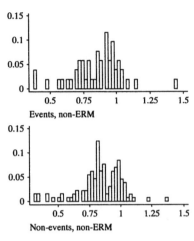

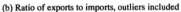

(b) Ratio of exports to imports, outliers included

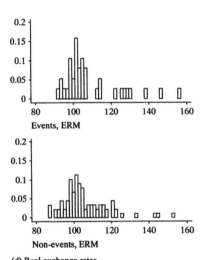

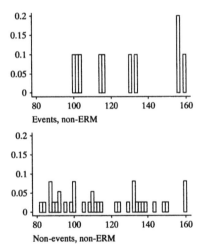

(d) Real exchange rates

Figure 7.3   (continued)

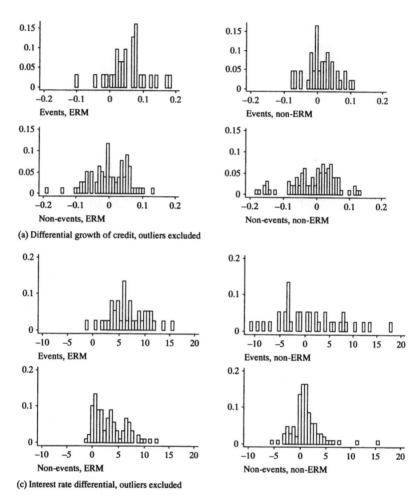

(a) Differential growth of credit, outliers excluded

(c) Interest rate differential, outliers excluded

Figure 7.4   Comparisons of events and non-events: histograms of financial variables (six-month window)

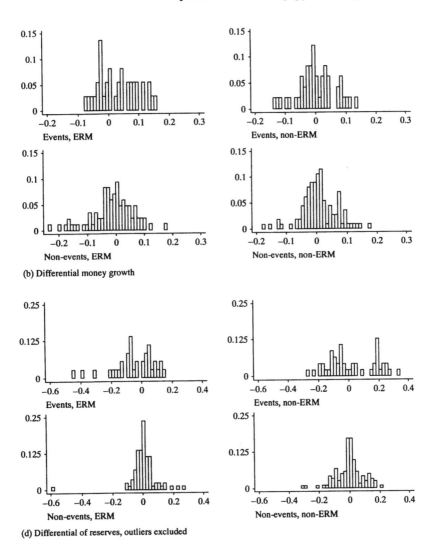

(b) Differential money growth

(d) Differential of reserves, outliers excluded

Figure 7.4 **(continued)**

Table 7.4.   Comparing actual events with non-events

Variable	Non-ERM			ERM		
	K–S	K–W	t	K–S	K–W	t
Fiscal ratio	.47	.29	−1.42	.12	.04	1.94
Real exchange rate	.27	.20	−1.26	.47	.39	−1.17
Inflation	.54	.55	−0.46	.00	.00	−4.12
X/M	.55	.60	−0.60	.00	.00	3.44
Credit growth	.08	.51	−1.09	.00	.00	−3.92
Money growth	.71	.64	0.53	.01	.00	−3.58
Interest rate	.00	.47	−0.02	.00	.00	−5.03
Reserve growth	.00	.96	−0.89	.00	.02	2.42

Notes:
'K–S' denotes probability computed under the null hypothesis (of equality of distribution across events and non-events), using the non-parametric Kolomo-gorov–Smirnov test. 'K–W' denotes probability computed under the null hypothesis (of equality of distribution across events and non-events), using the non-parametric Kruskal–Wallis test. 't' denotes a t-test of the null hypothesis of equality of first moments across events and non-events.
   Throughout, a six-month exclusion window and a three-standard deviation event delimiter are used. Events include: realignments; devaluations; flotations; and fixations.

populations but also of the t-tests for equal means. The opposite is true of the ERM observations. Except for the fiscal ratio and the real exchange rate, the test statistics reject the null of equality of distributions across events and non-events. The differences in sample first moments between ERM events and non-events are economically interesting as well. Inflation rates, money and credit growth rates, and interest rates are all higher for events than for non-events, while the export/import ratio and reserve growth are lower. These results are quite consistent with standard first-generation models of speculative attacks.
   The contrasts between tables 7.2 and 7.4 underscore the fact that some realignments and shifts from pegging to floating take place without speculative attacks, while not all attacks are successful. 'Events' and 'crises' are different, in other words. The evidence on 'events' is broadly supportive of first-generation speculative attack models but only for the ERM sub-sample. The evidence on 'crises' is also supportive of the first-generation model but more weakly and only for non-ERM observations. This is consistent with the notion that governments historically chose to realign ERM currencies on the basis of standard macroeconomic criteria but that speculators chose to attack ERM currencies for other reasons.[38]
   The fact that crises and events are not the same is corroborated in table

Table 7.5.   Comparing events with crises

Variable	Total		Non-ERM		ERM	
	K–S	K–W	K–S	K–W	K–S	K–W
Fiscal ratio	.00	.00	.29	.27	.29	.35
Real exchange rate	.81	.98	.85	.74	.56	.42
Inflation	.00	.04	.60	.60	.02	.01
X/M	.01	.01	.05	.06	.02	.01
Credit growth	.00	.00	.00	.03	.24	.08
Money growth	.93	.81	.25	.31	.05	.02
Interest rate	.00	.10	.01	.42	.64	.86
Reserve growth	.17	.98	.01	.52	.11	.18

Notes:
'K–S' denotes probability computed under the null hypothesis (of equality of distribution across events and crises), using the non-parametric Kolomogorov–Smirnov test. 'K–W' denotes probability computed under the null hypothesis (of equality of distribution across events and crises), using the non-parametric Kruskal–Wallis test.

Throughout, a six-month exclusion window and a three-standard deviation event delimiter are used. Events include: realignments; devaluations; flotations; and fixations.

7.5. The statistics tabulated there test the null equality of distributions and populations across events and crises for our eight macroeconomic and financial variables. The tests are performed for the ERM sub-sample, the non-ERM sub-sample, and the full sample. All the variables except the real exchange rate are distributed differently in crises and events.

We also tested for differences in the distributions of macroeconomic and financial variables before and after exchange-market disturbances. We compared their values six months before and six months after both 'crises' and 'events'. As table 7.6 shows, there are almost no statistically significant differences in the behaviour of our eight variables for either ERM or non-ERM observations.

The result is consistent with simple versions of the first-generation model, which posit that countries are running policies too expansionary to be compatible with indefinite maintenance of the exchange rate peg but do not specify a change in that policy following the collapse of the peg. It is incompatible, however, with the restrictive subclass of first-generation models that predict a deterministic future shift in policy in a more expansionary direction as the factor prompting the crisis. It is also incompatible with models of multiple equilibria that predict a shift towards looser policy following a successful attack.

Table 7.6.   Distributions six months before and six months after crises and events

Variable	Non-ERM K–S	Non-ERM K–W	ERM K–S	ERM K–W
Crises				
Fiscal ratio	.76	.59	.92	.56
Real exchange rate	.49	.28	.90	.56
Inflation	.68	.92	.31	.38
X/M	.68	.51	.59	.38
Credit growth	.02	.05	.43	.32
Money growth	.87	.71	.79	.51
Interest rate	.65	.74	.59	.24
Reserve growth	.03	.00	.90	.56
Events				
Fiscal ratio	.74	.69	.56	.50
Real exchange rate	.99	.66	.76	.65
Inflation	.27	.62	.60	.68
X/M	1.0	.92	.32	.31
Credit growth	.04	.10	.19	.35
Money growth	.77	.62	.04	.02
Interest rate	.04	.02	.12	.09
Reserve growth	.00	.05	.39	.16

Notes:
'K–S' denotes probability computed under the null hypothesis (of equality of distributions six months before crises/events to six months after events/crises), using the non-parametric Kolomogorov–Smirnov test. 'K–W' denotes probability computed under the null hypothesis (of equality of distributions six months before events/crises to six months after crises/events), using the non-parametric Kruskal–Wallis test.
   Throughout, a six-month exclusion window and a three-standard deviation event delimiter are used.

Thus, taken together with our other results, the analysis in table 7.6 points to empirical shortcomings of all existing classes of models of speculative attacks.

6   Conclusions and implications

We have analysed the behaviour of a range of macroeconomic and financial variables in the periods leading up to speculative attacks on pegged exchange rates. We consider data from official exchange rate pegs in the OECD countries since 1967, including the Bretton Woods System, the Snake of the 1970s, and the European Monetary System. Our results are noticeably different for the ERM and non-ERM sub-samples. For the non-ERM sub-sample we identify significant differences in the behaviour of budget deficits, inflation, export/import ratios, domestic credit growth, and international reserves in pre-attack and other periods. Only for the real exchange rate, money growth, and interest rates is it impossible to reject the null that the observations are drawn from a common underlying distribution. This is consistent with the predictions of first-generation speculative attack models such as that of Krugman (1979). For the ERM sub-sample, in contrast, there is a striking absence of differences between events and other observations. Aside from reserves and interest rates, which are two of the variables on whose basis we categorize episodes as events, we tend to be unable to reject the null of equal distributions for any variable, and where we reject that hypothesis the difference goes in the opposite direction from the predictions of first-generation models. It does not appear, in other words, that the policy imbalances to which first-generation models direct attention are obviously associated with the incidence of speculative attacks on ERM currencies. This absence of significant differences in the ERM sub-sample is consistent with the predictions of second-generation models emphasizing multiple equilibria and self-fulfilling attacks. The high capital mobility and abundant international liquidity of the relatively recent ERM period, which make self-fulfilling attacks relatively easy to launch, may explain this contrast.

When we compare actual realignments and changes in exchange rate regimes with tranquil periods, the results are strikingly different. The first-generation model works well in predicting the behaviour of macroeconomic variables for currencies participating in the ERM but not for the non-ERM observations.

Given the limitations of models of exchange rate determination and fundamental problems of observational equivalence, it is inevitably difficult to determine whether our findings are more easily reconciled with descendants of the first or second generation of balance-of-payments crisis models. In so far as the pre-attack behaviour of monetary and fiscal variables is at the heart of the distinction between them, we believe that where ERM crises are concerned our findings tend to shift the burden of proof toward the proponents of first-generation models. Admittedly, we also fail to turn up strong evidence favouring second-generation models, because we do not detect significant shifts in macroeconomic variables in the wake of speculative attacks. But, however our readers are inclined to interpret the results, we hope that we have convinced them that shedding additional light on these questions requires further empirical analysis of the sort we offer here.

Appendix: The context of EMS crises

One way of gauging the plausibility of our procedure for identifying speculative attacks is to relate the attack episodes identified by the index to historical events. In this appendix we do so for each country–month 'crisis' generated by our procedure when the components of our index are weighted to equalize volatilities, the sample is limited to ERM members since 1979, and a one and a half standard deviation threshold is used. We search the financial press for reports of speculative pressure on the currency in the month in question.

June 1979: Denmark
Germany's support of the DM pushed up the grid against other currencies, adversely affecting the weak members. European central banks were forced to sell DM to keep the Danish krone from falling through the bottom of its band.

March 1981: Denmark
The Danish economy was suffering a large current account deficit, putting downward pressure on the currency. Also, Italy's realignment and the resulting implications for competitiveness reinforced the weakness of the currency.

May 1981: France
The franc declined in response to an upward move in US interest rates and nervousness about a possible socialist victory in the second round of presidential elections.

October 1981: Italy
France and Italy devalued, while the DM and the Dutch guilder were realigned upward in the ERM.

March 1982: Belgium
Suffering high unemployment, a rising budget deficit, and a large current account deficit, Belgium devalued by 8.9 per cent.

June 1982: France
France devalued by 5.75 per cent, pushed in part by the strength of the dollar and waves of speculation against the franc that washed away more than two-thirds of the country's foreign exchange reserves.

December 1982: Ireland
Sterling's weakness raised questions about the stability of the punt.

January 1986: Ireland
A falling British pound (attributable to slumping oil prices), along with a large budget deficit (which the government announced in January would come to at least 8 per cent of GDP), put downward pressure on the punt.

August 1986: Ireland
Ireland devalued the punt by 8 per cent in order to encourage exports.

January 1987: France; Denmark; Italy
The eleventh realignment of the EMS was barely complete before speculators began betting on the next one. On 6 January the franc fell to the bottom of the ERM grid, spurred by student riots and public sector strikes. European finance ministers devalued the Danish krone by 3 per cent and the Belgian franc by 2 per cent. Italy announced plans to liberalize its exchange controls.

August 1992: United Kingdom
Reports that Helmut Schlesinger, the Bundesbank's president, had said that he felt that the pound should be devalued triggered heavy selling of sterling.

September 1992: Italy; France; Spain; Denmark; Belgium
A sliding dollar and anxiety over France's referendum on the Maastricht Treaty contrived to strain Europe's weak currencies. Sellers succeeded in driving the lira out of the ERM and obliged devaluation of the peseta. The Belgian franc was hurt by the country's close economic ties to France and the weakness of the French franc.

November 1992: Ireland
The punt displayed continued weakness in the wake of the September attack, the depreciation of sterling, realignments by Portugal and Spain, and the looming removal of Irish capital controls.

NOTES

We thank Florence Beranger and Lisa Ortiz for research assistance, and Matthew Canzoneri, Robert Cumby, Robert Flood, Jeffrey Frankel, Peter Garber, Alberto Giovannini, Vittorio Grilli, Assar Lindbeck, Torsten Persson, Jean Pisani-Ferry, Nouriel Roubini, Lars Svensson, Axel Weber, and seminar participants at UC Berkeley, ESSIM, IIES, the French Ministry of Finance, the Kiel Institute for World Economics, and CEPR's Conference on the New Transatlantic Economy for comments.
  1 These models derived from previous analyses of attacks on commodity-price stabilization schemes (Salant and Henderson, 1978; Salant, 1983). The subsequent literature developing these models is reviewed by Agenor *et al.* (1992) and Blackburn and Sola (1993). We are indebted to these reviews for our own survey of the literature.
  2 For discussion of this point see Flood and Hodrick (1986).
  3 We do this in more detail in the appendix to the paper.
  4 It is the supply of domestic assets following the attack rather than the pre-attack supply that determines the shadow exchange rate; the two differ because speculators swap a portion of their domestic asset holdings for foreign exchange when undertaking the attack that exhausts the central bank's remaining reserves and forces the transition to floating (see Grilli, 1986).

5 See also Flood and Hodrick (1986) and Wyplosz (1986).
6 Dellas and Stockman (1993) showed that the same result can obtain if an attack induces the authorities to impose capital controls on a regime of previously free international capital mobility.
7 George Soros, *International Investment Research*, 5 July 1994, p. 2. We thank Luis Freitas for bringing this statement to our attention.
8 See also Gros (1992) and Obstfeld (1994).
9 This contrast is subject to qualification by the problem of observational equivalence noted in the introduction. This paragraph refers to simple variants of first-generation models; more complicated variants of the first-generation model can suggest a deterministic shift in post-attack policy in a more expansionary direction.
10 A recent study that re-examines this episode is Goldberg (forthcoming).
11 This is an appropriate juncture at which to flag a point anticipated in the introduction. Any empirical model of crises requires a model of the asset demands from which the exchange rate is derived. Most investigators, such as Blanco and Garber, use standard money demand functions and assumptions akin to purchasing power parity. That such models fail adequately to track exchange rate movements is well known; the problem is equally debilitating in the present context, where it is reserves rather than the exchange rate that are permitted to move.
12 In addition, an increase in openness significantly reduces the probability of ending a peg, whereas higher trade concentration increases the probability that a peg will end. These findings are consistent with the literature on optimum currency areas, in which it is suggested that more open, less trade-diversified economies have a stronger desire to peg.
13 Other studies that follow this approach include Cooper (1971), Harberger and Edwards (1982), Kamin (1988), and Eichengreen (1991).
14 Once we construct a sample of 'events', it becomes possible to contrast their characteristics with those of successful attacks in which previously pegged exchange rates were abandoned, as a way of gauging the extent of such selectivity bias, as we do below.
15 Robert Flood has pointed out that this problem has an analogy in the literature on bubbles in foreign exchange markets. Bubbles are another instance of multiple equilibria analogous to the second-generation models of speculative attacks on pegged rates, the difference being that the exchange rate is freely determined in the exchange market bubbles literature whereas it is pegged and reserves are freely determined in the speculative attack literature (or rather, reserves, interest rates, and other policy instruments that can be used to defend the rate). Woo (1985) and West (1987) test for bubbles using monetary models of exchange rate determination. Their attempts to identify bubbles using this structural approach are no more convincing than their monetary model. Our less structured analysis can be seen as a counterpart of the non-parametric approach to analysing bubbles of authors such as Blanchard and Watson (1982).
16 We typically add exchange rate changes to a 0.08 multiple of reserve movements and a seven-fold multiple of interest rate differential movements.
17 Germany was the leading strong-currency country in the latter part of the Bretton Woods period and under the Snake as well as in the European

Monetary System. We also computed changes in most of our key macroeconomic variables relative to Germany.

18 This pattern in fact occurred in September 1992. Thus, when we attach a high weight to changes in relative reserves, our index identifies the guilder as one of the currencies that was attacked that month.

19 In future work, we hope to use weekly and daily data on interest rates and exchange rates to identify other possible periods in which speculative crises occurred.

20 For details, see Giavazzi and Giovannini (1989).

21 This may be thought of as a peso problem in second moments.

22 In 1987, for example, the finance ministers of the G7 countries agreed at the Louvre meeting to establish 'reference values' for the dollar and other currencies 'around current levels' but refused to reveal the width of the reference range. According to Funabashi (1988), they agreed to a narrow margin of plus or minus 2.5 per cent, after which intervention would be called for on a voluntary basis, and a wider band of plus or minus 5 per cent, at which point concerted intervention would be obligatory.

23 On the free float of the 1980s, see Frankel (1994).

24 In particular, we limit our tests below to countries with explicitly declared bilateral band widths of no more than 15 per cent.

25 Information on the events listed in table 7.1 is provided in the appendix.

26 This pattern becomes even more pronounced when we increase the weight on reserves when constructing our index, as discussed below.

27 The correlation between reserve changes and exchange rate changes is $-.13$ and between reserve changes and interest rate changes is $-.24$. The positive correlation between exchange rate and interest rate changes is a relatively low .04.

28 Our list of events also changes in a sensible way when we alter the weights on the three components of our index.

29 It would be interesting, but beyond the scope of this paper, to analyse the crises that occur closely together.

30 Crises are defined as observations where our measure of speculative pressure lies at least one and a half standard deviations above its sample mean; this threshold is used to create smoothness in the histograms. However, most of the statistical results (e.g. in table 7.2) use a three-standard deviation threshold. A sensitivity analysis shows that this cutoff point is arbitrary but not especially important.

31 All four histograms scaled so as to be directly comparable with one another.

32 Unlike the other variables, which are calculated for the 12 months preceding the event, the real exchange rate is considered in the month immediately preceding the event because it is constructed relative to its 1985 base.

33 The differences in reserve behaviour between events and non-events are more pronounced for the ERM cases. This is not surprising, because, as we noted above, the ERM requires mandatory intervention at the margin not only by the country in question but by the strong-currency country, typically Germany, our reference country against which the change in reserves is measured.

34 Sample size varies by variable owing to missing observations and different sample spans.

35 Only the difference in credit growth goes in the wrong direction.

36 The weak results on interest rate differentials may indicate that there is considerable measurement error inherent in the procedure that we use to identify speculative attacks, an issue to which we return later. However, we frequently find similar results for actual realignments and exchange rate regime switches.
37 An important limitation of these results (which we plan to rectify in future work) is that they are based on univariate analysis. An absence of differences in the distributions of monetary and fiscal variables in attack and non-attack cases when such variables are considered separately may disguise interactions among them that differ across categories.
38 We are grateful to Torsten Persson and Victor Rios-Ruell for leading us to this thought.

REFERENCES

Agenor, Pierre-Richard, Jagdeep S. Bhandari and Robert P. Flood (1992), 'Speculative Attacks and Models of Balance of Payments Crises', *Staff Papers* **39**, 357–94.
Bensaid, Bernard and Olivier Jeanne (1994), 'The Instability of Fixed Exchange Rate Systems When Raising the Nominal Interest Rate Is Costly', unpublished manuscript, ENPC.
Blackburn, Keith and Martin Sola (1993), 'Speculative Currency Attacks and Balance of Payments Crises', *Journal of Economic Surveys* **7**, 119–44.
Blanchard, Olivier and Mark Watson (1982), 'Bubbles, Rational Expectations and Financial Markets', National Bureau of Economic Research Working Paper No. 945.
Blanco, Herminio and Peter M. Garber (1986), 'Recurrent Devaluation and Speculative Attacks on the Mexican Peso', *Journal of Political Economy* **94**, 148–66.
Claessens, Stijn (1991), 'Balance of Payments Crises in an Optimal Portfolio Model', *European Economic Review* **35**, 81–101.
Committee of Governors of the Central Banks of the Member States of the European Economic Community (1993a), *Annual Report 1992*, Basle: Committee of Governors.
  (1993b), 'The Implications and Lessons to be Drawn from the Recent Exchange Rate Crisis: Report of the Committee of Governors', processed, 21 April.
Cooper, Richard (1971), 'Exchange Rate Devaluation in Developing Countries', Princeton Essays in International Finance No. 86, International Finance Section, Department of Economics, Princeton University.
Cumby, Robert E. and Sweder van Wijnbergen (1989), 'Financial Policy and Speculative Runs with a Crawling Peg: Argentina 1979–1981', *Journal of International Economics* **27**, 111–27.
Dellas, Harris and Alan C. Stockman (1993), 'Self-Fulfilling Expectations, Speculative Attacks and Capital Controls', *Journal of Money, Credit and Banking* **25**, 721–30.
Dornbusch, Rudiger (1993), 'Comment', *Brookings Papers on Economic Activity* **1**, 130–36.
Edwards, Sebastian (1989), *Real Exchange Rates, Devaluation and Adjustment:*

Exchange Rate Policy in Developing Countries, Cambridge, Mass.: MIT Press.

(1993), 'Devaluation Controversies in the Developing Countries', in Michael D. Bordo and Barry Eichengreen (eds.), *A Retrospective on the Bretton Woods System*, Chicago: University of Chicago Press, pp. 405–55.

Eichengreen, Barry (1991), 'Relaxing the External Constraint: Europe in the 1930s', in George Alogoskoufis, Lucas Papademos, and Richard Portes (eds.), *External Constraints on Macroeconomic Policy: The European Experience*, Cambridge: Cambridge University Press, pp. 75–117.

Eichengreen, Barry and Charles Wyplosz (1993), 'The Unstable EMS', *Brookings Papers on Economic Activity* 1, 51–143.

Eichengreen, Barry, Andrew K. Rose and Charles Wyplosz (1994), 'Is There a Safe Passage to EMU? Evidence from the Markets', unpublished manuscript, University of California at Berkeley and INSEAD.

Flood, Robert and Peter Garber (1984a), 'Collapsing Exchange-Rate Regimes: Some Linear Examples', *Journal of International Economics* 17, 1–13.

(1984b), 'Gold Monetization and Gold Discipline', *Journal of Political Economy* 92, 90–107.

Flood, Robert and Robert Hodrick (1986), 'Real Aspects of Exchange Rate Regime Choice with Collapsing Fixed Rates', *Journal of International Economics* 21, 215–32.

Frankel, Jeffrey A. (1994), 'Exchange Rate Policy', in Martin Feldstein (ed.), *American Economic Policy in the 1980s*, Chicago: University of Chicago Press, pp. 293–341.

Funabashi, Yoichi (1988), *Managing the Dollar*, Washington, DC: Institute for International Economics.

Giavazzi, Francesco and Alberto Giovannini (1989), *Managing Exchange Rate Flexibility: The European Monetary System*, Cambridge, Mass.: MIT Press.

Girton, Lance and Don Roper (1977), 'A Monetary Model of Exchange Market Pressure Applied to Postwar Canadian Experience', *American Economic Review* 67, 537–48.

Goldberg, Linda (1988), 'Collapsing Exchange Rate Regimes: A Theoretical and Empirical Investigation', unpublished dissertation, Princeton University.

(forthcoming), 'Predicting Exchange Rate Crises: Mexico Revisited', *Journal of International Economics*.

Goldstein, Morris and Michael Mussa (1994), 'The Integration of World Capital Markets', in Federal Reserve Bank of Kansas City, *Changing Capital Markets: Implications for Monetary Policy*, Kansas City: Federal Reserve Bank of Kansas City, pp. 245–314.

Grilli, Vittorio (1986), 'Buying and Selling Attacks on Fixed Exchange Rate Systems', *Journal of International Economics* 20, 143–56.

Gros, Daniel (1992), 'Capital Controls and Foreign Exchange Market Crises in the EMS', *European Economic Review* 36, 1533–44.

Harberger, A. and S. Edwards (1982), 'Lessons of Experience under Fixed Exchange Rates', in M. Gersovitz et al. (eds.), *The Theory and Experience of Economic Development*, London: Allen & Unwin.

Kamin, Steve (1988), 'Devaluation, External Balance and Macroeconomic Performance: A Look at the Numbers', Princeton Essays in International

Finance No. 62, International Finance Section, Department of Economics, Princeton University.

Klein, Michael W. and Nancy P. Marion (1994), 'Explaining the Duration of Exchange-Rate Pegs', National Bureau of Economic Research Working Paper No. 4651.

Krugman, Paul (1979), 'A Model of Balance of Payments Crises', *Journal of Money, Credit and Banking* **11**, 311–25.

Meese, Richard and Kenneth Rogoff (1983), 'Empirical Exchange Rate Models of the Seventies: Do They Fit out of Sample?' *Journal of International Economics* **14**, 3–24.

Obstfeld, Maurice (1984), 'Balance of Payments Crises and Devaluation', *Journal of Money, Credit and Banking* **16**, 208–17.

——— (1986), 'Rational and Self-Fulfilling Balance-of-Payments Crises', *American Economic Review* **76**, 72–81.

——— (1994), 'The Logic of Currency Crises', National Bureau of Economic Research Working Paper No. 4640.

Ozkan, F. Gulcin and Alan Sutherland (1994), 'A Model of the ERM Crisis', unpublished manuscript, University of York.

Portes, Richard (1993), 'EMS and EMU after the Fall', *The World Economy* **19**, 1–16.

Rose, Andrew and Lars Svensson (1994), 'European Exchange Rate Credibility Before the Fall', *European Economic Review* **38**, 1185–216.

Salant, Stephen W. (1983), 'The Vulnerability of Price Stabilization Schemes to Speculative Attack', *Journal of Political Economy* **91**, 1–38.

Salant, Stephen W. and Dale W. Henderson (1978), 'Market Anticipation of Government Policy and the Price of Gold', *Journal of Political Economy* **86**, 627–48.

West, Kenneth (1987), 'A Standard Monetary Model and the Variability of the Deutschemark–Dollar Exchange Rates', *Journal of International Economics* **23**, 57–76.

Williamson, John (1993), 'EMS and EMU after the Fall: A Comment', *The World Economy* **16**, 377–80.

Willman, Alpo (1988), 'The Collapse of the Fixed Exchange Rate Regime with Sticky Wages and Imperfect Substitutability Between Domestic and Foreign Bonds', *European Economic Review* **32**, 1817–38.

Woo, Wing T. (1985), 'The Monetary Approach to Exchange Rate Determination under Rational Expectations', *Journal of International Economics* **18**, 1–16.

Wyplosz, Charles (1986), 'Capital Controls and Balance of Payments Crises', *Journal of International Money and Finance* **5**, 167–79.

Discussion

ROBERT E. CUMBY

This paper presents systematic evidence on the behaviour of a number of macroeconomic variables during speculative crises and asks how well models of exchange rate crises correspond to our experience with exchange rate crises. Despite the obvious importance of the questions the authors ask and the fairly long-standing attention applied to exchange rate crises in the theoretical literature, surprisingly little systematic empirical research has been done to determine which of the insights from the theoretical literature appear to be consistent with the data.

The authors' approach to distinguishing a 'crisis' from other periods is a sensible one. They allow theory to guide their choices but do not adopt a tight (but possibly empirically suspect) specification that would be implied by any one particular model and are clearly correct in distinguishing crises from devaluations or realignments. Crises can end without a change in parities and parities can change without a crisis. Instead they identify crises with unusual behaviour of a linear combination of exchange rate, reserve, and interest rate changes. The particular linear combination(s) considered are aimed at allowing all three of these to contribute to the indicator of speculative pressure. This pragmatic approach to the problem of distinguishing crises appears to yield quite sensible results.

The authors adopt a similar strategy to determine which macroeconomic magnitudes to examine and how to examine them. Their choices would be suggested by a number of models but their methods do not adhere strictly to the specification implied by any particular model. Given the empirical problems with monetary models of exchange rates, which are commonly used in examining exchange rate crises, this seems like an extremely sensible way to proceed. But it is not without its costs. For example, one of the magnitudes that the authors examine is domestic credit growth. But it is the behaviour of domestic credit growth relative to money demand that plays a central role in monetary models of exchange rate crises. The problems encountered in identifying and estimating a stable money demand function suggest that the authors' choice is sensible, but leaves unanswered questions about whether differences in money demand growth between a country and the centre country (Germany) or changes in money demand might make it difficult to discern the role of domestic credit growth in exchange rate crises.

The main statistical analysis consists of comparing the distributions of each of the macroeconomic magnitudes during a period identified as a 'crisis' with the distributions of these variables during 'control' periods (all periods excluding a 'window' of six months on either side of a crisis). I will focus my discussion on the results from the ERM sample because they are probably the most relevant for answering the questions raised by the authors. Formal tests find that the distributions of money growth, interest rates, and reserve growth are all statistically significantly different during crisis periods. Crisis periods are distinguished by greater reserve losses, higher interest rates, and lower rates of money growth. In addition, inflation rates tend to be *lower* during crisis periods. This seemingly paradoxical difference in inflation rates is probably due to more crises taking place later in the sample (seven out of nineteen are in 1992, and twelve out of nineteen are in 1986 or later) when inflation rates were generally lower. Interestingly, the formal tests discern no statistically significantly different behaviour of the fiscal deficit (relative to GDP), real exchange rates, inflation rates, the ratio of exports to imports, or domestic credit growth.

How should we interpret the results of these tests? First, it is useful to ask whether the failure to reject the equality of distributions for a number of magnitudes is because the data are in fact close to the null hypothesis of equal distributions or because the data are essentially uninformative. The authors are to be commended for presenting histograms that permit the reader to supplement the formal test with informal, but informative, eyeball tests. The histograms of reserve growth differ most clearly when crisis and non-crisis periods are compared. The distributions of interest rates are also visibly different – smaller values of the interest rate differential are clearly missing during crisis periods. The most striking difference in the remainder of the histograms is that the distributions are flatter during crisis periods than in non-crisis periods, most likely reflecting the relatively small sample of crisis periods. Thus, for a number of the variables examined, the data simply do not provide enough information to allow us to distinguish differences in the distributions between crisis and non-crisis periods.

What conclusions can we draw from this evidence? One of the most interesting questions raised by the authors is whether or not ERM crises have been consistent with 'first-generation' models of exchange rate crises. The authors argue that the only reserve behaviour clearly different between crisis periods and non-crisis periods is in the ERM sample so that economic fundamentals do not differ between crisis and non-crisis periods. Consequently, they argue, the results are not consistent with first-generation models. Suppose, however, that all fixed exchange rates are doomed to lead to speculative attacks for Krugman–Flood–Garber reasons. How would crisis periods be distinguished from non-crisis periods? In such a world, the fixed parities are inconsistent with the rate of domestic credit creation. But in a Krugman–Flood–Garber setting, domestic credit growth follows the same process in both crisis and non-crisis periods. The crisis is triggered not by a *change* in domestic credit growth, but by the consequences of ongoing domestic credit creation that is inconsistent with the fixed rate. Thus one would not expect to find any difference between domestic credit growth in crisis and in non-crisis periods. Similarly, if fiscal policy is the source of domestic credit growth, one would not expect to find any difference in the budget deficit as a fraction of GDP in crisis and non-crisis periods. The control periods would look just like the crisis period for all variables except reserves and, in a stochastic model such as considered by Flood and Garber, nominal interest rates. Thus the data are consistent with the simplest versions of the first-generation speculative attack models.

The conventional wisdom about, for example, the speculative attack on the French franc in July 1993 differs somewhat from the simple Krugman–Flood–Garber version of first-generation models. A short version of the conventional wisdom is that the Bundesbank's disinflation policies confronted the French with either following a policy of tight money despite low inflation and an economy in recession or abandoning its ERM parity. The possibility of a change in exchange rate policy, driven not by a speculative attack but by domestic considerations, led investors to question the durability of the existing parity. In fact, relatively small probabilities of a small to moderate depreciation of the franc (say a 5 per cent chance of a 10 per cent depreciation in the next three months) are sufficient to explain the interest rate differential in mid-July 1993. This conventional wisdom attributes the crisis to the possibility of future changes in policy rather than to past policies. Speculative crises driven by such anticipations could generate results such as those found in the ERM sample.

Another version of this crisis attributes it to Anglo-Saxon elements – presumably the successors of the Gnomes of Zurich – that wrecked an otherwise perfectly good peg for the sport of it, or perhaps for fun and profit. Although economists generally approach such claims with well-placed scepticism, the 'second-generation' models provide a context in which a less conspiratorial version of these claims might have validity – the attack itself might trigger a change in the authorities' behaviour and create multiple equilibria and rational, self-fulfilling speculative attacks.

But, as the authors recognize, they cannot distinguish attacks that are consistent with these second-generation models from attacks that are driven by the consequences of exogenous fundamentals. The decision to realign or to abandon a fixed rate is fundamentally a choice. It could be a choice that would be triggered by an attack, as in the second-generation models. Alternatively, the attack could be driven by speculation that the choice to realign will be made for other reasons entirely. The key to distinguishing between a 'first-generation' and a 'second-generation' explanation of attacks driven by anticipated policy changes is whether the peg would be viable in the absence of an attack or whether the authorities might choose to abandon the peg even if no attack occurs. As the authors recognize, the evidence presented here will not allow us to distinguish between the two.

ROBERT P. FLOOD

As often happens in comments on papers delivered at conferences, I am taking the paper under discussion as a jumping off point to consider something that is suggested by the paper rather than the paper itself. The issue that fascinates me concerns the source of the enormous speculative pressures surrounding an attack. Such pressures were not really predicted by the original Krugman (1979) and Flood and Garber (1984a) models of speculative attacks on a fixed exchange rate except in the case of mismatched fundamentals processes. It is possible, however, to read later papers, e.g. Flood and Garber (1984b) or Obstfeld (1986), which develop the notion of a self-fulfilling speculative attack, as making such a prediction, since fundamental time-series processes are endogenous in these second-generation attack models. The authors of the paper under discussion find, however, that the macro data do not support a second-generation-style interpretation of the 1992 ERM attack and I agree. Here I want to sketch a model of speculative pressure that sidesteps the macro tradition and draws on the options pricing literature, but adds a twist from some newer empirical work by Flood and Rose (1994). The message I want to emphasize for this third-generation model is that the models of the first two generations were using the wrong conditional exchange rate volatility to assess attack pressure. Flexible rates are much more volatile than is predicted by fundamentals and consequently attack pressures have been badly understated.

The decision to fix an exchange rate is the same as the decision to give speculators an option to purchase the international reserves committed to the fixed rate's defence at a striking price equal to the fixed exchange rate. The reason that an attack becomes so frenzied is that the free option granted by the exchange authority does not immediately convey a private property right; it becomes privatized only in the event of the attack and then the rights convey to the first speculators in the attack line. There's no surprise then that there is quite a clamour to join in line when the attack begins.

The purpose of my discussion is to indicate why the standard attack literature would lead one to underestimate the pressure on a fixed rate that speculators put 'in play'. I shall use the language from the speculative attack literature and adopt some additional language from the options pricing literature. From the attack literature, the exchange rate prevailing immediately after a successful attack at time $t + 1$, next period, is known as the shadow exchange rate, $\hat{S}_{t+1}$, where S is the domestic currency price of foreign exchange. The currency will be attacked if and only if the shadow rate is above the fixed rate, $\bar{S}$.

The current value of the option that the foreign exchange authority gives to speculators by fixing the exchange rate at $\bar{S}$ is:[1]

$$\text{Option Value} = OV = \pi_t^*(E_t[\hat{S}_{t+1}|\hat{S}_{t+1} > \bar{S}] - \bar{S})^*R/(1 + i_t). \quad (1)$$

In this expression π_t is the probability attached at time t to an attack at $t + 1$; R is the quantity of reserves dedicated to defend the exchange rate peg, and i_t is the current one-period interest rate. In words, the option value is the expected value of the option given that the option is 'in the money' times the probability that the option is in the money. All of this is multiplied by $R/(1 + i)$ because R represents the number of options being given away by the exchange authority and because $1/(1 + i)$ is needed to convert future values to present values.[2]

As a simple indicator of pressure on a fixed exchange rate I propose to use OV from equation (1), and my point is that OV is *much* larger than speculative attack theory based on macro fundamentals would have one believe. Recall from option pricing theory that the value of a call option at a particular striking price is an increasing function of the variance of the price of the underlying asset. During the time that the exchange rate is fixed, its variance is zero. The fixed rate, however, is not the asset price relevant to pricing the free option. The relevant price is the shadow rate, and the variance of that price has been underestimated by an order of magnitude in the literature.[3]

The problem is that the literature, e.g. Flood and Garber (1984a), suggests that the short-run variance of the shadow flexible exchange rate is related to the variance of traditional fundamentals such as relative money supplies and relative outputs. Flood and Rose (1994) find, however, that such traditional fundamentals understate flexible exchange rate volatility by a factor of 10! The volatility of flexible rates is much higher than can be understood by looking at traditional macro fundamentals, and thus OV may be many times higher than appreciated by an onlooker attempting to assess the speculative situation by reference to traditional macro fundamentals.[4]

This observation is consistent with the paper under discussion. For the ERM sample the authors find no significant change in the behaviour of traditional fundamentals around the time of attacks. Two interpretations are possible in the context of existing models: first, that the attacks are of the first- or second-generation type and that fundamentals process misalignment or process change is simply not detectable in the small available samples; second, that the attacks are based only very weakly on macro fundamentals, but rather on a shift in non-traditional factors whose presence seems in little doubt but whose identity may be changing across episodes.

NOTES

1   See Hull (1993).
2   This option value is, in a way, familiar from Flood and Garber (1984a) (F&G). The π is identical to the probability in F&G so that OV in equation (1) is equal to the F&G expected rate of exchange rate change times the present value of the dollar value of reserves expended in a failed exchange rate defence.
3   Although the domestic interest rate will rise along with the expected rate of exchange rate change, such movement will, in the limit, mean that OV will approach its maximum $R^*\bar{S}$. See Flood and Garber (1984a) for a model of the domestic interest rate.

It was pointed out by John Williamson in oral discussion of these comments that the option value transfer to speculators under fixed rates is not the full general equilibrium effect on speculators of a move to fixed rates. Other parts of the speculator's business that involve facilitating international transactions may suffer under fixed rates.
4   In discussion of these comments it was suggested that the $\hat{S}$ may be inappropriate to use to value the implicit option if the authorities actually devalue the currency instead of allowing it to float. Although this is surely correct, the nature of the bias is that OV in equation (1) understates the value of the option because the devaluation, if successful, must always set the new parity above $\hat{S}$ (see Flood and Garber, 1984a).

REFERENCES

Flood, Robert and Peter Garber (1984a), 'Collapsing Exchange Rate Regimes: Some Linear Examples', *Journal of International Economics* **17**, 1–13.

(1984b), 'Gold Monetization and Gold Discipline', *Journal of Political Economy* **92**, 90–107.

Flood, Robert and Andrew Rose (1994), 'Fixing Exchange Rates: A Virtual Quest for Fundamentals', IIES Seminar Paper No. 529, Stockholm, Sweden.

Hull, John C. (1993), *Options, Futures and other Derivative Securities*, New Jersey: Prentice Hall.

Krugman, Paul (1979), 'A Model of Balance of Payments Crises', *Journal of Money, Credit and Banking* **11**, 311–25.

Obstfeld, Maurice (1986), 'Rational and Self-Fulfilling Balance of Payments Crises', *American Economic Review* **76**, 72–81.

8   Central banks and reputation: some transatlantic contrasts

BEN LOCKWOOD, MARCUS MILLER, and LEI
ZHANG

1   Introduction

The issue of delegating of monetary policy from government to central
bank is high on the political agenda in Europe. Both France and the UK
have recently given more autonomy to their central banks (CBs).
Moreover, the Treaty of European Union (1992) explicitly asserts that
those EU countries joining a European monetary union will collectively
delegate their monetary policy to a European central bank (ECB), whose
primary objective will be price stability.[1] It is not only in Western Europe
that delegation (and the appropriate targets for central bank monetary
policy) has been a key issue of debate. The success of the Baltic states of
Latvia and Estonia in checking inflation has coincided with establishing
monetary policy independence; while the high rates of inflation in other
newly independent states, such as Ukraine, are often associated with
central banks that are wholly subservient to political forces.

Two rather different ways of delegating monetary policy have attracted
academic attention. The starting point for both is the assumption that, in
the absence of any precommitment to a policy rule, discretionary
monetary policy leads to 'inflation bias' in the sense of Barro and
Gordon (1983) and Kydland and Prescott (1977). The first solution to
inflation bias is for the government to appoint a constitutionally
independent CB governor who is known to be more inflation averse (or
'conservative') than itself. Although this 'conservative bias' checks
expected inflation, it can also inhibit stabilization, leading to the notion
of an optimal degree of conservatism based on this trade-off, as in
Rogoff (1985). The idea of appointing a conservative central banker who
is nevertheless expected to help stabilize the economy may well reflect
American experience. (In any event, the paper referred to was largely
written when Rogoff was working at the Board of Governors of the
Federal Reserve System!)

236

The second solution to inflation bias, based more on microeconomic principal–agent theory, is for the CB governor to be appointed subject to a 'performance contract'. In this case, as Walsh (1992) and Persson and Tabellini (1993) point out, the terms of the contract can be set to induce an agent who is *not* conservative both to avoid inflation and to stabilize as appropriate. This contract-based approach to policy has found favour in some quarters because it gives less of a free hand to the governor (see Roll Report, 1993: 29). On the other hand, it has been criticized by Rogoff on the grounds that the *ex ante* contract is not 'time consistent': a government that threatens to punish inflation *ex ante* may nevertheless be inclined to reward an inflation surprise just before an election.

What light do these theories shed on the debate over delegation of monetary policy that is currently taking place in Europe? And what, in the light of these theories, can the European Union learn from the relative success of the US Federal Reserve both in establishing credibility and in stabilizing output and unemployment? These are the questions addressed in this paper. Our starting point is that the performance contract approach, although theoretically ingenious, is of limited interest in practice. Governments simply do not hire CB governors on performance contracts of the type required by the theory,[2] probably because of the time-consistency problem alluded to above, plus the fact that inflation is only partially under the control of the CB. Rather, CB governors are typically guaranteed some measure of constitutional independence to pursue specified goals. So, Rogoff's approach, where the 'goal' – as measured by the inflation aversion of the governor – can be specified, seems more appropriate.

In this paper, we focus in particular on two aspects of delegation where there are significant transatlantic contrasts: namely the reputation of the central bank and the structure of the economy. Specifically, we extend Rogoff's model of delegation to allow the CB to build *a reputation for low inflation*. We model reputation as a trigger strategy equilibrium in the repeated game between CB and private sector, where the CB keeps average price inflation low because it fears an increase in nominal wage inflation should it renege on its price inflation commitment.[3] In this case, the size of the reputation of the CB is related to its 'time-horizon', or, more precisely, inversely related to the rate at which it discounts the future. This seems a reasonable extension, because CBs tend, by and large, to take a 'longer view' of policy and its effects than do politicians.[4] Second, we investigate systematically the effect of the structure of the economy (in particular, nominal wage rigidity, NWR, and unemployment persistence) on optimal delegation.

Our main findings are as follows. First, we show that the longer time-horizons of CBs (as compared with politicians) provide an additional motive for delegation, i.e. governments may delegate in order to exploit the advantage of CBs in building a reputation. Second, a higher reputation *improves* the trade-off between low inflation and stabilization – a CB that is more forward looking can achieve more stabilization at a given average level of inflation. Third, we find that conservatism and reputation are 'substitutes'. More precisely, the higher the reputation of the CB, as measured by its discount factor, the less the optimal conservatism of the CB. Indeed, when reputation is high, it may be optimal for the government to delegate to a CB *less* inflation averse than itself (an *anti-conservative* CB). Finally, we show that the higher NWR, the greater conservatism; the more rigid are nominal wages, the greater the incentive for monetary expansion – and the need for a conservative bias to check inflation expectations.[5]

These results bear directly on the questions raised above. On the one hand, it is widely agreed that nominal wage rigidity is higher in the USA than in the EU, implying that the US Fed should be *more* conservative than any future ECB. On the other hand, the US Fed already has a well-established reputation for toughness on inflation, allowing it to be *less* conservative. In section 4 of the paper, we report numerical simulations that try to identify which of these two factors is dominant in the choice of the optimal 'conservatism' of the CB governor.

The rest of the paper is organized as follows. Section 2 discusses the modelling of reputation, and presents some evidence that CBs have some advantage in reputation-building. Section 3 provides a formal analysis of optimal delegation with reputation. Section 4 reports numerical simulations, and section 5 concludes.

2   Reputation in monetary policy

2.1   Modelling 'reputation' in monetary policy

Fudenberg and Tirole (1991) give a general definition of reputation in the context of game theory. A player has a reputation for a certain kind of play if, when 'the player always plays in the same way, his opponents will come to expect him to play in that way in the future and will adjust their own play accordingly'. There are in fact two different ways in which this concept can be made more precise. To fix ideas, we will review both of these in the context of the simple and familiar monetary policy game of Barro and Gordon (1983), where a monetary authority and a wage-setter interact over time and this interaction is modelled as a repeated game.

The first way of modelling reputation is as a 'trigger strategy' equilibrium. This is described more precisely below, but can be thought of as a kind of 'social contract', where the private sector and the monetary authority have an agreement – explicit or implicit – to keep price and wage inflation at some prescribed (low) level. If the monetary authority reneges on this agreement, it is 'punished' by the private sector increasing wage inflation (or, equivalently, inflation expectations). It is well known that the more weight the monetary authority attaches to the future, the lower the rate of inflation attainable as a trigger strategy equilibrium. So, the *degree* of reputation of the monetary authority can in this setting be parametrized by δ_b, the discount factor of the central bank. ($\$\delta_b$ is the present value of $1 received one period in the future.)

The second way of modelling reputation is in terms of beliefs on the part of the private sector about the *preferences* of the monetary authority, or, alternatively, about the *policy rules* that the authority may be committed to. Such models have been analysed by Backus and Driffill (1985) and by Vickers (1986). The common feature of these models is that the private sector believes the monetary authority is one of two types: either the *tough* type that places a large weight on the objective of price stability and a small weight (Vickers) or no weight (Backus and Driffill) on the objective of full employment; or the *weak* type that puts a large weight on the full employment objective.[6] The 'reputation' of the monetary authority in these models is usually taken to mean the subjective probability that the private sector attaches to the authority being tough (or, more generally, the distribution of private sector beliefs over possible types). This reputation is determined endogenously in the model and changes over time. However, the *initial reputation* (i.e. the prior belief that the authority is tough, or more generally the prior distribution of private sector beliefs) is obviously exogenous.

Both of these concepts of reputation have been criticized (see, e.g., Cuikerman, 1992), but it seems to us that they both capture different elements of what is meant by reputation in practice. The first notion captures the idea that, in a repeated game-setting, a CB whose preferences are well known can improve on what Barro and Gordon call the 'discretionary' outcome by acting in its own long-run interest. The second notion starts by assuming that the CB's true preferences are unknown and shows how appropriate behaviour can engender a favourable reputation.

Our concern here is how easily either concept can be introduced into Rogoff's model of monetary policy delegation. The 'trigger strategy' notion can be easily reconciled with Rogoff, as described below. In particular, the original Rogoff set-up, where the government chooses the weight on price stability in the CB's loss function, carries over. On the other hand, the 'prior belief' notion of reputation seems to complicate the delegation problem considerably, as the subsequent equilibrium between CB and private sector is determined not only by the actual 'type' of CB (as characterized by the weight on price stability in the CB's loss function), but also by the CB's initial reputation, as defined above. One possibility is that this initial reputation is taken as exogenous by the government; but this is not an attractive assumption because it is highly implausible that, when delegating monetary policy, the government is unable to affect this initial reputation. For example, as described by Swinburne and Castello-Branco (1991) and Roll Report (1993), the legislation for CBs proposed or enacted in recent years (e.g. European Central Bank, Banque de France, Reserve Bank of New Zealand, and CBs of Chile, Mexico, and Venezuela) in general stresses greater *transparency* of bank objectives and operations than the existing status quo. To reflect this reality, the Rogoff delegation model should really be extended to allow for government choice of an initial reputation for the CB, as well as a weight on price stability in the CB's objective. Modelling this adequately seems a challenge beyond the scope of this paper.[7] So we stick to the 'trigger strategy' concept of delegation.

2.2   Who discounts the future more: governments or central banks?

If we allow the monetary authority to have a reputation in the trigger strategy sense, the rates at which the government and the CB discount the future become an issue. Let the two discount factors be δ and δ_b respectively. In particular, as we show in section 3 below, (i) if δ is high enough, the government can achieve its 'precommitment' inflation outcome (defined more precisely below), and so does not need to delegate; (ii) if the government discount factor is high *relative* to that of the CB, then, even though it may not be able to achieve its precommit-ment, it may be able to 'reputation build' so much better than the CB that it prefers not to delegate.

Casual empiricism suggests that CBs take a 'long view' as opposed to politicians who have limited time-horizons. Such quantitative evidence as is available confirms this. Table 8.1 indicates that, in five out of the seven G7 countries, turnover rates of political parties are higher than those of CB governors; and, of course, turnover rates of those in government responsible for monetary policy are higher still. (For example, in the UK, although there have been no changes of government since 1979, over that period there have been five different finance ministers.) In so far as turnover rates affect discount factors, table 8.1 gives some evidence in favour of the proposition that $\delta_b > \delta$. On this basis, it seems reasonable

Table 8.1. Comparative turnover rates of political parties in office and CBs in G7 countries

Country	CB governor[1]	Party in office[2]
UK	0.10	0.17
Canada	0.10	0.17
Germany	0.10	0.13
USA	0.13	0.22
France	0.15	0.13
Japan	0.20	0.00
Italy	0.08	0.22

[1] Measured as average number of changes per annum over the period 1950–89. *Source*: Cuikerman (1992).
[2] Over the period 1959–92. Defined as number of elections at which a change in the party (or parties) of government occurred over the sample period, divided by the number of years in the sample. See Lockwood *et al.* (1994) for details.

to assume that governments are more myopic than CBs, which is what we assume below.

3 Delegation with reputation

3.1 The model

The economy evolves over an infinite number of time periods $t = 0, 1, 2, \ldots, \infty$. At time zero, the government appoints a central banker (CB), who is then responsible for monetary policy at $t = 1$ onwards. At every $t = 1, 2, \ldots$, inflation, the real wage, employment, and output are determined by the decisions of the CB and a trade union or other wage-setter. Within a period the order of events is as follows: first the wage-setter sets the log of the nominal wage, w_t, in order to achieve an employment target, $\bar{l}$, given rational expectations about the price level; then an independent identically distributed labour demand shock, ϵ_t, occurs, with $E_t\epsilon_t = 0, E_t\epsilon_t^2 = \sigma^2$.[8] Having observed the shock, the CB chooses the price level, p_t, or equivalently the rate of inflation, π_t. Finally, the log of employment is determined by labour demand, $l_t = p_t - w_t - \epsilon_t$.

It is well known that, once the CB is appointed, the CB and wage-setter can be thought of as playing a repeated game with the following structure. First, the stage-game strategy of the bank is an *inflation rule* mapping every shock ϵ_t into a choice of inflation level, π_t, while the strategy for the wage-setter is a choice of subjective expectation of inflation π_t^e before ϵ_t is realized. Second, unemployment varies around a fixed rate, u_n, according to the inflation surprises and labour demand shocks, i.e.

$$u_t = u_n - \beta(\pi_t - \pi_t^e) + \epsilon_t, \tag{1}$$

where $u_n = n - \bar{l}, n$ is the log of the labour force, and β is the response of unemployment to inflation surprises, usually called the coefficient of *nominal wage rigidity* (NWR). This is an important parameter in our analysis, and it is believed that β differs widely between the EU and the USA (see, e.g., table 8.2 or section 4 below). Stage-game expected losses for the two players are:

$$E_t\left[(1 - \lambda_b)u_t^2 + \lambda_b \pi_t^2\right] \quad \lambda_b \in [0, 1] \text{ (central bank)} \tag{2}$$

$$E_t\left[(\pi_t^e - \pi_t)^2\right] \qquad \qquad \text{(wage-setter)} \tag{3}$$

The second follows from the assumption of rational expectations on the part of the wage-setter. The parameter λ_b measures the CB's degree of aversion to inflation, and we assume that it is this parameter that the government chooses at time zero. The CB discounts the future at $\delta_b > 0$.

It remains to specify the preferences of the government. The government's per-period expected loss is

$$E_t\left[(1 - \lambda)u_t^2 + \lambda \pi_t^2\right] \quad \lambda \in (0, 1) \quad \text{(government)} \tag{4}$$

Note that this will differ from the CB's loss function if $\lambda \neq \lambda_b$, i.e. there is a difference in inflation aversion. Another difference can arise from discounting. The government discounts the future at some $\delta > 0$. On the basis of section 2.2, we assume that

(A1) *the government is more myopic than the CB:* $0 < \delta < \delta_b < 1$.

The two-stage model set out above can be solved backwards. Once appointed, the CB 'builds a reputation' with the wage-setter. So, we need to find the trigger strategy, or reputation equilibrium, at this stage. The reputation equilibrium condition then imposes a constraint on the government's action at the first stage, when the government chooses a central bank 'type', λ_b, to minimize its expected discounted losses subject to this incentive constraint. So, the first step is to solve for the reputation equilibrium in the game between CB and wage-setter. As a preliminary step, we solve for the stage-game Nash equilibrium in the game between

CB and wage-setter, which Barro and Gordon call the discretionary equilibrium (DE).

3.2   Discretionary equilibrium

To solve for the DE, we first derive the reaction functions of the two players. The CB chooses π_t to minimize (2) subject to (1) and π_t^e fixed, and similarly the wage-setter chooses π_t^e to minimize (3) subject to $E_t\pi_t$ fixed. This gives two first-order conditions $-(1 - \lambda_b)\beta u_t + \lambda_b\pi_t = 0$, all ϵ_t, and $\pi_t^e - E_t\pi_t = 0$, which can be solved to yield the DE inflation level,

$$\pi_t = \frac{1 - \lambda_b}{\lambda_b}\beta u_n + \frac{\beta(1 - \lambda_b)}{\lambda_b + \beta^2(1 - \lambda_b)}\epsilon_t. \tag{5}$$

This can be thought of as a linear inflation rule of the form $\pi_t = \phi u_n + s\epsilon_t$, where

$$\phi^n = \frac{1 - \lambda_b}{\lambda_b}\beta, \quad s^n = \frac{\beta(1 - \lambda_b)}{\lambda_b + \beta^2(1 - \lambda_b)}, \tag{6}$$

using the superscript 'n' to denote the Nash equilibrium. To interpret the rule (6), note that if the CB would *precommit* to a rule (ϕ, s) before π_t^e were set, it would choose $\phi_b = 0, s_b = \beta(1 - \lambda_b)/[\lambda_b + \beta^2(1 - \lambda_b)]$, i.e. zero expected inflation but optimal stabilization. So, it is clear from (5) and (6) that the discretionary equilibrium exhibits an 'inflationary bias', i.e. expected inflation is positive, as $\phi^n > 0$, but also that stabilization is the same as in the precommitment case.

3.3   Reputational equilibrium

In Barro and Gordon (1983), a reputational equilibrium (RE) is a low-inflation equilibrium sustained by a trigger strategy on the part of the wage-setters: as long as the CB sticks to a low rate of inflation, the wage-setter sets a corresponding low rate of wage increase, but, if the CB reneges at any date, wage-setters revert to a (higher) rate of wage increase from then on (the punishment). Let the higher rate be the discretionary equilibrium rate; more precisely, if the CB reneges, the wage-setter switches to inflationary expectation $\pi_t^e = \phi^n u_n$. Choosing this punishment ensures that the punishment is credible (technically, that the equilibrium is subgame-perfect).

So, the equilibrium condition consists of an incentive constraint that says that the CB has no incentive to renege at any date t following any shock ϵ_t, given this trigger strategy on the part of the wage-setter. We now briefly derive this equilibrium condition – it is a little more complex than the condition in Barro and Gordon (1983), because there is uncertainty in our model. First, in RE, the CB would like to commit to a *rule* for inflation that allows it to respond to shocks. Given the linear-quadratic structure, we can without loss of generality consider only linear rules of the form:

$$\pi_t = \phi u_n + s\epsilon_t, \tag{7}$$

where the $s\epsilon_t$ part of the rule allows for some stabilization of employment around u_n. If the CB sticks to the rule at time t, it is easy to calculate that its per-period loss would be

$$L_b(\phi, s, \epsilon_t) = (1 - \lambda_b)[u_n + (1 - \beta s)\epsilon_t]^2 + \lambda_b(\phi u_n + s\epsilon_t)^2, \tag{8}$$

using (1) and rational expectations on the part of the private sector, i.e. $\pi_t^e = \phi u_n$. Now suppose that the CB reneges on the rule at period t. Conditional on ϵ_t, its minimum per-period loss from reneging is simply the minimum of $(1 - \lambda_b)u_t^2 + \lambda_b\pi_t^2$ with respect to π_t, given that the private sector expects rule (ϕ, s), i.e. $\pi_t^e = \phi u_n$:

$$L_b^{min}(\phi, \epsilon_t) = \min_{\pi_t}\{(1 - \lambda_b)u_t^2 + \lambda_b\pi_t^2 \text{ s.t.(1) and } \pi_t^e = \phi u_n\}$$

$$= \frac{\lambda_b(1 - \lambda_b)(u_n + \beta\phi u_n + \epsilon_t)^2}{\lambda_b + (1 - \lambda_b)\beta^2}. \tag{9}$$

Finally, we calculate the expected per-period loss from time $t + 1$ onward in the event that the CB has reneged at t and so play has reverted to the discretionary equilibrium. From (6) and (8), in the DE, the CB suffers an *expected* per-period loss of

$$D_b(\phi^n, s^n) = (1 - \lambda_b)\frac{\lambda_b + \beta^2(1 - \lambda_b)}{\lambda_b}u_n^2 + \frac{(1 - \lambda_b)\lambda_b\sigma^2}{\lambda_b + \beta^2(1 - \lambda_b)}. \tag{10}$$

The condition for (ϕ, s) to be an RE rule is simply that the present value of losses from sticking to the rule be no more than the present value from reneging, at every date t and for any possible value of ϵ_t:

$$L_b(\phi, s, \epsilon_t) + E_t\left[\sum_{\tau=t+1}^{\infty} \delta_b^{\tau-t}L_b(\phi, s, \epsilon_\tau)\right]$$

$$\leq L_b^{min}(\phi, \epsilon_t) + \sum_{\tau=t+1}^{\infty} \delta_b^{\tau-t}D_b(\phi^n, s^n), \quad \text{all } t, \text{ all } \epsilon_t. \tag{11}$$

Following Barro and Gordon (1983), we assume that, at $t = 1$, the CB will then choose a rule to minimize its expected discounted losses subject to the RE equilibrium condition (11). In other words, the CB solves the following problem:

(PB) Choose ϕ, s to minimize $E_1\left[\sum_{t=1}^{\infty} \delta_b^{t-1} L_b(\phi, s, \epsilon_t)\right]$ subject to (11).

This is a complex problem, but can be considerably simplified if we restrict the RE rule (ϕ, s) to have the stabilization component $s_b = \beta(1 - \lambda_b)[\lambda_b + \beta^2(1 - \lambda_b)]^{-1}$ that the CB would choose if it could precommit to an inflation rule. In this case, the solution to (PB) can be straightforwardly characterized:

Proposition 1
(i) If $\delta_b \geq 1/[2 + \beta^2(1 - \lambda_b)/\lambda_b]$, then at the solution to (PB), the CB sets $\phi^* = 0$, $s^* = s_b$, i.e. the CB achieves its precommitment rule.
(ii) If $\delta_b < 1/[2 + \beta^2(1 - \lambda_b)/\lambda_b]$, then at the solution to (PB) the CB sets $s^* = s_b$, and

$$\phi^* = \phi^*(\lambda_b, \delta_b) = \frac{\beta(1 - \lambda_b)}{\lambda_b} \frac{1 - \delta_b - \delta_b[1 + \beta^2(1 - \lambda_b)/\lambda_b]}{1 + \delta_b\beta^2(1 - \lambda_b)/\lambda_b}. (12)$$

Also, ϕ^* is decreasing in δ_b.

Proof: see Appendix.

This result says that the CB can implement its precommitment rule if δ_b is high enough. Otherwise, it can achieve optimal stabilization, but has to tolerate a positive (expected) rate of inflation, i.e. $\phi^* > 0$. Note that unlike in the DE, ϕ^* in (12) is *not* necessarily decreasing in λ_b, the inflation aversion of the CB, a fact that will turn out to be important below. The reason for this is that a larger λ_b has the effect of lowering the DE inflation rate, ϕ_n (from (6)), which weakens the severity of the punishment in the RE constraint, (11). This in turn makes it harder to achieve a low inflation rate. This 'punishment' effect offsets the fact that a high-δ_b CB has a more intense dislike of inflation.

Proposition 1 allows us to draw a *delegation constraint* that will constrain the government's choice of CB, λ_b, at the delegation stage. This consists of the RE values of s and ϕ as λ_b varies from 0 to 1, and is shown in the top panel of figure 8.1. The constraint OA traces out feasible combinations of s and ϕ as λ_b varies from 1 to 0 in the benchmark case without reputation, i.e. when $\delta_b = 0$, so the DE prevails once the CB has been appointed. There, when $\lambda_b = 1$, $s = \phi = 0$ and as $\lambda_b \to 0$, $\phi_n \to \infty$, $s_n \to 1$ from (6). When $\delta_b > 0$, our main case of

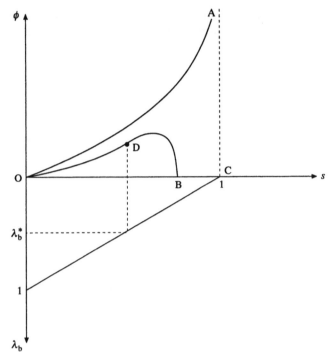

Figure 8.1   Time-consistent outcomes and the effect of reputation

interest,[9] the constraint OBC traces out values of s and ϕ that solve (PB), the CB's problem, as λ_b varies from 1 to 0.

   If delegation takes place, the government will choose a loss-minimizing point on OBC – say, at point D. Once this point is chosen, the implied type of CB, λ_b^*, can be read off the bottom panel of the diagram as shown for the case $\beta = 1$, using the fact that CB always chooses an $s = s_b = 1 - \lambda_b$.

3.4   Optimal delegation

The delegation problem for the government is a two-stage one. First, it must decide whether to delegate or not. (If δ is sufficiently high, it may choose to build a reputation without delegating.) Second, given that it has decided to delegate, it must choose a 'type' λ_b for the CB. We solve for this two-stage problem in the usual way, beginning with the second stage. Note that the government's expected per-period loss from a rule (ϕ, s) is

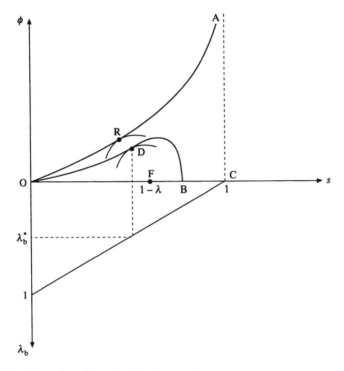

Figure 8.2   Delegation with and without reputation

$$EL_g(\phi, s) = E_t\{(1 - \lambda)[u_n + (1 - \beta s)\epsilon_t]^2 + \lambda(\phi u_n + s\epsilon_t)^2\}$$

$$= (1 - \lambda + \lambda\phi^2)u_n^2 + \sigma^2[(1 - \lambda)(1 - \beta s)^2 + \lambda s^2] \quad (13)$$

So, if the government decides to delegate, it will solve the following delegation problem:

(**D**)   *choose* λ_b *to minimize* $EL_g(\phi, s)$ *s.t.* $s = s_b = \beta(1 - \lambda_b)$
   $/[\lambda_b + \beta^2(1 - \lambda_b)]$, $\phi = \min\{0, \phi^*(\lambda_b, \delta_b)\}$.

Note that this is a generalization of Rogoff's (1985) delegation problem; his is the special case when $\delta_b = 0$, in which case the constraints reduce to $\phi = s/(1 - \beta s)$, $s = \beta(1 - \lambda_b)/[\lambda_b + \beta^2(1 - \lambda_b)]$. The solution to (D) can be illustrated by superimposing the iso-loss curves of (13) on figure 8.1. This gives figure 8.2. To interpret figure 8.2 note from (13) that the government precommitment inflation rule (ϕ_g, s_g), which minimizes L_g with respect to ϕ and s separately, is the rule with zero expected inflation $(\phi_g = 0)$ and optimal stabilization from the point of view of the government $(s_g = \beta(1 - \lambda)/[\lambda + \beta^2(1 - \lambda)])$. Figure 8.2 shows the concave iso-loss curves of L_g, centred at (ϕ_g, s_g), the point labelled F in the figure, again for the case $\beta = 1$.

So, the original Rogoff delegation solution is at the point R, where the iso-loss curve of L_g is tangent to the delegation constraint OA when $\delta_b = 0$. When $\delta_b > 0$, the government faces the constraint OBC as discussed above. Let $\bar{s}$ denote the value of s at B, where the constraint hits the horizontal axis. If $\bar{s} < s_g$, the government can obviously get to the first-best by not delegating. The more interesting case, where $\bar{s} > s_g$, is shown; there (assuming that there is an interior solution), the delegation solution is at the point D, where the iso-loss contour is tangent to OB. This implies a value λ_b^* for the type of the CB.

The government may also choose to build a reputation itself. In this case, it will solve the analogue of (PB), where λ_b, δ_b are replaced by λ, δ. The government will obviously delegate if and only if its expected loss from doing so is less than its expected loss from building its own reputation. We are interested in knowing when the government will delegate, and the properties of λ_b^*, the optimal degree of conservatism of the CB, when the government does delegate, and the inflation rule in each case. All this is given by Proposition 2.

Proposition 2

(i) *The government will choose not to delegate if and only if* $\delta \geq 1/[2 + \beta^2(1 - \lambda)/\lambda] = \delta^0$. *The inflation rule is the government's precommitment rule* $\phi_g = 0$, $s_g = \beta(1 - \lambda)/[\lambda + \beta^2(1 - \lambda)]$.

(ii) *If* $\delta < \delta^0 \leq \delta_b$, *the government will delegate, but to a CB no more conservative than itself, i.e.* $\lambda_b^* = \lambda$. *The inflation rule under delegation is the government's precommitment rule.*

(iii) *If* $\delta < \delta_b < \delta^0$, *then the government always delegates. The inflation rule under delegation,* ϕ^d, s^d *solves*

$$\phi^d, s^d = \mathrm{argmin}\ \{(1 - \lambda + \lambda\phi^2)u_n^2 + \sigma^2[\lambda s^2 + (1 - \lambda)(1 - \beta s)^2]\}$$

$$\text{s.t. } \phi = \phi^- = s\left(\frac{2(1 - \delta_b)}{1 - (1 - \delta_b)\beta s} - \frac{1}{1 - \beta s}\right),$$

$$s \in [0, \bar{s}],$$

$$\bar{s} = \frac{1}{\beta}\left(2 - \frac{1}{1 - \delta_b}\right).$$

The type of CB chosen by the government is $\lambda_b^* = \beta(1 - \beta s^d)/[\beta + (1 - \beta^2)s^d]$.

Proof:
(i) From Proposition 1, replacing δ_b, λ_b with δ, λ, it is clear that, when $\delta \geq \delta^0$, the government can achieve its precommitment rule without delegating. As it cannot do better than its precommitment rule, it will choose not to delegate.

(ii) As $\delta_b \geq \delta^0$, from Proposition 1, a CB of type $\lambda_b = \lambda$ will choose $\phi = 0$, $s = \beta(1-\lambda)/[\lambda + \beta^2(1-\lambda)]$ if delegated to; by setting $\lambda_b = \lambda$, the government can therefore achieve its precommitment rule only by delegating.

(iii) Suppose to the contrary that the government does not delegate, then, from Proposition 1, it will choose stabilization $s_g = \beta(1-\lambda)/[\lambda + \beta^2(1-\lambda)]$ and expected inflation $u_n \phi^*(\delta, \lambda)$. Now, from Proposition 1, as $\phi^*(\delta, \lambda)$ is decreasing in δ, and $\delta < \delta_b$, the government could achieve identical stabilization and a lower expected inflation by delegating to a CB with $\lambda_b = \lambda_b^*$, a contradiction. The second part follows directly from figure 8.2.

$$\text{QED}$$

The first part of this Proposition says that, when δ is high enough, the government does not need to delegate, because it can get to its precommitment inflation rule via its own reputation alone. The second part of the Proposition says that, when δ_b is high enough, it can get to its precommitment inflation rule by 'free-riding' on the CB's reputation. The third part points out that, even when the CB cannot achieve the government's precommitment rule, it still pays the government to 'free-ride' on the CB's superior ability to maintain a reputation. It also characterizes the delegation decision as the solution to a minimization problem.

Unfortunately, this minimization problem is not straightforward, because the constraint curve OBC is not convex (unlike the Rogoff case). First, there may be a corner solution at B. Second, even the portion of the constraint OB is not always less concave than the iso-loss contour of L_g, so that there can be several local minima of L_g along OB. This makes it impossible (for us!) to establish any properties of λ_b^*, s^d, and ϕ^d analytically. In particular, it is impossible to show whether or not the government will always choose a CB more conservative than itself, i.e. $\lambda_b^* > \lambda$.

Some computer simulations of λ_b^* as a function of the key parameters of the model, λ, β, and δ_b, are reported in figures 8.3 and 8.4.[10] The first figure is particularly interesting. It shows, first of all, that λ_b^* is increasing in λ. More surprisingly, however, it shows that, when λ is low, the government may delegate to a CB *less conservative* than itself. This is in

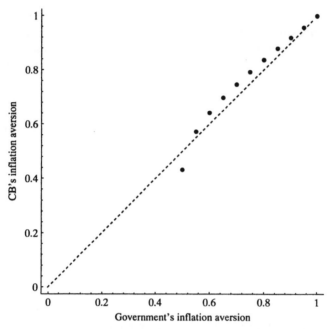

Figure 8.3   **How CB reputation can reduce the conservative bias of the central bank** ($u_n^2/\sigma^2 = \delta_b = 0.25$, and $\beta = 1$)

contrast to Rogoff's result. The reason for this is simple. Suppose $\lambda_b^* = \lambda$. Then, from the point of view of the government, stabilization is optimal at s^g, but expected inflation is too high. A small decrease in λ_b^* from λ will therefore have zero first-order effect on the government's expected loss via its effect on stabilization. On the other hand, a decrease in λ_b^* will reduce the government's expected loss if it reduces expected inflation, i.e. if $\partial\phi^*(\delta_b, \lambda_b)/\partial\lambda_b > 0$ where $\phi^*(\delta_b, \lambda_b)$ is defined in (12) above. It has been pointed out already that, owing to the 'punishment effect', it is possible that $\partial\phi^*/\partial\lambda_b > 0$.

Figure 8.4 indicates that, at least for the parameter values chosen, a high δ_b and a high λ_b are *substitutes*, i.e. if the CB discounts the future less, the government will typically choose it to be more conservative. This must be a general feature of the solution to (D) over some range of parameter values, as when $\delta_b = 0$, $\lambda_b^* > \lambda$, but when $\delta_b = \delta^0$, $\lambda_b^* = 1$, as asserted in Proposition 2.

Finally, figure 8.5 shows how the conservatism of the optimal CB varies with nominal wage rigidity, β. The dashed line shows the relationship when there is no reputation-building; conservatism is increasing in β. The

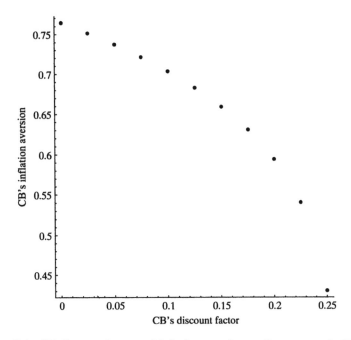

Figure 8.4   CB discount factor and inflation aversion: patience as a substitute for conservatism ($u_n^2/\sigma^2 = 1, \lambda = 0.5$, and $\beta = 1$)

intuition for this is well known; the higher β, the worse the inflation bias in the DE, the greater the incentive for the government to appoint a conservative CB. The solid line shows λ_b^* as a function of β for $\delta_b = 0.25$, where there is reputation-building by the CB. The striking finding here is that, with reputation, the link between nominal wage rigidity may be non-monotonic. Figure 8.5 shows that, when β is low, an interior solution (shown as D on figure 8.2) to the delegation problem obtains, and so the picture is qualitatively the same as in the case without reputation.[11] However, when β is high enough, a corner solution at B becomes optimal; it is clear from figure 8.2 that, at this point, λ_b^* will jump downwards.

4   Delegation, stabilization, and inflation: the USA and Europe compared

So far this paper has investigated the effects of both the structure of the economy (as measured by nominal wage rigidity) and reputation on the delegation of monetary policy. In this section, we combine this theory

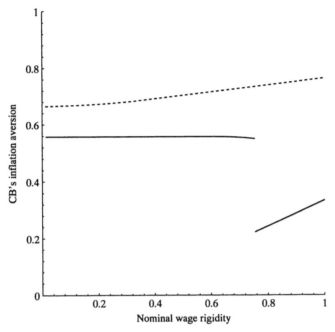

Figure 8.5   CB's inflation aversion and nominal wage rigidity ($u_n^2 / \sigma^2 = 1$, $\lambda = 0.5$, and $\delta = 0.25$)

with 'stylized facts' about the key parameters (β, δ_b, δ) to address two questions. How can extending the Rogoff model to take account of reputation help to explain the conduct of US monetary policy? And what does it imply about the likely conduct of any ECB?

We begin by noting that there are significant transatlantic differences in nominal wage rigidity. It is clear from the first two columns of table 8.2 that NWR is a good deal lower in the EU than in the USA: estimates of the parameter β in the EU are only about one-eighth of the US value in the short run, and about one-third in the long run.[12] Further, from column 3, it is apparent that there are considerable differences in unemployment persistence as well, with unemployment in the EU having a far more pronounced autoregressive structure.[13] The specific figures reported in the table are drawn from Layard *et al.* (1991), but many other studies have noted the same 'stylized facts'.

As regards differences in reputation, we note that whereas the Federal Reserve System has been in business for over eighty years (and acquired an enviable reputation for checking inflation and for stabilizing the economy), the ECB does not yet exist! This suggests surely that the ECB

Table 8.2. Nominal wage rigidity in the EC and USA

β	Nominal wage rigidity		Unemployment persistence
	Long-run (β_l)	Short-run (β_s)	
EU-9[1]	0.31	0.10	0.68
EMU-4[2]	0.24	0.09	0.77
USA	0.80	0.74	−0.02

Source: Layard *et al.* (1991). Long-run nominal wage rigidity taken from column 12 of their table 2, p. 407. Short-run nominal rigidity defined as the absolute value of the coefficient on $\Delta^2 p$ in equation (8), p. 407, and calculated using coefficient values reported in their table 2. The measure of persistence is taken from column 13 of this table.
[1] The nine EU countries for which estimates of nominal wage rigidity and unemployment persistence are available: Belgium, Denmark, France, Germany, Ireland, Italy, the Netherlands, Spain, and the UK.
[2] The four EU countries of the nine above most likely to form a European monetary union: Belgium, France, Germany, and the Netherlands.

will enjoy less credibility, at least initially, than the Fed currently commands.

What effects will these differences have on the conservativism of the CB in the USA and Europe? Because the labour market model in this paper is not dynamic, we leave on one side the differences in persistence and focus on nominal wage rigidity and reputation. (Appendix B to this paper contains a brief account of results we have derived elsewhere on delegation when unemployment persists.) Note that the differences in wage rigidity and in reputation have opposite implications for delegation. The higher nominal rigidity in the USA means that there will be a greater incentive to inflate: so the chairperson of the Federal Reserve Board should be relatively more conservative than their European counterpart. On the other hand, any ECB will have less of a reputation than the Fed, and will need greater conservatism to offset this reputational disadvantage.

Which of these two factors dominates can be further examined by numerical simulation for a variety of different values of δ_b and β (see table 8.3).[14] In the top panel, 8.3(a), we report the proportional conservative bias $(\lambda_b - \lambda)/\lambda$ for four of the β values in table 8.2 and for δ_b ranging from 0 to 0.5. In the first column, where there is no reputation-building, we can see how Rogoff's conservative bias varies with nominal wage rigidity. Specifically, the higher NWR in the USA leads to a bias of about 50 per cent as opposed to around 40 per cent for the EMU-4.

Table 8.3.   Inflation, stabilization, and conservative bias: the USA and the EU compared

β	δ_b		
	0.0	0.25	0.5
(a) *Conservative bias*, $(\lambda_b - \lambda)/\lambda$			
US-β_1	0.540	−0.146	0
US-β_s	0.526	−0.220	0
EMU-4 β_1	0.426	0.054	0
EMU-4 β_s	0.412	0.148	0
(b) *Coefficient of stabilization, s*			
US-β_1	0.201	0.577	0.488
US-β_s	0.197	0.624	0.478
EMU-4 β_1	0.094	0.205	0.218
EMU-4 β_s	0.037	0.066	0.085
(c) *Average inflation per unit unemployment,* ϕ			
US-β_1	0.239	0	0
US-β_s	0.230	0.201	0
EMU-4β_1	0.097	0.086	0
EMU-4β_s	0.038	0.033	0

How does the reputational advantage of the Fed affect this? In this stylized example it turns things round completely. For values of δ_b of 0.25 or 0.5,[15] which induce powerful reputational effects, the conservative bias in the USA falls essentially to zero (or slightly negative). So Rogoff's conservative bias is completely offset by what one might call the Greenspan effect! For the ECB without reputation, however, we leave the bias unchanged at the Rogoff solution. This would imply that the Fed is essentially able to implement the government's own precommitment stabilization policy without igniting fears of inflation, whereas the ECB would be constrained to be about 40 per cent 'more conservative' than the countries it represents!

These aspects of policy are shown in the next two panels. In 8.3(b), rows 1 and 2, we see how the stabilization policy chosen by a relatively conservative US central banker stabilizes about one-fifth of the supply shocks, while the precommitment policy chosen by a CB with lots of reputation and no bias stabilizes around 50 per cent of the shock. In rows 3 and 4, we find that the ECB without reputation will choose to stabilize only 4–9 per cent of the supply shocks. (Panel 8.3(c) gives the expected inflation in the various cases.)

Lastly, consider the case if the ECB were to enjoy the same sort of reputation as we have attributed to the Fed. Then it too should be able to 'substitute reputation for conservatism' and help to stabilize shocks to unemployment. From table 8.3, it is clear that, in this case, the reputation effect could in principle increase the stabilization coefficient s up to the range 0.09–0.22 and reduce the conservative bias to zero.

5 Conclusion

In this paper, Rogoff's account of monetary policy delegation is extended to take account of reputational factors – as captured in a trigger strategy equilibrium. In such a framework it turns out that the longer-run view taken by a central bank, relative to the finance minister, means that the former will be more concerned to protect its reputation. But this implies that the central bank has a comparative advantage in implementing monetary policy; for the central bank, unlike the ministry of finance, can respond actively to supply-side shocks without raising fears that this activism will be used to stimulate the economy beyond its non-inflationary equilibrium.

We have, in short, identified another reason for delegating monetary policy. But here it is the central bank's concern for reputation and not its conservative bias that checks inflationary expectations. With sufficiently good reputation, indeed, a central bank will in principle be able to implement the government's own first-best stabilization policy.

We have applied this idea to see how the conduct of policy might differ on either side of the Atlantic. First we noted that there was considerable nominal rigidity in the USA, substantially more than in Europe. On Rogoff's reasoning this should lead to a greater conservative bias in America – because the government there needs to offset a perceived greater temptation to spring monetary surprises. But there is little evidence of a more pronounced conservative bias in US monetary policy. On the contrary, the Fed seems to conduct a fairly active stabilization policy. That it can do this without stimulating inflation expectations is, we argue, because, in the USA, reputation (the 'Greenspan effect') is acting as an effective substitute for Rogoff's 'conservative bias'.

One can only speculate about future European monetary policy because the Maastricht Treaty has been signed but the ERM has meanwhile been largely suspended. Whereas the Fed has been in business for some eighty years, the European ECB is still very much on the drawing board. But this very observation might suggest that delegation in Europe will not be motivated by the perceived reputation of the ECB. More than likely, monetary delegation in Europe will be to a central bank with a pronounced conservative bias, for just the reason Rogoff described.

This could be highly significant because of a feature of European economies that we have noted but not specifically taken into account in this paper; namely, the marked persistence in European unemployment. If this persistence is due to insider power, the first-best policy would surely be to change the structure of the labour market – this was Mrs Thatcher's objective in the UK. But if this is not done – and there does not seem to be much stomach in Europe for labour market reform along Anglo-Saxon lines – then the (conditional) first-best policy is to increase stabilization as the persistence increases. But can one realistically expect a conservative ECB to play an active role in handling the hysteresis one observes in European unemployment? If not, can fiscal stabilization policy be used as a substitute? Or will that too fall foul of the Maastricht limits on debt and deficits?

These are vital questions that remain to be answered. In the meantime, an alternative *modus vivendi* is emerging, namely the development of independent national central banks, each gaining credibility by responding to local stabilization needs in an ERM with wide bands. Such credible players – or a subset of them – could at some time in the future choose to pool both sovereignty and credibility. Putting the ECB first, as in the Maastricht Treaty, runs the risk of putting the cart before the horse.

Appendix A: Proof of Proposition 1

First, we simplify the constraints (11). We note that, for $\tau \geq t$,

$$E_t L_b(\phi, s_b, \epsilon_t) = (1 - \lambda_b + \lambda_b \phi^2)u_n^2 + \sigma^2[(1 - \lambda_b)(1 - \beta s_b)^2 + \lambda_b(s_b)^2]$$
$$= (1 - \lambda_b + \lambda_b \phi^2)u_n^2 + \sigma^2(1 - \lambda_b)(1 - \beta s_b). \qquad (A1)$$

Also, after some simplification,

$$L_b(\phi, s_b, \epsilon_t) = (1 - \lambda_b + \lambda_b \phi^2)u_n^2 + 2u_n\epsilon_t(1 - \lambda_b)(1 + \phi\beta)(1 - \beta s_b)$$
$$+ (1 - \lambda_b)(1 - \beta s_b)\epsilon_t^2, \qquad (A2)$$

$$L_b^{\min}(\phi, \epsilon_t) = (1 - \lambda_b)(1 - \beta s_b)(1 + \phi\beta)^2 u_n^2 + 2u_n\epsilon_t(1 - \lambda_b)(1 + \phi\beta)$$
$$(1 - \beta s_b) + (1 - \lambda_b)(1 - \beta s_b)\epsilon_t^2. \qquad (A3)$$

Substituting (A1)–(A3) into (11), along with (10), we see that all terms in ϵ_t, ϵ_t^2, and s_b cancel from both sides of the inequality, and we get

$$(1 - \lambda_b + \lambda_b\phi^2)u_n^2 \leq \frac{\lambda_b(1 - \delta_b)(1 - \lambda_b)(1 + \phi\beta)^2 u_n^2}{\lambda_b + \beta^2(1 - \lambda_b)} + \delta_b\frac{1 - \lambda_b}{\lambda_b}$$
$$[\lambda_b + \beta^2(1 - \lambda_b)]u_n^2. \qquad (A4)$$

This is a simple quadratic inequality in ϕ and parameters. Next, the minimand of the CB in problem (PB) is simply the right-hand side of (A1). But this is increasing in ϕ^2, so (PB) is solved by setting $\phi = \phi^-$, if $\phi^- \geq 0$, and $\phi = 0$ otherwise, where ϕ^- is the smallest value of ϕ that satisfies (A4). Now ϕ^- can easily be calculated to be

$$\phi^- \equiv \phi^*(\lambda_b, \delta_b) = \frac{\{1 - \delta_b - \delta_b[1 + \beta^2(1 - \lambda_b)/\lambda_b]\}}{1 + \delta_b\beta^2(1 - \lambda_b)/\lambda_b} \frac{\beta(1 - \lambda_b)}{\lambda_b}. \quad (A5)$$

So, from (A5), $\phi^- > 0$ if and only if $1 > \delta_b + \delta_b[1 + \beta^2(1 - \lambda_b)/\lambda_b]$. This completes the proof.

QED

Appendix B: Introducing unemployment persistence

We have shown in the paper that NWR has a significant effect on the delegation decision, and furthermore that this effect may interact with the strength of the reputation of the CB. It seems likely that persistence will play an equally important role. The problem in investigating this is that, with the addition of persistence, the game between the CB and the private sector becomes a dynamic one, rather than a repeated one, and this makes analysis of the delegation decision much more difficult. Indeed, it turns out to be impossible to characterize the RE in Proposition 1, let alone obtain an analogue of Proposition 2. So we provide only a brief and informal discussion of the issue here.

As Alogoskoufis and Manning (1988) have argued, unemployment persistence can arise from two sources: (i) from the dynamics in the wage or employment targets of the monopoly wage-setter; or, alternatively, (ii) from costs of adjusting employment for firms. All these sources of dynamics give rise to an unemployment equation similar to the following form:

$$u_t = (1 - \rho)u_n + \rho u_{t-1} - \beta(\pi_t - \pi_t^e) + \epsilon_t. \quad (B1)$$

Note that ρ is the degree of persistence of unemployment; when $\rho = 1$ there is hysteresis in unemployment, and when $\rho = 0$ we are back to the static model. Next, u_n is the 'long-run natural rate' of unemployment (i.e. $Eu_t \rightarrow u_n$ as $t \rightarrow \infty$ if $\rho < 1$); we assume $u_n > 0$. We now try to identify informally what effects persistence may have on the delegation decision.

Consider the case[16] where the monetary authority (be it CB or government) *cannot* build a reputation, i.e. where the interaction between CB and wage-setter is modelled as a discretionary equilibrium (DE). In this setting, there are *two* potential differences from the static case, which can easily be explained. First, if the CB cares about the future, i.e. $\delta_b > 0$, s/he faces a genuinely intertemporal problem at stage 2, as a 1 per cent inflation surprise at t will reduce not only current unemployment by 1 per cent at t, but also future (expected) employment by ρ per cent at $t + 1$, ρ^2 per cent at $t + 2$, etc. This implies that a CB of a given degree of aversion to inflation, λ_b, will inflate *more* in the dynamic case, because the marginal (present-value) benefit of inflation has risen, but the marginal cost is unchanged relative to the static case. This implies in turn that the government must appoint a *more conservative* central banker to achieve a given level of inflation.

On the other hand, there is a second effect that goes the other way. If $\rho > 0$ in (B1), the unemployment effects of a temporary adverse shock to labour demand will persist, and the present-value cost of the shock will be larger than in the static case ($\rho = 0$). So the incentive to inflate to offset the shock is higher if $\rho > 0$. This suggests that the government will desire more stabilization, and hence a *less conservative* CB.

Numerical simulations in Lockwood *et al.* (1993) for plausible parameter values (i.e. when δ_b is large relative to δ) suggest that the first effect dominates; so increasing persistence tends to increase conservatism. It seems likely that this will continue to be the case when reputation is introduced,[17] though we have not yet carried out a detailed analysis of the effects of persistence in the presence of reputation.

NOTES

We are grateful for discussions with Jonathan Thomas and for comments received at the conference, from Stanley Black in particular.

 1 Since the treaty was concluded, of course, the quasi-fixed exchange rate system it was designed to reinforce has broken down: Italy and the UK have quit the exchange rate mechanism (ERM) and the margins for those remaining within it have been dramatically widened (to $\pm$ 15 per cent around central ECU rates). Nevertheless, the Treaty remains in being.
 2 The only relevant empirical example is the governor of the CB of New Zealand, who may be dismissed if he should fail to meet an inflation target. However, this contract bears little resemblance to those in the theory.
 3 As is well known, this is not the only way of modelling reputation; an alternative, and in some ways more satisfactory, model is the incomplete information one of Backus and Driffill (1985) and Vickers (1986). These modelling issues are fully discussed in section 2 below.
 4 We offer some evidence in favour of this hypothesis in section 2 below.
 5 The effects of increasing unemployment persistence are discussed more informally in this paper, using results from an earlier paper of ours (Lockwood *et al.*, 1993).
 6 In the Backus and Driffill model, we can think of the tough type as being committed to a zero-inflation rule, because it is a dominant strategy for the tough type always to choose zero inflation.
 7 Our conjecture is that, even with the 'prior belief' notion of reputation, our main results would still go through. In particular, we expect reputation and conservatism to be substitutes. We intend to investigate this in our future work.
 8 E_t denotes the expectation taken conditional on all inflation values and outputs over periods $\tau = 1, \ldots, t - 1$.
 9 Points on OB correspond to values of λ_b where $\delta_b < 1/[2 + \beta^2(1 - \lambda_b)/\lambda_b]$, so $\phi^* > 0$; points on BC correspond to values of λ_b where $\delta_b \geq 1/[2 + \beta^2(1 - \lambda_b)/\lambda_b]$; the constraint hits the horizontal axis at the critical value $\bar{s} = (1 - 2\delta_b)/(1 - \delta_b)$. Note finally that OBC always lies to the right of OA as ϕ^* is always smaller than ϕ^n. It is possible to show that the curve OB is described by $\phi = [s/(1 - s)] \cdot [(s - \bar{s})/(s - \hat{s})]$, where $\hat{s} = 1/(1 - \delta_b)$.
10 In this exercise, the parameter values are not based on any empirical information; for calibration of u_n, σ, and β, see section 5 below.
11 Note, however, that at a given β conservatism is lower with reputation,

highlighting the fact (already mentioned) that reputation and conservatism are substitutes.

12 The LNJ model allows for nominal inertia and partial adjustment in both wage- and price-setting, and is thus more general than most other studies of this type.

13 For example, Blanchard and Summers (1986) found the first-order auto-regressive coefficients for European unemployment to be almost twice as large as that for the USA (around unity for European countries as opposed to about a half for the USA). The term 'Eurosclerosis' has been coined to describe the sluggishness of labour markets on this side of the Atlantic.

14 Other variables are set as described in table 8.3. The value for σ/u_n is the midpoint of a range of 0.35–1.40; this range is calculated as described in Lockwood et al. (1993).

15 It is clear from Proposition 2 that no conservatism is desirable as long as $\delta_b \geq 0.5$.

16 This case has been analysed in depth by Lockwood et al. (1993) on whose analysis we draw here.

17 In a special case when δ_b is high enough, we can formally verify that the CB can attain its precommitment outcome.

REFERENCES

Alogoskoufis, George and Alan Manning (1988), 'Unemployment Persistence', *Economic Policy* 7, 429–69.

Backus, D. and J. Driffill (1985), 'Information and Reputation', *American Economic Review* 75, 530–9.

Barro, Robert and David Gordon (1983), 'Rules, Discretion and Reputation in a Model of Monetary Policy', *Journal of Monetary Economics* 12, 101–21.

Blanchard, Olivier and Larry Summers (1986), 'Hysteresis and the European Unemployment Problem', *NBER Macroeconomics Annual*, 15–78.

Cuikerman, Alex (1992), *Central Bank Strategy, Credibility, and Independence: Theory and Evidence*, Cambridge, Mass., and London: MIT Press.

Fudenberg, D. and J. Tirole (1991), *Game Theory*, Cambridge, Mass.: MIT Press.

Kydland, Finn and Edward Prescott (1977), 'Rules Rather Than Discretion: The Inconsistency of Optimal Plans', *Journal of Political Economy* 85, 473–91.

Layard, Richard, Stephen Nickell and Richard Jackman (1991), *Unemployment: Macroeconomic Performance and the Labour Market*, Oxford: Oxford University Press.

Lockwood, Ben, Marcus Miller and Lei Zhang (1993), 'Delegating Monetary Policy when Unemployment Persists', mimeo, University of Warwick, November.

Lockwood, Ben, J. Maloney and K. Hadri (1994), 'Does Central Bank Independence Smooth the Political Business Cycle? Some OECD Evidence', mimeo, University of Exeter.

Persson, Torsten and Guido Tabellini (1993), 'Designing Institutions for Monetary Stability', mimeo, presented at CEPR/ESF European Summer Symposium on Macroeconomics, Spain, May.

Rogoff, Kenneth (1985), 'The Optimal Degree of Commitment to an Intermediate Monetary Target', *Quarterly Journal of Economics* 100, 1169–90.

Swinburne, Mark and Marta Castello-Branco (1991), 'Central Bank Independence: Issues and Experience', IMF Working Paper, WP/91/58, June.
Roll Report (1993), *Independent and Accountable: A New Mandate for the Bank of England*, London: Centre for Economic Policy Research.
Vickers, J. (1986), 'Signalling in a Model of Monetary Policy with Incomplete Information', *Oxford Economic Papers* 38, 443–55.
Walsh, C. (1992), 'Optimal Contracts for Central Bankers and the Inflation Bias of Monetary Policy', mimeo, University of California at Santa Cruz.

Discussion

STANLEY W. BLACK

The paper by Lockwood, Miller, and Zhang (LMZ) addresses three important issues: (1) how to avoid *inflationary bias* when central banks interact with the public in the Barro–Gordon (1983) model; (2) what difference it makes to this process if there is *nominal wage rigidity* in the wage-bargaining process; and (3) what the implications are of these findings for the *European Central Bank* (ECB).

Several solutions have been suggested in the literature for the problem of inflation bias. Rogoff (1985) shows that a rational public that is aware of the bias problem will choose a more *conservative* central banker to offset the bias. LMZ describe this process as *delegation* of policy (by government, not by the public) to a central banker. Using LMZ's notation for the central bank's policy rule,

$$\pi = \phi u_n + s\epsilon,$$

in a *discretionary* Nash equilibrium, inflation π (equivalently money growth) will be proportional to the excess of the natural rate of unemployment u_n over the central bank's target rate of zero unemployment, with the proportionality factor $\phi^n = \beta(1 - \lambda_b)/\lambda_b$, where λ_b is the weight of inflation in the central banker's objective function and β is the coefficient of nominal wage rigidity. But in addition to the bias term, which can be made smaller by increasing λ_b towards unity, there is a stabilization term, $s\epsilon$, that involves using monetary policy to reduce the impact of temporary shocks to unemployment, ϵ, by a factor $s^n = \beta(1 - \lambda_b)/[\lambda_b + \beta^2(1 - \lambda_b)]$. Thus, reducing bias also reduces stabilization along the trade-off line OA in LMZ's figure 8.1. The preferred anti-inflation weight λ_b for the central banker exceeds the government's own λ. The result is less stabilization than would be optimal if ϕ could be arbitrarily set at zero, but also less inflation bias than would result from using the government's lower value of λ.

Lohmann (1992) modifies the result of this linear decision rule analysis by noting that stabilization losses will be greatest for large shocks, so that an escape clause should allow more stabilization of large shocks, leading to a non-linear decision rule. Another approach to reducing inflation bias is to rely on an incentive-compatible *performance contract* with the central banker, as in the case of New Zealand.

LMZ offer an alternative approach to the issue, based upon the acquisition of *reputation* by the central banker in a repeated game situation involving a *trigger strategy*.[1] In this repeated game the government and central banker have discount factors δ and δ_b with, as plausibly argued by LMZ, a higher discount factor or longer horizon for the central banker than for the government. With δ_b positive, the central banker cares about the future as well as the present and so has to worry about her reputation. The choice of ϕ and s by the central banker in this case is subject to an incentive compatibility (or delegation) constraint to guarantee that the central bank will not cheat, forcing the public to revert to the discretionary Nash equilibrium ϕ^n, s^n. This constraint is shown as the curve ODBC in figures 8.1 and 8.2. Notably, it falls well below the Nash equilibrium possibilities on OA. As LMZ show in Proposition 2, if δ_b is large enough (greater than $\lambda_b/[\beta^2 + (2 - \beta^2)\lambda_b]$), zero inflation bias may be achieved along the segment BC, while otherwise inflation bias may be significantly reduced. In fact it is clear that, if the government's own δ exceeds its own $\lambda/[\beta^2 + (2 - \beta^2)\lambda]$, there is no reason to choose a more conservative central banker, because the government on its own can achieve the first-best $\phi = 0$ and $s = \beta(1 - \lambda)/[\lambda + \beta^2(1 - \lambda)]$. That is to say, *reputation* alone is sufficient to eliminate the inflation bias, because the government will fear the punishment to be imposed by the public in the event of an inflationary outcome. If δ is not that high but δ_b is, the government will prefer to appoint a central banker whose reputation will again allow the achievement of the first-best outcome. In this case the central banker need not be more conservative. Finally, if neither discount factor is high enough, the government will delegate to a more conservative central banker. All of these results are achieved by use of the trigger strategy concept in conjunction with incentive compatibility for the central banker.

A related interesting result shows that a higher value of δ_b can substitute for a lower value of λ_b, that is, patience is a substitute for conservatism in central bankers. And, figure 8.3 shows, λ_b can be less than λ; the central banker can even be *less* conservative than the government if λ is low enough. Also, from figure 8.5, increasing nominal wage rigidity, which raises the inflation bias, requires a more conservative central banker. But this is true only up to a certain limit, at which zero inflation bias is again an option, so that conservatism can be reduced. These rather striking results all flow from the assumption that a trigger strategy can be used to enforce the contract between the central bank and the public.

The question that must be asked is whether or not these results are believable? Is the trigger strategy the correct model of reputation for central banks? This use of the trigger strategy concept has been discussed earlier by Persson and Tabellini (1990), who use it to show that, in an infinitely repeated game, a zero inflation equilibrium can be achieved by an appropriately chosen punishment strategy. However, Persson and Tabellini go on to point out that the trigger strategy requires a 'formidable' coordination problem for the central bank and all private agents and can in addition support a large number of alternative equilibria.

At a more descriptive level, high real interest rates in the United States are often explained as involving the risk that in future the Federal Reserve, in collusion with Congress, will inflate away the public debt rather than raise taxes or reduce spending. This type of risk is better modelled by Bayesian learning about the true intentions of the central bank, with the public uncertain whether it is 'wet' or 'conservative'. In such a model, even a long run of actual low inflation will not completely eliminate the chance of reversion to high inflation.

In the context of European monetary unification, can one believe in a low inflation regime enforced by a punishment strategy? Or is it more likely that the public does not know whether to believe that the politicians really mean what they say about going all the way to EMU? Italy has had to keep its interest rates high because the public has doubted the lira would remain absolutely pegged to the Deutschmark.

If credibility has to be *earned* by evidence that the central bank is *really* hardnosed on inflation, then there is no cheap way to achieve first-best results or even reduced inflation bias without loss of stabilization. This seems closer to actual experience in both the United States and Europe, where EMS central banks have had to accept continued high unemployment simply to sustain the fiction that they are as tough as the Bundesbank.

LMZ's table 8.1 presents convincing evidence that central banks indeed have longer horizons and therefore higher δ's than do governments. The model implies that this is an optimal choice for governments to make, in many circumstances. This is the most convincing evidence presented in favour of the model.

Table 8.3 provides some interesting simulations of the optimally chosen degree of conservative bias for the central bank under various alternative degrees of nominal wage rigidity and reputation (as measured by the discount factor) for the central bank. With high nominal wage rigidity, as in the United States, reputation in the sense of a higher weight for future outcomes can substitute for the high degree of conservatism required to offset the substantial inflation bias. Utilizing this reputational effect allows the central bank to reduce inflation bias significantly while retaining a large element of stabilization. On the other hand, with a low degree of nominal wage rigidity, as in Europe, these effects are less pronounced. The suggestion is that the Fed's reputation allows it to choose a first-best policy, while the ECB's lack of reputation will cause it to be too conservative.

Appendix B of the paper briefly analyses a model with persistence in unemployment, as appears characteristic in Europe. In combination with the repeated game environment, this gives rise to a peculiar intertemporal trade-off that influences the central bank to inflate *more* because the benefits in terms of reduced unemployment will last longer. In this case, the model suggests that a *myopic* central banker would be the best choice to avoid this temptation. This result seems to be an artefact of the trigger strategy approach. It seems to me that persistent unemployment simply makes the horns of the inflation–unemployment dilemma sharper. Again, the Bayesian learning approach may prove to be more realistic.

Policy issues

Let us assume that the European Central Bank is selected to have high δ_b and λ_b. Will it begin with a strong reputation, or will it have to earn one the 'old-fashioned' way? Just because it is located in Frankfurt will not solve the problem. With a non-German majority on the board, the ECB is likely to have to prove to the markets that it means business, just as the new chairman, Greenspan, had to do at the Federal Reserve. He was, after all, taking over an *existing* institution with a good record and he *still* had to prove himself.

If the trigger strategy suggested by the model does not work for the ECB, it will, according to Rogoff's argument, have to be staffed with very conservative central bankers. But many governments may not want to accept the implications of such choices and therefore may not be willing to carry out the Maastricht Treaty. One may also question whether inflation bias is really the problem in Europe today.

In the United States, President Clinton's appointees to the Federal Reserve Board in the spring of 1994 are believed to have lower λ's than their Republican predecessors. Will their long terms in office be sufficient to enable them (and the Fed) to overcome inflation bias? The model suggests they could, but the behaviour of long-term interest rates suggests that the markets believe otherwise, because of anticipated *future* inflation. Thus suggests that President Clinton should be wary of replacing Chairman Greenspan with Vice Chairman Blinder, who will have to earn his reputation all over again. This reminds me of the advice to vote against the reformers and keep the 'old pols' in office, because they already have their swimming pools.

NOTE

1   Technically, LMZ say that their game has a subgame perfect equilibrium. But, as pointed out by Persson and Tabellini (1990), a game between a central bank and a large number of participants among the public cannot be expressed in full extensive form, so the concept of subgame perfection should be replaced with sequential rationality.

REFERENCES

Barro, Robert, and David Gordon (1983), 'Rules, Discretion, and Reputation in a Model of Monetary Policy', *Journal of Monetary Economics* 12, 101–21.

Lohmann, Susan (1992), 'The Optimal Degree of Commitment: Credibility versus Flexibility', *American Economic Review* 82, 273–86.

Persson, Torsten and Guido Tabellini (1990), *Macroeconomic Policy, Credibility, and Politics*, Chur, Switzerland: Harwood Academic Publishers.

Rogoff, Kenneth (1985), 'The Optimal Degree of Commitment to an Intermediate Monetary Target', *Quarterly Journal of Economics* 100, 1169–90.

9   Trade liberalization and trade adjustment assistance

K. C. FUNG and ROBERT W. STAIGER

1   Introduction

Successive rounds of multilateral trade negotiations under the General Agreement on Tariffs and Trade (GATT) have been important for transatlantic economic relations over the post-war period. The prospects for continued progress seem unsure, however, as multilateral trade liberalization has encountered increasingly rough sailing over the past several decades. It is therefore important that alternative policy tools and initiatives be evaluated with regard to their potential for fostering greater success in multilateral trade liberalization. In this paper, we explore the potential for trade adjustment assistance to serve this role.

The provision of trade adjustment assistance poses an interesting puzzle in its own right. A programme of adjustment assistance to trade-impacted import-competing sectors in an amount over and above what is normally available to displaced resources was first introduced into United States law in the Trade Expansion Act of 1962. Trade adjustment assistance (TAA) in some form has been a part of US trade law ever since. Nor is US law unique in this regard; many countries offer some form of special assistance to trade-impacted resources, and such programmes have been interpreted as consistent with the 'escape clause' (Article XIX) of GATT. More recently, however, the prospect of offering special benefits to workers displaced for trade-related reasons has come under renewed scrutiny. Whereas US policy seems to be moving *away* from providing trade-impacted workers with special programmes on the grounds that there is no basis for treating such workers differently from other displaced workers, Bhagwati (1988) has argued for *strengthening* trade adjustment assistance programmes as a key area of unilateral and multilateral reform. Since the rationale for trade adjustment assistance rests on the case for treating trade-impacted workers differently from other displaced workers within the context of a broader adjustment programme, a crucial question in this debate is why trade-impacted import-competing resources might be deserving of special treatment.

An important component of the answer to this question may be that adjustment assistance offered to trade-impacted import-competing workers can facilitate trade liberalization. This interpretation is suggested by the legislative history of TAA in the United States. Before 1962, the United States relied solely on authority provided under GATT's Article XIX to raise tariffs temporarily from GATT-negotiated levels in the event that negotiated tariff reductions threatened import-competing industries with serious injury. However, the right to reverse negotiated tariff reductions through these 'escape clause' proceedings bred scepticism among US trading partners concerning the US commitment to lower trade barriers negotiated under GATT (see, for example, Preeg, 1970: 48). By providing the United States with an alternative to escape clause proceedings that was more acceptable to its trading partners, the introduction of TAA in the Trade Expansion Act of 1962 offered US trading partners additional assurance that tariff reductions negotiated under the Kennedy Round would not later simply be undone.

We explore in this paper the possibility that trade adjustment assistance can facilitate reciprocal trade liberalization. Our basic observation is that there may well be strategic benefits associated with a worker's decision to exit a trade-impacted sector when countries are engaged in a process of reciprocal trade liberalization but are restricted to self-enforcing agreements, and that adjustment assistance to facilitate relocation outside the sector can internalize these externalities. In this paper, we focus on an externality that is essentially static, reflecting the static misallocation of resources across sectors that is brought about by the presence of tariffs. Specifically, a programme of trade adjustment assistance introduced by one country as part of a broader cooperative trade agreement can reduce the distortionary costs of its trading partner's remaining tariffs under the agreement, increasing the value to the trading partner of maintaining the integrity of the agreement, and thereby tempering enforcement problems. If each country implements such a programme, enforcement problems associated with maintaining international cooperation are symmetrically relaxed, and tariffs can be symmetrically lowered as a consequence. This is the basic message of the paper.

Our approach to distinguishing trade-impacted import-competing industries from the rest of the economy for purposes of adjustment policy is related in spirit if not methodology to a view of trade adjustment assistance associated with the political economy literature (see, for example, Richardson, 1982), which focuses on the ability to secure protective trade policies as the distinguishing feature of import-competing sectors.[1] According to this view, trade adjustment assistance can be thought of as a bribe offered to the import-competing sector in return for 'good behaviour', i.e. going along with liberal trade policies. By making possible the reduction of tariffs at home, domestic trade adjustment assistance will also help to bring about tariff reductions abroad through a process of reciprocal tariff concessions. It is the latter that is presumably the major source of national welfare gains to a country that introduces a programme of trade adjustment assistance.

In this paper, rather than focusing on the conflicting interests *within* countries as to the determination of trade policy, and on how trade adjustment assistance can affect the outcome of this *domestic* conflict, we focus on the trade policy conflicts *between* countries and on how trade adjustment assistance can affect the outcome of this *international* conflict. In agreement with the political economy view, we find that trade adjustment assistance can serve as a bribe for cooperative behaviour. However, we find that the bribe embodied in trade adjustment assistance accrues directly to *foreign* interests, and is contingent on the continuation of liberal *foreign* trade policies. In essence, each country's trade adjustment assistance programme expands the tax base for tariff revenue collected by its trading partner, but is made available only as long as trading-partner tariffs remain at a low cooperative level. Thus, each country's programme of trade adjustment assistance rewards cooperative tariff behaviour by its trading partners, allowing greater tariff coopera- tion and higher welfare to be achieved by all countries in equilibrium as a result.

We begin in section 2 by introducing a simple model of resource adjustment in response to trade shocks. We solve for the most cooperative tariffs sustainable in the absence of trade adjustment assistance. Section 3 explores the impact of a programme of trade adjustment assistance on equilibrium tariffs and welfare. Section 4 concludes.

2   A model of sectoral adjustment

2.1   *Basic assumptions*

We begin by describing the basic model in the absence of trade adjustment assistance. We will consider economies that are faced with a periodic need to move resources out of a declining sector, and that are attempting to sustain cooperative but self-enforcing tariff levels in the face of these adjustment needs. Institutionally, one might think of the self-enforcing cooperative tariff levels as those codified in GATT, of the temporary tariff response to protect declining sectors as consistent with that provided for under the escape clause, and of the use of trade adjustment assistance as an alternative government response that can be used in conjunction with temporary protection.[2]

Specifically, we consider two economies, home (no *) and foreign (*), that trade with each other in the products of an infinite sequence of a pair of one-period-lived industries. One of the industries in each country (industry x abroad and industry y at home) has a stable technology over the period. However, the other industry (industry y abroad and industry x at home) is a 'sunrise' industry, with its rise and decline corresponding to two distinct industrial phases within the period. Each period begins with a 'sunrise' phase, during which each country has a strong productivity advantage relative to the other country in its sunrise industry, and ends with a 'sunset' phase in which this productivity advantage erodes. We assume that each country is also endowed with a traded numéraire good that enters linearly into utility and is consumed in positive amounts by both countries, and we therefore restrict our analysis to a partial equilibrium setting.

We assume that, in each country and in each period, there is a fixed amount of labour (one unit) to be allocated across production in the two industries, x and y. For simplicity, all consumption occurs at the end of each period, so there is no need to discount within-period activities, i.e. between phases one and two.[3] Production technologies for x and y in the home and foreign country are given by

$$Q_x = v_0 L_x; \ Q_y = L_y; \ Q_x^* = L_x^*; \ Q_y^* = v_0 L_y^*$$

in the sunrise phase and by

$$Q_x = v L_x; \ Q_y = L_y; \ Q_x^* = L_x^*; \ Q_y^* = v L_y^*$$

in the sunset phase, with Q_i and L_i denoting output and employment in sector $i \in \{x, y\}$, and where $v_0 > 1$ and $v \in (0, 1)$ represent labour productivity parameters in each country's sunrise industry.

Thus, in the sunrise phase of any period, the home (foreign) country has a relative productivity advantage in x (y), while in the sunset phase this productivity advantage is reversed. For simplicity, we assume that both v_0 and v are completely deterministic and known at the time of initial labour allocation. Domestic demand for x and foreign demand for y are taken to be infinitely elastic at $P_x = P_y^* = 1$, while there is no demand for y at home or for x abroad. Thus, each country consumes only the numéraire good and its sunrise good, and local prices of both goods consumed in each country are fixed at unity. These artificial demand assumptions allow us to focus on the supply side of the model, where the resource movements that are central to trade adjustment assistance can be isolated. Under our assumptions on demand, if trade occurs, x will be imported by the home country at a domestic price of unity and y will be imported by the foreign country at a foreign price of unity. Henceforth, we will refer to industry x abroad and y at home as the 'export sector' of the respective country.

Each country can set trade taxes at the beginning of each phase. The demand assumptions assure that export taxes are never advantageous, since the incidence of such taxes would fall completely on the exporters. For any (specific) domestic import tariff τ_x and foreign import tariff τ_y^*, the respective exporting country prices are given by

$$P_x^*(\tau_x) = 1 - \tau_x; \; P_y(\tau_y) = 1 - \tau_y^*.$$

At the beginning of the first (sunrise) phase of any period in a given country, workers must make an initial (costless) decision about whether to locate in industry x or y. The location decision is made to maximize expected labour income over the period. Once allocated, workers produce in their chosen industry during the sunrise phase and then, at the beginning of the period's sunset phase, are free to change jobs for sunset-phase production. However, they face a cost in moving between x and y. In particular, a worker of type λ who moves between x and y at the beginning of the sunset phase of the period spends the amount λ on moving costs. These moving costs vary across individuals, and embody the real resources of a moving industry in the rest of the economy that turns numéraire goods into moving services with a linear technology. For simplicity, we take worker types (and thus λ) to be distributed uniformly on the unit interval.

In either phase, workers are hired by each industry up to the point where the industry wage equals the value of labour's marginal product. With w denoting the wage paid to labour, the equilibrium labour hiring conditions imply

$$w_{x0} \geq v_0; \; w_{y0} \geq 1 - \tau_{y0}^*; \; w_{x0}^* \geq 1 - \tau_{x0}; \; w_{y0}^* \geq v_0$$

in the sunrise phase, and

$$w_x \geq v; \; w_y \geq 1 - \tau_y^*; \; w_x^* \geq 1 - \tau_x; \; w_y^* \geq v$$

in the sunset phase, with equalities holding for any industry in which employment is strictly positive in that phase. Thus, provided employment in each industry is strictly positive, the wage paid to workers in the sunrise industry falls in the sunset phase as productivity falls to v, while the wage paid to workers in the export industry is a declining function in the tariff that the industry faces on its sales abroad. Here and throughout, '0' subscripts denote sunrise phase values.

2.2   Labour allocation in the sunrise phase

We now establish conditions under which, in the sunrise phase of each period, workers choose to locate in the sunrise industry in each country. With this initial allocation, we then study the incentive for workers to reallocate out of the industry in its sunset phase. It is with respect to this labour reallocation that we will later consider the role of trade adjustment assistance.[4]

Consider for a moment the location decision in the sunrise phase for workers of type $\lambda = 1$. These are workers for whom moving out of the sunrise industry as its productivity erodes in the sunset phase is not worthwhile: by staying, such a worker avoids moving costs and gets $v > 0$ in the second phase, whereas, by leaving, the domestic (foreign) worker would receive $-\tau_y^* \leq 0$ ($-\tau_x \leq 0$). Thus, a worker of type $\lambda = 1$ will be the least likely of all types to choose to locate initially in the sunrise industry because, for such a worker, locating in the sunrise industry implies staying there during the sunset phase.

To establish conditions under which all workers choose initially to locate in the sunrise industry of their country in any period, we thus need only establish when a worker of type $\lambda = 1$ would choose to do so. Note that a worker of type $\lambda = 1$ who locates initially in the sunrise industry of his country will receive a wage over the period of $v_0 + v$. Alternatively, such a worker who chooses to locate initially in the export sector (and stay there) would receive a wage over the period of $2 - (\tau_{y0}^* + \tau_y^*)$. Since this amount is no greater than 2 (for non-negative tariffs), all labour will choose to locate initially in the sunrise industry of each country in each period provided that

$$v_0 + v > 2,$$

a condition that we assume is met. In words, we require that the productivity advantage for the sunrise industry in its sunrise phase be sufficiently great relative to its future decline. Hence, under this condition, each country will be specialized in the production of its sunrise industry in the sunrise phase (home specializes in x and foreign specializes in y), and there is no trade in either good. Accordingly, the first-phase tariff policy is irrelevant, and we simply set $\tau_{x0} = \tau_{y0}^* = 0$.

2.3   Labour allocation in the sunset phase

Now consider the relocation decision of workers at the beginning of the sunset phase of the period. Workers with lower λ's (lower moving costs) will be the first to leave the sunrise industry as it enters its sunset phase, with the marginal moving worker in each country given by

$$\lambda(v; \tau_y^*) = w_y - w_x = 1 - \tau_y^* - v; \quad \lambda^*(v; \tau_x) = w_x^* - w_y^* = 1 - \tau_x - v.$$

The equilibrium allocation of labour in the sunset phase of the period and the associated sunset-phase production is, under the uniform distribution of worker types (λ's), then given by

$$L_x(v; \tau_y^*) = v + \tau_y^*; \quad Q_x(v; \tau_y^*) = vL_x(v; \tau_y^*)$$
$$L_y(v; \tau_y^*) = 1 - \tau_y^* - v; \quad Q_y(v; \tau_y^*) = L_y(v; \tau_y^*)$$

for the domestic country and by

$$L_y^*(v; \tau_x) = v + \tau_x; \quad Q_y^*(v; \tau_x) = vL_y^*(v; \tau_x)$$
$$L_x^*(v; \tau_x) = 1 - \tau_x - v; \quad Q_x^*(v; \tau_x) = L_x^*(v; \tau_x)$$

for the foreign country, with total moving costs incurred by domestic and foreign labour, respectively, given by

$$M(v; \tau_y^*) = [L_y(v; \tau_y^*)]^2/2; \quad M^*(v; \tau_x) = [L_x^*(v; \tau_x)]^2/2.$$

Finally, domestic and foreign tariff revenues are given, respectively, by

$$T(v; \tau_x) = \tau_x Q_x^*(v; \tau_x); \quad T^*(v; \tau_y^*) = \tau_y^* Q_y(v; \tau_y^*).$$

Figure 9.1 illustrates the equilibrium sectoral allocation of labour in the sunset phase for the domestic country as a function of the foreign tariff choice. With labour measured on the horizontal axis and starting from the initial sunrise phase allocation in which all of the (one unit of) labour is located in the sunrise sector x, the value of labour's marginal product in the import-competing sector x in the sunset phase is given by the horizontal line drawn at v, while its value if located in the export sector y, facing a sunset-phase import tariff abroad of τ_y^*, is given by the horizontal line through $1 - \tau_y^*$. With labour ordered along the horizontal axis in order of decreasing moving costs, the wage earned in the export sector by each worker after its moving costs have been netted out is then given by the 45 degree line through the point $(1, 1 - \tau_y^*)$. The equilibrium allocation of labour remaining in the import-competing sector is then

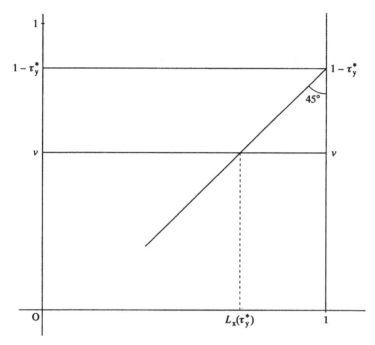

Figure 9.1   Sunset-phase labour allocation

determined to be $L_x(\tau_y^*)$ where, net of moving costs, the marginal worker earns v regardless of his location choice.

We define per-period welfare for each country as the surplus generated in the two sectors over the period. Because consumer surplus is zero, this amounts to the sum of producer surplus (which is simply the value of production at local prices) associated with production in the sunrise phase (denoted for the domestic country by W_0 and for the foreign country by W_0^*) plus producer surplus and tariff revenue minus labour moving costs in the sunset phase. Thus, each government's respective per-period welfare function is defined by

$$\bar{W}(v; \tau_x, \tau_y^*) = W_0 + Q_x(v; \tau_y^*) + P_y(\tau_y^*)Q_y(v; \tau_y^*) + T(v; \tau_x) - M(v; \tau_y^*)$$
$$\bar{W}^*(v; \tau_x, \tau_y^*) = W_0^* + P_x^*(\tau_x)Q_x^*(v; \tau_x) + Q_y^*(v; \tau_x) + T^*(v; \tau_y^*) - M^*(v; \tau_x).$$

2.4   Non-cooperative tariffs

We first consider the optimal tariffs that are set when countries do not attempt to cooperate. These will serve both as a benchmark from which to measure the gains from tariff cooperation, and as credible (subgame perfect) threats that can be used to support cooperation in the infinitely repeated tariff game to be studied next.

As noted above, since there is no trade between the two countries in these two industries in the sunrise phase of any period, tariffs in the sunrise phase are irrelevant. The first- and second-order conditions of the domestic and foreign welfare functions defined above yield the non-cooperative Nash equilibrium tariffs to be applied at the beginning of the sunset phase in each period. In fact, each country's optimal tariff choice is independent of the choice of its trading partner (i.e. tariff reaction curves are flat), owing to our partial equilibrium focus and the fact that we have ruled out export taxes. Assuming that workers reallocate after observing tariff choices,[5] the non-cooperative Nash tariffs are given by

$$\tau_x^N = \tau_y^{*N} = (1 - v)/2.$$

Thus, the greater the sunset-phase productivity decline in each country's import-competing sector, the greater the Nash tariff response to the resulting surge in each country's imports. This simply reflects the fact that, when productivity declines in a country's import-competing sector, labour is induced to relocate into the export sector, increasing the underlying free trade volume of exports $(1 - v)$ and, with export supply linear in price, reducing the export supply elasticity. Hence, a productivity decline in one's import-competing sector is associated with the relocation of labour toward the export sector, a greater volume of exports as a result, and rising non-cooperative tariffs abroad in response to the export surge and associated fall in export supply elasticity.

Finally, it is straightforward to show that each country would prefer the maintenance of (symmetric) free trade throughout the sunset phase of each period $(\tau_x = \tau_y^* = 0)$ to the non-cooperative Nash tariff outcomes of the sunset phase described above. In fact, for symmetric tariff levels $\tau_x = \tau_y^* = \tau$, we have

$$d\bar{W}(v; \tau_x = \tau, \tau_y^* = \tau)/d\tau = d\bar{W}^*(v; \tau_x = t, \tau_y^* = \tau)/d\tau = -\tau,$$

which is strictly negative for $\tau > 0$. Hence, both countries would monotonically prefer symmetric reductions of their sunset-phase tariffs in the direction of free trade, but the non-cooperative Nash equilibrium has both countries imposing strictly positive symmetric tariffs during this phase in each period and suffering the consequent per-period welfare loss. The tariff reaction curves and Nash equilibrium tariff in the sunset phase are illustrated in figure 9.2, along with the per-period welfare levels associated with symmetric free trade, unilateral optimal tariff-setting, and

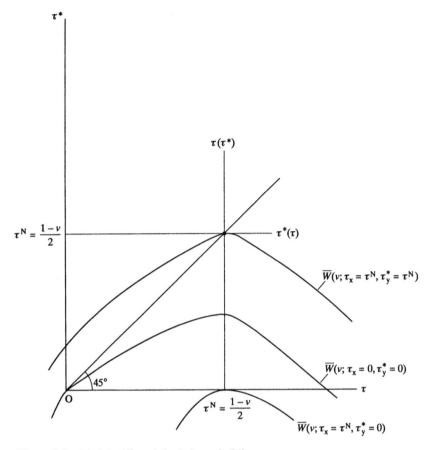

Figure 9.2   Nash tariffs and the Prisoner's Dilemma

the Nash tariff equilibrium. Although extremely stylized and simple, the model therefore captures an environment in which intersectoral resource movements and tariff policy interact in a Prisoner's Dilemma setting.

2.5   Cooperative tariffs

We now consider attempts by the two countries to move cooperatively away from the non-cooperative Nash tariff equilibrium of the sunset phase toward the maintenance of more liberal sunset-phase trade policies. We restrict our attention to agreements in which both countries set a symmetric and stationary sunset-phase tariff τ^c below τ^N, with the agreement held in force by the credible (subgame perfect) threat to revert to τ^N forever if any party defects from the cooperative agreement. Although while the multiplicity of such equilibria is well known, we focus on the 'most cooperative' equilibrium tariff, i.e. the lowest non-negative tariff, sustainable by this threat, denoted by $\hat{\tau}^c$. This is a natural focus in this context, both because GATT may be viewed as a coordinating vehicle to help countries achieve this equilibrium (see, for example, Bagwell and Staiger, 1990), and because our ultimate interest is in exploring the role that trade adjustment assistance plays in increasing the extent of tariff cooperation achievable by countries. We choose to focus on equilibria supported by Nash reversion rather than other, possibly more severe, punishments (such as the optimal symmetric punishments of Abreu, 1986, 1988) because of the simplicity of Nash punishments and because we believe that our results on the role of trade adjustment assistance are robust to other punishments.

In sustaining a symmetric cooperative tariff τ^c below τ^N, countries must ensure that the one-time payoff to each country in deviating from τ^c is no greater than the discounted value of avoiding the non-cooperative trade war that would follow a deviation. This is the basic incentive constraint that will determine the degree of sustainable tariff cooperation in the sunset phase of each period. Since countries are completely symmetric and the model is stationary (each period is like every other), we characterize this incentive constraint from the domestic country's point of view and from the vantage point of a representative period.

We first define the one-time payoff in defecting from a cooperative tariff, τ^c, for the domestic country:

$$\Omega(v; \tau^c) \equiv \bar{W}(v; \tau_x = \tau^N, \tau_y^* = \tau^c) - \bar{W}(v; \tau_x = \tau^c, \tau_y^* = \tau^c)$$
$$= T(v; \tau_x = \tau^N) - T(v; \tau_x = \tau^c) = (\tau^N = \tau^c)^2.$$

Hence, the one-time payoff from defection is measured by how far cooperative tariff revenues (those collected under τ^c) are from individually optimal (non-cooperative) tariff revenues (those collected under τ^N). However, a defection would bring the end of cooperation and the beginning of a trade war. The per-period value of maintaining cooperation at τ^c and avoiding a trade war is given by:

$$\omega(v; \tau^c) = \bar{W}(v; \tau_x = \tau^c, \tau_y^* = \tau^c) - \bar{W}(v; \tau_x = \tau^N, \tau_y^* = \tau^N)$$
$$= [(\tau^N)^2 - (\tau^c)^2]/2.$$

Defining δ as the discount factor and $\Delta \equiv \delta/(1 - \delta)$, the incentive constraint that ensures that τ^c will be self-enforcing is

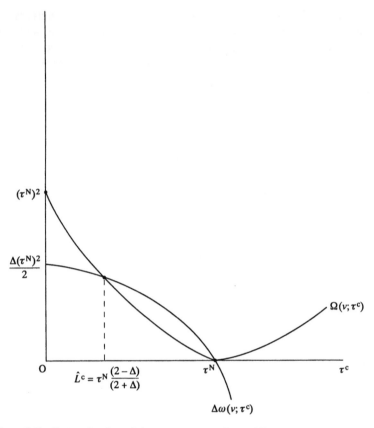

Figure 9.3　Determination of the most cooperative tariff

$$\Omega(v;\tau^c) \le \Delta w(v;\tau^c).$$

Figure 9.3 depicts $\Omega(v;\tau^c)$ and $\Delta w(v;\tau^c)$ as functions of τ^c. As the figure depicts, $\Omega(v;\tau^c)$ is decreasing and convex in τ^c for $\tau^c \in [0,\tau^N]$, equal to $(\tau^N)^2$ when $\tau^c = 0$ and equal to zero when $\tau^c = \tau^N$. On the other hand, $\Delta w(v;\tau^c)$ is decreasing and concave in τ^c, equal to $[\Delta(\tau^N)^2]/2$ when $\tau^c = 0$ and equal to zero when $\tau^c = \tau^N$. Figure 9.3 illustrates the determination of the most cooperative tariff $\hat{\tau}^c$, which is the lowest non-negative tariff satisfying the incentive constraint, for the case of $\Delta \in (0,2)$. In the figure, this is determined by the (lowest) point of intersection of $\Omega(v;\tau^c)$ and $\Delta w(v;\tau^c)$. Explicit calculation yields

$$\hat{\tau}^c = \tau^N \frac{(2-\Delta)}{(2+\Delta)}.$$

Thus, for $\Delta \geq 2$, free trade is sustainable as a cooperative equilibrium in the presence of a decline in import-competing sectors and the inter-sectoral resource movements that this decline implies. However, for $\Delta \in (0,2)$, the decline of import-competing sectors requires a tariff response $\hat{\tau}^c > 0$ in the cooperative equilibrium, because free trade can no longer be maintained as an incentive-compatible policy.

3   Trade adjustment assistance

In this section we consider the role of a programme of trade adjustment assistance. We model trade adjustment as a programme that offers a relocation subsidy to displaced workers in the sunset phase in proportion to their moving costs. We begin by establishing that a programme of adjustment subsidies will not raise the welfare level of the country that implements it if it has no effect on equilibrium tariff choices. Hence, there is no rationale in the model for a country to implement its own trade adjustment assistance programme unless by doing so it can alter equilibrium tariff choices in the sunset phase. Next, we show that non-cooperative Nash tariffs will be unaffected by a trade adjustment assistance programme that takes this form, so that a country has nothing to gain from implementing such an adjustment assistance programme when tariffs are set non-cooperatively. We then show that each country does stand to gain *directly* (i.e. with tariffs held fixed) from a trade adjustment assistance programme implemented by its trading partner, so that each country would gain under non-cooperative Nash tariff-setting if both implemented small symmetric adjustment programmes. Finally, we establish that there is an additional *trade liberalization* gain from the implementation of small symmetric adjustment programmes when countries set tariffs cooperatively, provided only that the discount factor is below a critical level, and therefore provided only that sunset-phase tariff cooperation in the absence of an adjustment programme is sufficiently hindered by weak enforcement abilities at the international level.

Throughout we focus on *small* adjustment assistance subsidies because they can be implemented unilaterally and entail no enforcement mechanisms, i.e. they do not require the threat of future punishments to maintain. While there is no explicit reason in our model for countries to limit themselves to small amounts of adjustment assistance that can be implemented unilaterally and without international enforcement provisions, our focus does conform to the lack of explicit international cooperation with regard to the implementation of trade adjustment assistance programmes, as distinct from tariff reduction, that one observes in practice (though see the comments of Syropoulos on this paper for an extension of our results to the interesting case in which countries enter into self-enforcing agreements over both tariffs and trade adjustment subsidies). At the same time, a focus on small adjustment subsidies serves our purpose of illustrating the formal possibility that trade adjustment assistance can facilitate trade liberalization without explicitly considering the optimal design of such a policy.

3.1   A potential role for trade adjustment assistance

As before, we continue to exploit the symmetry of the model and characterize all magnitudes from the domestic country perspective. In a domestic industry to which trade adjustment assistance has been granted, we suppose that displaced workers who relocate into the export sector receive subsidies equal to a fraction of their moving costs. Thus, the moving cost faced by a domestic worker of type λ who moves from x to y at the beginning of the sunset phase of x is now $(1 - s)\lambda$, with $s \in [0, 1]$ denoting the adjustment subsidy rate. Hence, in the presence of trade adjustment assistance, the marginal mover in the domestic country equates the wage in x to the wage received in y net of the unsubsidized portion of his moving costs, or

$$w_x = w_y - (1 - s)\tilde{\lambda}.$$

This yields an expression for the marginal moving worker in the presence of trade adjustment assistance of

$$\tilde{\lambda}(v; \tau_y^*, s) = \frac{1 - \tau_y^* - v}{(1 - s)}.$$

The equilibrium allocation of domestic labour in the sunset phase of the period under a programme of domestic trade adjustment assistance and the associated sunset-phase production is then given by

$$L_x(v; \tau_y^*, s) = \frac{v + \tau_y^* - s}{(1 - s)}; \quad Q_x(v; \tau_y^*, s) = vL_x(v; \tau_y^*, s)$$

$$L_y(v; \tau_y^*, s) = \frac{1 - \tau_y^* - v}{(1 - s)}; \quad Q_y(v; \tau_y^*, s) = L_y(v; \tau_y^*, s)$$

with magnitudes for the foreign economy defined symmetrically. The total moving costs incurred by the domestic economy, a portion of which is now financed by the trade adjustment assistance programme, are then

$$M(v; \tau_y^*, s) = [L_y(v; \tau_y^*, s)]^2/2$$

with domestic tariff revenues given by

$$T(v; \tau_x, s^*) = \tau_x Q_x^*(v; \tau_x, s^*).$$

All other domestic and foreign variables are as before. Finally, because the direct impact of domestic trade adjustment assistance subsidies is simply a transfer from the government to the domestic private sector, domestic and foreign welfare under a programme of domestic trade adjustment assistance is defined as before and given by

$$\bar{W}(v; \tau_x, \tau_y^*, s, s^*) = W_0 + Q_x(v; \tau_y^*, s) + P_y(\tau_y^*)Q_y(v; \tau_y^*, s)$$
$$+ T(v; \tau_x, s^*) - M(v; \tau_y^*, s)$$
$$\bar{W}^*(v; \tau_x, \tau_y^*, s, s^*) = W_0^* + P_x^*(\tau_x)Q_x^*(v; \tau_x, s^*) + Q_y^*(v; \tau_x, s^*)$$
$$+ T^*(v; \tau_y^*, s) - M^*(v; \tau_x, s^*).$$

Now consider the impact of a small programme of domestic adjustment assistance on domestic welfare. For fixed tariffs, it is straightforward to calculate that

$$\partial \bar{W}(v; \tau_x, \tau_y^*, s^*, s = 0)/\partial s = 0; \ \partial^2 \bar{W}(v; \tau_x, \tau_y^*, s^*, s = 0)/\partial s^2 < 0,$$

and symmetrically for the foreign country. Thus, in the absence of any effect of the adjustment programme on equilibrium tariffs, there is nothing to be gained by either country from implementing its own adjustment assistance programme. This is because, for fixed tariffs and therefore fixed domestic prices, and from the point of view of national welfare, a country's workers allocate efficiently across the two sectors in the sunset phase.

Second, note that the non-cooperative Nash tariffs are unaffected by an adjustment programme of this form, because export supply elasticities are not affected. That is, we have τ^N defined by

$$\partial \bar{W}(v; \tau_x = \tau^N, \tau_y^*, s, s^*)/\partial \tau_x = \partial T(v; \tau_x, \tau^N, s^*)/\partial \tau_x$$
$$= \frac{(1 - v - 2\tau^N)}{(1 - s^*)} = 0$$

so that

$$\tau^N(s, s^*) = (1 - v)/2 = \tau^N,$$

and similarly for the foreign country. Thus, in the non-cooperative Nash equilibrium, equilibrium tariffs are independent of the adjustment subsidies. This simply reflects the fact that we have modelled trade adjustment assistance in a way that leaves export supply elasticities, and hence optimal non-cooperative Nash tariffs, unaffected. This is, of course, not general, but it serves as a useful benchmark from which to evaluate the role of trade adjustment assistance when countries set tariffs under a (self-enforcing) cooperative agreement. In particular, with Nash tariffs unaffected by the programme of trade adjustment assistance, we have

$$d\bar{W}(v; \tau_x = \tau^N, \tau_y^* = \tau^N, s^*, s=0)/ds = 0; d^2\bar{W}(v; \tau_x = \tau^N, \tau_y^* = \tau^N, s^*, s=0)/ds^2 < 0.$$

That is, neither country would gain from implementing a small trade adjustment programme on its own if tariffs are set non-cooperatively.

Nevertheless, even with mixed tariffs, each country does stand to gain from a small adjustment programme implemented by its trading partner. For fixed tariffs, the impact on domestic welfare of a small foreign adjustment programme is given by

$$\partial\bar{W}(v; \tau_x, \tau_y^*, s^* = 0, s)/\partial s^* = \partial T(v; \tau_x, s^* = 0)/\partial s^*$$
$$= T(v; \tau_x, s^* = 0),$$

which is positive provided the domestic tariff is positive. Thus, even with fixed tariffs, each country can reduce the distortionary cost to the other of the other's own tariff policy by implementing a small trade adjustment assistance programme. This is because each country's marginal worker fails to internalize the additional tariff revenue it could generate for the other country were it to locate in the export sector rather than the import-competing sector. Consequently, at no cost to itself, each country can help the other by internalizing this externality with a small adjustment subsidy. This suggests in turn that small symmetric programmes of trade adjustment assistance – implemented along with a cooperative self-enforcing tariff agreement and maintained as long as cooperative tariff policies were maintained – could increase the benefits to both countries of maintaining a given level of cooperative tariffs under the arrangement, thereby diminishing enforcement problems and allowing greater tariff liberalization. We now explore formally this possibility.

3.2   Trade adjustment assistance and tariff liberalization

To characterize the impact on equilibrium most cooperative tariffs of a small symmetric trade adjustment programme implemented in each country, we assume that each country offers to subsidize a small fraction

$s = s^* = s^c$ of the relocation costs of its trade-displaced workers as long as tariff cooperation continues. More precisely, we assume that (i) along the equilibrium path, and at the beginning of the sunset phase of each period, each government offers a small symmetric relocation subsidy rate, s^c, to its injured import-competing workers and sets a symmetric cooperative tariff level, τ^c, and (ii) if a deviation from s^c or τ^c is observed, then in all future periods countries set the adjustment subsidy rate s to zero and set tariffs at their Nash level, τ^N.

In fact, as noted above, although each country derives no direct benefits from its own adjustment assistance programme, for small s^c the programme carries no social costs either, so that enforcement of each country's obligation to provide a small adjustment subsidy is not an issue. We thus focus again on the incentive constraints associated with the maintenance of τ^c, but now in the presence of a small symmetric adjustment programme.

The one-time payoff in defecting from an agreement over τ^c and any s^c is given by

$$\Omega(v; \tau^c, s^c) = \bar{W}(v; \tau_x = \tau^N, \tau_y^* = \tau^c, s = 0, s^* = s^c) - \bar{W}(v; \tau_x$$
$$= \tau^c, \tau_y^* = \tau^c, s = s^c, s^* = s^c).$$

To find how the one-time payoff in defecting from τ^c is affected by the introduction of a small adjustment subsidy, it is easily checked that

$$\partial\Omega(v; \tau^c, s^c = 0)/\partial s^c = \Omega(v; \tau^c, s^c = 0) = (\tau^N - \tau^c)^2 > 0 \text{ for } \tau^c \in [0, \tau^N).$$

Hence, the one-time payoff to defection from τ^c is larger in the presence of a small symmetric adjustment programme than in its absence. The reason is that each country's adjustment programme expands its export sector, which increases the tax base for its trading partner's tariff collections and makes defection from τ^c to the optimal tariff more tempting. This by itself would suggest that trade adjustment assistance would hinder the ability to maintain low cooperative tariffs during the sunset phase. Note also that

$$\partial^2\Omega(v; \tau^c, s^c = 0)/\partial s^c\partial\tau^c = \partial\Omega(v; \tau^c, s^c = 0)/\partial\tau^c < 0 \text{ for } \tau^c \in [0, \tau^N).$$

Thus, the higher the cooperative tariff (i.e. the closer τ^c is to τ^N), the smaller the upward shift in $\Omega(v; \tau^c, s^c = 0)$ from a small increase in s^c, i.e. the smaller would be the rise in the one-time payoff from defection associated with the introduction of a small programme of trade adjustment assistance.

However, defection would trigger a trade war, and it remains to determine the per-period value of maintaining cooperation and avoiding a trade war in the presence of a small trade adjustment assistance programme in each country. For τ^c and any s^c, this is given by

$$\omega(v; \tau^c, s^c) = \bar{W}(v; \tau_x = \tau^c, \tau_y^* = \tau^c, s = s^c, s^* = s^c)$$
$$- \bar{W}(v; \tau_x = \tau^N, \tau_y^* = \tau^N, s = 0, s^* = 0).$$

To find out how the per-period value of maintaining cooperation is affected by the introduction of a small adjustment subsidy, we note that

$$\partial\omega(v; \tau^c, s^c = 0)/\partial s^c = \tau^c(2\tau^N - \tau^c) > 0 \quad \text{for } \tau^c \in (0, \tau^N].$$

Hence, the per-period benefit of maintaining cooperation at τ^c and avoiding a trade war is also increased with the implementation of small symmetric adjustment assistance programmes in each country. This reflects once again the expanded tax base from which cooperative tariff revenues can be collected and the fact that the adjustment programme providing this expansion would be forfeited in a trade war. Finally, note also that

$$\partial^2\omega(v; \tau^c, s^c = 0)/\partial s^c \partial t^c = 2(\tau^N - \tau^c) > 0 \quad \text{for } \tau^c \in [0, \tau^N].$$

Thus, the higher the cooperative tariff (i.e. the closer τ^c is to τ^N), the greater the upward shift in $\omega(v; \tau^c, s^c = 0)$ from a small increase in s^c, i.e. the higher would be the rise in value of maintaining cooperation associated with the introduction of a small programme of trade adjustment assistance.

If liberalization is facilitated by a small symmetric programme of trade adjustment assistance, then the most cooperative tariff sustainable under a small symmetric adjustment assistance programme must be smaller than that sustainable in the absence of such a programme. Since both $\Omega(v; \tau^c, s^c = 0)$ and $\Delta\omega(v; \tau^c, s^c = 0)$ are increasing in s^c, establishing conditions under which the most cooperative tariff $\hat{\tau}^c$ falls with the introduction of a small readjustment subsidy amounts to finding conditions under which

$$\partial\Omega(v; \hat{\tau}^c(s^c = 0), s^c = 0)/\partial s^c < \Delta\partial\omega(v; \hat{\tau}^c(s^c = 0), s^c = 0)/\partial s^c.$$

This condition holds for $\Delta \in (0, 2/\sqrt{3})$. Recalling that $\hat{\tau}^c(s^c = 0) = \tau^N [2 - \Delta]/[2 + \Delta]$, this implies that a small symmetric programme of trade adjustment assistance will facilitate mutually beneficial trade liberalization provided that cooperation in the absence of such a

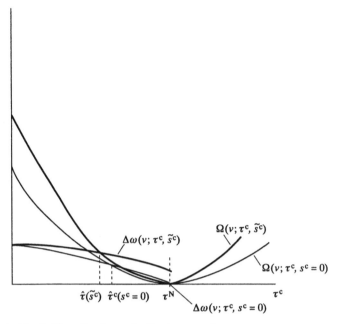

Figure 9.4   Trade liberalization and adjustment assistance

programme would yield a most cooperative tariff in the range
$\hat{\tau}^c \in ([\sqrt{3} - 1)/(\sqrt{3} + 1)]\tau^N, \tau^N)$.

Figure 9.4 illustrates the facilitating effect that a small symmetric
programme of trade adjustment assistance can have on trade liberalization. The most cooperative sunset-phase tariff sustainable in the
absence of trade adjustment assistance is determined by the (lowest)
intersection of the $\Omega(v; \tau^c, s^c = 0)$ and $\Delta\omega(v; \tau^c, s^c = 0)$ functions,
depicted by the light curves in figure 9.4. This determines $\tau^c(s^c = 0)$. For
$\Delta \in (0, 2/\sqrt{3})$, the introduction of a small trade adjustment assistance
subsidy $\tilde{s}^c$ will shift $\Delta\omega(\bullet)$ up by more than $\Omega(\bullet)$ at $\hat{\tau}^c(s^c = 0)$.
Consequently, as figure 9.4 depicts, $\hat{\tau}^c(\tilde{s}^c) < \hat{\tau}^c(s^c = 0)$. Hence, there can
be a trade-liberalizing role for a programme of trade adjustment
assistance, although this role is limited to situations in which cooperation
is sufficiently poor in the absence of such a programme.

Finally, note that the welfare impacts of the small symmetric trade
adjustment programme we have considered are composed of two effects.
There is a direct effect (holding tariffs fixed) of each country's programme
on the other's welfare, which is strictly positive for any (fixed) positive
cooperative tariffs. And there is a trade-liberalizing effect, which

facilitates joint trade liberalization (and hence has a strictly positive welfare effect) for $\Delta \in (0, 2/\sqrt{3})$ but which hinders joint trade liberalization (and hence has a strictly negative welfare effect) for $\Delta \in (2/\sqrt{3}, 2)$. Since free trade is sustainable during the sunset phase in the absence of trade adjustment assistance for $\Delta \geq 2$, this implies that the overall rationale for trade adjustment assistance depends on the degree of tariff cooperation being sufficiently modest in its absence.

4   Conclusions

We have proposed and formalized a particular view of the way in which trade adjustment assistance can affect an economy. Our focus has been on the ability of trade adjustment assistance to enhance tariff cooperation between countries. By rewarding one's trading partners for cooperative behaviour, we have shown that a small symmetric programme of trade adjustment assistance can enhance efficiency, leading to greater tariff cooperation, lower tariffs, and higher welfare worldwide. In the process, we have also identified two separate potential welfare benefits of trade adjustment assistance: a direct welfare benefit, which occurs at fixed tariffs as each country's adjustment programme enhances the efficiency with which its trading partner collects tariff revenue; and an indirect welfare benefit that comes with the trade-liberalizing effects of the adjustment programme. We have argued that both effects will yield positive welfare benefits provided that tariff cooperation in the absence of an adjustment programme is sufficiently modest, but that, for sufficiently high levels of cooperation, trade liberalization can be hindered by a trade adjustment assistance programme and the overall welfare effects of introducing a small programme of trade adjustment assistance could be negative.

Although we have ignored in this paper many other relevant dimensions of trade adjustment, we close with a number of implications concerning the design of trade adjustment assistance programmes that are suggested from our stylized analysis. First, our analysis points to the importance of the overall degree of international cooperation in trade policy as an input into the design of an efficiency-enhancing trade adjustment assistance programme. In particular, where international cooperation in trade policy is achieving only modest success, an efficiency argument for trade adjustment assistance can be made, but when cooperative tariffs are sufficiently low, the efficiency role for adjustment assistance is weakened, and efficiency may even be served by an adjustment tax on movements of resources from the import-competing to the export sector rather than a subsidy. Second, our results suggest that the efficiency rationale for trade adjustment assistance depends not in a fundamental way on the causes of injury to import-competing resources, but rather only on the fact that injury has occurred and resources are exiting the import-competing sector and entering export sectors. This stands in stark contrast to the focus on injury-due-to-increased-imports that characterizes the actual practice of trade adjustment assistance in the United States and elsewhere. In fact, although the model depicts resources flowing from the import-competing to the export sector, the efficiency arguments for adjustment assistance we have considered have more to do with appropriate policy regarding resources moving into export sectors than with resources moving out of import sectors, although in practice the two will often be linked. Third, our results indicate that the efficiency properties of trade adjustment assistance will depend crucially on how such assistance affects the relocation decisions of workers. In this regard, although some elements of the US TAA programme are clearly designed to encourage worker relocation, other elements may work to discourage it, and existing empirical evidence regarding the programme's effect on relocation is inconclusive (see, for example, Corson *et al.*, 1993: 110–12). Thus, although our results are suggestive of an efficiency-enhancing role for adjustment policies that treat resources differently when traded sectors are involved, the relation such adjustment policies have to what is actually embodied in trade adjustment assistance programmes is less clear.

NOTES

We thank Bill Ethier and participants in CEPR's Conference on the New Transatlantic Economy for helpful comments, and our discussant Costas Syropoulos for especially detailed and helpful suggestions and for pointing out an error in an earlier draft.

1   Other attempts to model the impact of adjustment assistance include Diamond (1982), Mussa (1982), and Neary (1982).
2   Prior to 1974, eligibility for escape clause protection and/or trade adjustment assistance required that negotiated trade 'concessions' (tariff reductions) had to constitute a major cause of the rising imports that were themselves the major cause of injury. The Trade Act of 1974 eliminated the so-called 'double causality' standard and allowed rising imports from any cause to be considered in the injury determination. The post-1974 law is closer in spirit to the interpretation of temporary protection and adjustment assistance that we have in mind below, although see also note 4.
3   Allowing consumption to occur in each phase of a period would simply necessitate the introduction of a within-period discount factor in addition to the between-periods discount factor that we consider below.
4   In our model, the need for resource reallocation in the sunset phase is

generated by a purely domestic (productivity) shock, and workers are not in fact dislocated from the import-competing sector owing to increased imports. Whereas existing trade adjustment assistance programmes require a link to be established between import increases and injury in order for trade adjustment assistance to be forthcoming, our results suggest that the *cause* of the dislocation is not a crucial part of the rationale for providing workers who are displaced from import-competing sectors with special adjustment programmes. We will return to this point in the concluding section. We also note here that, by focusing on the case of complete sunrise-phase specialization in the absence of adjustment assistance, we are abstracting from a potentially important distortion that could accompany the introduction of trade adjustment assistance, namely, its effect on the initial (sunrise-phase) allocation of resources in the economy.

5   Hence, we ignore the time-consistency issues associated with the optimal tariff that were raised by Lapan (1988).

REFERENCES

Abreu, D. (1986), 'Extremal Equilibria of Oligopolistic Supergames', *Journal of Economic Theory* **39**, 191–225.

   (1988), 'On the Theory of Infinitely Repeated Games with Discounting', *Econometrica* **56**, 383–96.

Bagwell, Kyle and Robert W. Staiger (1990), 'A Theory of Managed Trade', *American Economic Review* **80** (September), 779–95.

Bhagwati, Jagdish (1988), *Protectionism*, Cambridge, Mass.: MIT Press.

Corson, Walter, Paul Decker, Phillip Gleason and Walter Nicholson (1993), *International Trade and Worker Dislocation: Evaluation of the Trade Adjustment Assistance Program*, Mathematica Policy Research, Princeton, NJ, April.

Diamond, Peter (1982), 'Protection, Trade Adjustment Assistance, and Income Distribution', in Jagdish Bhagwati (ed.), *Import Competition and Response*, Chicago and London: University of Chicago Press, pp. 123–45.

Lapan, Harvey E. (1988), 'The Optimal Tariff, Production Lags, and Time-Consistency', *American Economic Review* **78**, 395–401.

Mussa, Michael (1982), 'Government Policy and the Adjustment Process', in Jagdish Bhagwati (ed.), *Import Competition and Response*, Chicago and London: University of Chicago Press, pp. 73–122.

Neary, J. Peter (1982), 'Intersectoral Capital Mobility, Wage Stickiness, and the Case for Adjustment Assistance', in Jagdish Bhagwati (ed.), *Import Competition and Response*, Chicago and London: University of Chicago Press, pp. 39–69.

Preeg, Ernest H. (1970), *Traders and Diplomats*, Washington, DC: The Brookings Institution.

Richardson, J. David (1982), 'Trade Adjustment Assistance Under the United States Trade Act of 1974: An Analytical Examination and Worker Survey', in Jagdish Bhagwati (ed.), *Import Competition and Response*, Chicago and London: University of Chicago Press, pp. 321–57.

Discussion

CONSTANTINOS SYROPOULOS

Trade liberalization causes relative product and factor prices to change. These changes alter the proportions at which producers mix factor inputs, create incentives for resources to relocate between industries, and generally influence the distribution of income. Typically, sectoral adjustment is costly and, depending on the flexibility of markets, can be a friction-ridden process. In democratic societies, factor owners register their support for or lobby in opposition to specific trade accords, usually with a view towards enhancing their own well-being or that of their associates. Similarly, self-interested politicians pursue their election or re-election objectives, and it seems that only when the wider interest of the public coincides with the goals of governments are efficient policies adopted. Therefore, whether countries' attempts to liberalize trade are successful or not seems to depend on the objectives of competing parties and the environment within which the economic goals of individuals and interest groups are expressed.[1]

The literature on sectoral adjustment has investigated how factor markets adjust to exogenous shifts in comparative advantage or policy-related disturbances in the presence of distortions (e.g. wage rigidities or monopsony power in labour markets, asymmetric information in employer–employee relations, capital market imperfections), and what optimal policy ought to be. There is also considerable work on the effects of multilateral and preferential trade arrangements and how in particular the extent of liberalization depends on the objectives of governments and their instruments of policy. An important issue that is closely related to the above considerations is how exogenous swings in technology influence the ability of benevolent governments to sustain self-enforcing trade agreements in the presence of adjustment costs. This is precisely what the paper by Fung and Staiger is about. It is concerned with the effects of adjustment assistance subsidies on policy incentives and is an attempt to identify circumstances in which such subsidies are likely to facilitate trade liberalization.

Fung and Staiger have provided us with a stimulating paper that constructs an ingeniously simple model to formalize the validity of what, I think, is a novel point. If welfare-maximizing governments do not value the future highly, then the provision of adjustment assistance to workers affected by productivity shocks and faced with moving costs can raise their incentives to reduce protective tariffs. The analysis is positive, but, as we shall see, it has several interesting normative implications.

When I first tried to determine what to include in the discussion, my inclination was to probe the structure of the model and study the sensitivity of the principal result to alternative assumptions on the structure of the model. I am now convinced that a more useful alternative is to take the analysis of Fung and Staiger one step further and explore the normative implications of their model. This approach helps us gain appreciation for several features of their model and may also illustrate some of its limitations. Perhaps more importantly though, it helps illustrate that the normative case for adjustment assistance subsidies is strong.

The salient features of the model can be summarized as follows. There are a composite numéraire that enters consumer preferences linearly and two unrelated traded goods that are produced under constant returns to scale by a specialized input, labour, that incurs moving costs when it relocates between the two industries. All markets are perfectly competitive. Two anti-symmetric countries are involved in a perpetual trading relationship where they exchange the two goods. Within each period, exogenous technological change alters relative productivities and comparative advantage so that labour in each country has an incentive to relocate from its 'sunset' to its 'sunrise' industry. The heterogeneous moving costs for labour prevent complete specialization in production; and the demand assumptions ensure the existence of monopoly power in import, but not export, markets. Governments intervene in trade with specific import tariffs; and, being immune to political economy forces, their goal is to maximize national welfare. Policy interactions are repeated infinitely, and this allows planners to utilize history-dependent strategies (here, trigger strategies) to sustain cooperative outcomes in an otherwise non-cooperative environment. Thus, tariff agreements have the attractive feature that they are self-enforcing. As usual, the well-known problem of multiplicity of subgame-perfect equilibria is present here. The authors finesse this problem by considering anti-symmetric trading partners so that symmetric policy outcomes are focal points. Infinitesimally small adjustment assistance subsidies proportional to workers' moving costs are then introduced by the authors as part of the agreement in order to examine whether or not such subsidies facilitate trade liberalization, and, if so, how.

Let s and τ denote the symmetric adjustment assistance subsidy and tariff adopted by both countries under a given agreement. The authors show that the optimal subsidy and tariff of every country under unilateral defection and in the one-shot Nash equilibrium are $s^N = 0$ and

$\tau^N = (1 - v)/2$, respectively. The symmetry of the model implies that world welfare, $W(s, \tau)$, is identical to a representative country's welfare – provided, of course, that both countries adopt symmetric subsidies s and tariffs τ. Let $\Phi(\tau, s; \Delta) \equiv \Omega(\tau, s) - \Delta\omega(\tau, s)$ where Ω, ω are the welfare gain to defection and the per-period welfare loss when the agreement collapses, respectively. $\Delta \equiv \delta/(1 - \delta)$ is the discount parameter (δ is the discount factor). The problem that a world planner who wishes to maximize world efficiency faces can now be described as follows:

$$\underset{s, \tau}{\text{maximize }} W(s, \tau) \tag{1}$$

$$\text{subject to: } \Phi(s, \tau; \Delta) \leq 0, \tag{2}$$

where (2) is the incentive compatibility constraint. As it turns out, the problem in (1) and (2) is straightforward to solve algebraically. For expositional clarity my analysis below will mostly be graphical. To solve the above optimization problem, it is helpful to graph the iso-welfare contours and the incentive compatibility constraint in the (s, τ) space, as shown in figure 9D.1.

Consider the world welfare function, $W(\bullet)$, first. Rearranging terms appropriately, $W(\bullet)$ can be rewritten in the following form:

$$W(s, \tau) = (1 - 2\tau^N) + 2\tau^N f(s, \tau) = \frac{1}{2} f^2(s, \tau), \tag{3}$$

where $f(s, \tau) \equiv (2\tau^N - \tau)/(1 - s)$ with $f_s > 0$ and $f_\tau < 0$. Direct calculation reveals that

$$\frac{\partial W}{\partial f} = \frac{\tau - 2s\tau^N}{1 - s} \quad \text{and} \quad \frac{\partial^2 W}{\partial f^2} = -1 < 0. \tag{4}$$

Thus, if $\tau = \tilde{\tau}(s) \equiv 2s\tau^N$ then world welfare is the largest it can be. Interestingly, this level of welfare coincides with the level of welfare under no intervention in any market. That is, $W(s, \tilde{\tau}(s)) = W(0, 0)$. The incentive compatibility constraint aside for the moment, this implies that there exist pairs (s, τ) that can reproduce the free trade level of efficiency. When this is true, tariffs are related linearly to subsidies, as shown in (4). Thus, all (s, τ) pairs that reproduce the free trade welfare level will lie along the straight line OO' in figure 9D.1, whose slope is $2\tau^N$. Similarly, it is straightforward to verify from (3) and (4) that any iso-welfare contour with welfare lying in the range $(W(0, \tau^N), W(0, 0))$ will also be positively sloping and linear – as shown, for example, by schedule GG' in figure 9D.1. The linearity of the iso-welfare contours is a consequence of the special structure of the model and the particular choice of policy

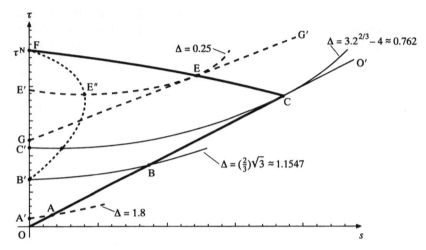

Figure 9D.1   Welfare-maximizing adjustment assistance subsidies and tariffs

instruments. Linearity simplifies the problem but is not essential to the analysis. When $\tau \geq \bar{\tau}(s)$, the iso-welfare schedules are upward sloping because increases in the tariff τ reduce world welfare, whereas increases in the subsidy s raise world welfare.[2]

Consider now the incentive compatibility constraint in (2). This constraint is the heart of the Fung and Staiger paper and is worth visualizing with the help of figure 9D.1. I will discuss some features of this constraint later. For now it is sufficient to note that (2) defines a convex set of (s, τ) pairs, the exact shape of which depends on the discount parameter Δ. Figure 9D.1 depicts four boundaries of (s,τ) pairs that satisfy (2) with equality. For example: if $\Delta = 0.25$, then every pair (s, τ) that lies above the EE′ contour will satisfy (2). This set is enlarged when Δ is raised (see, e.g., schedules CC′, BB′, and AA′) and the reason is simple. For any given adjustment assistance subsidy s, larger discount parameters raise every country's discounted value of future losses if cooperation breaks down, and this enables them to sustain a wider range of trading regimes. In particular, if $\Delta = 2$ then the (s, τ) pairs of the $\Phi(\bullet; \Delta = 2) = 0$ boundary will lie below OO′ but will also include the no intervention point O.

The optimization problem described in (1) and (2) can now be solved – in fact, explicit solutions can be found. Figure 9D.1 illustrates how the solution depends on the discount parameter Δ. As Fung and Staiger argue, free trade will be sustainable if $\Delta \geq 2$. This is so because the incentive constraint in (2) is not binding. Furthermore, the linearity of the iso-welfare contour, OO′, and the convexity of the incentive compatibility sets of (s, τ) pairs imply that there is a point of tangency, C, as shown in figure 9D.1. Though tedious, it is straightforward to find that $\Delta \approx 0.762$ at point C. The distinguishing feature of point C is that it identifies a unique pair $(s, \tau) > (0, 0)$ which induces a level of world welfare equal to that under no intervention. If adjustment assistance subsidies were absent, then the maximum sustainable level of world welfare would be at point C′, which is clearly Pareto dominated by point C. Therefore, adjustment assistance subsidies can alter the incentive compatibility constraint; and this may help countries sustain more efficient trade acords.

However, the validity of the above point is more general than it might appear at first sight. Suppose for example, that $\Delta \in [0.762, 2)$. Then, as figure 9D.1 illustrates, the no-intervention (i.e. free trade) level of welfare will always be possible to reproduce with an appropriate combination of adjustment subsidies and tariffs along segment OC of iso-welfare schedule OO′. On the other hand, if $\Delta \in (0, 0.762]$ then points of tangency between iso-welfare schedules and incentive compatibility contours can be obtained. These points will lie on curve CF of figure 9D.1 (see, e.g., point E when $\Delta = 0.25$). Once again, if finite adjustment assistance subsidies are used as part of the trigger strategy, more efficient agreements are possible to sustain. Of course, in reality such intervention schemes are hard to implement because of informal problems and because they are subject to political economy influence and manipulation by special interests. To my knowledge, this normative argument for adjustment assistance is new, and Fung and Staiger deserve credit for proposing a simple model that lays the necessary building blocks to obtain it.

Fung and Staiger note that reciprocal adjustment assistance subsidies can be welfare improving for two reasons. First, at constant tariffs, an increase in the subsidy s expands every country's tax base and raises welfare as long as s and its increase are sufficiently small. As shown in (4), the precise condition for such an improvement in welfare is $\tau \geq \tilde{\tau}$. Second, an increase in the subsidy s may relax the incentive compatibility constraint and thus make trade liberalization easier to sustain. If so, tariffs will fall and welfare will rise. It is the latter effect that Fung and Staiger explore in detail for the case of infinitesimally small subsidies. I shall illustrate how their argument is modified when finite subsidies are considered.

First, as figure 9D.1 indicates, tariffs and subsidies need not be monotonically related along an incentive compatibility boundary. However, as long as the discount parameter Δ is sufficiently low, it is possible to find an interval of subsidy rates so that increases in these rates cause the most cooperative tariff to decline. Precisely, if $\Delta \in (0, 2 \cdot 3^{-1/2})$

then any incentive compatibility constraint schedule associated with this Δ will contain a pair (s, τ) with the tariff being the lowest it can be (see, e.g., point E″ along GG′ in figure 9D.1). The dotted curve B′E″F in figure 9D.1 is the locus of such (s, τ) pairs that discount parameters in $(0, 2 \cdot 3^{-1/2})$ generate. As long as (s, τ) pairs remain to the left-hand side of B′E″F, increases in the subsidy rate cause the most cooperative tariff to fall along a given incentive compatibility constraint. Thus, even though Fung and Staiger consider only an infinitesimally small increase in the subsidy rate, their argument remains valid for a range of finite subsidy rates. It is also useful to note that the relationship between subsidies and tariffs along any incentive compatibility constraint is positive in the neighbourhood of policies that maximize world efficiency.

The intuition behind the above extension of the Fung and Staiger result can be sharpened by examining more closely how the incentive compatibility constraints change when the levels of instruments adjust. This can be done with the help of figure 9D.2. Suppose, for example, that $\Delta = 0.25$ and let $s = 0$ initially. Then, as shown in figure 9D.1, the most cooperative tariff is equal to the interval OE′. Now consider figure 9D.2. The dark, solid-line, convex and concave curves depict the per-period benefit to defecting from any symmetric tariff agreement and the welfare loss if cooperation breaks down, respectively. Their intersection at point E′ ensures that $\Phi(\bullet; \Delta = 0.25) = 0$ and thus gives the most cooperative sustainable tariff.[3] As long as $\tau^N > \tau > \tilde{\tau}$ and Ω and Δw depend on tariffs as shown in figure 9D.2, a tariff increase will relax the incentive constraint (i.e. $\Phi_\tau < 0$) at any point on a boundary $\Phi(\bullet; \Delta) = 0$. In contrast, when the subsidy s changes, its effect on the incentive constraint is ambiguous. In the most interesting case, where the most cooperative tariff τ falls as the subsidy s rises, we must have $\Phi_s \equiv \Omega_s - \Delta w_s < 0$. This is equivalent to having w and Ω shift as shown with the dashed and the thin solid curves in figure 9D.2. But what is happening in the background?

Recall that welfare $W(s, \tau)$ will rise (fall) when the subsidy s is raised if $\tau > \tilde{\tau}$ $(\tau < \tilde{\tau})$. Since welfare at the single-period Nash equilibrium is invariant to changes in the subsidy s, the direction of changes in Δw will match the changes in $W(s, \tau)$.[4] On the other hand, an increase in s will raise Ω for the following reasons. The increase in the other country's subsidy rate expands the reference country's tax base more when this country defects than when it cooperates. This raises Ω. At the same time, however, the increase in the reference country's subsidy reduces that country's welfare. This reinforces the initial increase in Ω. Since increases in the subsidy s raise both Ω and Δw, its effect on the incentive constraint (i.e. the sign of Φ_s) is ambiguous. As both figures 9D.1 and 9D.2 suggest,

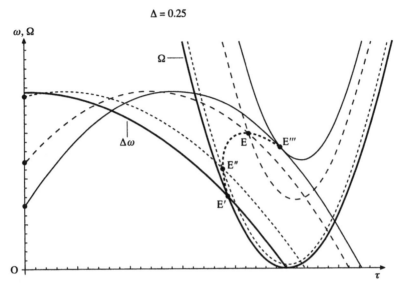

Figure 9D.2 Adjustment assistance subsidies and the incentive compatibility constraint

Φ_s can be negative, but this will be true only for a certain range of values in the subsidy s and the discount parameter Δ. Starting at point E′, the tariff falls until E″ but eventually increases until point E‴. Welfare is maximized at point E.

My reaction to my first reading of the paper was mixed. I was satisfied that the principal point of enquiry was well motivated, that the analysis was solid, and that the economic intuition was clearly explained. I enjoyed reading the paper. Yet I was sceptical about how robust the argument was and unsure about how seriously we should take it. After numerous readings and experiments with the structure of the model, several of my reservations have subsided. Recall, Fung and Staiger warn us that their primary goal is not to provide a general analysis of the relationship between adjustment assistance and self-enforcing trade agreements. All along, their main goal has been to illustrate that there exist circumstances in which adjustment assistance subsidies facilitate cooperation in trade. The authors have provided us with an argument that is intuitive, compelling, and capable of surviving several checks of robustness.[5] Perhaps more importantly, they have given us an exemplary illustration of how good theorists construct simple models to analyse problems that, at least on first sight, seem unmanageably complex. In this analysis, I have explored the normative side of the problem and shown that the case for adjustment assistance subsidies can be even stronger than Fung and Staiger suggest. Regardless of how they affect self-enforcing tariff agreements, adjustment subsidies can enhance world efficiency.

NOTES

I am indebted to Beverly Jonnes for valuable comments and suggestions.

1   The Uruguay Round of the GATT negotiations, recent efforts of European countries to consolidate and deepen their integration of product and factor markets, and the North American Free Trade Agreement (NAFTA) are all examples of movements towards freer trade at the multilateral and regional levels.

2   An increase in the domestic subsidy reduces domestic welfare because it causes excessive relocation of workers into the export sector. On the other hand, an equal increase in the country's adjustment subsidy increases the tax base of the reference country and raises welfare. If subsidy rates are sufficiently small, the latter effect dominates. Of course, it is equal to the former when $\tau = 2s\tau^N$. When this relationship is satisfied, the resulting allocation of labour across the two industries is identical to the one we would observe under free trade. This implies that moving costs are identical across the two regimes. It also implies that the value of domestic production plus tariff revenues evaluated at domestic prices is equal across the two regimes as well.

3   It can be shown that the shapes of Ω and $\Delta\omega$ depicted in Figure 9D.2 arise under a wide variety of specifications in consumer preferences and production functions. However, the shapes of the Ω and $\Delta\omega$ schedules can be quite different if other trade policy instruments (e.g. export or import quotas) are considered. This is more likely in general equilibrium settings where incentives to defect from trade agreements differ markedly.

4   Notice that the peak of the $\Delta\omega$ curves remains invariant because the value in s is such that $\tau = \tilde{\tau} \equiv 2s\tau^N$.

5   A fundamental conceptual problem arises when asymmetries (e.g. asymmetric shocks in technology across countries) are considered. Symmetric tariffs need no longer be focal points and the rules about the implementation (as opposed to the sustainability) of concrete agreements become important.

10 Trade liberalization as politically optimal exchange of market access

AYRE L. HILLMAN and PETER MOSER

1 Introduction

The northern transatlantic economic relationship has in the course of the second half of the twentieth century evolved from the days of 'dollar shortage' and protectionist policies into a liberal trading environment compromised only by occasional trade conflicts regarding sensitive industries, generally in agriculture (for example, the issue of hormones in beef) and also environmentally related issues (such as US prohibition of imports of Mexican tuna processed in Europe but caught in fishing nets harmful to dolphins). The liberal transatlantic trading environment has developed out of the GATT (General Agreement on Tariffs and Trade) rounds of multinational negotiations, and also has been facilitated by GATT mechanisms for resolution of trade disputes. The Uruguay Round of negotiations and the World Trade Organization succeeding the GATT have confirmed the basis for the liberal trade policies of the northern transatlantic trading partners.

The question we wish to address here is, what have been the motives underlying liberalization of transatlantic trade? Why, or how, did the liberal trading environment emerge? The answer has implications for how liberal policies can be sustained, and for possible causes of protectionist reversion.

A first explanation for liberalization points to the classical gains from free trade. These gains, were they to form the basis for trade policy, would lead governments to liberalize trade *unilaterally* without engaging in negotiations with other governments. Unilateral liberalization does take place; a much-studied instance is the nineteenth-century repeal of the English corn laws (see, for example, Schonhardt-Bailey, 1991), and, more recently, trade in developing countries has been unilaterally liberalized in compliance with World Bank conditionality (see Papageorgiou *et al.*, 1990). In the transatlantic relation, liberalization has however not

295

been unilateral, but reciprocal. To explain transatlantic trade liberalization, we therefore need to look for motives for reciprocating behaviour.

Motives for reciprocal liberalization are to be found in the tariff-bargaining literature, which models strategic interaction in intergovernmental trade negotiations. This literature views trade liberalization as the outcome of the elimination or reduction of trade barriers that were imposed to improve countries' terms of trade, that is, for optimum tariff reasons. Governments are here benevolent maximizers of aggregate welfare, and liberal trade policies are motivated by the desire to avoid the welfare losses that arise from retaliatory imposition of tariffs. The substantial literature that takes this view has been surveyed by McMillan (1986) and Vousden (1990); more recent formulations include Riezman (1991), Kovenock and Thursby (1992), and Bond and Syropoulos in this volume (ch. 4).

These tariff-bargaining models are consistent with observed international trade negotiations and consequent liberalization. The models exclude domestic income distribution concerns and political motives from government objectives (the exception is Mayer, 1984, who includes lobbying in a tariff-bargaining model). The benevolent social-welfare-maximizing view of government is of course at variance with documented income distribution motives for protectionist policies (see the surveys by Hillman, 1989, and Magee et al., 1989). Beyond the motives underlying policy decisions, the tariff-bargaining literature is at variance with observed behaviour in offering no role for the market access concerns that are prominent in trade policy negotiations.

In distinction to the tariff-bargaining literature, we present here a view of reciprocal trade liberalization as has characterized the transatlantic relationship, set in the context of the political economy view of protectionism with trade liberalization described as exchange of market access. The motive underlying policy decisions is described as enhanced domestic political support deriving from each country's government conferring benefits on the other country's exporters. Although governments could make transfers to exporters unilaterally by means of export subsidies, the subsidies would form the basis for countervailing duties by an importing country's government. Exchange of market access, on the other hand, offers mutual political gain, while avoiding claims for countervailing duties. This view of the motives for reciprocal trade liberalization is consistent with (i) the objectives of international trade negotiators in seeking to improve or maintain foreign market access for their exporters, (ii) the presumption in international trade negotiations that a country's producers have pre-eminent rights to sell in their own home markets, and (iii) the position that, in liberalizing trade, governments make 'concessions' that violate these pre-eminent rights by allowing foreign producers access to domestic markets.

Models based on optimum tariffs and models based on political support and income distribution both predict mutually beneficial trade liberalization. But, we would ask, beneficial to whom? The optimum-tariff-bargaining literature assumes that the benefits and policy motives pertain to the country as a whole. Our story is one of mutual political gain to governments cognizant of how the income distribution effects of policies affect election prospects. Policies are then adopted not because aggregate welfare increases but because of political-support considerations.

To describe the mutual political gains from exchange of market access, we shall employ a two-country specific-factors model that identifies industry interests as gainers and losers from trade policies. Formally, we could just as well have used the Heckscher–Ohlin model, which identifies gainers and losers from trade policies as intersectorally mobile factors of production. Then the beneficiaries of foreign market access are not individuals whose real incomes are tied to relative prices of the output of export sectors, but individuals deriving incomes from claims to economies' relatively abundant factors of production. The Heckscher–Ohlin framework does sometimes identify interested parties; for example, organized labour in the USA had a self-interest position with regard to the North American Free Trade Agreement. We, however, choose the specific-factors model in consistency with the evidence (see Hillman, 1989; Magee et al., 1989) that industry interests rather than coalitions of cross-industry factors of production are in general the interested parties in the politically endogenous determination of trade policy. In particular, in the case of the transatlantic trading relationship, it is not at all evident how a Heckscher–Ohlin framework would be applied and whether such a framework would be pertinent. Significantly, the principal protectionist means in the European Union have been industry-specific anti-dumping procedures, which the evidence indicates have been applied in a manner that suggests the exercise of political discretion (see Messerlin, 1989; Tharakan, 1991; and Schuknecht, 1992).

Our model makes no explicit reference to third countries. We accordingly omit consideration of potential trade diversion losses from discriminatory trade liberalization.[1] We note, however, that trade diversion possibilities were reduced by the most-favoured-nation provision of the GATT.

We also focus on the motives for broad agreements on the reciprocal exchange of market access such as have liberalized northern transatlantic trade, and do not here consider industry-specific deviations from the principle of reciprocal liberalization.[2] Explaining these deviations would require a model where liberalization occurs simultaneously with protection for particularly favoured import-competing industries. Our two-good model with only one import-competing industry does not provide the setting for addressing the question why some import-competing industries are more exposed to foreign competition via agreements to exchange of market access than others; this discrimination among industries is, however, the principal question addressed by the theory of endogenous protection and the literature on the political economy of protection.[3]

We wish to make clear that we are not introducing a new insight in viewing trade liberalization as the exchange of market access. The novelty is only in contrast with the policy motives assumed in the tariff-bargaining literature. In describing trade liberalization in terms of market access concerns, we are following an institutionally oriented literature that includes among others Hauser (1986), Moser (1990), and Finger (1988, 1991). Our model also has similarities with Mayer (1984).

2   Income distribution and trade policies

Since the background is the familiar specific-factors model of international trade, we shall need to add only the elements required for our two-country formulation. In each of two economies, competitive production of (potential) export and import-competing goods takes place employing an industry-specific factor and an intersectorally mobile factor of production with constant-returns-to-scale technologies. A competitive market allocates the mobile factor between employment in the two sectors. Factors of production are internationally immobile.

Although the 'small country' assumption is common in the literature, producers in countries no matter how 'small' appear to have market access concerns. Our two countries are *not* 'small' in the sense of confronting given world prices at which producers can sell any quantities they wish in 'world' markets.

In the 'home' economy, we denote the relative domestic price of output by $P^d(\equiv P_X^d/P_Y^d)$ and total real incomes of specific factors in the export and import-competing sectors by I_X and I_Y respectively. The latter incomes consist of real factor returns, respectively R_X and R_Y in the export and import-competing sectors, which respectively increase and decrease with increases in the domestic relative price P^d, plus contributions to income of shares of tariff revenues, respectively G_X and G_Y, from a tariff t levied by the home government:

$$I_i = R_i(P^d) + G_i \qquad i = X, Y. \tag{1}$$

The role of tariff revenue in determining real incomes here merits some comment. We do not view the tariff revenue component of real incomes as discretionary lump sum transfers. Distribution of tariff revenues is not a significant consideration in determining trade policy in developed economies, and we wish our model to reflect this. We perceive tariff revenue to accrue to the Treasury in the first instance, and to contribute to payment for government services or to be a reduction from other taxes that we do not explicitly model. Formally, we view the contributions of benefits G_X and G_Y from tariff revenue to an individual's total real income to be small relative to earned income. Although changes in tariff revenue reflect conditions of foreign market access and terms of trade changes, and thereby affect aggregate national real income, our assumption is that contributions to income from tariff revenues are not manipulable for assignment to designated beneficiaries. This means that tariff revenue cannot be concertedly distributed to counter or neutralize the primary effects on sector-specific incomes of relative price changes, which is then consistent with the non-assignability of tariff revenues to designated beneficiaries in contemporary developed economies.

We denote the relative price of output in the foreign market by $P^f(\equiv P^f_X/P^f_Y)$. The *foreign* tariff is T, defined when there is no domestic tariff by $P^d = P^f(1 - T)$. T reflects the role of the foreign tariff as a cost of market access for home-country exporters; exporters receive the proportion $(1 - T)$ of the (relative) foreign market price for their foreign market sales. The home-country tariff, t, levied on the domestic import-competing good, with no foreign tariff present, is defined by $P^d = P^f/(1 + t)$. When both the home and foreign governments levy tariffs, we have, with $t > 0$ and $T > 0$, the relation

$$P^d = P^f \frac{(1 - T)}{(1 + t)}. \tag{2}$$

Adding a market-clearing condition for balanced trade between the two countries, substituting (2) into (1), and observing that tariff revenue depends on the volume of imports as determined by both domestic and foreign tariffs, allows sectoral real incomes to be expressed as functions of trade policies t and T in both countries:

$$I_i(t, T) = R_i(t, T) + G_i(t, T) \qquad i = X, Y. \tag{3}$$

The properties of the specific-factors model readily establish how these real incomes are influenced by trade policies in the two countries.

Unilateral liberalization at home decreases the domestic relative price of import-competing output,[4] while the foreign relative supply price of imports increases, deteriorating the terms of trade. Aggregate welfare declines or increases depending respectively on whether the home country's tariff is below or above the level of the optimum tariff, but, whichever is the case, sectoral real incomes are affected asymmetrically: given the level of protection, T, abroad, unilateral liberalization results in a decline in real incomes in the import-competing sector and an increase in real incomes in the export sector.

Similarly, unilateral trade liberalization abroad increases the relative price of the home economy's exported goods, improving the home country's terms of trade and increasing aggregate welfare; again there are asymmetric income distribution effects, with the domestic import-competing sector losing and the export sector gaining.

Since these same effects apply to the foreign economy, it follows that trade liberalization in either country decreases real incomes in both countries' import-competing sectors and increases real incomes in both export sectors. Producers in the import-competing sectors in both countries thus have a common interest in protection in either economy, and producers in each country's export sector have an interest in trade liberalization at home and abroad.

Given these income distribution effects of trade policies in the two countries, a government can respond to protectionist policies abroad by liberalizing its own trade policy, to offset the disadvantageous effects of foreign protection on export sector incomes. However, a response of unilateral liberalization cannot completely countervail the effects of foreign protection, because a restriction on foreign market access deteriorates the terms of trade. Further, by responding to foreign protection by liberalizing its own trade policy, the home government deteriorates its terms of trade further, and would be granting improved conditions of market access to foreign exporters in response to denial of market access for its own exporters. Given these considerations, how do we expect governments concerned with the political-support consequences of their policies to respond to trade policies abroad? An answer requires a specification of the objectives underlying policy decisions.

3   Policy interdependence

We shall assume that policy endogeneity takes the form of maximization by an incumbent government of a political-support function based on real incomes in import-competing and export sectors. This is of course but one of a number of possibilities for modelling endogenous policy (see Ursprung, 1991). We could alternatively endogenize trade policy in a model of political competition between candidates choosing policies to maximize election probabilities (as, for example, in Hillman and Ursprung, 1988). Or politicians could be viewed as concerned not just with election prospects but also with personal income, and as therefore trading off probabilities of election for increased income (Ursprung, 1990). Or election prospects could be altogether downplayed as politicians are portrayed as using ensured incumbency to maximize their income by letting it be known that 'protection is for sale' (see Grossman and Helpman, 1994).

We proceed here with the familiar political-support-maximization approach that models governments as seeking to optimize with regard to re-election prospects by trading off support (the precise form of which is left unspecified) from the gainers and losers from policy decisions. With the policy abroad, T, given, the government chooses its own policy, t, to maximize the function $M[t, T] = M[I_X(t, T), I_Y(t, T)]$ where $M_i > 0$, $M_{ii} < 0$, $i = I_X, I_Y$, and $M_{I_X I_Y} \geq 0$. Political support is thus increasing (at a decreasing rate) in the real incomes of individuals whose incomes derive from rents of specific factors in the export and import-competing sectors. M_i reflects a sector's political importance, and the cross-term an envy effect.

Observe that we are assuming here that intersectorally mobile factors do not influence trade policy. Such factors have 'natural insurance' in their ability to respond to relative price changes via intersectoral mobility, and consequently have lower stakes in policy outcomes than do sector-specific factors (Hillman, 1989: ch. 9). We therefore do not view mobile factors as having the same intensity of preferences regarding policy outcomes as sector-specific factors; and of course we cannot establish the trade policy position of mobile factors without reference to their consumption preferences. Although we proceed here on the assumption that governments are concerned only with how policies affect industry-specific incomes, in principle there is no reason to exclude mobile factors from the political-support function; to express the basis for the motive of exchange of market access, we require however to focus only on industry-specific interests.

The home-country tariff chosen to balance domestic political support from export and import-competing industry interests (for $t > 0$) follows from the solution to

$$R(t, T) = \frac{\partial M(t, T)}{\partial t} = M_{I_x} \frac{\partial I_X(t, T)}{\partial t} + M_{I_Y} \frac{\partial I_Y(t, T)}{\partial t} = 0, \qquad (4)$$

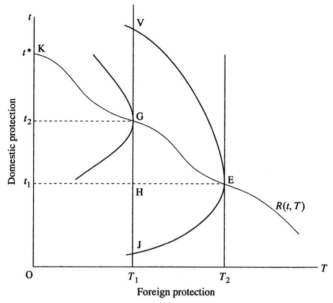

Figure 10.1   Domestic protection as a reaction to foreign protection

which describes how home-government policy, t, responds to the policy, T, adopted by the foreign government.[5]

In figure 10.1, the policy reaction function $R(t, T)$ expressed by (4) has a negative slope.[6] An intuitive explanation for this negative slope is based on established characteristics of policy responses to exogenous changes affecting income distribution (Hillman, 1989: ch. 2). In figure 10.1, the policy chosen in response to the foreign level of protection T_2 is t_1. Were the foreign government unilaterally to liberalize by reducing protection to T_1, the home government would be moved off its reaction curve, to the point H. The benefits of such unilateral foreign trade liberalization are in the initial instance captured by the export sector via improved conditions of foreign market access. To restore political equilibrium, the government transfers part of the export sector's gain to the import-competing sector, which has lost as the consequence of foreign liberalization. The redistribution is achieved by increasing protection to t_2, at the point G on the reaction curve. The import-competing sector thereby shares in the gains from improved foreign market access for exporters.

Political support is greater at G than at E, because real incomes in *both* the export and import-competing sectors have increased. From G on the reaction curve, the government can return to the lower level of political support at E, either by increasing protection to V to disadvantage the

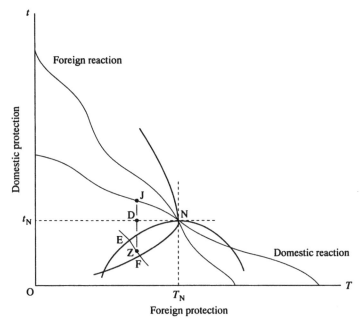

Figure 10.2   The interaction between domestic and foreign protection

export sector by more than the import-competing sector gains, or by liberalizing to J, to disadvantage the import-competing sector by more than the export sector gains. Political support on the reaction curve is maximal at the endpoint K, where there are no barriers to foreign market access.

4   Exchange of market access

Figure 10.2 depicts a unique non-cooperative Nash equilibrium (t_N, T_N). Along EF, both countries' trade policies are more liberal and both governments enjoy superior political-support outcomes than at the Nash equilibrium. Let Z on EF be the achieved reciprocal liberalization equilibrium.[7] As in the optimum-tariff-bargaining literature, reputation in repeated games can be used to explain cooperation to liberalize trade from the Nash equilibrium (see, for example, Riezman, 1991); or we can just as well appeal to the credibility of sovereign commitment.

Let us consider now unilateral foreign liberalization as in a move from N to D in figure 10.2. As we have observed, the home government's unilateral optimizing response is to *increase* protection, to the point J on its reaction function, thereby sharing the benefit of unilateral foreign liberalization between the export sector interests (whom the initial change advantaged) and import-competing sector interests (whom the initial change disadvantaged). In committing to exchange market access, however, the home government obligates itself to respond to foreign liberalization not by moving to J but by moving to Z. Both governments have an incentive to defect from Z (reflecting the Prisoner's Dilemma present here), but cooperation to provide mutual market access is superior to mutual defection to N.

The conclusion that governments have an incentive to liberalize from the non-cooperative Nash tariff equilibrium is of course central to the tariff-bargaining literature, which explains trade liberalization with reference to aggregate welfare. In our version, governments are moved to liberalize trade not because overall welfare has increased, but because of income distribution consequences for political support.

The source of the mutual political benefit is that reciprocal liberalization lowers the political cost of liberalization, because the political cost of lowering incomes in the import-competing sector is counterbalanced against the political gain from increased incomes in the export sector owing to the enhanced foreign market access that each government provides the other's exporters. The scope for mutually beneficial reciprocal liberalization is reflected in the characteristics of the iso-political-support contours. Along the reaction curve, $M_t = 0$. Reciprocal liberalization moves policies into a range where political support from the import-competing sector along an iso-political-support contour can be increased by increasing protection (that is, where $M_t > 0$). The incentive to reciprocate liberalization depends on the magnitude of M_T, that is, the offsetting marginal political benefit from improved foreign market access for exporters. There are a number of possibilities. In figure 10.3(a), a free trade agreement is a politically feasible outcome (if aggregate welfare maximization were to underlie trade liberalization, free trade would always be feasible). In figure 10.3(b), liberalization incentives in both countries are small, reflecting minor political influence of export sectors in either economy. In figure 10.3(c), asymmetric political influence of export sectors in the two countries results in asymmetric mutually beneficial liberalization possibilities; this latter case suggests why governments have incentives to exaggerate the political sensitivity of disadvantaging import-competing sectors (see Feenstra and Lewis, 1991).

5   Unilateral liberalization

We turn now from negotiated reciprocal liberalization to an exogenous change in policy preferences that leads one government to favour more

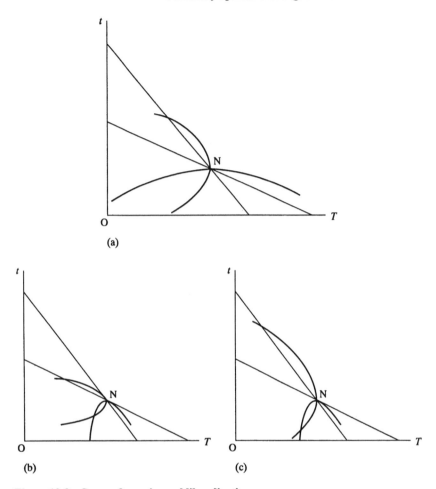

Figure 10.3   Scopes for reciprocal liberalization

liberal trade policies. Figure 10.4 depicts such a change as a downward shift of the now more liberally inclined (home) government's reaction function, from $R(t, T)$ to $R'(t, T)$. The shift reflects an altered perception by the home country's government of the gains and losses from pursuing policies that assist or disadvantage domestic export and import-competing industries. Since the home government now chooses a lower level of protection for any level of foreign protection, the Nash equilibrium moves from N to N', where the home government adopts a more liberal trade policy and the foreign government a more protec-

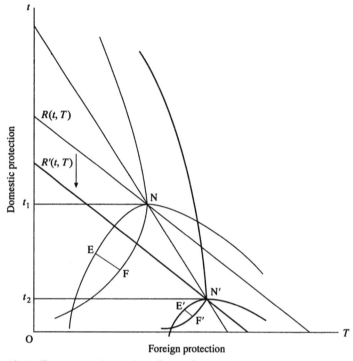

Figure 10.4   Exogenous change in policy preferences

tionist policy. The range of policy outcomes consistent with politically
mutually beneficial exchange of market access is also asymmetrically
biased toward a more liberal policy at home and more protectionist
policies abroad, as indicated by the locations of EF and E'F'.

   Consequently, when one government unilaterally revises its position
to prefer a more liberal trade policy, the political-support-maximizing
foreign response is not reciprocal liberalization but increased protectionism. The potential now arises for international conflict over trade
policy, because the liberalizing government confronts a protectionist
response by its trading partner. Such potential conflict is reflected in
section 301 of the US Trade Act, which provides a basis for
compelling foreign liberalization by threat of withdrawal of US market
access. As noted by McMillan (1990: 45), reciprocity implies 'if you
help me, I'll help you' (to which our model gives a political-support
connotation), whereas section 301 implies 'unless you help me, I'll hurt
you'.

6   Predetermined conditions of reciprocity

We have thus far considered *negotiated* reciprocal market access. For some countries, the discretion to negotiate may, however, not be present, and the choice may be to agree to conditions of predetermined reciprocity or to forgo reciprocal liberalization. This is the case when a government decides whether or not to participate in a multilateral GATT-sponsored liberalization round, or when the option is to join a pre-existing trading bloc under predetermined multilateral reciprocity conditions. These circumstances are portrayed in figure 10.5, which depicts a function

$$T = h(t), \tag{5}$$

representing a designated reciprocal trade liberalization rule. The function presupposes (as is not always the case) that a government can choose the extent to which it wishes to participate in reciprocal liberalization; in accord with the rule, the more liberal the conditions of access to the domestic market, the more liberal are market access conditions for the country's own exporters abroad.

Whether a government has an interest in exchange of market access under these conditions depends, as before, on achievable outcomes in terms of domestic political support. Maximization of political support subject to (5) yields the tangency outcome at S (a Stackelberg equilibrium) in figure 10.5. This outcome, which is the best the government can achieve by agreeing to reciprocal liberalization, need not be superior to confronting a default foreign level of protection. Since points along the segment of the reaction function MN are preferable to points along SF on $h(t)$, for levels of foreign protection in the range $T \in [T_0, T_1]$, the government has no interest in reciprocal liberalization. A level of foreign protection in excess of T_1 does, however, provide an inducement to agree to exchange market access (i.e. to choose the Stackelberg equilibrium at S).

It is the developing countries[8] that have been the beneficiaries of unilateral concessionary trading arrangements via the Generalized System of Preferences (GSP)[9] and other such preferential arrangements. If preferential access offers an outcome in the range MN of the reaction function, these countries have no incentive to participate in liberalization programmes based on reciprocity. Graduation (or exit) from preferential status (see Cassing and Hillman, 1991), on the other hand, provides an incentive for reciprocal liberalization, and hence has a liberalizing influence on trade policy. The transatlantic trading partners have not

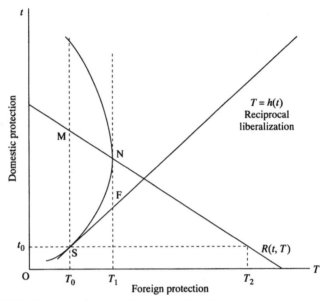

Figure 10.5   Predetermined conditions of reciprocity

provided each other with unilateral concessions that counter the incentive to agree to predetermined liberalization rules; and, more importantly, they have been instrumental in determining the reciprocal liberalization rules.

7   Concluding remarks

Since, subject to trade diversion qualifications, reciprocal trade liberalization is Pareto improving and increases the aggregate potential welfare of the inhabitants of liberalizing economies, the motives for liberalization can be posited as independent of income distribution considerations. Yet, since protectionist policies are explained by producer or industry interests rather than by benefit to the broad population of voters or consumers, we would for consistency wish an explanation for trade liberalization also to acknowledge the political incentive to respond to producer interests. To this end, our version of the explanation for reciprocal trade liberalization encompasses the role of producer interests, income distribution, and governments' political-support sensitivities in determining policy decisions. This allows us to base the motives for liberalization not on mutual aggregate welfare gains from reducing tariffs imposed for terms of trade reasons, but on *mutual political gains* to governments from reciprocating market access for each other's exporters.

Of course, the mutual political gains on which we base motives for reciprocal trade liberalization could as well be associated with aggregate welfare, if the electorate rewarded the government for increasing total real income without regard for income distribution; but it is the consequences for individuals' personal incomes that in general determine their support for policies.

Liberalization as has occurred for transatlantic trade is consistent with exchange of market access and income distribution motives underlying policy, as we have described, and with aggregate welfare maximization based on terms of trade effects as assumed in the tariff-bargaining literature. The choice of explanation exists because of the ambiguity that both benevolent aggregate-welfare-maximizing governments and also politicians choosing policies with concern for how income distribution consequences affect election prospects have incentives to liberalize trade from the non-cooperative Nash equilibrium. One may choose to tell the aggregate welfare version of the story, because that provides the more enlightened and educational (and hence the more politically correct) view of the exercise of policy discretion. Adhering to this version could, however, require closing one's eyes to the actual nature of policy determination under representative democracy.

Beyond the available evidence that governments in democracies are concerned with the political-support implications of their policies, there is a compelling indirect basis for differentiation between the two versions of the motives for trade liberalization, related to rent transfers. Our view of liberalization motives implies that the possibilities for reciprocal liberalization are contained when foreign exporters have already previously secured the rents from trade restrictions. This occurs in the presence of voluntary export restraints. The political benefits from exchange of market access are then limited, because, in a prospective liberalizing country, rents from trade restrictions have already been transferred to foreign exporters. In the policy equilibrium that has been established, the foreign producers, having moved closer to joint profit-maximizing output as a consequence of the voluntary export restraints, may then well lose rather than gain from trade liberalization (see Hillman, 1989: ch. 8). Mutual incentives for rent transfers by governments to each other's exporters by exchange of market access then are compromised, and reciprocal liberalization does not take place. We thus have a contributing explanation for why the northern transatlantic trading partners have been more successful in reciprocally liberalizing trade than has been the case in their trade relations with East Asian countries, for which significant trade has been subject to voluntary export restraints.

NOTES

We thank Wilfred Ethier and Martin Richardson for helpful comments.
1 For a model of endogenous protection with preferential trading policies, see Richardson (1993).
2 For a review of empirical studies of these protectionist deviations, see Hillman (1989: ch. 11).
3 The same contrasting views of policy motives arise here as in explaining protection in general and trade liberalization; Bagwell and Staiger (1990) present a theory where governments maximizing social welfare functions undertake protectionist reversions from negotiated liberalization agreements. Bagwell and Staiger's portrayal of policy motives underlying protectionist reversions is thus that of the benevolent apolitical governments in the tariff-bargaining literature.
4 We rule out the Metzler paradox (that protection may reduce rather than increase the domestic relative price of import-competing output).
5 This condition includes revenue distribution in the neutral manner we have described. For a more explicit treatment of political-support maximization with tariff revenue distribution, see Long and Vousden (1991).
6 The slope of the reaction function $R(t, T)$ is

$$\frac{\mathrm{d}t}{\mathrm{d}T} = -\frac{M_{tT}}{M_{tt}}.$$

Since the choice of trade policy t maximizes M, $M_{tt} < 0$. Expanding yields $M_{tT} < 0$, where signs of terms follow the relation between trade policies t and T and industry-specific incomes and the properties of the political-support function, with additional sufficient conditions $I^i_{tT} \leq 0$, $i = X, Y$.
7 We shall not model the negotiations that establish Z. Again here the concerns are the same as in the optimum-tariff literature.
8 Many developing countries are not or have not been democracies, which may compromise the assumption of our model that governments are sensitive to political support. None the less, political-support concerns are also important in one-party states and dictatorships – the procedures whereby governments change differ.
9 Here, too, domestic political-support considerations have influenced policies in the preference-granting economies; see Ray (1987).

REFERENCES

Bagwell, Kyle and Robert W. Staiger (1990), 'A Theory of Managed Trade', *American Economic Review* 80, 779–95.
Cassing, James H. and Ayre L. Hillman (1991), 'Equalizing the Cost of Success: Equitable Graduation Rules and the Generalized System of Preferences', *Journal of International Economic Integration* 6, 40–51.
Feenstra, Robert C. and Tracey R. Lewis (1991), 'Negotiated Trade Restric-

tions with Private Political Pressure', *Quarterly Journal of Economics* **106**, 1287–307.

Finger, J. Michael (1988), 'Protectionist Rules and Internationalist Discretion in the Making of National Trade Policy', in Hans-Jürgen Vosgerau (ed.), *New Institutional Arrangements for the World Economy*, Heidelberg: Springer-Verlag, pp. 310–23.

—— (1991), 'The GATT as an International Discipline over Trade Restrictions', in Roland Vaubel and Thomas D. Willett (eds.), *The Political Economy of International Organizations*, Boulder, Colo.: Westview Press, pp. 125–41.

Grossman, Gene and Elhanan Helpman (1994), 'Protection for Sale', *American Economic Review* **84**, 833–50.

Hauser, Heinz (1986), 'Domestic Policy Foundation and Domestic Policy Function of International Trade Rules', *Aussenwirtschaft* **41**, 171–84.

Hillman, Ayre L. (1989), *The Political Economy of Protection*, Chur, Switzerland: Harwood Academic Publishers.

Hillman, Ayre L. and Heinrich W. Ursprung (1988), 'Domestic Politics, Foreign Interests, and International Trade Policy', *American Economic Review* **78**, 729–45.

Kovenock, Dan and Marie Thursby (1992), 'GATT, Dispute Settlement, and Cooperation', *Economics and Politics* **4**, 151–70.

Long, Ngo Van and Neil Vousden (1991), 'Protectionist Responses and Declining Industries', *Journal of International Economics* **30**, 87–103.

McMillan, John (1986), *Game Theory in International Economics*, Chur, Switzerland: Harwood Academic Publishers.

—— (1990), 'The Economics of Section 301: A Game Theoretic Guide', *Economics and Politics* **2**, 45–57.

Magee, Stephen P., William A. Brock and Leslie Young (1989), *Black Hole Tariffs and Endogenous Policy Theory: Political Economy in General Equilibrium*, Cambridge: Cambridge University Press.

Mayer, Wolfgang (1984), 'The Political Economy of Tariff Agreements', *Schriften des Vereins für Socialpolitik* **148**, 423–37.

Messerlin, Patrick (1989), 'The EC Anti-dumping Regulations: A First Economic Appraisal', *Weltwirtschaftliches Archiv* **125**, 563–87.

Moser, Peter (1990), *The Political Economy of the GATT*, Grüsch: Verlag Ruegger.

Papageorgiou, Demetrios, Armeane M. Choksi and Michael Michaely (eds.) (1990), *Liberalizing Foreign Trade*, Oxford: Basil Blackwell.

Ray, Edward (1987), 'The Impact of Special Interests on Preferential Trade Concessions by the U.S.', *Review of Economics and Statistics* **69**, 187–95.

Richardson, Martin (1993), 'Endogenous protection and trade diversion', *Journal of International Economics* **34**, 309–24.

Riezman, Raymond (1991), 'Dynamic Tariffs with Asymmetric Information', *Journal of International Economics* **30**, 267–83.

Schonhardt-Bailey, Cheryl (1991), 'Specific Factors, Capital Markets, Portfolio Diversification, and Free Trade: Domestic Determinants of Repeal of the Corn Laws', *World Politics* **43**, 545–69.

Schuknecht, Ludger (1992), *Trade Protection in the European Community*, Chur, Switzerland: Harwood Academic Publishers.

Tharakan, P. K. M. (1991), 'The Political Economy of Anti-dumping Undertakings in the European Community', *European Economic Review* **35**, 1341–59.

Ursprung, Heinrich W. (1990), 'Public Goods, Rent Dissipation, and Political Competition', *Economics and Politics* **2**, 115–32.
  (1991), 'Economic Policies and Political Competition', in Ayre L. Hillman (ed.), *Markets and Politicians: Politicized Economic Choice*, Boston and Dordrecht: Kluwer Academic Publishers, pp. 1–25.
Vousden, Neil (1990), *The Economics of Trade Protection*, Cambridge: Cambridge University Press.

Discussion

MARTIN RICHARDSON

I am very pleased to have been asked to comment on this paper as I think it broaches a subject that is both extremely important and timely. To my mind, this paper identifies exactly the practical motive behind bilateral trade liberalization.

The notion that trade policy is driven by income distributional and other so-called 'political economy' goals is increasingly unarguable. The *Economist* magazine, a couple of years ago in a piece on endogenous growth theory, noted that one implication of new theory was that government policies might affect long-term growth rates. The magazine remarked that 'it takes many years of training for this idea to seem odd'. The same might be said for the theory of endogenous policy but, nevertheless, it is by now firmly established in international trade theory. Our understanding of not only *why* countries restrict trade but why they choose the *means* they do has been greatly enhanced, I think, by work in the vein of the present paper. To paraphrase Paul Krugman, the only intellectually respectable argument for trade restriction in classical theory, the optimal tariff argument, is probably the least relevant to the actual formation of trade policy. Additional support for this idea is given by some recent computable general equilibrium (CGE) simulations (Perroni and Whalley, 1993), which suggest that the optimal European Union tariff on the USA is 931 per cent and US tariff on the EU is 426 per cent! Now, there's a slim chance that the CGE estimates might be a little off, so divide these numbers by ten; one still ends up with tariffs over four times greater than actual tariffs. Clearly something else drives trade policy and also, therefore, trade liberalization.

In this context particularly, income distributional goals are of paramount importance and again the *Economist*'s dictum seems fairly accurate. Formal models of preferential trading areas have long stressed the gains to the *importing* country from tariff reduction, yet the non-economist's understanding of the gains from such agreements is almost always that we gain access to foreign markets for our exports (and, indeed, that reciprocal access is a concession we grant). Whatever the reason for this understanding, it is important to build models that reflect it and this is what the present paper does. In doing this, I think the authors have made a solid contribution.

However, it would be very useful if the authors could pursue their analysis a little further to distinguish the implications of the political economy approach from those of more standard analyses of bilateral liberalization. I think it is safe to say that, whatever the shortcomings of economic analysis, one problem we do not have is the inability to explain unobserved phenomena! Indeed, some might argue that in the international trade literature we have been explaining unobserved phenomena for over 150 years now and I think that a large part of the recent growth in study of the 'political economy' of trade policy has stemmed from dissatisfaction with the positive, as opposed to normative, power of more 'traditional' analysis. It is from this view of the role of endogenous policy models that I think the present analysis could go a little further. The authors choose a well-known specific-factors framework to motivate a 'reduced form' tariff function and then look at trade liberalization in a two-country world. However, as the authors are aware, their paper very much parallels work by Mayer (1981) on trade negotiations (itself based on Johnson's, 1953–4, seminal work on tariff wars). The core of Mayer's paper conducts much the same exercise but in a model where tariffs are motivated solely by terms of trade considerations.[1] The central results of the current paper are present in Mayer too: first, international negotiation can avoid non-cooperative outcomes of a Prisoner's Dilemma nature; and, second, tariffs are strategic substitutes, and unilateral tariff reduction by one country that shifts its tariff reaction function will elicit *increased* protection from the other.

Now, I agree with the authors that providing a basis for these results grounded in a political economy model is desirable in itself for consistency with the notion that distributional goals drive trade policy. Furthermore, I am not making an instrumentalist methodological argument suggesting that 'realism of assumptions' is irrelevant and only 'prediction' matters. Nevertheless, I would have liked to see a little more discussion of how the current analysis might be distinguished, in terms of observable predictions, from the more usual analysis. Along these lines, the authors' concluding remarks are promising.

To get more into the details of the analysis, I would have liked to see some more detailed discussion on the nature of the contract curve in this setting: what determines its location and shape? Further, what are the underlying parameters that determine the size of the 'trading lens': the set of tariffs that are mutually beneficial compared with the non-cooperative outcome? There is some brief discussion of figures 10.3(a–c), but a more complete characterization would be useful in explaining in what *circumstances* the mutual gains from bilateral liberalization are small or large.

The authors, quite correctly in my view, downplay the role of tariff revenues in motivating political actors to seek protection or liberalization. However, taking the allocation of tariff revenues as purely exogenous does lead to a couple of problems. In particular, the authors note in note 6 that a sufficient condition for downward-sloping tariff reaction functions in this model is that specific-factors incomes are concave in the price of the good they produce. Ignoring tariff revenues, this condition is not innocuous and will not hold in many cases unless the other component of specific-factor income specified in equation (1) in the paper – its share of tariff revenues – falls sufficiently, for a price increase, that it more than offsets the usual convexity of these returns in their own-good price.

The paper refers briefly to repetition as a means of achieving cooperation but, of course, there will generally be an infinity of possible outcomes of differing degrees of implicit cooperation that can be sustained by appropriate punishment strategies. In the context of multilateral negotiations it has been argued that GATT's principle of reciprocity serves to provide, by means of the tariff-reduction formulas that have been negotiated in some rounds, a 'focal point' for avoiding non-coordination in the presence of multiple equilibria.

This might also be the role of the authors' $h(t)$ function when they discuss predetermined conditions of reciprocity in section 6 of the paper, but I must confess to some unease with that section. The entire analysis of the paper posits only two countries,[2] but the analysis in section 6 is presented in terms of a many-country world. In a truly two-country setting, the use of a Stackelberg-type equilibrium concept *for each participant country* is inappropriate unless the $h(t)$ rule is chosen (or adjusted) so that each country's decision *given* the rule is mutually consistent. In that case, however, the outcome must be Pareto efficient from the governments' perspectives and we are back to the analysis of the earlier part of the paper. The thrust of section 6 is that a country may choose not to participate in mutual liberalization if foreign tariffs are already sufficiently low, but this seems readily apparent. The argument that the GSP may induce non-involvement in mutual liberalization follows from this but implies that non-participation is still in an LDC's best interests (as defined by the political-support function.) A rather more surprising interpretation can be placed on the GSP: it might prevent mutual liberalization that *is* in the interests of the LDC simply because it removes the reciprocity condition – with GSP, an LDC cannot commit to giving reciprocal access to its own market and is therefore simply left out of the negotiations (McMillan, 1987).

There are a number of issues that the authors deliberately sidestep in order to focus on their central point and I think some are of considerable interest and might usefully be the subject of future work. Some major issues are avoided by focusing essentially on liberalization in a two-country world. The unilateral tariff reduction (UTR) critique of traditional models of bilateral liberalization between small countries is something that might usefully be addressed in a three-country version of the present model. Much traditional analysis of customs unions makes what Corden (1984) calls the 'non-optimality assumption' about external tariffs, and the UTR critique notes that, in many settings, one member might do better than joining a customs union by simply abolishing all its tariffs unilaterally. The structure of the present model is clearly immune to this critique. Adding a third country, however, might present other problems of a more technical nature. For instance, external tariff reaction functions in a free trade area will often involve discontinuities when such tariffs are discriminatory. This can present problems for the existence of equilibrium in traditional models (see Richardson, 1995) and it is unlikely that the current specification of policy-setting would avoid that. For instance, suppose we take the current setup but use it to model external tariff-setting in a free trade area. Then the objective function $M[t,T]$ in equation (4) may be discontinuous at $t = T$: a small decrease in t has no effect on domestic producers, who simply choose to sell in the partner's market at $p^* + T$ (where p^* is the external price), but gives a large, discrete increase in tariff revenue in the home country.

All up, I think this paper gives some useful insights into the reality of trade liberalization but I also think it is very much a first step in the analysis and that there are a lot of interesting extensions that future work might consider. In closing, I must take issue with one remark the authors make in their conclusion. The notion that political economy approaches are somehow heretical in the economics literature is surely no longer tenable, largely as a result of the work of Professor Hillman and others over recent years. Although the implications of the 'aggregate welfare version' of this story (*à la* Mayer) are much the same as the implications of this political economy version, I think that the suggestion that a preference for the former reflects deliberate myopia and a submission to 'political correctness' is a little extreme.

NOTES

1 In a concluding section, Mayer also considers 'political economy' policy-setting.
2 I suggest below, however, that I think the three-country extension would be very valuable.

REFERENCES

Corden, W. Max (1984), 'The Normative Theory of International Trade', in Ronald W. Jones and Peter B. Kenen (eds.), *Handbook of International Economics*, vol. 1, Amsterdam: North-Holland.
Johnson, Harry G. (1953–4), 'Optimum Tariffs and Retaliation', *Review of Economic Studies*.
McMillan, John (1987), 'International Trade Negotiations: A Game Theoretic View', mimeo, World Bank, Washington DC.
Mayer, Wolfgang (1981), 'Theoretical Considerations on Negotiated Tariff Adjustments', *Oxford Economic Papers* 33, 135–43.
Perroni, Carlo and John Whalley (1993), 'The New Regionalism: Trade Liberalization or Insurance?' Paper presented at NBER Conference on International Trade Rules and Institutions, December, Cambridge, Mass.
Richardson, Martin (1995), 'Tariff Revenue Competition in a Free Trade Area', *European Economic Review* 39(7), 1429.

Index

317

tariff liberalization 280–4
Lockwood, Ben 241, 258, 259
Lohmann, Susan 261
Long, Ngo Van 310
lumpy countries and trade liberalization
148, 164–5
immobile factors 151–6
mobile labour with amenities 156–9
mobile labour with a production subsidy
159–64
Luxembourg 190

Ma, Y. 14
Maastricht Treaty, *see* Treaty of European
Union
McDonald, D. 46
McKinnon, Ronald I. 54, 55–6, 57, 76, 84,
93, 94, 100, 108
McMillan, John 296, 306, 315
Magee, Stephen P. 296, 297
Manning, Alan 257
Marion, Nancy P. 199
market access, trade liberalization as
politically optimal exchange of, *see*
under liberalization of trade
market size and direct investment
asymmetric countries and convergence
hypothesis 180
preliminary results: symmetric countries
179
markups and direct investment
model, specification 175
preliminary results: symmetric countries
179
Markusen, James R. 172, 176, 188
Marston, R. 70, 77
Masson, P. 9, 14
Mastropasqua, Christina 70, 71, 73, 111
Mayer, Wolfgang 296, 298, 313
Meese, Richard 200
MERCOSUR 118
Meredith, G. 9
Messerlin, Patrick 297
Metzler paradox 310n.4
Mexico 198
Micossi, S. 111
migration
trade liberalization, effects on trading
blocs 156–9, 163, 164
unified Germany 42–3
Mishkin, Frederic 109
monetary policy
central banks and reputation 236, 238–41
EMS coordination 106, 107–8
G3 coordination 91, 92
transatlantic coordination 25–9

monetary union, EU 2
American concerns 3
money market rates
EMS policy coordination 104
G3 policy coordination 85
Moser, Peter 298
MPS/GE software 172
MULTIMOD, policy coordination 13–14,
16, 47, 49
wage inflation 29–30
multinational firms, and direct investment
172, 187, 190
asymmetric countries and convergence
hypothesis 180, 181, 182, 183, 184
model, specification 173, 174, 175
preliminary results: symmetric countries
178, 179
Mussa, Michael 79, 193, 285

national firms, and direct investment 172,
187
asymmetric countries and convergence
hypothesis 181, 182
model, specification 173–4, 175
preliminary results: symmetric countries
178, 179
Neary, J. Peter 285
Netherlands
exchange rate management 109
coordination 100
sterilization 95
interest rate policy coordination 104, 107
speculative attacks 202, 222
Neumann, Manfred J. M. 70, 73, 77
New Zealand, central bank governor
258n.2, 261
nominal wage rigidity (NWR), central
banks and reputation, *see under*
wages
non-cooperative policies 10, 17–19, 20–1,
48–9
transatlantic interactions 25
North American Free Trade Agreement
(NAFTA)
formation 118
'new regionalism' 2
policy bloc 40
trade liberalization 148, 294n.1
as politically optimal exchange of
market access 297
subsidies 160

Obstfeld, Maurice 55, 70, 77, 81, 85, 111,
192, 193, 196, 224, 232
options pricing theory 233
Oudie, G. 15

326   **Index**

For EU product safety concerns, contact us at Calle de José Abascal, 56–1°,
28003 Madrid, Spain or eugpsr@cambridge.org.

www.ingramcontent.com/pod-product-compliance
Ingram Content Group UK Ltd.
Pitfield, Milton Keynes, MK11 3LW, UK
UKHW042211180425
457623UK00011B/155